Social Protection for the Poor and Poorest

Social Protection for the Poor and Poorest

Concepts, Policies and Politics

Edited by

Armando Barrientos

and

David Hulme

palgrave
macmillan

in association with the Brooks World
Poverty Institute at the University of
Manchester and the Chronic Poverty
Research Centre

University of Texas
at San Antonio

First published in 2008 by
PALGRAVE MACMILLAN
Houndmills, Basingstoke, Hampshire RG21 6XS and
175 Fifth Avenue, New York, N.Y. 10010
Companies and representatives throughout the world.

PALGRAVE MACMILLAN is the global academic imprint of the Palgrave Macmillan division of St. Martin's Press, LLC and of Palgrave Macmillan Ltd. Macmillan® is a registered trademark in the United States, United Kingdom and other countries. Palgrave is a registered trademark in the European Union and other countries.

ISBN-13: 978–0–230–52530–6 hardback
ISBN-10: 0–230–52530–X hardback

This book is printed on paper suitable for recycling and made from fully managed and sustained forest sources. Logging, pulping and manufacturing processes are expected to conform to the environmental regulations of the country of origin.

A catalogue record for this book is available from the British Library.

Library of Congress Cataloging-in-Publication Data

Social protection for the poor and poorest : concepts, policies and politics / edited by Armando Barrientos, David Hulme.
     p. cm.—(Palgrave studies in development)
   Includes bibliographical references and index.
   ISBN-13: 978–0–230–52530–6 (hdbk)
   ISBN-10: 0–230–52530–X (alk. paper)
     1. Social security. 2. Public welfare. 3. Poverty. 4. Poor—Services for.
   I. Barrientos, Armando. II. Hulme, David.

HD7091.S547 2008
362.5—dc22   2008000185

10 9 8 7 6 5 4 3 2 1
17 16 15 14 13 12 11 10 09 08

Printed and bound in Great Britain by
CPI Antony Rowe, Chippenham and Eastbourne

Contents

Part I   Introduction

Part II   Conceptual Frameworks for Social Protection: Risks, Needs and Rights

Part III   What Policies Work for the Poorest?

List of Tables

List of Figures

List of Abbreviations

ACCs	Area Coordinating Committees
ADB	Asian Development Bank
ANC	African National Congress
ARVs	Anti-retrovirals
BDP	Botswana Democratic Party
BNF	Botswana National Front
BPL	Below Poverty Line
BRAC	Bangladesh Rural Advancement Committee
CBPWP	Community Based Public Works Programme
CCTs	Conditional cash transfers
CEDAW	Convention on the Elimination of All Forms of Discrimination Against Women
CFW	Cash for work
CMED	Central Motor Engine Department
CPRC	Chronic Poverty Research Centre
DFID	Department for International Development (UK)
DSW	Department of Social Welfare
DSWO	District Social Welfare Officer
DWAC	District Welfare Assistance Committee
EFA	UNESCO's Education for All
EPWP	Expanded Public Works Programme
FAO	Food and Agriculture Organization
FFD	Free food distribution
FFW	Food for work
GDP	Gross domestic product
GEMA	Gikuyu, Embu and Meru Association
GoM	Government of Maharashtra
GTZ	Deutsche Gesellschaft für Technische Zusammenarbeit
HPI	Human Poverty Index
ICESCR	International Covenant on Economic, Social and Cultural Rights
IFOCC	Instituto de Fomento a la Comercialización Campesina
IFPRI	The International Food Policy Research Institute
IFRC	International Federation of Red Cross and Red Crescent societies
IGSS	Instituto Guatemalteco de Seguridad Social
IGVGD	Income Generation for Vulnerable Group Development (Bangladesh)
ILO	International Labour Office

ILTPWP	Improving Livelihoods Through Public Works Programme
IMF	International Monetary Fund
MASAF	Malawi Social Action Fund
MCDSS	Ministry of Community Development and Social Services of the Republic of Zambia
M+E	Monitoring and evaluation
MDC	Movement for Democratic Change
MDG	Millennium Development Goals
MEGS	Maharashtra Employment Guarantee Scheme
MFI	Micro Finance institution
NER	Net enrolment ratio (primary education)
NFBS	National Family Benefit Scheme
NFRF	National Famine Relief Fund
NGO	Non-governmental Organisation
NMBS	National Maternity Benefit Scheme
NOAPS	National Old Age Pension Scheme
NSAP	National Social Assistance Programme
NSUP	Non-selected ultra-poor households
NVF	New variant famine
OVCs	Orphans and vulnerable children
PEAP	Poverty Eradication Action Plan (Uganda)
PF-ZAPU	Patriotic Front-Zimbabwe African People's Union
PLWA	People living with AIDS
PPA	Programme partnership agreement
PPP	Purchasing power parity
PRI	Institutional Revolutionary Party (Mexico)
PRS	Poverty reduction strategies
PRSP	Poverty Reduction Strategy Paper
PSWO	Provincial Social Welfare Officer
PWAS	Public Welfare Assistance Scheme
SEWA	Self-Employed Workers Association
SP/SAG	Social Protection Sector Advisory Group
SRM	Social risk management
SSA	Sub-Saharan Africa
SSC	Social Security Committee
SSN	Social safety net
SUP	Selected ultra poor households
TLU	Tropical livestock units
TUP	Targeting the Ultra Poor programme (Bangladesh)
UN	United Nations
UNDG	United Nations Development Group
UNDP	United Nations Development Programme
UNICEF	United Nations Children's Fund

UPE	Universal Primary Education
USAID	United States Agency for International Development
VAC	Village Assistance Committees
WFP	World Food Programme
WHO	World Health Organisation
WIDER	World Institute for Development Economics Research
ZANU	Zimbabwe African National Union
ZANU-PF	Zimbabwe African National Union-Patriotic Front
ZAPU	Zimbabwe African People's Union

List of Web Resources

Chronic Poverty Research Centre: www.chronicpoverty.org
Crisis States Programme Development Research Centre: www.crisisstates.com
Expanded Public Works Programme (South Africa): www.epwp.gov.za
Office of the United Nations High Commissioner for Human Rights:
www.ohchr.org/english/
Pilot Social Cash Transfer Scheme, Kalomo District: www.socialcashtransfers-
zambia.org
SMERU Research Institute (Indonesia): www.smeru.or.id
United Nations Development Programme: www.undp.org
UNICEF: www.unicef.org
World Food Programme: www.wfp.org

Acknowledgements

This book would not have been possible without the support and assistance of colleagues from across the world. It has its origins in a conference on 'Social Protection. Risk, Needs and Rights' we organised at the University of Manchester in February 2005. That conference was part of the Chronic Poverty Research Centre's (CPRC) research programme and benefited enormously from the encouragement and ideas of co-workers in the CPRC and of conference participants. Papers from the conference and further details are available on the CPRC website (www.chronicpoverty.org). Thanks also to the Institute for Development Policy and Management (IDPM) at the University of Manchester for hosting the conference and providing financial support. The conference also received financial support from DFID's Reaching the Very Poorest Team, to whom we are grateful. In addition, this book has benefited from a dissemination grant from the Brooks World Poverty Institute at the University of Manchester.

A number of people have been particularly generous with their time, ideas and expertise. We must single out Karen Moore and Debbie Whitehead at IDPM. Karen has provided us with excellent research assistance during both the conference phase and during the drafting of this book. She helped to edit the contributions to the book, and has provided ideas and insights that are woven into its arguments. Debbie, with her colleagues at IDPM, organised the conference and managed post-conference administration. She was the 'invisible hand' that made the conference such a stimulating and enjoyable event, as everything ran so smoothly. Armando thanks Debora Shenton and Nadine Beard at the Institute of Development Studies (IDS) at the University of Sussex. Deborah managed the completion of the final manuscript with her usual efficiency, resourcefulness and good humour. At IDPM, David also wishes to thank Denise Redston, who provided personal assistance throughout the writing of this book. Without their generous contributions, this book would still be on the drawing board!

It is also relevant to mention the many people in developing countries, many of them in poverty, who have helped us in our work. Over the years they have patiently answered our questions about their vulnerability, their understandings, and potential remedies. They have generously provided us with the insights that inform our analysis. We hope that we have built on this knowledge in ways that will reduce vulnerability more generally.

Finally, mention must be made of our families who supported us in different ways, and who have provided us with the time and space to complete this task with only occasional grumbles. Armando thanks Stephanie,

Kim and Rici for unstinting support, intellectual stimulation, informed criticism and advice. David thanks his children – Ed, Jazzi and Saffi – for tolerating his frequent absences from home and for the increasing amount of time they devote to upgrading his computer skills and keeping him online, and Georgina for all her support and care over the years and for keeping the home fires burning.

Notes on the Contributors

Armando Barrientos is Senior Research Fellow at the Brooks World Poverty Institute at the University of Manchester, and Senior Researcher with the Chronic Poverty Research Centre, leading work on insecurity, risk and vulnerability. He is also Co-Director of the Centre for Social Protection. His research interests focus on the interaction of labour markets and welfare production, poverty, and social protection.

Sami Bazzi was Visiting Luce Fellow at SMERU Research Institute, Jakarta, from September 2005 to July 2006. He is currently a Research Assistant at the Center for Global Development in Washington, DC, where his research focuses on foreign aid effectiveness and the development consequences of skilled migration.

Christina Behrendt is the regional Social Security Specialist in the International Labour Organization's Regional Office for Arab States in Beirut, Lebanon. Prior to this, she worked in the ILO's Social Security Department in Geneva, Switzerland, and at the University of Konstanz, Germany. Her research interests have focused on basic social protection, public and private pensions, social assistance, and the effectiveness of social security benefits in alleviating poverty.

Tessa Bold is a Research Fellow in Development Economics at the University of Oxford. Her research interests include applied microeconomic theory, development economics, and applied econometrics.

Cesar Calvo teaches economics at Piura University, Peru, and is a Research Associate at Oxford University.

Michael R. Carter is Professor of Agricultural and Applied Economics at the University of Wisconsin, Madison, USA. He is also director of the BASIS Collaborative Research Support Program studying rural poverty alleviation strategies across the developing world. Author of numerous articles and books, his research focuses on the nature of growth and transformation in low-income economies, paying particular attention to how inequality in the distribution of assets shapes, and is shaped by, economic growth. His current projects include longitudinal analysis of income distribution in South Africa, and a pilot study of index-based agricultural insurance in Peru.

Stefan Dercon is Professor of Development Economics at the University of Oxford. He has written extensively on risk and poverty. Currently, he is involved in a number of projects studying long-term poverty dynamics in

Ethiopia, India and Tanzania. A recent book, *Insurance against Poverty* (Oxford University Press, 2004), discusses how risk may cause poverty, and how interventions designed as part of social protection policies can help poor people to escape poverty.

Stephen Devereux is a Research Fellow at the Institute of Development Studies at the University of Sussex and Co-Director of the Centre for Social Protection. His research interests include famine, food security and social protection in Sub-Saharan Africa.

Tatiana Feitosa de Britto is a researcher in the field of poverty and social policies, with a focus on conditional cash transfers. She is associated with the UNDP International Poverty Centre and the University of Brasilia.

Sam Hickey lectures in international development at the Institute for Development Policy and Management, University of Manchester. His research focuses on the politics of development, particularly the links between politics and poverty reduction, issues of citizenship and participation, and the role of civil society and NGOs in development. Recent papers have appeared in *World Development* and *Development and Change*, and he is co-editor of books on participation (2004) and NGOs (2007), both published by Zed Books. He currently co-ordinates research into the politics of exclusion within the Chronic Poverty Research Centre.

David Hulme is Professor of Development Studies at the University of Manchester, Director of the Chronic Poverty Research Centre and Co-Director of the Brooks World Poverty Institute at the University of Manchester. His interests include global poverty reduction, rural development policy and planning, poverty reduction strategies, finance for the poor, the sociology of development, the role of community organisations and NGOs, evaluation of technical assistance, environmental management, and public sector reform. Recent publications include *Challenging Global Inequality* (Palgrave 2007) and *Understanding Poverty Dynamics* (OUP 2008).

Peter D. Little is Professor of Anthropology at Emory University. His research interests include economic and ecological anthropology; development and change; political economy; pastoralism; social theory and organisation; East Africa and the Horn of Africa.

Anna McCord is an economist in the Southern Africa Development and Research Unit (SALDRU) in the School of Economics at the University of Cape Town, managing the Public Works Research Project, which carries out policy-orientated research relating to public works and social protection in South Africa and the region. Her research focuses on the micro-level impact of social protection interventions, and the implications for programme selection and design.

Tewodaj Mogues is a Research Fellow at the IFPRI. She joined the Development Strategy and Governance division in February 2005 to undertake research on public investment for poverty reduction in Ethiopia and other countries. Her research interests include returns to public investment for poverty reduction, long-term effects of shocks on household assets and welfare, and social capital.

Karen Moore is a Research Associate at the Chronic Poverty Research Centre and is based in the Institute for Development Policy and Management, University of Manchester. Her research interests include chronic and intergenerational poverty; childhood; gender and development; economic psychology; livelihoods approaches; and microfinance.

Ngonidzashe Munemo is an Assistant Professor of Political Science in the Department of Political Science at Williams College, MA, USA. His current work examines the political economy of drought relief across Sub-Saharan Africa. Broadly, his research on this topic focuses on how changes in state-society configurations produce different regimes of social protection.

Lauchlan T. Munro is Director of Policy and Planning at the International Development Research Centre in Ottawa, Canada. Before joining IDRC in 2003, he worked for thirteen years with UNICEF, mainly in Africa. His recent research and publications have covered poverty and social security; human rights and public policy; and public sector management.

Workneh Negatu is Associate Professor in agricultural economics and development at the Institute of Development Research (IDR), Addis Ababa University, Ethiopia. His research interests include agricultural technological innovation and institutional changes, food security, and pastoral development.

Sony Pellissery is Associate Professor at the Institute of Rural Management, Anand, India. His research interests include social policyprocesses, local governance, rural economies and social protection in the context of informal labour markets.

Rachel Sabates-Wheeler is a development economist and IDS Fellow with extensive experience in rural development, institutional analysis and social policy. Although her geographical research focus has been primarily in Eastern Europe and Central Asia, since joining IDS she has become involved with poverty analysis work relating to PRSPs, social protection and migration in Africa. She is currently involved in a number of studies that explore understandings of risk and vulnerability, both conceptually and empirically.

Bernd Schubert is a development researcher and practitioner. Since 1986 he has focused on research and advisory work in social protection and social transfers. As a GTZ and UNICEF consultant he designed the Social Cash

Transfer Scheme called GAPVU/INAS in Mozambique (1989 to 1994). As a consultant for GTZ and for CARE International he designed Pilot Social Cash Transfer Schemes in a number of districts in Zambia (2003 to 2006). Since April 2006 he has worked as a UNICEF consultant designing Pilot Social Cash Transfer Schemes in Malawi and advises the Government of Malawi on social protection policy issues.

Rachel Slater is a Research Fellow at the Overseas Development Institute in London. Her work is mainly on southern and eastern Africa. Her specific research interests include risk and vulnerability, the linkages between agricultural growth and social protection, and the use of different social protection instruments to tackle HIV/AIDS and chronic food insecurity.

Sudarno Sumarto is Director of the SMERU Research Institute, Jakarta. He is an economist and his research focuses on poverty analysis, social protection, wage and labour employment and other socio-economic-related issues. His work has been published in a number of international journals, including *Asian Economic Journal*, *Journal of International Development*, *Bulletin of Indonesian Economic Studies*, *World Development* and *Review of Income and Wealth*.

Asep Suryahadi is Senior Researcher at the SMERU Research Institute, Jakarta. His research interests focus on poverty, vulnerability, labour, and social protection issues. He has written for several publications, including the *Bulletin of Indonesian Economic Studies*, *Asian Economic Journal*, *Review of Income and Wealth*, *Applied Economics*, *Journal of International Development*, *World Development*, *Development and Change*, *Education Economics* and the *European Journal of Development Research*.

Glossary

Beneficiaries: Direct recipients of support from social assistance programmes.

Cash for work: Cash transfers distributed to vulnerable individuals or households in exchange for labour.

Categorical targeting: Selection of programme beneficiaries based on individual or household characteristics or assets; for example, age, disability, landlessness.

Conditional cash transfer: Cash distributed to vulnerable individuals or households on condition that they undertake specified activities; for example, that children attend school, or that mothers attend primary health centres.

Evaluation: Process of assessing whether a programme is fulfilling its objectives.

Fee waiver: Exemptions from payment of fees (for example, school fees, exam fees or fees for medical treatment) for selected vulnerable individuals or groups.

Food-based transfer: Food distributed to vulnerable individuals and households to alleviate poverty or malnutrition.

Food for work: Food distributed to vulnerable individuals or households in exchange for labour.

Geographical targeting: Selection of beneficiaries on the basis of their residence in poorer regions or locations.

Grant: A sum of money or in-kind subsidy awarded to compensate for specified contingencies; for example, resettlement, old age, disability.

Gross domestic product (GDP): A measure of the value of all the resources produced by a country in a year.

In-kind transfer: Non-cash transfers (for example, wheat or flour) distributed to vulnerable individual or households (see Food-based transfer).

Leakage: The extent to which a programme includes beneficiaries not in the target group. The leakage rate of a poverty programme measures the proportion of beneficiaries that are not poor.

Means or Income test: A test applied to determine eligibility for programme benefits. It usually defines a threshold above which applicants are not eligible for support. The threshold can be based on the income or assets, or both, of the applicant and his/her immediate family (spouse, household). The test can also help to determine the value of the benefit paid; for example, the difference between current income and the threshold.

Near cash transfer: A non-monetary transfer to vulnerable individuals or households that can be exchange for goods or services – for example, food stamps or school vouchers.

Pilot project: A small-scale project undertaken in an effort to determine whether a larger-scale project should be undertaken at a later date.

Poverty gap: The difference between the current income or expenditure of those in poverty and the poverty line.

Poverty headcount: The proportion of a population who are in poverty.

Programme coverage: The population reached by a programme. Coverage rate measures the extent to which programmes reach their target population.

Proxy index: A test of whether individuals or households are eligible for participation in a programme, based on an index calculated from several variables (quality of housing, assets, household composition, etc.) but excluding income or expenditure. Households are then ranked according to their index value, and programme beneficiaries are selected if their index value is below a threshold.

Self-targeting: Applies to programmes lacking explicit eligibility requirements but including design features that attract some target population only; for example, public works that pay wages lower than the market wage will only attract the unemployed or underemployed.

Social assistance: Programmes providing cash or in-kind support for individuals or households in poverty, normally tax-financed.

Social insurance: Programmes providing pre-specified support for affiliated individuals in the event of specific contingencies, such as work-related injury or sickness, old age, and disability. Social insurance programmes are normally financed through contributions from employees and employers.

Social pension: Applies to non-contributory pensions, and describes unconditional cash transfers paid to older or disabled people, normally tax-financed.

Targeting: The method and process of selection of programme beneficiaries.

Unconditional cash transfer: Cash transferred to vulnerable individuals and/or households without conditions or requirements.

Vulnerability: The probability that individuals and households will be in poverty in the future.

Foreword

Social protection aims to protect poor people from the grave hazards they face and thereby prevent households descending into abysmal poverty as a result of adverse shocks. Ill-health, drought, natural hazards, market fluctuations and violent conflict can each cause a catastrophic loss of income for poor households. These hazards have been getting worse: climate change is increasing the magnitude and incidence of shocks such as flooding and drought; globalisation has increased vulnerability to technology change and market fluctuations; 'new' diseases such as HIV/AIDS threaten progress on health, while ageing is presenting a new source of vulnerability. The need for social protection has thus recently become a priority of development policy, supported by the donor community as well as many developing country governments. The increasing acceptance of its importance stems from the recognition that poverty eradication goals, such as the MDGs or Human Rights realisation, *cannot* be achieved without social protection since the poor, and those who have just escaped poverty, are highly vulnerable to shocks that throw them back into poverty. In recognition of this, among the most important political struggles of the late nineteenth and early twentieth century in Europe was the, at first piecemeal, introduction of measures of social protection culminating in near universal coverage for citizens who have survived some recent retreat from the welfare state model. It is now recognised that universal protection, albeit modest, is essential and affordable for developing countries too and cannot be postponed until they achieve developed country status.

This book represents a timely review of social protection concepts and policies in developing countries. It shows that a wide range of policy approaches can be classified under the social protection mantle including, among others, social risk management; cash transfers towards children, the old, and the ultra-poor; public works; and insurance-based schemes. Some are universal entitlements, while others are conditional or targeted. Most countries have several schemes in operation. A critical question then is the *comprehensiveness* of the social protection coverage in a country, taking all schemes available together. It is the comprehensiveness of approach which should differentiate social protection from the old-style (1980s and 1990s) social safety nets, which for the most part covered a small fraction of the population in need. The limited coverage was due to financial constraints combined with excessive targeting, especially where the schemes were introduced with the support of donors rather than being home grown. It is shown in this book, however, that comprehensive coverage *is* affordable.

The challenge then is to introduce low-cost schemes and effective design to ensure comprehensiveness.

Social protection has two legs: there is the leg of hazard prevention and that of compensation. Prevention includes, for example, tackling global warming; providing comprehensive preventative health care; generating decent work; and introducing policies to reduce violent conflict. These are all clearly difficult to achieve, and therefore compensation is essential. Yet it is important not to forget about prevention because – if it works – it is likely to be much more satisfactory than compensation. Who would not prefer to avoid floods, to remain in good health, to continue in employment and so on than to suffer personal disasters and then receive (normally inadequate) compensation?

The book ends by exploring the politics of social protection. Essentially, social protection has to be fought for as European history shows. The struggle was by unions, intellectuals and progressive politicians, inspired by a hatred of poverty and a growing recognition that universal protection made not only economic but also political sense. This represents the views of the authors of this book – which should play an important role in the struggle for social protection in poor countries.

Frances Stewart
Professor of Development Economics,
University of Oxford

Part I
Introduction

1

Social Protection for the Poor and Poorest: An Introduction

Armando Barrientos and David Hulme

What is social protection?

There is an emerging consensus around the view that social protection provides an effective response to poverty and vulnerability in developing countries.[1] This is finding expression in the growing number of national governments adopting social protection strategies, and in the rapidly expanding set of policies and programmes being implemented in developing countries.[2] There is also rising interest in social protection among development researchers, with social protection being viewed increasingly as the emerging paradigm for social policy in developing countries.

Social protection has been around for some time. It is defined as 'public actions taken in response to levels of vulnerability, risk, and deprivation which are deemed socially unacceptable within a given polity or society' (Conway, de Haan and Norton 2000). In the work of the ILO it has been associated with a range of public institutions, norms and programmes aimed at protecting individuals and their households from poverty and deprivation. Broadly, these can be grouped under three main headings: social insurance, social assistance, and labour market regulation. *Social insurance* consists of programmes providing protection against contingencies arising from life-course contingencies such as maternity and old age, or from work-related contingencies such as unemployment or sickness. *Social assistance* provides support for those in poverty. Normally, social insurance is financed from contributions by workers and their employers, whereas social assistance (in some countries known as public assistance) is tax-financed. Finally, *labour market regulation* ensures basic standards at work, and extend rights to organisation and voice.

In the 1990s, social protection underwent a significant transformation, especially in the context of developing countries. Against a background of economic crises, structural adjustment and globalisation, social protection increasingly defines an agenda for social policy in developing countries. There are several distinguishing features of the emerging paradigm. Social protection has a strong focus on poverty reduction and on providing support to the poorest (de Haan 2000). It seeks to address the causes of poverty, and not simply its symptoms (World Bank 2001). It is based on the view that a primary cause of poverty is to be found in the constraints faced by the poor in taking advantage of economic opportunity arising from their vulnerability to the impact of economic, social and natural hazards. In the absence of social protection, these hazards impact directly on living standards, but can in addition motivate risk-averse behaviour among the poor and poorest that is detrimental to their long-term welfare. By focusing on vulnerability – that is, the likelihood of being in poverty in the future – social protection places us in a better position to understand the dynamic nature of poverty. In its new guise, and in particular in the context of developing countries, social protection must perform three main functions: (i) to help protect basic levels of consumption among those in poverty or in danger of falling into poverty; (ii) to facilitate investment in human and other productive assets that alone can provide escape routes from persistent and intergenerational poverty; and (iii) to strengthen the agency of those in poverty so that they can overcome their predicament (Barrientos forthcoming).

Social protection and development: linking policy to conceptual frameworks

Beyond its role as a policy framework addressing poverty and vulnerability, social protection embodies and extends alternative approaches to economic and social development. In developing countries in particular, all public policy is concerned with social transformation, and social protection is not an exception. It is important to trace back alternative approaches to social protection to the different perspectives on social transformation in which they are rooted. Some locate the basis of social protection in a rights perspective to human development, others locate it in the context of the satisfaction of basic needs, and yet others ground it in the context of lifting the constraints to human and economic development posed by social risk. A conceptual focus on risks, needs and rights can support alternative views of social protection. Munro's chapter in this volume discusses these alternative frameworks for social protection in detail.

Here, we can illustrate this point by considering the different perspectives on social protection proposed by multilateral organisations. The ILO understands social protection as arising from human rights. It is defined by 'entitlement to benefits that society provides to individuals and households – through public and collective measures – to protect against low or declining living standards arising out of a number of basic risks and needs' (van Ginneken 2000, p. 34). The international community acknowledged that social protection is a basic human right to be enshrined in the Universal Declaration of Human Rights agreed by the United Nations General Assembly in 1948. In the words of the Declaration, 'everyone has the right to a standard of living adequate for the health and well-being of himself and of his family'. The ILO's recent reformulation of its mission statement as involving work to 'secure decent work for women and men everywhere' is an affirmation of their rights perspective and reflects the Declaration's commitment to extend social protection to all.[3]

The UN defines social protection as 'a set of public and private policies and programmes undertaken by societies in response to various contingencies to offset the absence or substantial reduction of income from work; to provide assistance to families with children as well as provide people with basic health care and housing' (United Nations 2000, p. 4). It is underpinned by shared 'fundamental values concerning acceptable levels and security of access to income, livelihood, employment, health and education services, nutrition and shelter' (United Nations 2000, p. 4). This approach extends the role of social protection to securing basic needs as a precondition for human and economic development.

The Social Protection Strategy Paper from the World Bank moves beyond 'traditional' social protection in defining a 'social risk management' framework adding macroeconomic stability and financial market development to typical social protection programmes. Social risk management consists of public interventions 'to assist individuals, households and communities in better managing income risks' (Holzmann and Jorgensen 1999, p. 4). The emphasis on risk assumes that vulnerability to hazards is a significant constraint on economic and human development, and that efforts to reduce the likelihood of hazards, or to ameliorate their effects on living standards are essential to growth and development.

As can be seen from this brief review, the different definitions of social protection adopted by these organisations in fact reflect the different perspectives on development on which they are grounded. It is important to explore the conceptual underpinnings of the different policy frameworks that agencies or individuals propose, as these determine what practical actions are (or are not) emphasised in the framework. Because it focuses purely on the concept of risk, the World Bank is often accused of having a narrow framework focused on 'safety nets'. By contrast, Sabates-Wheeler and Devereux (Chapter 4 in this volume) weave together the concepts of rights, needs, and empowerment to produce an all-encompassing policy framework of 'transformative social protection'.

The rise of social protection in development policy

What are the main drivers of social protection? Current interest in social protection among policy-makers developed in the context of the sharp rise in poverty and vulnerability in the 1980s and 1990s. This led to a better understanding of the human and developmental costs associated with not having adequate social protection policies and programmes in developing countries. More recently, the Millennium Development Goals (MDGs) have focused attention on poverty and vulnerability reduction, and as a result the social protection agenda has been given a high profile.

Social protection as a response to global insecurity and vulnerability

A number of factors explain the rise of social protection as a dominant agenda for social policy, but the effects of globalisation and rapid economic transformation are the most important. Globalisation has been a significant factor in the emergence of social protection, as it raises the demand for social protection (Rodrik 1997, 2001). The greater openness of developing economies implies increased vulnerability to changes in global markets, and a greater concentration of social and economic hazards on the less powerful participants. In the 1980s and 1990s, economic transformation unfolded at a rapid pace in Latin America and East Asia. The 1980s were characterised by acute and sustained economic and financial crises as well as structural adjustment in the economies of Latin America. The financial crisis in 1997 affected in similar ways the countries in East Asia. The transition economies underwent deep structural reforms and transformation.

In all cases, the outcomes of these changes were at first a rapid rise in poverty and vulnerability, which laid bare the glaring gaps in social protection in developing countries. In the countries affected, the adverse impacts of transformation were concentrated on the more vulnerable sectors. The immediate impact of the crises and transformation on poverty and vulnerability, and the threat of conflict and social unrest they presaged, focused attention on strengthening social protection policies and programmes. Sumarto *et al.* (Chapter 6 in this volume) track the hasty introduction of safety nets in Indonesia as the financial crises in 1997 led to the incidence of poverty doubling from 15 per cent to 33 per cent by the end of 1998. Relatedly, Britto (Chapter 9 in this volume) examines the emergence of conditional cash transfer programmes in Latin America as a response to the 1980s crises. Increasing poverty and vulnerability arising from globalisation and economic transformation are therefore key drivers for social protection. In addition, the continuing and perhaps rising levels of violent conflict in many parts of the world (especially Afghanistan, Iraq and Sub-Saharan Africa) further increase vulnerability and insecurity across those regions.

For Africa, and perhaps in the future for parts of Asia, HIV/AIDS has become a major factor that increases vulnerability. As Slater (Chapter 7 in this volume) describes the high incidence of HIV/AIDS in some countries has had catastrophic effects on household, community and national human security.

The cost of not having social protection

The rise in poverty and vulnerability has facilitated an improved understanding of the costs associated with the glaring gaps in social protection in developing countries. In fact, an extensive literature is available measuring these costs in a variety of settings (Morduch 1998; Dercon 2005). Table 1.1 extracts some estimates from this literature.

Table 1.1 The cost of not having social protection: selected estimates

Sources of vulnerability and nature of adverse impact	Estimates of impact
Exposure to natural, economic, and political (conflict) shocks reduces growth and development	An IMF report identified the negative impact of shocks on GDP growth as follows: Cambodia (drought/flood 1994) less than 1%; Zimbabwe (drought, 1992) 8.5%; Mali (export price shock, 1992–1993) 1.8% per year; Uganda (export price shock, 1987 1992) 3.5% per year for 6 years; Honduras (hurricanes, 1987–1992) 13,700 people dead or missing and direct damages estimated at 47% of 1997 GDP (IMF 2003)
Transient poverty can be attributed to direct exposure to employment, health and other idiosyncratic hazards	In China, it was estimated that transient poverty accounts for half of the squared poverty gap (Jalan and Ravallion 2001)
	In rural Ethiopia, transient poverty accounts for 45% of the squared poverty gap (Dercon and Krishnan 2000)
Exposure to hazards can also cause chronic poverty through behavioural responses to risk by the poor. For example, through:	
• lower farm productivity from choosing low-return/low-risk crops	In India, providing the poorest quartile with the same protection against rainfall time variation as the top quartile would improve their farm profits by 35% (Rosenzweig and Binswanger 1993)
	In rural Tanzania, the cost to the poorest quintile arising from growing low-return/low-risk crops is lower returns by 20% compared to the wealthiest group (Dercon 2005)
• the impact of hazards on the asset base of the poor	IIn Ethiopia's famine years (1984–1985) 60% of households reported having had to sell livestock, and herds declined by 40%; 90% of households reported having cut back on food consumption. By 1994, herds were still only 87% of pre- famine size (Dercon 2005)

Continued

Table 1.1   Continued

Sources of vulnerability and nature of adverse impact	Estimates of impact
• the impact of hazards on human capital	The negative impact of crises on child labour and schooling has been observed in a wide range of developing countries, and in particular among larger countries such as Brazil, India and Indonesia (Priyambada, Suryahadi and Sumarto 2002)
	The impact on nutrition has also been observed for many countries. In Zimbabwe, a severe drought resulted in poor nutrition and stunting, with permanent loss of 1–2 cm of height on average (Hoddinott and Kinsey 2001)
	In Mexico, there is evidence that crises result in cuts in spending on health care and nutrition for both young and old, leading to higher mortality rates for these groups (Cutler, Knaul, Lozano *et al.* 2000)

The Table provides an indication of the substantial welfare gaps arising from the absence of social protection in developing countries.[4] There are large direct costs associated with economy-wide, and sometimes region-wide, natural, economic and political hazards. The extent of transient poverty provides a good indicator of the losses associated with the absence of social protection. On the assumption that appropriate social protection could help to stabilise income and consumption in the event of idiosyncratic health or employment hazards, say, transient poverty could in principle be eradicated by social protection. Transient poverty itself therefore provides a good measure of the gaps in social protection.

Gaps in social protection can also be responsible for chronic poverty, especially in situations where the social protection instruments available to those below or near the poverty line are limited, and as a result they are forced to adopt alternatives with detrimental long-run effects. Taking children out of school, cutting down on health care, sub-standard nutrition, or less productive employment or crops, can push households into persistent poverty. This brief review of estimates of the impact of hazards strongly suggests that there are large losses associated with not having adequate social protection, and consequently large gains to be captured by establishing strong social protection institutions. An improved understanding of these losses and potential gains has been an important driver for social protection.

The Millennium Development Goals and social protection

The adoption of the Millennium Declaration in 2000 has focused the attention of international organisations, poor and rich country governments, and the citizens and celebrities of Europe and North America, on poverty and vulnerability reduction more than any other global initiative in the past (Greig, Hulme and Turner 2007, pp. 129–161). Leaving aside an assessment of the desirability of the enterprise,[5] or the extent to which it sits comfortably with ongoing initiatives such as Poverty Reduction Strategies (PRSs), the focus on poverty has being a strong driver for the extension of social protection in many developing countries.

While all the MDGs can contribute to reduced vulnerability and poverty reduction, a number of the MDG targets have particular significance for social protection (see Table 1.2).

Table 1.2 The MDGs and social protection

Goal/target	Objective	Implications for social protection
Goal 1 Target 1	Halve the proportion of people whose income is less than US$1 a day (1990–2015)	While the MDGs assume that this will be achieved largely by economic growth, this also promotes cash transfers to those not benefiting from growth
Goal 1 Target 2	Halve the proportion of people suffering from hunger (1990–2015)	This supports nutritional interventions (humanitarian aid, mid-day meals) and/or basic income grants
Goal 2 Target 3	Universal primary education by 2015	More concerted efforts to reduce the withdrawal of children from school as a vulnerability coping mechanism
Goal 4 Target 5	Reduce the under-5 mortality rate by two-thirds (1990–2015)	Promotes improved access to basic health services for children and free provision or improved health insurance schemes
Goal 5 Target 6 Goal 6	Reduce the maternal mortality ratio by three-quarters (1990–2015)	Promotes improved access to basic health services for women and free provision or improved health insurance schemes

Continued

Table 1.2   Continued

Goal/target	Objective	Implications for social protection
Targets 7 & 8	Halt and reverse the spread of HIV/AIDS, malaria and other diseases by 2015	Supports more effective disease prevention and improved access to health services
Goal 7 Target 10	Halve the proportion of people without access to safe water and basic sanitation by 2015	Encourages basic infrastructural development leading to fewer health shocks and reduced morbidity and mortality
Goal 7 Target 11	Significant improvements in the lives of at least 100 million slum dwellers by 2020	Promotes initiatives to reduce the vulnerability of slum dwellers

Source: UN Millennium Development Goals, http://www.un.org/millenniumgoals.

Table 1.2 reveals the potential encouragement that the MDGs provide for an increased emphasis on social protection policies. However, three limitations to this must be considered. First, the rich world has not matched its promises to support the MDGs with increased aid and related policy reforms (trade and debt). Second, the relatively high rates of pro-poor economic growth assumed in the MDG scenario have not occurred in some regions, particularly Sub-Saharan Africa, where growth has been based on oil and mineral extraction. Finally, while the governments of developing countries have signed up to the MDGs, and this is reflected by the inclusion of social protection policies in PRSs, policy implementation in many counties has been ineffective. This has been particularly the case in countries where the need for social protection is greatest.

Main actors

The policy agenda around social protection involves key development actors: multilateral and bilateral organisations, international NGOs, national governments and agencies, and research institutes. This section discusses their recent contributions.

Among multilaterals, the ILO has traditionally taken the lead in advocating and supporting social protection, and has been in large part responsible for the spread of social protection institutions in developing countries (Usui 1994). Its tripartite governance system, involving trade unions, employers' associations and governments has proved effective in gathering support for the extension of social protection for organised workers. However, the growth in informality, and the relative decline of organised formal employment in recent times has been particularly challenging to these structures. Concerns with the capacity of traditional approaches and institutions to extend social protection coverage to workers in informal employment, a majority of workers in the South, has encouraged important shifts in perspective. It has led to a new focus on 'decent work' as a framework for extending basic rights to all workers, regardless of their employment relationship (ILO 2001b). Decent work is defined as productive and secure employment, with respect for labour rights, providing adequate income and social protection, and enabling dialogue and participation. There are direct linkages to social protection and poverty reduction, in so far as decent work includes protection and provides a direct escape from poverty. Social protection is not restricted to the employment relationship, and extends to all. The ILO has recently advocated a basic package of social protection measures among low-income countries (ILO 2006).

The World Bank developed a social protection strategy in the mid-1990s as a response to the impact of structural adjustment on developing countries, and the failure of 'social dimensions' and safety net approaches. The Bank established a Social Protection Group, initially focused on labour market and pension reform, and safety nets, but more recently focused on a wider range of instruments, including cash transfers.[6] The World Bank is now a major player in social protection, leveraging change through technical assistance and financial support.[7] Its role as a bank restricts its social protection work in both low-income countries and middle-income countries with high debt levels. Partnerships with bilaterals, such as the Social Protection Trust Fund established by DFID to support joint initiatives, provide a facility with which to influence policy developments in these countries. The risk-based approach to social protection embraced by the World Bank at times enforces a more technocratic approach.[8]

Other parts of the UN family have adopted social protection policies, including UNDP, UNICEF, WHO (United Nations 2000). Bilaterals such as DFID, GTZ and USAID are increasingly developing and supporting social protection policies. DFID is a large player through the funding of social protection initiatives of multilaterals (DFID 2005).

Increasingly, national governments are developing social protection strategies in an effort to consolidate and institutionalise cross-sectoral policies. In middle-income countries, social protection strategies have involved the reform of social insurance schemes and a stronger effort to develop effective social assistance. This is especially true of transition economies, but also of countries in Latin America and the Caribbean. In low-income countries, national social protection strategies have developed around second-generation PRSs, in an effort to develop pro-active and integrated social protection policies. In low-income countries in Africa, pilot programmes focused around cash transfers are also spearheading efforts to establish social protection strategies and institutions (Barrientos forthcoming). An important recent change in many countries has been the growing interest of ministries of finance because of donor financial support for social protection. This can be beneficial, as the welfare ministries that traditionally oversee social assistance often have limited capacity for policy analysis and evaluation.

Apart from humanitarian relief and assistance,[9] the adoption of social protection among international NGOs has been slower. Receptiveness to the social protection agenda has been greater among international NGOs committed to poverty reduction and advocating policies directed at groups whose vulnerability arises from life-course conditions. Help Age International, and more recently Save the Children, have embraced the social protection agenda (Beales and German 2006). The 'Grow Free from Poverty Coalition' and 'Pensions not Poverty' are interlinked advocacy platforms gathering support for the extension of social protection in developing countries. NGOs involved in the delivery of development programmes, on the other hand, have been slower to adopt social protection, in part because their experience and orientation is focused on piecemeal programmes with a fixed time-frame. There are some elements of the social protection policy agenda that are inimical to their orientation, especially the often acknowledged need to move beyond fragmented programmes delivered by structures running in parallel to, or independent from, government agencies. Nevertheless, some change can be observed among NGOs focused on delivery; for example, OXFAM's involvement in the Orphans and Vulnerable Children (OVCs) Cash Transfer Programme in Kenya, or the involvement of CARE in the delivery of pilot cash transfers in Zambia.

Interestingly, it is among the NGOs involved in delivering emergency and humanitarian assistance that a receptiveness to social protection as a longer-term response to conflict and emergency is strongest (Harvey 2005). Beyond advocacy, the role of NGOs in social protection in the medium and longer term is not well defined. Social protection acknowledges, in both principle and practice, the advantages of mixed provision, but at the same time it assigns to public agencies a primary role in policy development, co-ordination and regulation. NGOs engaged in social protection will need to adjust to this parameter.

An important constraint in the development of social protection in developing countries is the absence of a strong research base in universities and leading development institutes. Compared to the related areas of education or health, it is difficult to identify an equivalent institutional research and policy base for social protection. Social policy has never become established as a discipline outside Europe, and the sub-discipline of 'social development' (see Booth 1994) which might have filled this institutional and intellectual vacuum, focused on participation, and has a suspicion of delivery programmes by public agencies. In terms of academic research, social protection works under the twin disadvantages of its multidisciplinarity and its strong policy focus. Moreover, the evolution, institutions and policies that characterise social protection in developed countries are hard to replicate in developing countries, even among the most advanced. Typically, in developed countries, researchers engaged with social protection are based in development studies institutes or think tanks. Despite the significant role and profile of social protection within the current development policy agenda, there are few researchers specialising in this area, even fewer in developing countries, and they are scattered across countries and institutions.[10] A challenge for the development of social protection in developing countries will be the need to strengthen research capacity promoting the development of an epistemic community that engages directly with policy, and to integrate the range of expertise needed to advise developing countries.[11]

At present, and in the future, institutional partnerships to devise, advocate and deliver social protection seem likely. These can involve national governments, national and international NGOs, bilateral and multilateral aid agencies and research institutes. Each can contribute its strengths – national coverage, links to poor people, finance, analytical and monitoring capacity etc. Such partnerships are not without their problems, however– for example, when a donor tries to impose its model of social protection on a recipient government.

Key issues

In this section we focus on the main issues emerging from the ongoing expansion of social protection in developing countries since the early 1990s. We focus on issues of scale, scope, integration, financing and politics.

Scale

Without doubt, by far the most important issue in social protection is the scale of recent initiatives. Whereas since the early to mid-1990s the coverage of social insurance in developing countries has stagnated or declined, the coverage of social assistance programmes has risen at a staggering pace. Take a handful of recent income transfer initiatives: the Child Support Grant in South Africa implemented in stages since 2003 now reaches 7.2 million children; the Minimum Living Standards Scheme in China rose from 2.6 million beneficiaries in 1999 to 20.6 million in 2002, and 22.4 million in 2006. Mexico's *Oportunidades*, which replaced *Progresa* in 2002, now reaches 5 million households. *Bolsa Familia*, which replaced *Bolsa Escola* in 2004, now reaches 11 million households in Brazil; Indonesia's Safety Net cash transfer scheme introduced in 2005 reaches more than 15 million households. The Employment Guarantee Scheme, aiming to provide 100 days' guaranteed income for the rural poor in India, is currently being implemented and is expected to reach around 26 million households when fully operational. Admittedly, these are countries with large populations, and a more comprehensive list would need to include a large number of programmes recently introduced in other countries in Latin America and the Caribbean, Asia and Africa,[12] but they show the extent and speed of growth in the global coverage of social assistance. It is apparent from this brief list that the recent growth in social protection in developing countries has the potential to make a very significant contribution to the reduction of poverty and vulnerability on a global scale.

Scope

We have grouped these programmes under social assistance because they are focused on the poorest, rely mainly on income transfers, and are tax-financed; but it would be wrong to see them in the same light as compensatory social assistance programmes in developed countries. Increasingly, social assistance programmes in developing countries are based around regular and predictable transfers, and combine a range of developmental interventions addressing the multidimensional and persistent nature of poverty. Social assistance programmes in developing countries are widening in terms of their scope too. This is particularly the case among programmes targeting households in extreme or persistent poverty.

A couple of examples may be helpful. Mexico's *Progresa* is a targeted conditional cash transfer programme. It pioneered income transfers, directed towards the poorest, that were conditional on households sending children to school and attendance at health centres with early childhood and nutrition interventions. *Progresa* was designed to reflect an assessment that the incidence and persistence of poverty in rural Mexico resulted not only from consumption deficits but also from insufficient investment in human capital. The extension of *Progresa* to the rest of the country in 2006 as *Oportunidades* also widened the scope of the programme. It now includes subsidies supporting education beyond secondary school, skills training for the unemployed in urban areas, additional subsidies for people aged over 70, and a range of micro-saving and micro-enterprise development components.[13]

In Bangladesh, BRAC (the largest NGO working on poverty reduction in South Asia) accumulated experience with micro-finance and micro-enterprise development interventions over three decades, and concluded that the poorest are unable to benefit from conventional asset accumulation programmes because of their social exclusion, acute deficits in nutrition and health, and low borrowing capacity. This led to the design of a poverty reduction programme specifically for the poorest – the Targeting the Ultra Poor (TUP) programme, introduced in 2001 following a multi-stage approach combining a monthly cash stipend boosting the consumption of the poorest households, confidence building, social development in the form of health interventions, and income-generating skills training promoting an economic project for each participant household. The objective is to combine a range of interventions strengthening the productive capacity of beneficiaries up to a level where they can make full use of conventional asset accumulation programmes. Hulme and Moore, in Chapter 10 in this volume take a closer look at BRAC's experience with the TUP programme. Widening the scope of social protection programmes is the most effective approach to addressing the multiple causes of chronic poverty, and its persistence (Barrientos, Hulme and Shepherd 2005).

Integrating social protection in national development strategies

Social assistance programmes in developing countries are necessarily 'productivist' in so far as they must combine interventions aimed at strengthening the productive capacity of the poor and poorest, as an essential component of an integrated poverty reduction and development strategy.[14] In this context, the integration of social protection interventions becomes a crucial issue. The integration of multiple interventions based on an assessment of the factors generating persistent poverty in different countries or regions is increasingly a feature of social protection interventions. In many countries, a widening of the scope of the programmes has followed directly from the lessons emerging from the evaluation of narrower, sectoral, and fragmented programmes. *Chile Solidario*, for example, combines interventions along seven different dimensions of poverty: income, employment, health, education, housing, registration, and intra-household dynamics, in an effort to eradicate extreme poverty (Barrientos 2006b).

It is likely that, in low-income countries at least, the evolution towards a comprehensive social protection system for developing countries will be led by the kind of social assistance programmes reviewed above. The widening of the scope of social assistance beyond income transfers provides important clues as to the future evolution of these programmes. Assumptions about the evolution of social protection systems in developing countries often takes it for granted that they will follow the pathway used by present-day developed countries. In these countries, social insurance gradually extended to larger sections of the population, with social assistance becoming largely residual. In low-income countries, a different evolutionary pathway seems probable, moving outwards from social assistance and with a strong 'productivist' orientation. Tracking the integration and dynamics of the social protection mix is a priority for further research, and is an issue that we shall come back to in the context of the politics of social protection (see Chapters13 by Hickey and Chapter 14 by Munemo in this volume).[15]

Financing social protection

What are the options for financing the expansion of social protection in developing countries? Finance is rightly perceived as one of two main constraints, the other being political commitment, on the expansion of social protection, especially in low-income countries. It will help our discussion to distinguish between two separate issues: (i) determining the level of financing required to ensure a minimum level of social protection; and (ii) finding out how developing countries might finance this.

As regards the first issue, the ILO's Social Security Department has performed some simulations for low-income countries in Africa and Asia to indicate the resources required to provide a basic social assistance package for low-income countries. These are reported in Chapter 15 by Berendt in this volume. Their main findings are that the cost of a basic package including a universal pension covering old age and disability and a child benefit would absorb, on average, around 2–3 per cent of GDP.[16] Naturally, the cost of the same package in different countries would differ in line with demographic, macroeconomic and fiscal conditions. At the same time, varying the level of the benefit and targeting only the poor could reduce the size of the resources required significantly. We could also take a positive approach to determining the resources required by considering the cost of existing social assistance programmes. With the exception of the Minimum Living Standards Scheme in China, social assistance programmes in developing countries aim to cover only a fraction of household consumption.[17] The targeted conditional cash transfer programmes introduced in Latin America and the Caribbean absorb less than 1 per cent of GDP. As a rough rule of thumb, around 1–2 per cent of GDP appears to be the level of resources required to finance a basic level of social assistance in developing countries.

Financing this basic level of social assistance appears to be affordable for most developing countries, but it is bound to be more difficult to achieve for low-income countries with low revenue mobilisation capacity. Uganda, for example, only manages to collect taxes equivalent to 13 per cent of GDP, and therefore allocating 1 per cent of GDP for social protection would require a substantial budget change. Economic growth could generate additional resources, while at the same time a reduction in demand for social assistance would reduce fiscal pressures. Aside from growth, there are two main options to be considered: raising tax revenues as a proportion of GDP through improvements in the efficiency of tax-collection agencies.[18] Another option would be to switch expenditure from poorly performing poverty budget allocations. However, in low-income countries there is only very limited scope for expenditure switching. It would make little sense to divert resources supporting the provision of basic services, or supporting productive investment, to finance social assistance. The latter relies on basic service infrastructure and growing economic opportunity. There is a case for using official development assistance to finance the start-up costs of social protection programmes and to ease financial constraints in their initial stages. In the medium and longer run, sustainable and effective social protection has to be financed from domestic resources. In middle-income countries, there is greater scope for expenditure switching, especially in countries devoting considerable resources to poorly performing poverty reduction interventions, or to subsidise financially unsustainable and highly unequal social insurance schemes.[19]

The politics of social protection

Extending social protection in developing countries also requires a propitious political environment in which demand for social protection can translate into appropriate government responses. It is useful to make a distinction between the political conditions needed for the adoption of social protection initiatives, and those required for the sustainability of programmes.

Considering the adoption of social protection programmes, there is surprisingly little research on developing countries. Public choice models of policy processes are perhaps not very helpful in this context, especially low-income countries. They rely on assumptions about the existence of a competitive political system in which voters signal preferences over different policy alternatives, and politicians have no option but to respond. In developing countries, and in particular low-income ones, the shortcomings of median voter models of policy adoption are apparent. Voters are ill-informed about the relative advantages of policy options, and the promises of politicians have little or no credibility (Keefer and Khemani 2003). Patronage, clientelism and corruption undermine the basis for competitive politics. The political system is, as a result, less effective in aggregating voter preferences than in protecting and nurturing patron–client relationships. Hickey's Chapter 13 in this volume reflects on these issues in the context of Africa.

This underscores the importance of factors exogenous to the political system, such as major disasters or crises, or the intervention of donors and NGOs, in forcing social protection into the political agenda. It is not surprising that the adoption of social protection programmes often reflects a desire on the part of policy-makers to counteract real or perceived opposition to government policy, and the threat of social unrest. Social protection programmes can play a very significant part in facilitating social and economic transformation, especially where the associated losses are large and up-front. A good example is the introduction of Bolivia's *Bono Solidario*. The government used the pension programme as a means of ensuring political support for the privatisation of utilities, by promising to use the proceeds from privatisation to fund a pension scheme (Gray-Molina 1999). Interestingly, the government suspended the pension entitlement after successfully completing the privatisation process, but reinstated it later under public pressure, with a reduced level of benefits. Later, renewed public pressure led a new government to reinstate the pension in full (Barrientos 2006a). The rapid expansion of China's Minimum Living Standards Scheme or Argentina's *Jefes y Jefas* constituted a response to rapidly rising unemployment and the threat of unrest.

The political conditions required for the political sustainability of social protection programmes are less demanding, but this can be problematic. Discussing the spread of income transfer programmes in Latin America, Britto (Chapter 9 in this volume) notes how quickly political support can be gathered for poverty reduction programmes that are perceived to be both effective in reaching the poor and efficient in the use of resources. Social protection programmes can quickly build coalitions of support. This can also be a disadvantage in so far as social protection shows strong path dependence, with the implication that often it will be difficult to reform them or replace them with better alternatives.

Structure of the book

The book is divided into three main sections. The first section focuses on the conceptual frameworks supporting social protection: risks, needs and rights. As noted above, there is very little discussion in the social protection literature on the deeper theoretical underpinnings of social protection. Social protection is usually considered as a policy framework, but we have argued that policy frameworks need to be grounded in theories of economic and social development. We have also demonstrated that differences in the approach to, and definition of, social protection in multilateral agencies can be tracked down to differences in their development perspectives. Chapter 2 by Munro unpacks the three main conceptual frameworks for social protection, taking care to identify and discuss the main areas of agreement and disagreement existing between them. We are then better placed to understand divergent perspectives on social protection. As he puts it, it 'is important to understand why we support what we support'. Even more importantly for our purposes, it facilitates the task of reconsidering these perspectives in the context of extreme and chronic poverty.

The next three contributions focus on these perspectives and their interactions. Dercon, Bold and Calvo, in Chapter 3, expand on the risk perspective in order to examine the impact of risk on those in poverty, including the risks associated with the limited provision of insurance for the poorest, and to consider ways in which improved insurance instruments may be deployed effectively to support them. Sabates-Wheeler and Devereux adopt a rights perspective in Chapter 4 to argue for a transformative social protection, understood as 'policies that integrate individuals into society, allowing everyone to take advantage of the benefits of growth and enabling excluded or marginalised groups to claim their rights'. Carter, Little, Mogues and Negatufocus in Chapter 5 on the way in which the impacts of natural hazards on rural households are mediated by social and economic institutions. They find that environmental shocks could generate 'poverty traps' among those with high sensitivity to shocks, and low resilience. Their contribution highlights how effective social protection strategies needs to integrate concerns with risks, needs, and rights.

The second section includes several chapters discussing social protection policies and programmes that show promise in working for the poor and poorest. Sumarto, Suryahadi and Bazzi provide in Chapter 6 an insightful and comprehensive discussion of the design and evolution of social protection in Indonesia as a response to the 1997 financial crisis. Their contribution tracks the evolution of social protection from the immediate response to the crisis, which consisted of a range of temporary safety nets, to the design and implementation of more permanent social protection programmes targeting human development. The chapter raises three important themes that are discussed through the book: the tensions and dynamics shown by the rapid development of social protection policies and programmes; the significance of external factors, lesson learning, and political institutions in shaping these dynamics; and the shift in focus from risk responses to human development strengthening over time. In Chapter 7, Slater considers the extent to which social protection has a role to play in developing a comprehensive response to the spread of HIV/AIDS in developing countries, while in Chapter 8 McCord provides a critical assessment of short-term public works as a response to persistent poverty and vulnerability. In Chapter 9, Britto traces the origins of conditional cash transfer programmes in Latin America, and outlines the policy environment in which they were implemented. Slater, McCord and Britto agree that, to be effective, social protection requires stable and longer-term institutional structures, focused beyond immediate responses to shocks and external factors.

The final two chapters in this section examine the role and effectiveness of social protection in low-income countries. In Chapter 10, Hulme and Moore discuss BRAC's Targeting the Ultra-Poor (TUP) Programme, which offers support to the very poorest in Bangladesh. TUP is one of several path-breaking poverty reduction initiatives in the developing world aiming to develop interventions that are effective in supporting households in extreme and persistent poverty to find pathways out of their predicament. In Chapter 11, Schubert discusses another such initiative, a cash transfer programme in the Kalomo district of Zambia, focused on the poorest 10 per cent of households. Chapters 10 and 11 illustrate the feasibility and constraints involved in extending social protection for the poorest in low-income countries.

The third section tackles the thorny issues of the politics and finance of social protection. In Chapter 12, Pellissery provides an insightful account of the micro-politics and process deficits associated with the delivery of the National Social Assistance Programme in India. Based on the findings of detailed field research, he brings to the fore the influence of powerful elites, government officials and private intermediaries on the delivery of public assistance to the poorest. Hickey, in Chapter 13, takes a broader perspective on the macro-politics of extending social protection in Africa, in the context of fragmented and clientilistic political systems. His analysis suggests that the process of arriving at social contracts between the governed and the governing is a necessary condition for the development of comprehensive social protection in that region. In Chapter 14, Munemo points to the significance of politics in the selection of policy responses to drought relief in Africa. His analysis finds that a secure political environment for incumbents facilitates a longer-term view of the advantages of public works, whereas an insecure environment is more conducive to incumbents relying on food relief, to make short-term political gains. Taken together, these three chapters underscore the significance of politics in the design, development and effectiveness of social protection in developing countries.

The remaining two chapters in this section discuss the financing of social protection. Behrendt reports in Chapter 15 on detailed simulations, conducted by the Social Security Department of the ILO, of the finance required for a basic package of social protection in low-income countries in Africa. Her conclusion is that most developing countries can afford programmes that ensure basic living standards among the poorest, especially the young, the old and those affected by disabilities. Barrientos argues in Chapter 16 that financing the extension of social protection in developing countries requires changes to the financing mix, from a strong reliance on out-of-pocket household financing to an increased role for tax financing, supported in low-income countries by international aid. It is important that the financing mix mobilises sufficient resources for the extension of social protection, but also that it ensures appropriate incentives and secures legitimacy for the relevant institutions and policy.

In the Conclusion, we return to the main themes of the book and consider the future of social protection in developing countries. We begin by discussing regional trajectories with regard to social protection policies, in order to locate firmly current trends and innovation. It is apparent that there is a good measure of diversity in social protection policies across the different regions, and even within regions. There are many, and diverse, pathways for the extension of social protection. Some common features also emerge. With few exceptions, the extension of social protection is dominated by the introduction, or expansion, of social assistance programmes and institutions, focused on poor and poorest households. Within these, income transfers also dominate. It is remarkable both the speed and spread of social assistance in the developing world is remarkable and promises to make a measurable dent on global poverty and vulnerability. The second section examines key policy issues – programme design, beneficiary selection, affordability and implementation capacity. The final section points out that while the medium- and long-term impact of this extension of social protection cannot be predicted reliably, strong and durable partnerships among all the main stakeholders involved, led by national governments and nurtured by energetic debates within civil society about the means and ends of social policy, could ensure that the emerging institutions of social protection are sustained and supported into the future.

Notes

1. This is acknowledged by many multilateral and bilateral organisations, national governments and NGOs (IADB 2000; United Nations 2000; World Bank 2001; ADB 2001; ILO 2001a; HAI 2003; DFID 2005).
2. For a database of social protection programmes in developing countries, see Barrientos and Holmes (2006).
3. The more recent *Social Security. A New Consensus*, notes that one 'of the essential features of the decent work approach is that everybody is entitled to basic social protection' (ILO 2001a, p. 39). This is taken to be an extension of the 1948 Universal Declaration of Human Rights' article 22, via the 1966 International Covenant on Economic, Social and Cultural Rights', article 9 stating 'the right of everyone to social security, including social insurance' (ILO 2001a).
4. Behind these statistics are the harrowing accounts of individual human suffering that tens of millions of people have experienced because social protection has not been available – hunger, social stigma, lives constrained by withdrawal from education and easily preventable deaths.
5. For critiques, see Clemens *et al.* (2004) and Saith (2006).
6. For a discussion of the evolution of social protection in the Bank, see Social Protection Sector Strategy: From Safety Net to Springboard (World Bank 2001). For a discussion of social policy and social protection in the Bank, see Hall (2007).
7. A recent review of social safety nets (social assistance) work by the World Bank in the period 2002–2006 concluded that 9 per cent of all Bank projects (lending and analytical) involved safety nets; that safety nets absorbed 3 per cent of total Bank lending; and that safety nets absorb one half of the social protection portfolio (Milazzo and Grosh 2007).
8. This is explored briefly in Sabates-Wheeler and Devereux (Chapter 4 in this volume).
9. Many NGOs have decades of experience in responding to emergency and humanitarian crises, and some are global leaders in this field.
10. South Africa is considering instituting what to our knowledge is the first-ever Chair in the Economics of Social Protection.
11. A new Centre for Social Protection launched at IDS in the UK in November 2006 aims to strengthen research and policy links across the South.
12. See Barrientos and Holmes' Social Assistance in Developing Countries database posted at www.chronicpoverty.org for a regularly updated list (Barrientos and Holmes 2006).
13. For example, beneficiaries aged 30–69 can open a retirement savings account to which the federal government contributes counterpart amounts. In effect, this extends government subsidies to workers affiliated to pension plans (mainly workers in formal employment) to the beneficiaries of *Oportunidades*, who commonly work in the informal sector.

14. Barrientos (2007) makes the point that, in developed countries, social assistance is a residual component of social protection, coming into play only where basic services, labour market regulation and social insurance have failed. In the eyes of researchers and policy-makers in developed countries, the very presence of social assistance is an embarrassment. In developing countries, on the other hand, where basic services are often inadequate, labour market regulation extends at best to a minority of the labour force, and social insurance covers a fraction of the population, social assistance is the main component of social protection.

15. Even in middle-income developing countries, such as Mexico or China, with established social insurance schemes, the social protection mix shows considerable flux. In Mexico, the administration at the time of writing has committed itself to shifting public expenditure from supporting social insurance to extending social assistance. In China, the restructuring of state enterprises has meant a rapid dismantling of employment-based protection, and the expansion of the Minimum Living Standards Scheme.

16. If, in addition, a basic health insurance is added, it would absorb on average an extra 2 per cent of GDP.

17. Many programmes aim to transfer an additional 20 per cent of household consumption, for the average beneficiary household.

18. Warlters and Auriol argue convincingly that improvements in the efficiency of tax collection are likely to be more effective than expanding the tax base as a means of raising revenues in low-income countries (Auriol and Warlters 2002; Warlters and Auriol 2005).

19. Sumarto *et al.* (Chapter 6 in this volume) discuss how the expansion of social protection in Indonesia was financed by switching resources away from petrol subsidies. Chapter 9 by Britto (in this volume) makes reference to Brazil's partially successful efforts to switch government subsidies from generous pensions for civil servants to programmes such as *Bolsa Escola* targeting the poor.

References

ADB (2001) *Social Protection Strategy*. Manila: Asian Development Bank.

Auriol, E. and M. Warlters (2002) 'Taxation base in developing countries', Mimeo. Toulouse: ARQADE.

Barrientos, A. (2006a) 'The missing piece of pension reform in Latin America: Poverty reduction', *Social Policy and Administration*, 40(4), 369–384.

Barrientos, A. (2006b) 'Protecting capability, eradicating extreme poverty: The future of social protection?', Mimeo. Brighton: IDS, University of Sussex.

Barrientos, A. (2007) 'Tax-financed social security', *International Social Security Review*, 60(2), 99–117.

Barrientos, A. (forthcoming) 'Introducing basic social protection in low income countries: Lessons from existing programmes', in P. Townsend (ed.), *Challenging the Development Paradigm: Rethinking the Role of Social Security in State Building*. Geneva: ILO.

Barrientos, A. and R. Holmes (2006) *Social Assistance in Developing Countries Database*. Brighton: Institute of Development Studies.

Barrientos, A., D. Hulme and A. Shepherd (2005) 'Can social protection tackle chronic poverty?', *European Journal of Development Research*, 17(1), 8–23.

Beales, S. and T. German (2006) Situation analysis of social protection and cash transfers in Africa, Report. London: Development Initiatives and Help Age International.

Booth, D. (ed.) (1994) *Rethinking Social Development: Theory, Research and Practice*. London: Longman.

Clemens, M. A., C. J. Kenny and T. J. Moss (2004) 'The trouble with the MDGs: Confronting expectations of aid and development success', CGD Working Paper No. 40. Washington, DC: Centre for Global Development.

Conway, T., A. de Haan and A. Norton (eds) (2000) *Social Protection: New Directions of Donor Agencies*. London: Department for International Development.

Cutler, D. M., F. Knaul, R. Lozano, O. Méndez and B. Zurita (2000) Financial crisis, health outcomes and aging: Mexico in the 1980s and 1990s, Working Paper 7746. Cambridge, Mass.: National Bureau of Economic Research.

de Haan, A. (2000) 'Introduction: The role of social protection in poverty reduction', in T. Conway, A. de Haan and A. Norton (eds), *Social Protection: New Directions of Donor Agencies*. London: Department for International Development, pp. 5–20.

Dercon, S. (ed.) (2005) *Insurance Against Poverty*. Oxford: Oxford University Press.

Dercon, S. and P. Krishnan (2000) 'In sickness and in health: Risk sharing within households in rural Ethiopia', *Journal of Political Economy*, 108(4), 688–727.

DFID (Department for International Development) (2005) Social transfers and chronic poverty: Emerging evidence and the challenge ahead, DFID Practice paper. London: DFID.

van Ginneken, W. (2003) Extending social security: Policies for developing countries, ESS Paper 13. Geneva: ILO.

Gray-Molina, G. (1999) La economía política de reformas institucionales en Bolivia, Working paper R-350. Washington, DC: Inter-American Development Bank.

Greig, A., D. Hulme and M. Turner (2007) *Challenging Global Inequality: Development Theory and Practice in the 21st Century*. London: Palgrave.

HAI (Help Age International)(2003) Population Ageing and Development: New Strategies for Social Protection, Report. London: Help Age International.

Hall, A. (2007) 'Social policies in the world bank: Paradigms and challenges', *Global Social Policy*, 7(2), 151–175.

Harvey, P. (2005) *Cash and Vouchers in Emergencies*. London: ODI.

Hoddinott, J. and B. Kinsey (2001) 'Child health in the time of drought', *Oxford Bulletin of Economics and Statistics*, 63, 409–436.

Holzmann, R. and S. Jorgensen (1999) 'Social protection as social risk management: Conceptual underpinnings for the social protection strategy paper', *Journal of International Development*, 11, 1005–1027.

IADB (Inter-American Development Bank) (2000) *Social Protection for Equity and Growth*. Washington, DC: Inter-American Development Bank.

ILO (International Labour Office) (2001a) *Social Security. A New Consensus*. Geneva: International Labour Office.

ILO (International Labour Office) (2001b) Social Security: Issues, Challenges and Prospects, Report VI. Geneva: International Labour Office.

ILO (International Labour Office) (2006) Social Security for All: Investing in Global Social and Economic Development, Discussion paper 16. Geneva: Social Security Department.

IMF (International Monetary Fund) (2003) Fund Assistance for Countries Facing Exogenous Shocks, Report. Washington, DC: IMF.

Jalan, J. and M. Ravallion (2001) 'Is transient poverty different? Evidence for rural China', *Journal of Development Studies*, 36(6), 82–99.

Keefer, P. and S. Khemani (2003) 'The Political Economy of Public Expenditures', Mimeo. Washington, DC: The World Bank.

Milazzo, A. and M. Grosh (2007) Social safety nets in World Bank lending and analytical work: FY2002-2006, Social Protection Discussion paper 0705. Washington, DC: The World Bank.

Morduch, J. (1998) 'Between the state and the market: Can informal insurance patch the safety net?', *The World Bank Research Observer*, 14(2), 187–207.

Priyambada, A., A. Suryahadi and S. Sumarto (2002) What happened to child labor in Indonesia during the economic crisis? The trade-off between school and work, Working paper. Jakarta: SMERU.

Rodrik, D. (1997) *Has Globalization Gone Too Far?* Washington, DC: Institute for International Economics.

Rodrik, D. (2001) 'Por qué hay tanta inseguridad económica en America Latina?', *Revista de la CEPAL*, 73, April, 7–31.

Rosenzweig, M. R. and H. Binswanger (1993) 'Wealth, weather risk and the composition and profitability of agricultural investment', *Economic Journal*, 103(416), 56–78.

Saith, A. (2006) 'From universal values to Millennium Development Goals: Lost in translation', *Development and Change*, 37(6), 1167–1199.

United Nations (2000) Enhancing social protection and reducing vulnerability in a globalizing world, Report of the Secretary General to the Thirty-ninth Session E/CN.5/2001/2. Washington, DC: United Nations Economic and Social Council.

Usui, C. (1994) 'Welfare state development in a world system context: Event history analysis of first social insurance legislation among 60 countries, 1880–1960', in T. Janoski and A. M. Hicks (eds), *The Comparative Political Economy of the Welfare State*. Cambridge: Cambridge University Press, pp. 254–277.

van Ginneken, W. (2000) 'The extension of social protection: ILO's aim for the years to come', in T. Conway, A. de Haan and A. Norton (eds), *Social Protection: New Directions of Donor Agencies*. London: Department for International Development, pp. 33–48.

Warlters, M. and E. Auriol (2005) The Marginal Cost of Public Funds in Africa, Policy Research Working paper WPS 3679. Washington, DC: The World Bank.

World Bank (2001) Social Protection Sector Strategy: From Safety Net to Springboard, Sector Strategy paper. Washington, DC: The World Bank.

Part II

Conceptual Frameworks for Social Protection: Risks, Needs and Rights

2
Risks, Needs and Rights: Compatible or Contradictory Bases for Social Protection

Lauchlan T. Munro

Introduction[1]

Justifications for the welfare state in general, and for social protection and the attack on chronic poverty in particular, have traditionally come from three sources: an analysis of uninsurable risks and other market failures; doctrines of human rights – specifically, economic and social rights; and needs-based doctrines. The risk school emphasises failures in insurance markets, specifically the inability of private and communal insurance mechanisms to provide cover against all forms of risk, often due to asymmetrical or incomplete information. These important failures in insurance markets are compounded by other failures in markets for labour, credit and human capital. The social and economic rights school focuses on the obligations of the state derived from the assertion that citizens possess social and economic rights that are legally enforceable claims on the state. These rights are usually said to be defined in the Universal Declaration of Human Rights (UN 1948) and the International Covenant on Economic, Social and Cultural Rights (UN 1996a), among other sources of international law, and are frequently asserted as coming from natural law. The needs-based doctrine stresses the practical and moral importance for poor and non-poor alike of eliminating (or at least alleviating or reducing) chronic poverty, and asserts both moral and economic claims in favour of social protection measures.

Perhaps because the three discourses of risks, needs and rights arose from different academic disciplines, the three tend to run in parallel, with remarkably few intersection points. In public policy debates, the three discourses tend to come into and fall out of fashion, only to return later. The rights-based argument, for example, is currently in the ascendancy, at least with certain UN agencies and many development-orientated NGOs. In the 1970s, the needs-based approach held sway, and it has enjoyed something of a revival recently in the form of the Millennium Development Goals. From the 1930s to the 1960s, market failures were used as the grounds for a considerable expansion of the state's economic roles, including the growth of the modern welfare state. The recent granting of the Nobel Prize to three leading figures in the economics of asymmetrical information (with its implications for insurance markets, among other things) attests to the continuing power of the risk-based tradition.

Given these political and intellectual dynamics, those who support social protection and reduction of chronic poverty need to understand each of these three discourses, including the areas where they are mutually supportive or where they are mutually contradictory. Certainly, the critics of increased social protection will pick and choose their counter-arguments, and many of them will be tempted to pick apart arguments from one source to discredit the entire project of social protection and poverty reduction. This chapter begins by outlining each of the three main sources of support for social protection, and then explores those areas where the three discourses provide mutual support or mutual contradiction. The main purpose of this chapter is to help proponents of social protection to understand these areas better. A secondary objective is to suggest areas where members of the three traditions might usefully co-operate.

The three discourses explained

Uninsurable risks and market failures

In neo-classical economics, it is universally admitted that real world markets – as opposed to the perfectly competitive ones found in elementary textbooks – frequently suffer from market failure. The traditional list of market failures includes public goods, externalities, incomplete markets, imperfect competition, imperfect information and (less frequently) merit goods. Variations of this list are found in every textbook of public economics (for example, Barr 1998: 78–85; Stiglitz 2000: 76–88).

Nicholas Barr was the first to point out that the traditional list of market failures might explain many types of government intervention in the economy, but did little to explain or justify the emergence of a comprehensive welfare state. His 'main conclusion is how thin, at least in utilitarian terms, is the traditional justification for large-scale, publicly organized welfare state services. To the extent that the traditional market failures support welfare state institutions at all, they justify only a residual welfare state' (Barr 1992: 749). Extensive public provisioning in health care, education and social security is justified in large part by 'information failures' – that is, incomplete and/or asymmetrical information between (would-be) parties to a transaction (Barr 1992: 749).

> Many parts of the welfare state are a response to pervasive technical problems in private markets, and therefore serve not only the distributional

and other objectives (of)...poverty relief,...equity, dignity and social solidarity, but also efficiency objectives such as income smoothing and the protection of accustomed living standards in the face of uninsurable risks and capital market imperfections... [T]here is an *efficiency* case for a universal welfare state. (Barr 1998: 98; emphasis in original)

Commercial insurance will not cover a large number of risks, or will cover them only incompletely. These are related to principal–agent problems between the insurer and the insured, asymmetrical information about intentions and states of health, uncertainty about the future, and moral hazard problems. Together, these explain why the private sector is generally loath to insure against unemployment or pregnancy, or to cover certain types of health risks (Barr 1998: 108–126; Stiglitz 2000: 359–363). Paradoxically, commercial insurance may deny cover to low-risk cases while providing it to higher-risk cases, which violates the risk-sharing principle underlying insurance (Barr 1998: 117; Stiglitz 2000: 316–317).

Since the profitability of insurance companies depends on the independence of risks between insured parties, the existence of strong covariant risks is a strong discouragement to the formation of insurance markets. If all (or many) of the insured parties make claims at the same time, the insurer may be bankrupted. Typical covariant risks include many 'natural' disasters such as droughts, floods, some pest infestations (for example, locusts), and armed conflict. The private insurance company is unlikely to provide full cover for such areas without state guarantees, or without strict limitations on the type and level of liability.[2] Commercial insurers do not provide unemployment insurance either, and again the reason is largely covariant risk; a recession resulting in widespread unemployment could bankrupt the insurer.[3]

Similar problems affect other markets. Uncertainty about future earnings means that banks will not generally lend money to students without state guarantees or collateral from parents.[4] This amounts to an imperfection in the market for human capital formation, since children from poor households are too great a risk for most lenders. Uncertainty about future earnings and the risk of operative failure also explains why banks do not lend money to help poor people to pay for expensive, but life-saving, medical procedures.

These and many other, often overlapping, market failures help to explain why the richer countries have built comprehensive welfare states. While developing countries do not have the comprehensive welfare systems of the West, they often do have free or subsidised education and health care, state pensions, food subsidies, various conditional and unconditional cash transfers, and disaster relief, for similar reasons.

In the risk-based school, social protection measures are justified 'in utilitarian terms' (Barr 1992: 749) on the basis of real or potential welfare losses arising from market failures and the ability of public action to prevent or compensate for these losses. Deciding on the appropriate nature and scope of social protection measures is a pragmatic exercise based on the costs and benefits, judged in utilitarian terms, of various possible government interventions (for example, taxation, subsidisation, regulation or direct provisioning) versus the costs of leaving the problem to the market.

There is little talk of rights or needs in this discourse. Indeed, the index to Stiglitz's major textbook (Stiglitz 2000) contains no entries for 'rights', 'human rights', 'needs' or 'basic needs'. Barr, a leader in the risk-based literature on social protection, goes further than most, but he subsumes rights under statements of 'value judgement' and 'ideology'. '[T]he proper place of ideology is in the choice of aims, particularly in the definition of social justice and in its trade-off with economic efficiency; but, *once these aims have been agreed*, the choice of method should be regarded as a technical issue' (Barr 1998: 98; emphasis in original). 'There is wide acceptance of the value judgement that people have a right to adequate nutrition and health care. These are *aims*; but the existence of these rights does not, per se, have any implications for the best method of achieving them' (Barr 1998: 100).

The neo-classical risk-based literature is much concerned with poverty, though it defines this solely in terms of income; within the income poverty school, its concern is usually absolute poverty. There is an extensive literature on possible public policy interventions to alleviate inadequate incomes (see, for example, Barr 1998, Stiglitz 2000 and the sources they cite). The risk-based school has only just begun to grapple with chronic poverty. There is often the (reasonable) assumption that chronic poverty is linked to depth of poverty. To the extent that this is true, the very poor and/or the chronically poor may suffer from several overlapping and mutually reinforcing market failures that prevent them from using the market to manage risk. Social protection measures are particularly important for such people.

Rights-based arguments for social protection

Since the Universal Declaration of Human Rights (UN 1948) declared the existence of economic and social rights, the discourse on rights and social protection has taken root. In essence, this literature suggests that the state should provide social protection to its citizens as a matter of right.[5]

But where do human rights come from? One can discern three traditions within the human rights school:

- natural law;
- constitutional law and international law, especially international human rights law; and
- a theory of human needs as a basis for human rights.

Natural law has a quasi-theological character and is rooted in the Judeo-Christian tradition. Natural law is based on a few axioms or articles of faith. In this tradition, all humans have rights because of their inherent human dignity. The respect of that dignity implies a system of rights and obligations, or duties. One of the clearest expressions of the natural law tradition comes from the American Declaration of Independence: 'We hold these truths to be self-evident, that all men are created equal, that they are endowed by their Creator with certain unalienable Rights'. The natural law tradition is now widely (though not universally)[6] held to include economic and social rights, as well as the more traditional civil and political rights of classical liberalism.

The second source of human rights is constitutional and international law. Since the Second World War, there has developed a large corpus of international law, including international human rights law and international humanitarian law. For the purposes of this chapter, the most important parts of the corpus are the Universal Declaration of Human Rights (UN 1948) and the International Covenant on Economic, Social and Cultural Rights (ICESCR) (UN 1966a).[7] National constitutions also frequently enshrine rights for their citizens. This 'legalistic' interpretation of rights says that human rights exist because the great majority of the world's states have ratified a certain number of human rights treaties, or because national constitutions confer rights on their citizens.[8]

Rights are not about charity or morality; they are binding legal obligations, in this view. The UN High Commissioner for Human Rights put it this way: 'the power or human rights lies not just in the expression of an aspiration ... but in the articulation of a legally binding framework' (Arbour 2005: 5). This emphasis on rights being grounded in law is an attempt to give rights, especially economic, social and cultural rights, the political and policy traction that they might not otherwise have. Contrary to what some liberal critics of economic and social rights have argued in the past (see, for example, Barry 1990: 80), economic and social rights are justifiable. Courts in Canada, India and South Africa have ruled that economic and social rights are justifiable (see, for example, Rights and Democracy 2003).

Natural law and the legalistic traditions of human rights are often linked; for example, the preambles of the main human rights treaties allude to the natural law principle of the inherent dignity of the human person (UN 1948: Preamble; UN 1966a: Preamble).[9]

But natural law and legalistic traditions can also contradict each other; for example, on the question of whether laws give rise to rights, or whether rights exist prior to (and without) law. Jeremy Bentham believed the former, saying that '*Right*, the substantive *right*, is the child of law ... from laws of nature [can come only] *imaginary* rights' (Bentham 1998; emphasis in original). The drafters of the American Declaration of Independence took the latter view, saying that it is 'self-evident' that 'Governments are instituted among Men' to 'secure these rights'.

The third tradition within the human rights school is sceptical about both the faith-based character of natural law and the legalistic grounding of human rights. Since natural law is essentially faith-based, what can one do about non-believers? What does one say to the drafters of the American Declaration of Independence if one does not accept that these 'truths' are 'self-evident'? And of the legalists one could ask what would happen if enough states withdrew their ratifications of these human rights conventions: would human rights then cease to exist? Indeed, if rights are based on the existence of conventions and constitutions, were there no rights before the conventions or constitutions came into force? This third tradition asserts that the notion of human rights can only be grounded on a theory of basic human needs (Doyal and Gough 1991; Taylor-Gooby 1991; Munro 2000; see also Sen 2004).

The needs-based theory of rights sees human rights as part of moral philosophy. To have any system of moral philosophy, one must have a moral agent. A moral agent is a person who is capable of making choices, specifically of choosing between good and bad. Going back to Thomas Hobbes (1651), the mere existence of human life is not enough to ensure a decent existence; for that, security of the person and his/her property are essential. Therefore, the survival and 'avoidance of serious harm' (Doyal and Gough, 1991: 40) to the moral agent are the basis for any system of moral philosophy, whatever its ends may be. Human needs can be defined as those things that are required to avoid serious harm to the moral agent. Though the boundaries of this set of things may be fuzzy, the core set is clear enough: physical and psychological security, the ability to participate in decisions that affect oneself and one's community, health care, basic education, adequate nutrition, an adequate livelihood. To say that someone has a 'right' to any of these things is merely to say that he or she needs them in order to be and remain a moral agent.[10] The realisation of rights is thus essential to any moral philosophy; indeed to any system of law. In short, a convincing theory of rights can be built without recourse to natural law, constitutions or international treaties.

In relation to social protection, the International Labour Office got close to this theory in 1942, when it defined a social safety net as 'a form of social security which provides assistance to persons of small earnings granted *as of right* in amounts (that should be) sufficient to meet a minimum standard of *need*' (ILO 1942: 84; italics added).

In all three versions, human rights theory holds that rights are binding obligations. This means that someone is obligated. For every rights holder there must then be a duty bearer. Sometimes the duty is simply to forbear from acting: for example, I must abstain from hitting you unless you attack me first. But this is merely respecting your rights, and, to be meaningful, rights must be respected, protected and fulfilled. There are therefore also duties to protect rights; for example, a policewoman is duty-bound to protect a person who is being hit. And there are duties to fulfil rights: the state is obliged to help people who have been hit – for example by providing medical care and counselling.

But not all rights are claims against the state. Sometimes the claims may be against other citizens. Take the case of a girl's right to an education (UN 1948: Article 26; UN 1966a: Article 13; UN 1989: Article 28). This right implies that the state has a duty to 'take steps ... to the maximum of its available resources, with a view to achieving progressively the full realisation of the [girl's] right' (UN 1966a: Article 2) to schooling of adequate quality near the girl's home. The girl has claims against the state in that sense. But the girl also has claims against her family and her community. The girl's parents are obliged to allow the girl to go to school. They must not put any obstacles in her way. Similarly, members of the girl's community are constrained from taking any steps to prevent the girl attending school – for example, by harassing her on the way to and from school.

All rights, including civil and political rights, have resource implications; elections cost money, as do police forces and judicial systems. But many economic and social rights (for example, education, health care, social security) are particularly resource-intensive. Rights-based thinkers acknowledge the scarcity of resources in the face of an unlimited number of possible demands; all rights cannot be realised immediately for all people everywhere. Hence the international human rights instruments incorporate the doctrine of the progressive realisation of rights. They accept that scarcity is a problem, but insist that governments and other duty bearers must make a concerted effort over time to allocate resources to the fulfilment of their duties to rights holders. The ICESCR requires that 'Each State Party to the present Covenant undertakes to take steps ... to the maximum of its available resources, with a view to achieving progressively the full realization of the rights recognised in the present Covenant' (UN 1966a: Article 2). But how much effort is enough? What are 'the standards and processes for monitoring ... [the] core minimum obligations of State parties and the progressive steps required' (O'Neill and Bye 2002: 29)? Neither the statute law nor the subsequent case law clarifies the issue much (Robertson, 1994; O'Neill and Bye 2002: 31–32, 42).

A rights-based approach to development is now the official policy of many development organisations. Several United Nations agencies have developed a 'common understanding' of the human rights-based approach to programming (UNDG 2003). Among the NGOs, the BRAC, Oxfam, the Save the Children Alliance, and World Vision are the leaders in the rights-based approach to development. All these organisations are trying, with varying degrees of difficulty and success, to understand the implications of incorporating human rights into the daily business of project and programme planning in general (Brouwer 2005; Courdesse and Hemmingway 2005; Goulden *et al.* 2005; Ljungman and Forti 2005; Munro forthcoming) and into concrete domains such as social protection in particular. UNICEF took the lead in designing a 'rights-based approach to programming' (UNICEF 1998) including in situations of social protection. It includes a sophisticated, rights-based situation analysis for identifying when and how violations of rights are occurring, and hence, who is responsible (UNICEF 2000a,b, 2004). The UNICEF tool and other project-level tools like it (for example, NORAD 2001) are useful in designing individual interventions, including in social protection. Since the doctrine of human rights is loath to create a hierarchy of rights, however, such project-level tools are of little use in deciding which violation(s) of rights are the most serious. It is unclear what their role should be in broader public policy debates– that is, at programme and policy levels (Munro forthcoming). The risk-based thinkers, with their concepts of welfare losses and opportunity costs, have much less difficulty.

Needs-based arguments for social protection

The concept of human needs stretches back at least as far as Thomas Hobbes (1651), who insisted that security of the person and of property was necessary for any kind of decent life. The poverty studies of the nineteenth and twentieth centuries described the poor diet and insecure and unhealthy living conditions of the poor (for example, Engels 1845; Riis 1890; Rowntree 1901). These authors used words such as 'necessity' to describe such things as a basic diet, adequate shelter, sanitary living conditions and simple clothing. At the same time, they used words such as 'insufficiency' and 'lack' to describe their absence.

Such studies laid the foundation for the now established tradition of poverty surveys based on poverty lines. These surveys establish and cost out a list of basic needs, including a minimum diet, defined by the level of caloric intake needed to remain alive and economically active, and usually some other necessities such as clothing and shelter. Often health care and education costs are included as well. People whose income is below the level required to purchase this set of commodities are deemed to be 'poor'.

The 1970s saw the ascendancy of the 'basic human needs' school of development policy (Afxentiou 1990).[11] The basic needs school set itself up in contrast to the earlier fixation of development economics with the growth of income per capita. The basic needs school redefined development in a more humanistic fashion, as the extent to which people's basic needs for health, nutrition, literacy, shelter, clothing, employment and security were met. The list of basic human needs they used has its roots in the nineteenth- and early twentieth-century poverty studies, and to later poverty line studies: people living below the poverty line are unable to meet their basic needs.

The basic needs school relied, usually implicitly, on Maslow's hierarchy of human needs (Maslow 1943), which was popular throughout the social sciences in the 1960s and 1970s. The usual 1970s list of basic needs corresponded closely with the bottom two levels of Maslow's hierarchy, namely 'physiological' needs (health, nutrition, clothing, shelter) and 'safety' needs (adequate income, security).

The seminal article in the basic needs school was Dudley Seers' 'The meaning of development' (Seers 1969), which questioned whether the growth of GNP (gross national product) per capita was an adequate measure of development. Seers suggested not that GNP per capita is irrelevant, but that distributional issues are also important. Most importantly, growth is possible, they asserted, without any improvement – and possibly with a deterioration – in the levels of things that really matter for the quality of human life: the basic needs of health, nutrition, literacy, shelter, clothing, employment and security. The job of social protection is to ensure that these needs are met if they cannot be met through individual or community effort. Indeed, the objective of public policy generally should be to ensure that basic human needs are met.

There are three arguments in favour of basic needs: a moral or intrinsic argument for the satisfaction of basic needs, an instrumental argument for the satisfaction of basic needs, and a political argument (Streeten *et al.* 1981). The moral case asserts that the satisfaction of basic needs is a good thing in, and of, itself. The mental and physical suffering caused by the lack of satisfaction of basic needs is largely avoidable, given modern wealth and technology. The obstacles to the universal satisfaction of basic needs are mainly social, political and economic (and thus amenable to public policy), not technical or scarcity-based. Continuing to allow current levels of unsatisfied basic needs when they can be satisfied is morally repugnant.

The original proponents of the basic needs school in the 1970s were mainly economists, agronomists, nutritionists and medical professionals (for example, McHale and McHale 1977). The moral and political theory underlying the basic needs school was not very sophisticated, and the legal arguments were conspicuous by their absence. Some leading lights of the basic needs school even argued that basic needs could *not* be seen as human rights (Streeten *et al.* 1981: 184–192). The basic needs school relied on an intuitive approach to morality based on a sense of human solidarity and compassion in the face of unnecessary suffering. Social protection, at least in the sense of providing basic human needs to all, especially to those who are least able to support themselves, is thus a moral imperative.

The second argument is that the satisfaction of basic needs is good not only intrinsically, but also instrumentally. Expenditure on primary health care, basic education, sanitation and nutrition is not consumption, but rather investment, with high rates of private and social return. Healthy, well-nourished and well-educated people are more productive, can support themselves, are able to pay more taxes, and are less likely to spread disease or engage in socially undesirable behaviours. In the 1970s and early 1980s, it was widely believed that the satisfaction of basic needs on a mass scale might even promote faster economic growth.[12]

It is no accident that the basic needs school flourished in the decade after economists discovered 'human capital'. The evidence of high rates of return to investment in human capital (especially in education) helped the basic needs school to appeal both to mainstream economists and to the moralists. Prominent proponents of basic needs pitched their arguments to both camps simultaneously (for example, Streeten *et al.* 1981). Proponents of basic needs sometimes bolstered their arguments on the affordability of basic needs by linking them to the then popular appropriate (or intermediate) technology movement. Many basic needs for sanitation, shelter, clothing, energy and health care can be met using low-cost appropriate technology (McHale and McHale 1977: 148–154, 163–164). The affordability of, and high rates of return on, investments in basic needs meant that satisfying basic needs was both economically rational in the short run and likely to reduce the demand for social protection in the future.

There was a third, more overtly political, argument put forward for basic needs. Proponents argued that satisfying basic needs could benefit rich and poor alike, at least in the medium– to long term.[13] For example, both rich and poor benefit from the control of epidemic diseases. The entrepreneurial upper classes benefit from having access to a more educated, better skilled and healthier labour force. With proper political management, basic needs could thus form a viable political platform.

The basic human needs school ran out of intellectual steam by the late 1970s, making no new intellectual contributions until the launch of UNDP's human development index (UNDP 1990), but its political influence continued. UNICEF, under the leadership of James Grant from 1980 to 1995, used the basic needs literature as a jumping-off point for a powerful moral and political narrative on the need for the world to invest more in its children (Jolly and Cornia 1984; Cornia *et al.* 1987; UNICEF 1987; Vandemoortele 2000). UNDP's human development index draws greatly on the basic needs literature; the index can be read as a measure of the satisfaction of basic needs in a society, combining income (a proxy for command over commodities necessary to satisfy basic needs), literacy (a basic need in itself), and longevity (as a proxy for health and nutrition needs). Basic needs thinking underpins the Millennium Development Goals (MDGs). Indeed, the MDGs are merely the 1970s basic needs literature writ large.

One blind spot of the basic human needs literature is the lack of a specific analysis of social protection in general, and of chronic poverty in particular. Social protection is seldom dealt with explicitly in the basic needs literature. Implicitly or explicitly, the basic needs school assumed a strong role for the state in assuring basic needs, either as regulator, facilitator or direct provider, especially for the poorest and those chronically in need. Equally, however, there was an assumption that the role of the state must be to step in only where the market and individual or community effort were insufficient to satisfy basic needs, and where public action could improve the situation in welfare terms. In this sense, there was a strong residualist tendency in the basic needs school, especially in the branch affiliated to the World Bank in the 1970s. The risk-based school, also residualist in its approach, was, however, much more rigorous in spelling out how and where social protection measures would be appropriate. Given the economics background of members of both the basic needs and risk-based schools, however, it is unlikely that they would come to radically different conclusions on how and where the state should intervene.

Interactions between the risks, needs and rights schools

Risks

As mentioned above, there is surprisingly little interaction between the risks, needs and rights schools. The economists who drive the risk-based set of justifications for social protection rarely concern themselves with rights or needs. When they are confronted with a rights-based discourse demanding social security, health care, adequate nutrition and so on, their reaction is similar to that of the economists in the needs-based school (see below). Being firmly rooted in neo-classical economics, the risk-based thinkers on social protection prefer to avoid all talk of needs; using standard utilitarian terminology, they prefer to speak of 'preferences'. Since preferences are based on expected utility, and since interpersonal comparisons of utility are impossible, their concern is not unmet needs, but rather 'welfare losses' measured in terms of potential utility that cannot be realised because of market failures. Chronic poverty, to the extent that it is based on market failures, is, then, a chronic welfare loss, and proof of the chronic economic inefficiency. To speak of 'needs' is to imply a hierarchy. Neo-classical economists are loath to introduce such a hierarchy, since it implies interpersonal comparisons of utility.

The risk-based economists see claims of rights as one of several possible value judgements or statements regarding the proper aims of public policy. Once these aims are agreed upon, the determination of the best method to achieve these aims is a technical exercise, not an ideological one. This implies a separation of means and ends. Rights-based theorists reject such a separation, since any method for achieving a public policy target (even one intended to promote human rights) cannot violate human rights.

One interesting, and unexplored, avenue for collaboration between the utilitarian risk-based school and the rights-based school comes from Jacob Viner (1949). Bentham (1789) tried to build a new social science without any basis in the preceding tradition of natural law by insisting on 'the principle of utility' as the primary objective of public policy. The question (asked by Viner but not by Bentham) was why anyone should expect utility to be the primary objective of public policy. One possible answer is that people have a right to utility, and that it is the duty of the state to uphold rights. If this is the case, then the welfare losses, measured in utilitarian terms by the risk-based school of economists, also become rights violations.

Rights

The rights-based supporters of social protection think of poverty as a violation of human rights. Chronic poverty is then an ongoing violation of rights. One can infer that, if poverty is a violation of rights, then there must be a right to get out of poverty. Indeed, in 1986, the UN General Assembly declared that human beings have 'a right to development', and this right has been reiterated in numerous UN declarations since. Poverty reduction is thus not a policy option that a state might take on or not, as it sees fit, but is a duty of states to their citizens, since rights are binding legal obligations.

When they are confronted with rights-based arguments, the economists – either from the risk-driven school or the basic needs school – view the rights-based claims with great scepticism.[14] They point out that no amount of legal obligation can get around the tough questions of trade-offs in economic and social policy-making in a world characterised by material scarcity and infinite wants. More of one thing means less of another, and more of one thing today may mean less of everything tomorrow. The absolutist language of the rights discourse – for example, 'there are no small rights' (UNICEF 2000a: 4), 'all rights for all children' (UNICEF 2005) – is unconvincing to those reared on the doctrine of scarcity, the production possibility curve and associated opportunity costs. When economists point these things out, the rights-based thinkers can only respond with the doctrine of the progressive realisation of rights, which has its own problems, as seen above.

The legalistic tradition in human rights thinking views the binding legal obligations implied by rights as its trump card. The legalistic rights-based thinkers thus tend to denigrate needs-based arguments as being paternalistic, based on charity and moralism – soft ground compared to legal obligations. 'Benevolent and charitable actions, while good in themselves, are insufficient from a human rights perspective' (UNICEF 2000b: 9–10; see also UNICEF 2004: 11–12.) The legalistic rights-based thinkers tend to ignore the risk-based economic arguments of neo-classical economics, or dismiss them as 'welfarist' and thus, again, as being weaker than arguments based on law.

The only ones who address the link between rights and needs systematically are those who think that rights must be based not in natural law or the whims of nation states when they make international law, but on a theory of human needs. Like the risk-based economists, they also address the problem of moral hazard in social protection. Economists and moralists have often stressed moral hazard as a potential problem in social protection. The existence of a social safety net may distort patterns of work and levels of savings and effort, and social protection schemes incorporate mechanisms intended to avoid such problems. Many of these mechanisms, however, have the effect of denying coverage to those who should be getting benefits from the social protection scheme (Munro 2002). Economists have explored the welfare losses involved in both failing to cover the whole target group of a social protection scheme and in providing benefits to too many (ineligible) people (Cornia and Stewart 1993). Rights-based thinkers usually ignore the moral hazard issue in discussions of the design of social protection measures. A few, however, have grappled with the issue, most notably Peter Taylor-Gooby (1991, ch. 8). Admitting that moral hazard is a problem, Taylor-Gooby insists that a rights-based framework can cope with moral hazard. Since rights come with correlative duties, one of the duties of the rights holder is not to abuse his/her rights. This implies not only the usual injunction not to invoke one's own rights to the detriment of the rights of others, but also the injunction to invoke one's right to social protection (and hence invoke the state's duty to provide it) if and only if one has made a good-faith effort to support oneself to the best of one's ability. By implication, it is reasonable for the state to design social protection measures with this in mind. Taylor-Gooby's argument opens a terrain for fruitful conversations between the three schools on how social protection mechanisms should be designed.

Needs

The needs-based group is the least theoretically sophisticated of the three schools considered here. The definition of 'needs' is largely intuitive, or bio-medical. The satisfaction of needs is taken as a strong moral imperative, albeit one that also has the benefit of being useful for instrumental purposes as well. Initially seen as a progressive and humanistic approach to development in general, and to economics in particular, the needs-based school is now denigrated as being paternalistic or welfarist by the rights-based thinkers. The needs-based approach has been called 'the cattle rearing approach to development': make sure they are adequately nourished, fully vaccinated and well housed, and everything will be all right.[15] Somewhat unfairly, the basic needs school has been accused of ignoring the rights and dignity of the poor, and of avoiding issues of agency and participation.[16]

Coming from economics, albeit from a somewhat heterodox end of the profession, the needs-based thinkers speak a common language with the risk-based neo-classical economists, at least up to a point. Both can talk of returns to investment in human capital, for example, and both see that welfare losses resulting from market failures can have both static and long-term effects. Both schools acknowledge the problem of scarcity in the face of unlimited wants, and so both feel comfortable addressing issues such as trade-offs, rates of return to various types of investment, and the long-term effects of resource allocations.

The two schools may diverge, however, over the issue of Pareto optimality. Pareto optimality is politically conservative in that it suggests that welfare improvements should be sought (or can only be proved to have taken place) if the welfare of one party can be increased without reducing the welfare of another. Risk-based thinking on social protection tends to rely heavily on Pareto optimality as a benchmark. The needs-based thinkers have often had a strong leaning towards redistributionist policies to increase the welfare of the many, even if it is to the (temporary) detriment of the few. Furthermore, some close allies of the basic needs school have shown that, under certain plausible assumptions of unemployment and landlessness, a Pareto optimal equilibrium can reduce some citizens to below starvation levels (Coles and Hammond 1995).

The needs-based thinkers can also communicate with the rights-based thinkers. For example, both the needs-based and the rights-based approaches call attention to the links between those in need and those who already have enough. The needs-based thinkers assert, for example, that even the materially well off in developing countries would be still better off in several ways if their fellow citizens were better educated, healthier and more secure. Rights-based thinkers also sometimes stress the common interest that rights holders and duty bearers have in realising everyone's rights (see, for example, UNICEF 2004: 11–12), though many think this is politically naïve (Table 2.1).

Conclusions

It is important to understand why we support what we support. The fact that the ends are the same (or very similar) does not mean that the pathways taken to get there were the same. The three pathways to social protection and poverty eradication – risks, needs and rights – twist and turn. At times they approach each other, occasionally they intersect, but then they diverge again. Opponents of social protection may wish to take advantage of the diverse paths taken by its proponents to sow confusion and to paint a portrait of intellectual confusion surrounding social protection. Those who believe in social protection need to know how to defend it. To do so, they need to understand how risks, needs and rights support and contradict each other as justifications for social protection. This has been the main objective of this chapter.

Table 2.1 Compatibility and contradiction between the risks, needs and rights schools

	Areas of compatibility	Areas of contradiction
Risks and rights	Everyone has the right to utility	(1) Market failures provide no legal grounding for social protection
		(2) Risk-based economists separate the ends from the means of policy; rights-based theorists find this ends–means separation unacceptable
Rights and needs	(1) Development is about people, not commodities	(1) Natural law and legalistic theories of rights reject needs-based arguments as charity, paternalism, welfarism and/or moralism
	(2) Both rights and needs involve social relations	(2) The rights-based school's doctrine of 'progressive realization' of rights is poorly specified compared to the economists' language of scarcity, trade-offs and opportunity costs
	(3) One theory of human rights is based on human needs, not international or natural law	
	(4) Rights and needs both have a strong moral dimension	

Source: Author.

Another objective of the chapter has been to point out how and where the proponents of these three views of the bases of social protection might begin to talk to each other. A striking feature of the three schools is the different levels at which they operate. The risk-based school is highly technical and operational; the rights-based school is highly theoretical and not much concerned with the details of design and implementation of social protection schemes.[17] Debate on the design of social protection schemes has traditionally been dominated by the risk-based school – that is, by economists concerned with moral hazard – or by the needs-based school, who have looked at how needs are met or unmet under various schemes. What has been missing is the human rights element. Advocates of the rights-based approach to social protection need to leave their ivory towers, roll up their sleeves and contribute ideas for a rights-based design of social protection schemes.

Second, the underlying basis of utility, essential to risk-based analysis, is philosophically underdeveloped, as is the underlying basis of the basic human needs school. The rights-based school has a comparative advantage here, though its tendency to become hyper-legalistic, literalist and pedantic should not be underestimated.[18] A needs-based theory of human rights seems to offer a fruitful basis for dialogue. Any takers?

Third, the needs and rights-based schools need to develop (better) analytical and design tools. The needs- and rights-based schools do a good job of proving the desirability for social protection in principle, but do a much less convincing job in analysing individual social protection situations. Where they do provide tools for the analysis of such situations, these are usually in the form of a needs- or rights-based critique. Furthermore, the two schools provide little, if any, concrete guidance on, for example, the role of social protection in public policy more generally.

Finally, the attentive reader will have noted that the treatment of chronic poverty, a core theme of this book and part of its title, has been uneven in the course of this chapter. Far from being an accident, this is a reflection of the state of the literature. Chronic poverty is a relatively new concern (or at least a new terminology), and it has entered the mainstream of public policy-making only after many of the classics of the literature on risks, needs and rights and social protection have been written. An important task for scholars today is to reconsider, and to rewrite, the classics of the field using chronic poverty as a starting point.

Notes

1. The views expressed in this chapter are personal, and should not be attributed to any organisation with which the author is or has been affiliated.
2. Witness the recent debates about insurance coverage against terrorist attacks, especially for airlines.
3. Asymmetrical information about the insured person's intentions is the other reason why the private sector does not provide insurance against unemployment (or pregnancy) (Cullis and Jones,1998: 224).
4. An exception is commercial lending to students in professional and graduate schools of, say, medicine, law and business administration. Here future earnings are likely to be high, and previous high performance in undergraduate studies serves as an indicator of future performance.
5. And, in some cases such as refugees, to the citizens of other states as well.
6. The US government is one of the main proponents of the view that there are no economic, social or cultural rights. Of course, various stripes of economic liberals and social conservatives also support this view.
7. Among the other important elements of the corpus of international human rights law are the International Covenant on Civil and Political Rights, the Geneva Conventions, the Convention on the Elimination of All Forms of Discrimination against Women, and the Convention on the Rights of the Child.
8. William O'Neill and Vegard Bye (2002: 17), consultants to the UN Office of the High Commissioner for Human Rights, refer to a 'legalistic approach to human rights [that relies]...on legal jargon and obscure references to arcane procedures that no one has the time to remember'. Sarah Forti (2005) calls it the 'legal centralist approach to human rights'.

9. The religious origins of the natural law tradition are obvious in the naming of two of the main UN human rights treaties, which are called 'covenants' (UN 1966a; UN 1966b).
10. And all of these things are found, albeit under different names, in the Universal Declaration of Human Rights.
11. Also frequently known simply as 'basic needs'.
12. Subsequent research has shown that the relationship between growth and the satisfaction of needs is varied and complex (Afxentiou 1990; Mehrotra and Jolly 1997).
13. In the short term, some redistribution might be needed via the fiscal system.
14. Or from just about any other school of modern economics, for that matter.
15. David Hulme anecdote told at the opening of the Conference on 'Winners and Losers from Rights-Based Approaches to Development', University of Manchester, 21 February 2005.
16. This is actually a caricature of the basic needs school. The 1970s basic needs school (for example, Streeten *et al.* 1981) dealt systematically with dignity, security, agency and participation.
17. Or of any other public policy mechanism outside of the realm of judicial and quasi-judicial institutions.
18. See endnote 7.

References

Afxentiou, Panayiotis (1990) 'Basic needs: A survey of the literature', *Canadian Journal of Development Studies*, XI(2), 241–257.

Arbour, Louise (2005) 'Introduction by the High Commissioner' in Office of the High Commissioner for Human Rights *Annual Appeal 2005: Overview of Activities and Financial Requirements*. Geneva, OHCHR.

Barr, Nicholas (1992) 'Economic theory and the welfare state: A survey and interpretation', *Journal of Economic Literature*, XXX(2), 741–803.

Barr, Nicholas (1998) *The Economics of the Welfare State*, 3rd edition. Oxford: Oxford University Press.

Barry, Norman (1990) *Welfare Concepts in the Social Sciences Series*. Milton Keynes, UK: Open University Press.

Bentham, Jeremy (1789) *An Introduction to the Principles of Morals and Legislation*. Oxford: Clarendon Press (many modern editions).

Bentham, Jeremy (1998) *Anarchical Fallacies*, Headline Series, Foreign Policy Association 318, 56–68.

Brouwer, Marjolein, (2005) 'RBA: A duty to cooperate?' Paper presented to the Conference on 'Winners and Losers in the Rights-based Approach to Development, University of Manchester, 21 February.

Coles, Jeffrey L. and Peter J. Hammond (1995) 'Walrasian equilibrium without survival: Existence, efficiency and remedial policy' in K. Basu *et al.* (eds) *Choice, Welfare and Development: Festschrift for Amartya Sen*. Oxford: Clarendon Press.

Cornia, Giovanni Andrea and Frances Stewart (1993) *Two Errors of Targeting*, Innocenti Occasional Papers, Economic Policy Series, No. 36, Fiscal Policy and the Poor Subsidies, UNICEF, Florence. Reprinted in Dominique van de Walle and Kimberly Nead (eds) (1995) *Public Spending and the Poor: Theory and Evidence*. Baltimore and London: Johns Hopkins University Press for the World Bank.

Cornia, Giovanni Andrea, Richard Jolly and Frances Stewart (1987) *Adjustment with a Human Face*, two volumes. Oxford: Clarendon Press.

Courdesse, Laure-Anne and Sarah Hemingway (2005), 'A human rights-based approach to development in practice: Some lessons learned from the rights-based municipal assessment and planning project in Bosnia and Herzegovina' Paper presented to the Conference on 'Winners and Losers in the Rights-based Approach to Development', University of Manchester, 21 February.

Cullis, John and Philip Jones (1998) *Public Finance and Public Choice*. Oxford and New York: Oxford University Press.

Doyal, Len and Ian Gough (1991) *A Theory of Human Needs*. London: Macmillan.

Engels, Friedrich (1845) *Die Lage der Arbeitenden Klasse in England*, O. Wigand, Leipzig, (English translation 1892 *The Condition of the Working Class in England in 1844*. London: Allen and Unwin).

Forti, Sarah (2005) 'Challenges in the implementation of women's human rights: Field perspectives on domestic violence and HIV/AIDS' Paper presented to the Conference on 'Winners and Losers in the Rights-based Approach to Development', University of Manchester, 21 February.

Goulden, Jay, Brigitte Bode and Elsa Martinez (2005) 'Putting rights-based development into context: CARE's programming approaches in Malawi and Bangladesh' Paper presented to the Conference on 'Winners and Losers in the Rights-based Approach to Development', University of Manchester, 21 February.

Hobbes, Thomas (1651) *Leviathan*. London: Oxford University Press. (Many modern editions.)

International Labour Office (ILO) (1942) *Approaches to Social Security: An International Survey*, Series No. 18. Montreal: McGill University.

Jolly, R. and G. A. Cornia (1984) *The Impact of World Recession on Children: A UNICEF Report*. New York: Pergamon Press.

Ljungman, Ceclia and Sarah Forti (2005) 'Applying a rights-based approach to development: Concepts and principles' Paper presented to the Conference on 'Winners and Losers in the Rights-based Approach to Development', University of Manchester, 21 February.

Maslov, A. H. (1943) 'A theory of human motivation', *Psychological Review*, 50(4), 370–396.

McHale, John and Magda Cordell McHale (1977) *Basic Human Needs: A Framework for Action*, Report to the UN Environment Programme. New Brunswick, NJ: Transaction Books.

Mehrotra, Santosh and Richard Jolly (eds) (1997) *Development with a Human Face: Experiences in Social Achievement and Economic Growth*. Oxford: Clarendon Press.

Munro, Lauchlan T. (2000) 'Is there a liberal case for the comprehensive welfare state?' *Discussion Paper No. 61*, Institute for Development Policy and Management, University of Manchester, May.

Munro, Lauchlan T. (2002) 'Social protection', in Colin Kirkpatrick, Ron Clarke and Charles Polidano (eds), *Handbook on Development Policy and Management*. Cheltenham, UK and Northampton, MA: Edward Elgar, pp. 182–192.

Munro, Lauchlan T. (forthcoming) 'The "human rights-based approach to programming": A contradiction in terms?', in Sam Hickey and Diana Mitlin (eds), *Rights, Wrongs and Realities: Reflections on the Rights-Based Approach*.

NORAD (2001) *Handbook in Human Rights Assessment: State Obligations, Awareness and Empowerment*. Oslo: Norwegian Agency for Development Cooperation.

O'Neill, William and Vegard Bye (2002) 'From High Principles to Operational Practice: Strengthening OHCHR Capacity to support UN Country Teams to Integrate Human Rights in Development Programming', Consultancy report to the UN Office of the High Commissioner for Human Rights, Geneva.

Rights and Democracy (2003) 'Economic and social rights: Canada's Supreme Court disappoints' *Libertas*, Issue 9, International Centre for Human Rights and Democratic Development, Montreal, January.

Riis, Jacob A. (1890) *How the Other Half Lives: Studies among the Tenements of New York*. New York: Charles Scribner.

Robertson, Robert E. (1994) 'Measuring state compliance with the obligation to devote "the maximum available resources" to realizing economic, social and cultural rights', *Human Rights Quarterly*, 16, 693–714.

Rowntree, S. (1901) *Poverty: A Study in Town Life*. London: Macmillan.

Seers, Dudley (1969) 'The meaning of development', *International Development Review*, 11(4), 2–6.

Sen, Amartya (2004) 'Elements of a theory of human rights', *Philosophy and Public Affairs*, 32(4), 315–357.

Stiglitz, Joseph E. (2000) *Economics of the Public Sector*, 3rd edition. New York and London: W.W. Norton and Co.

Streeten, Paul, Shahid Javed Burki, Mahbub ul Haq, Norman Hicks and Frances Stewart (1981) *First Things First: Meeting Basic Human Needs in Developing Countries*. Oxford and New York: Oxford University Press.

Taylor-Gooby, Peter (1991) *Social Change, Social Welfare and Social Science*. London and New York: Harvester-Wheatsheaf.

UN (1948) *Universal Declaration of Human Rights*. New York and Geneva: United Nations.

UN (1966a) *International Covenant on Economic, Social and Cultural Rights*. New York and Geneva: United Nations.

UN (1966b) *International Covenant on Civil and Political Rights*. New York and Geneva: United Nations.

UN (1989) *Convention on the Rights of the Child*. New York and Geneva: United Nations. (Downloaded from http://www.ohchr.org/english/law/crc.htm, on February 2005).

UNDG (2003) *The Human Rights Based Approach to Development Cooperation: Towards a Common Understanding among Un Agencies*. New York: UN Development Group Office. (Downloaded from www.undp.org/governance/docshurist/030616CommonUnderstanding.doc, on 27 February 2005).

UNDP (1990) *Human Development Report 1990*. New York: Oxford University Press.

UNICEF (1987) *Children on the Front Line: The Impact of Apartheid, Destabilisation and Warfare on Children in Southern and South Africa*. Geneva and New York: UNICEF.

UNICEF (1998) *Guidelines for Human Rights-Based Programming Approach – A Human Rights Approach to UNICEF Programming for Children and Women: What It Is, and Some Changes It Will Bring*, CF/EXD/1998–004. New York: UNICEF, 17 April.

UNICEF (2000a) *Poverty Reduction Begins with Children*, Division of Evaluation, Policy and Planning. New York: UNICEF, March.

UNICEF (2000b) *Programme Policy and Procedures Manual: Programme Operations*, Programme Division. New York: UNICEF, January.

UNICEF (2004) *Programme Policy and Procedures Manual: Programme Operations*, Revised Edition, Division of Policy and Planning. New York: UNICEF, June.

UNICEF (2005) *All Rights for All Children: UNICEF in Central and Eastern Europe and the Commonwealth of Independent States*, Communication and Partnership Section, UNICEF Regional Office for CEE/CIS, Geneva, (Downloaded from http://www.unicef.org/publications/index_25088.html on 22 April 2005).

Vandemoortele, Jan (2000) *Absorbing Social Shocks, Protecting Children and Reducing Poverty: The Role of Basic Social Services*, Staff Working Papers, Evaluation, Policy and Planning Series No. EPP-00-001. New York: UNICEF.

Viner, Jacob (1949) 'Bentham and J.S. Mill: The utilitarian background', American Economic Review, XXXIX(2), 360–382.

3
Insurance for the Poor?

Stefan Dercon, Tessa Bold and Cesar Calvo[1]

Introduction

Households in developing countries are exposed to high risks, with important consequences for their welfare. It has long been acknowledged that shocks, ranging from individual-specific (such as illness, theft or unemployment) to economy-wide (such as droughts or recessions), have important implications for consumption and nutrition, not least among the poor. Policy responses have mainly focused on safety nets or other social security mechanisms. This chapter goes beyond this view by arguing, first, that the costs associated with these risks are much higher than those estimated from their short-term impact and, second, that expanding insurance provision for the poor could result in substantial long-term welfare benefits. To illustrate this possibility, we use examples, mainly from Latin America, starting from a consideration of how risk affects the poor and the ways in which they respond to it. The chapter assesses the most promising insurance instruments, while emphasizing that expanding insurance provision should not be seen as a panacea, but instead be viewed as part of a comprehensive extension of protection of the poor.

In addressing the case for extending insurance to the poor, a number of key questions need to be answered. Is risk prevalent? What are the main risks faced by the poor? Thinking about the design and promotion of specific insurance products requires a careful understanding of the risks the poor face, and their consequences. Recent surveys have highlighted the variety of risks faced by the poor (Morduch, 1995; Townsend, 1995; World Bank, 2000; Dercon, 2002; Fafchamps and Lund, 2003). Some of these risks are relatively straightforward to insure, such as funeral or health costs, while in the case of others – say, country-wide recessions or crime – several factors come into play. Any discussion about insurance for the poor will need to acknowledge the shortcomings of an insurance-related approach and the need for alternative mechanisms to deal with the implications of particular shocks. We argue here that there is a need to think in terms of complementarities with other mechanisms to reduce and to cope with risk, including safety nets. The first section will take up these issues in more detail.

The poor try actively to manage risk and to cope with its consequences. A study of the strategies employed to manage and to cope with risk helps us to understand the implications of risk for welfare as well as for the design of policy responses, including insurance. Much research has been conducted in recent years on these strategies and their implications, but more work is definitely needed. These strategies typically involve households trying to shape the risk they face through managing their activity and asset portfolios. A typical example is diversification of activities. Combining economic activities with returns that are imperfectly correlated reduces overall exposure to risk. This also implies accepting lower mean returns, which could effectively perpetuate poverty in the long run. Other strategies involve risk-coping mechanisms – for example, self-insuring through accumulating assets in good years to be drawn on in bad years, or entering into informal mutual assistance arrangements within families or communities. Most evidence suggests, nevertheless, that risk management and coping is rather imperfect, and shocks result in substantial fluctuations in welfare outcomes, which also undermine the asset base of households for future wealth creation, not just in terms of physical and financial assets, but also nutrition and human capital (Morduch, 1995; Dercon, 2002; Dercon and Hoddinott, 2004).

The impact of shocks and the limited range of risk strategies available to those in poverty in developing countries significantly undermine their ability to grow out of poverty, and have important implications for their welfare. The overall result is not only fluctuations in welfare levels, but also a loss of efficiency in that the poor are induced to use their assets less efficiently than the rich. Theoretical models such as the one developed by Banerjee and Newman (1993) build on this feature to show that risk may well result in poverty traps, a situation in which those who cannot escape poverty by their own means end up living in permanent poverty, even if other sectors of the economy are growing). The implication is also that there is no trade-off between equity and efficiency when measures are taken to avoid those poverty traps. In other words, there is a case for providing insurance at subsidized rates so that some do not slip into poverty.This point is expanded on further in the second section.

In the third section , the case for strengthening insurance and insurance substitutes is made, but it is also acknowledged that insurance products can be costly and, more importantly, that they cannot solve all the problems facing the poor. Alternative (complementary) measures are discussed as well, not least in response to the realization that some economic shocks or social and political risks usually cannot be insured by insurance markets, or at least that alternative measures may be more cost-effective. Still, the scope for insurance products for the poor remains strong.

The fourth section discusses general issues related to the design of insurance for the poor. A key issue to be considered is that one must ensure that the poor are reached effectively, which suggests the need to involve local and grass-roots organizations with established links to the poor. Equally important is that the system should be able to provide a cost-effective service and be sustainable. Insurance provision is a specialized service, and should involve private (and possibly public-sector) institutions with the experience and financial capacity to operate such schemes. A 'partner-agent' model is likely to be the most effective institutional arrangement. The final section notes the main conclusions.

Risk and the poor

There are a number of ways of classifying risks faced by the poor. Two issues are relevant for our purposes: the extent to which the poor are affected by these sources of risk, and the extent to which developing more insurance is an appropriate response. To discuss the first point, the section discusses covariance of risks across a population, and the frequency of risks over time. Insurance contracts are offered most easily if risks within the relevant population are not covariate – that is, risks do not affect a large proportion of the population at the same time. Insurance for rare and infrequent events is also typically more difficult to offer. Taken together, insurance contracts are less likely to be on offer for rare and covariate shocks.

Turning to the typology of risks, in recent years a number of studies have highlighted the risks facing the poor. The focus has largely been on data from South Asia and, more recently, from Africa (Morduch, 1995; Dercon, 2002). One key difference between these regions and Latin America and the Caribbean is the urban nature of poverty in the latter. Whereas poverty is mainly a rural phenomenon in Africa and Asia, in Latin America and the Caribbean urban areas account for most of the poor. There are risks that are specific to the urban poor but not to the rural poor, and vice versa, or at least risks that have a different intensity from those in a rural setting.[2] The discussion that follows attempts to give at least equal weight to both types of settings.

Few studies have tried to record systematically the sources of risk faced by the poor. As part of a more extensive World Bank study on poverty in Guatemala, the analysis by Tesliuc and Lindert (2002) provides a unique insight into those sources and their consequences in that country, based on a specifically designed household survey combined with focus group interviews, conducted in the year 2000. It should be noted that Guatemala is one of the most rural economies in Latin America, presenting the lowest percentage of urban poor, so these findings need to be supplemented by other sources for a more complete picture. Although no serious economic crises or natural disasters occurred in 2000, Tesliuc and Lindert found that about

Table 3.1   Incidence of reported shocks, Guatemala, 2000

Frequency reported	Types of shocks
15 or more	Pests, lost harvest
6–14 per cent	Income drop, accident of breadwinner, job losses, drought
2–5 per cent	Loss of terms of trade, crime, floods
0–2 per cent	Hurricane, bankruptcy, landslide, death of breadwinner, enterprise closure, land dispute, fire, earthquake

Source: Tesliuc and Lindert (2002).

53 per cent of the households interviewed reported one or more shocks: 23 per cent mentioned a 'natural' shock (from pests to forest fires and floods); 17 per cent reported an economic or other human-related shock; and 13 per cent reported both. The most commonly reported shocks were related to agriculture, but many different types of shocks were identified (see Table 3.1). Some of these shocks were largely 'rural' – pests, lost harvest and drought are the obvious ones here, while others are common in urban areas – including crime and job losses, which had more than double the incidence in urban areas. Accidents and floods have a similar incidence in both rural and urban settings, with no apparent differences in the overall reported incidence of shocks across both areas. Other studies in the same period confirm the high incidence of shocks. For example, Gaviria and Pages (1999) report that, in the first half of 2000, 36 per cent of urban Guatemalans reported a shock causing a loss of income. A study on Peru (Chacaltana, 2002) reported about 30 per cent of households facing a significant shock to income or wealth in 2001. In short, all available evidence suggests that shocks are prevalent in both rural and urban households in Latin America and the Caribbean.

The study by Tesliuc and Lindert (2002) has other striking findings. First, in 2000, all these shocks were typically idiosyncratic; that is, only a sub-section of a local population was affected. It should nevertheless be recalled that this was largely a year without serious 'large' and covariant shocks. During the previous five years, some shocks had a much higher incidence, including hurricanes (Hurricane Mitch was included in this period), with 44 per cent reportedly being affected, while forest fires hit 17 per cent at least once over a five-year period. These types of risks are largely covariant, affecting typically whole communities or neighbourhoods. Second, there was a rather high incidence of households being affected by more multiple shocks – a phenomenon known as 'bunching' of risk, which may exacerbate the consequences of shocks. Agricultural shocks, such as drought and pests, tend to come together, as do economic shocks, such as job losses and accidents, or the death of a breadwinner. They also find that the poorest are more affected by

Table 3.2 Effects of natural disasters in Latin-American and Caribbean countries, 1970–2001

	Caribbean	Central America	South America	Total
Affected (000s)	19,774	20,146	104,980	144,900
Killed	5	85	156	247
Injured	8	202	276	486
Homeless	971	2,664	4,240	7,875
Damage (US$ 000s)	10,187,949	23,121,364	35,192,517	68,501,830
Annual damage	318,373	722,543	1,099,766	2,140,682

Source: From Chacaltana (2002), based on CRED data.

shocks. In terms of asset or welfare loss, the poor are typically hit hardest. This is especially the case for shocks related to agricultural risks.

In Tesliuc and Lindert (2002), health shocks were not analysed in their survey, which does not mean that they are irrelevant. For example, in a rural sample in Mexico (reported in Ibarra, 2003), it was found that about 48 per cent of households reported a shock in wealth or welfare related to a drop in yields (largely a result of weather-related events), while the second main cause was illness of the farmer or a member of his/her family (reported by about 15 per cent of households). This is consistent with surveys from across the world where illness is typically the second most frequent risk in rural settings after crop failures (see Dercon, 2002), and before many other risks (such as loss of livestock, crime or fire).

In sum, a discussion of the risks faced by the poor in Latin-American and Caribbean countries will need to consider those risks with high incidence and with serious consequences. 'Natural' risks are clearly at the top of the list, but not only for rural settings. Some are obviously rural, such as those related to harvest losses caused by drought or pests, but floods or hurricane risks, and other large-scale natural disasters, are also relevant to urban settings. Data on the impact of large-scale natural disasters over a thirty-year period (see Table 3.2) suggest that their impact on households – ranging from death, injury, homelessness and physical damage – is substantial.

Market failures and household responses to risk

If these risks are substantial and the consequences are as serious as suggested above, one questions why insurance markets are not offering insurance contracts to the poor. There are a number of reasons why this may not occur. Information asymmetries undermine the provision of insurance. Insurance contracts are exposed to adverse selection (hidden information) and moral hazard (hidden action). These have been held responsible for the failure of crop insurance systems (Binswanger, 1986; Braverman and Guasch, 1986), or the lack of insurance against natural disasters or economic recessions. However, it remains to be explained why these asymmetries might be considered more perverse when policyholders are poor.

Insurance providers mitigate information asymmetry by promoting group insurance (against adverse selection) and by requiring co-payments and deductibles (against moral hazard). Although insuring large groups is a feasible strategy, co-payments and deductibles may well discourage the poor from buying the product. In any case, these payments and deductibles will probably need to be lower than the values needed to separate 'good risks' from 'bad risks' (the so-called second-best separating-equilibrium values). As contracts will still allow for significant moral hazard, insurers will require high premiums and thus discourage the poor.

A related issue is that as the poor do not usually participate in the formal economy, formal insurers also face enforcement problems and/or the poor confront extra costs. For example, claiming for home insurance when there are no formal titles to land or homes imposes extra verification costs, which discourages firms from offering contracts to the poor or makes them less attractive. Similarly, the assets of the poor may be of relatively low value, so the transaction costs involved in valuation would be relatively high relative to the size of the contract. Costs related to providing birth and death certificates may also make insurance contracts less attractive to the poor.

Supplying the poor with insurance implies further high transaction costs. For example, micro-credit experiences suggest that the poor find it easier to deal with frequent repayment in small instalments.[3] This suggests that payments of premiums may also occur ideally in small instalments, adding transaction costs to insurance provision.

Furthermore, it has been suggested that the poor sometimes have difficulty in fully understanding their rights in insurance contracts. McCord *et al.* (2001) report several cases where the poor did not file their claims after being affected by an event covered by their policies. In other cases, some policyholders have expected coverage beyond the scope of their contract.

Finally, many of the most serious risks faced by the poor may well be covariant and therefore not easily insured by an emerging insurance market. The fact that a sizeable part of the population is dependent on agriculture, and that macroeconomic instability is substantially higher in developing rather than in richer countries (resulting in serious covariate shocks in the economy) is bound to limit the emergence of private insurance focused on poorer segments of the population.

The lack of market-based insurance could in principle have been compensated for by 'social insurance' – or public-sector-based insurance provision as part of broader social security programmes. In practice, the coverage of these programmes for the poor is minimal in most Latin-American and Caribbean countries. For example, a recent review of Guatemala's social insurance system concluded that the 'system provided minimal coverage of the population, risks financial crisis, faces allegations of corruption and is regressive' (World Bank, 2003). The Instituto Guatemalteco de Seguridad Social (IGSS) covers workers in the formal private and public sectors only, and runs a number of programmes. Programmes analysed, such as the accident–maternity–sickness (IVS) programme, were shown not only to be in deficit but also regressive in terms of the incidence of benefits.

The lack of formal insurance or social insurance systems does not mean that the poor are passive towards the risks they face. Much of their livelihood is centred around ways to reduce, mitigate and cope with risks. The poor use risk management and risk coping strategies to alleviate risks. Table 3.3 describes these strategies and their shortcomings. By risk management we mean that they try to reduce their exposure to risk, or mitigate the risk of some income sources by combining them with others. Diversification of crops and other sources of income is one typical example. Other common strategies involve migration and relative specialization in low-risk activities, even at the cost of lower returns. Risk-coping strategies effectively try to smooth consumption given income fluctuations linked to risk. These

Table 3.3 Risk management and coping strategies

Strategy	Examples	Shortcomings
Managing and reducing risk resulting from changes in sources of income	Crop diversification Specialization in low-risk activities	Sacrifice of expected income
	Migration of some members of the household	
Asset management	Savings as self-insurance	Lack of suitable saving assets (risky or bulky assets, insecurity)
		Focus on liquid, less productive assets
		Long building-up time
		Covariance in asset price and income
Informal insurance	Reciprocal gifts/ loans from friends/ relatives	Incomplete protection
		Vulnerability to covariant risks
Market-based	Insurance	Typically not available

Source: Based on Dercon (2002), Holzmann and Jorgensen (2000) and World Bank (2000).

strategies include self-insurance – that is, building up suitable liquid assets in good years that can be drawn on during a bad year. An alternative strategy is to enter into informal 'risk-sharing arrangements' – that is, informal insurance arrangements based on reciprocal gifts or contingent credit.

Risk management and coping strategies are always present in the life of the household. However, if a serious crisis occurs, households resort to more extreme actions – that is, survival strategies: 'emergency' actions to be taken when a reduction in income is unavoidable. See Table 3.4 for a summary of such strategies.[4]

Some striking conclusions emerge from the empirical literature on this issue. Households cope with risk mainly by using income-based strategies – such as diversification of income sources – and assets for buffering consumption. Informal insurance and credit is also used, but only in a relatively limited number of cases. These strategies are not without cost. As has been widely documented, both income and asset-based strategies imply efficiency losses in the generation of income, and thus may lead to poverty traps (see, for example, Rosenzweig and Binswanger, 1993; Rosenzweig and Wolpin, 1993; Dercon, 2002).[5] Lack of formal or informal insurance provision forces households to choose a safe portfolio of activities and assets, which typically implies a lower mean return. Lack of insurance provision precludes the poor from taking risks to raise their income, thus perpetuating their poverty. The process is exacerbated by shocks as asset holdings are difficult to rebuild after they are depleted. In emergency cases, households are also forced to sacrifice human capital, as is the case when children drop out of school and start working (Pizarro, 2001). In Peru, Jacoby (1994) finds that 'children from households with lower income … and greater childcare responsibilities begin withdrawing from school earlier'. In urban areas, issues of privacy in the household arise as families rent out rooms, or children come back to live in the parental house in order to rent out their own

Table 3.4   Survival strategies

Strategy	Examples	Shortcomings
Changes in sources of income	Child labour	Sacrifice of human capital
Asset management	Selling/pawning of real/productive assets	Long time to replace them
Informal insurance	Charity	Incomplete protection Vulnerability to covariant risks
Market-based	Bank loans for consumption credit	Usually not available

Source: Based on Dercon (2002), Holzmann and Jorgensen (2000) and World Bank (2000).

houses (Zaffaroni, 1999). In fact, after analysing data on Guatemala, Tesliuc and Lindert (2002) concluded that 'the poor have lower resilience than the rich to the effects of shocks. The probability of restoring household income to the level that prevailed before the occurrence of the shock rises with income'(p. 37).

In short, the restricted risk strategies available to the poor result in efficiency losses (Rosenzweig and Binswanger, 1993). It also means that the welfare losses caused by lack of insurance are well beyond those arising from income fluctuations and other transient effects in consumption. They involve permanent or chronic effects on poverty, implying substantially higher welfare costs and lower efficiency. These efficiency losses also mean that effective interventions could be implemented without involving a trade-off between efficiency and equity, since increasing equity (spending focused on the poor), also raises efficiency.[6] If providing insurance could enable the poor to take on riskier, but higher-return activities, then in principle support for the poor could be financed by improvements in efficiency. This makes a case for interventions to encourage insurance with public (and aid) money based on efficiency considerations (see Dercon, 2004).

Scope for insurance provision to the poor

Instruments that could provide incentives and means for the poor to protect themselves *ex ante* against hardship include better insurance products, self-insurance via savings, and access to credit in order to facilitate asset building and properly manage those risks that might affect income. *Ex ante* measures should also focus on reducing risk itself. *Ex post* measures would provide a genuine safety net, targeted appropriately at the poor but large enough in scale and coverage to provide broad social protection to assure a minimal and sustainable standard of living. Such measures could be part of a more general welfare support system, or be targeted specifically to respond to risk-related hardship.

The potential role of these complementary *ex ante* measures should be stressed here. One set of measures involves reducing directly the risks faced by the poor – for example, policies supporting health prevention and sanitation. Better information systems on prices and weather conditions could have substantial benefits, while investments in technology could reduce certain types of risk, with irrigation systems and drought-resistant crops being very good examples of the latter. Indeed, these types of measures could make certain risks, at present too large or covariate to be offered viable insurance cover, more easily insurable in a cost-effective way. They clearly highlight the need for multisectoral approaches to deal with risk and insurance.

Other financial products can also play a part in coping with risk. Savings instruments, for example, have been largely undervalued as an effective instrument for protection against hardship (Dercon, 2002; Morduch, 2004). While credit provision to the poor has received much attention, relatively little has been directed towards savings, even when theses do present many advantages as an area for subsidized intervention and regulation. For example, they are not affected by the information or reinsurance problems concerning credit and insurance, and transaction costs involved in these operations, while not negligible, are likely to be largely restricted to the administrative handling of savings. One of the key issues is that insurance via financial assets may be risky, especially given the endemic risks of inflation in developing countries. Typically, financial savings are not tailored to the poor, offer low or negative returns, and involve extremely high transaction costs imposed on the saver. Savings should not be considered as just a means of building a credit-worthy reputation or mobilize capital aside from the normal economic activity of the household. Typical products are tailored to long-term deposits, with highly punitive returns for those looking for flexible instruments to respond to unexpected hardship.

Credit products could also help to provide better protection against risk. Credit can act as an insurance substitute, and products for this purpose should be part of the standard portfolio of financial instruments offered to the poor. Furthermore, credit can help to diversify the source of income and build up assets. It can also increase income, reduce risk in income, and enhance the ability to cope with shocks that might affect income. Financial products for the poor should be flexible and take into account the fact that they face substantial risks. Linked credit and insurance contracts are one option – for example, linking credit and health insurance. This form of insurance is not the focus of the present chapter, but there is a definite need for more research on such products.

As part of a general system of protection against risk-induced poverty, there is clear scope for insurance targeted at the poor. Furthermore, evidence suggests that the best method for offering insurance to the poor is the partner-agent model, in which an established insurer, possibly with public-sector support, co-operates with local microfinance institutions. Existing informal institutions are also potential agents.

Insurance involves the pooling of risk over a large number of similar units and is most appropriate for uncertain and high losses, which are greater than the amount a household can save for, or repay. When the loss and the degree of uncertainty decrease, insurance loses out to credit and saving. Insurance therefore involves exchanging the uncertainty of large losses for the certainty of small regular payments. Policyholders pay for the losses incurred by others, while the costs and risk are assumed by the insurer. For less uncertain or smaller losses, savings or credit may be more appropriate.[7]

Brown and Churchill (2000) suggest that there is scope for insurance provision only when the following criteria are met: (i) a large number of similar units exposed to risk; (ii) limited policyholder control over the insured event; (iii) the existence of insurable interest; (iv) losses can be identified and measured; (v) losses should not be catastrophic: reinsurance becomes increasingly difficult with increasing covariance across people (such as a hurricane or a flood); (vi) availability of historical information on a sufficiently large number of people or property exposed to the same risk, so that probability of loss can be estimated; and (vii) premiums are affordable. They propose a rule of thumb by which, if the probability of a loss exceeds 40 per cent, premiums will definitely be too high to be affordable.

There are numerous examples of insurance schemes that have been introduced without meeting these criteria, one of the most infamous examples being the crop insurance programmes introduced in the early 1980s in different parts of the world. Many of the criteria included above apply to both poor and rich insurance clients. However, some of them make it particularly difficult to insure the poor profitably. The need for premiums to be economically affordable often means that the policy portfolio cannot in fact be covered by contributions, or that insured amounts are so small that they make little difference to the vulnerability of the poor. Self-Employed Workers Association (SEWA), an Indian health and life insurer, is a case in point, with payouts so low that they only cover about 10 per cent of losses caused by illness-related shocks. Insurance to the poor is traditionally fraught, with high per-unit transaction costs, because premiums need to be small and be collected frequently, while the total amounts of policies are also small. Problems such as moral hazard and adverse selection are not necessarily more damaging among the poor, but the higher transaction costs in dealing with them may mean that these issues make insurance unprofitable. None the less, a number of small-sized (microfinance) institutions already cater to the poor. Their successful experiences may help to develop some best-practice guidelines for potential entrants into the small-scale insurance market who want to target the poor.[8] Some of these lessons are discussed in the fourth and fifth sections of this chapter.

A key lesson is that *ex ante* measures, in the form of a savings, credit and insurance system, may provide substantial protection to the poor, but ultimately they cannot fully insure individuals and families. In short, some *ex post* measures that entail transfers to those affected by uninsured risk would still be necessary as part of a comprehensive system to protect the poor against risk. Insurance products for the poor need to be simple, insuring only specific, highly observable risks with measurable losses, while high-risk groups may need to be excluded by design for the scheme to be sustainable.

All self-protection strategies require some outlay beforehand, and self-insurance fails if shocks occur in successive periods. Credit as a substitute for insurance may not be available either. Certain highly covariate and rare events are very difficult to insure. This means that some 'natural' risks, such as catastrophes, may not be covered easily by a pure insurance system. Other risks require that other types of measures be applied, and market-based insurance products are unlikely to be the most sensible or the only response: 'social' risks such as crime or enforcement of property rights are examples. While it is possible to design products that insure against the consequences of these risks, they only address part of the problem.

But even if there are clear limits to insurance provision for the poor as a solution for their vulnerability to risk, insurance is definitely an option worth focusing on. In particular, life and health insurance, as well as forms of property and asset insurance, are possibilities, and even insurance against some covariate risks, such as drought or, in general, weather insurance.

Implementing insurance for the poor

Some key issues pertaining to insurance management need to be addressed when implementing insurance programmes for the poor. This section addresses institutional arrangements and issues such as financial management, premium calculation, distribution of services, and reinsurance, with a particular focus on targeting the poor.

It is paramount that agents involved in insurance schemes have very close contact with the poor. This is unlikely to be achieved by either government agencies or by standard private insurance providers. As such, institutions with close links to grassroots organizations or NGOs may be ideal agents – for example, microfinance institutions (MFIs), which are relatively widespread within developing countries. But, since purchasing insurance involves a payout only in the case of an adverse shock, it is critical that insurance customers clearly know and understand the benefits to which they are entitled. This requires a simple and clearly stated policy, swift processing of claims, and careful financial management of the insurance portfolio by the insurance provider. To inspire trust among the clientele, adequate reserves need to be held and financed through underwriting, reinsurance and investment. To be financially viable, insurers need to have a sufficiently diversified investment portfolio. This is something that MFIs or other institutions working closely with the poor may often find hard to achieve.

A partner-agent arrangement, in which a local institution or the MFI undertakes only the distribution of insurance services, linked with a private or possibly public-sector insurance provider, may therefore be more appropriate when targeting poor customers. One of its advantages is that it eliminates agent risk and allows the institutions involved to focus on their particular strengths. It also allows local institutions and MFIs to offer greater benefits to policyholders at a similar cost. The most important drawback of this model is the limited availability of potential partners. Fostering these relationships is an issue that public policy should address, by providing a clear institutional and regulatory environment. This point is discussed in further detail in the sixth section, below. Within the context of a partner-agent arrangement, mutual insurance funds may overcome some of the resistance to insurance, since they mimic features of informal insurance arrangements in which funds are often returned to members at regular intervals. Exiting informal arrangements may, however, become a part of an MFI's established set of procedures.

Turning to the issue of premium-setting, most of the existing insurers surveyed by Brown and Churchill (2000) calculated their premiums either in house or by partnering with an established insurer to gain access to the required expertise. Brown and Churchill also found that MFIs that co-operate with established insurers are usually able to offer coverage at better prices. Instituto de Fomento a la Comercialización Campesina (IFOCC) in Peru searched for partners with the actuarial expertise they lacked, but they were unable to find an established insurer willing to provide a product for the low-income market. Instead, they used their own simple calculations based on historical mortality statistics within their credit portfolio. ASA in Bangladesh, however, followed a different and far more risky approach, basing their premiums on customer demand, starting out with very high premiums on their mandatory insurance policy. Numerous complaints were received from their clients, however, so premiums were then lowered successively until complaints stopped. While this ensures that clients are able to afford premiums and are satisfied with the rates offered, it obviously entails a higher risk than the calculation of premiums based on actuarial principles.

As Rutherford (1999) points out, one of the most important demands the poor make on their financial services is easy access and regular small payments, which impose the necessary payment discipline. An agency employing home service distribution and collecting premiums on a weekly basis would be well suited to the needs of low-income households, although this may incur high transaction costs. Integrated distribution, as practiced by SEWA in India, where life insurance is distributed through already existing fixed deposit accounts, could help to curb these costs.

Reinsurance is one element that is almost completely absent in micro-insurance and similar insurance institutions focused on the poor. One of its many benefits is that it can improve the ability of insurers to grow, helps to stabilize financial results, protects against catastrophic losses, and improves underwriting expertise. Reinsurance in low-income markets can also open up markets for some of the large-scale covariant risks such as many natural disasters (Skees et al., 2004). However, to attract reinsurance, it is of critical importance that primary insurers have sound pricing policies and controls to deal with abuse. According to respondents in the Brown and Churchill survey, all partner institutions in partner-agent arrangements and some co-operative insurers were likely to have reinsurance contracts. However, few of the MFIs and other smaller organizations in their study have reinsurance, which leaves them highly exposed to sudden increases in claims, and prevents them from having access to a potentially valuable source of expertise.

There is substantial scope for the government to effectively support the insurance market serving the poor. A favourable policy environment can support the proliferation of insurance services among the poor by facilitating the establishment of local (micro) finance institutions, and making insurance provision to the low-income segment of the market more attractive to established insurers. The strategy is unlikely to involve large-scale subsidies, but government spending will need to be directed towards establishing the necessary infrastructure, institutions and regulatory environment to promote this segment of the market. Unfortunately, such a policy environment does not exist in most parts of the world and, in fact, some of the existing regulations actually present a bias against the use of finance and insurance products targeted at the poor (see Dercon *et al.*, 2005) for a further discussion).

Conclusions

The poor face substantial risk, in the form of natural, health, social and economic risks, and are also more likely to be affected by these. In general, the poor use sophisticated strategies to cope with these risks, but the measures are inadequate and welfare losses substantial. The strategies themselves come at an additional cost in terms of long-term welfare. Risk, and how the poor respond to it, contributes to the persistence of poverty. There is a clear need for policies to reduce risk and its consequences for the poorest. Indeed, there may well be an efficiency argument for providing subsidized insurance and protection, given risk-induced poverty traps.

This chapter has argued for the need to foster insurance provision, not as panacea to solve all problems, but as part of a comprehensive system. The current focus on *ex post* measures in the form of some kind of safety net is not cost-effective or sufficient to reach the poor. Other components of such a system would be *ex ante* measures to stimulate and protect self-insurance through savings, reducing risk and fostering credit for the poor as a form of insurance and to allow a stronger asset base to grow out of persistent vulnerability to risk. These efforts need to be supplemented by a careful and well-designed safety net, since some risks should not be addressed by 'ex ante' insurance-related mechanisms – examples are certain covariate economic or catastrophic risks. A high proportion of risk, including economic and social risk, is also largely human-made, and reducing the impact of this requires actions to address its causes – inflation, crime or waste-related risks are examples. Providing protection only against the consequences of such risks is unlikely to be cost-effective.

In terms of the basic institutional arrangement for insurance provision, the partner-agent model appears to be the most suitable, so that an established insurer (the partner, from the private sector, possibly in partnership with the public sector) links up with an institution with local financial connections, such as a microfinance institution (MFI). The advantage is that this would include a mechanism to provide easy access and terms to the poor, while costs are reduced and sustainability is protected by reinsurance and contracting with an established insurer. Judging from case studies, it appears that a number of products might be suitable for promotion, including life, property, health, weather or price insurance, possibly linked to credit. One should be cautious about the likely success of these schemes. In terms of types of coverage, the experience of existing insurers catering to the poor shows that it is difficult to offer profitable comprehensive coverage to low-income households. In part, this can be explained by the financial capacity of clients and the lack of opportunities for diversification. Term life insurance is the most sustainable type of insurance, but the support of governments, donors and NGOs is necessary to branch out into other profitable products. Product features should include group policies, mandatory insurance and incentives to cope with moral hazard and adverse selection – for example, by rewarding members who do not submit any claims during the year.

While subsidized insurance for the poor can be an attractive option on efficiency grounds, an important role for the government would be to establish a more effective regulatory framework to foster the establishment of micro-insurers at the local level, while maintaining overall stability and credibility of the entire financial system. While relaxing entry requirements for MFIs to enter the insurance market may be beneficial, incentives should be also provided so that MFIs partner with established insurers, through the partner-agent method.

Finally, objectives should be clearly defined when extending insurance to the poor. Uninsured risk means that poverty is perpetuated, with the possibility that a risk-induced poverty trap might occur. Extending insurance, as part of a credible comprehensive system of social protection, should allow the poor to sustain their assets and to enter into more profitable, riskier activities. In short, it would allow the poor to focus on long-term strategies to get out of poverty.

Of critical importance are the credibility and sustainability of insurance provision as part of a broader social protection system. These cannot be underestimated. Often, institutions in developing countries are not transparent or sustainable, and therefore well-intentioned measures may lack the credibility and public support to succeed. Credibility cannot be acquired easily, and governments face an uphill struggle in this regard. There is a key role for the government in the development and support of an appropriate regulatory and institutional framework for such programmes, and sustainable and transparent institutions to monitor these activities.

Notes

1. This chapter is based on work initially financed by the Inter-American Development Bank and by the World Institute of Development Economics Research (WIDER). We would like to thank Luis Tejerina for insightful comments.
2. It should be pointed out here that the urban poor face *different* risks, not *more* (or fewer) risks. For example, in an LSMS in Peru in 2001, 30.1 per cent of urban households reported having suffered a shock. In the rural sample, it was 29.6 per cent (Chacaltana, 2002).
3. In fact, Armendariz and Morduch (2000) argue that theoretical literature on micro-credit has exaggerated the focus on joint liability and dynamic incentives, and neglected the importance of the repayment schedule. This comment is bound to be relevant for insurance provision as well.
4. More information on this can be found in Dercon (2002), while the Social Risk Management Approach is discussed in Holzmann and Jorgensen (2000) and in World Bank (2000).
5. It is worth noting that most studies focus on poverty traps in the rural sector. Hence, the effect of risk exposure on urban investment decisions remains to be explored. This research is especially relevant for Latin America.
6. For a more detailed discussion, see Dercon (2004). For a theoretical discussion on poverty traps induced by risk, see Banerjee (2004).
7. This feature may also explain why the poor in Latin America may be unwilling to purchase some of the existing 'formal' insurance products available and instead prefer to rely on 'autarkic solutions', including self-insurance, since the lack of appropriately targeted and designed products would make existing products relatively too costly for the poor, possibly outweighing the benefits.
8. The survey by Brown and Churchill (2000) provides a number of examples.

References

Armendariz, B. and J. Morduch (2000) 'Microfinance beyond group lending', *The Economics of Transition*, 8(2), 401–420.

Banerjee, A. V. and A. F. Newman (1993) 'Occupational Choice and the Process of Development', *Journal of Political Economy*, 101(2), 274–298.

Banerjee, A. V. (2004) 'The Two Poverties', in S. Dercon (ed.), *Insurance against poverty*. Oxford: Oxford University Press, pp. 59–75.

Binswanger, H. (1986) 'Risk aversion, collateral requirements and the market for credit and insurance in rural areas', in P. Hazell, C. Pomareda and A. Valdés (eds), *Crop Insurance for Agricultural Sectors: Issues and Experience*. London: John Hopkins University Press.

Braverman, A. and J. L. Guasch (1986) 'Rural Credit Markets and Institutions in Developing Countries: Lessons for Policy Analysis from Practice and Modern Theory', *World Development*, 14(10–11), 1253–1267.

Brown, W. and C. Churchill (2000) *Providing Insurance to Low-income Households*. Washington DC: USAID.

Chacaltana, J. (2002) Social Funds and the Challenge of Social Protection for the Poor in Latin America. (Conference on Social Protection), ADB-IADB.

Dercon, S. (2002) 'Income Risks, Coping Strategies, and Safety Nets', *World Bank Research Observer*, 17(2), 141–166.

Dercon, S. (ed.) (2004) *Insurance against Poverty*. Oxford: Oxford University Press.

Dercon, S. and J. Hoddinott (2004) 'Health, Shocks and Poverty Persistence', in S. Dercon (ed.), *Insurance against Poverty*. Oxford: Oxford University Press, pp. 124–136.

Dercon, S., T. Bold and C. Calvo (2005) 'Insurance for the Poor', *QEH Working Paper* 125. Oxford: Department of International Development.

Fafchamps, M. and S. Lund (2003) 'Risk-sharing networks in rural Philippines', *Journal of Development Economics*, 31(1), 261–287.

Gaviria, A. and C. Pages (1999) 'Patterns of Crime Victimization in Latin America Research Department', *Working Paper* 408, Inter-American Development Bank.

Holzmann, R. and S. Jorgensen (2000) Social Protection as Social Risk Management: A new conceptual framework for social protection and beyond, Social Protection Discussion Paper 6. Washington, DC: The World Bank.

Ibarra, H. (2003) 'Comments on Risk Managed Challenges in Rural Financial Markets' by J. Skees. Mimeo. AGROASEMEX.

Jacoby, Hanan G. (1994) 'Borrowing Constraints and Progress through School: Evidence from Peru', *The Review of Economics and Statistics*, 76(1), 151–160.

McCord, M. J., J. Isern and S. Hashemi (2001) *Microinsurance: A Case Study Example of the Full Service Model of Microinsurance Provision*, Self-Employed Women's Association. MicroSave-Africa.

Morduch, J. (1995) 'Income Smoothing and Consumption Smoothing', *Journal of Economic Perspectives*, 9 (Summer), 103–114.

Morduch, J. (2004) 'Consumption Smoothing Across Space: Testing Theories of Risk-Sharing in the ICRISAT Study Region of South India', in S. Dercon (ed.), *Insurance Against Poverty*, Oxford: Oxford University Press, pp. 38–56.

Pizarro, R. (2001) 'La vulnerabilidad social y sus desafíos: una mirada desde América Latina', *Serie Estudios Estadísticos y Prospectivos*, 6. ECLAC.

Rosenzweig, M. and H. Binswanger (1993) 'Wealth, Weather Risk and the Composition and Profitability of Agricultural Investments', *Economic Journal*, 103, 56–78.

Rosenzweig, M. and K. Wolpin (1993) 'Credit Market Constraints, Consumption Smoothing, and the Accumulation of Durable Production Assets in Low-Income Countries: Investments in Bullocks in India', *Journal of Political Economy*, 1001(2), 223–244.

Rutherford, S. (1999) *The Poor and Their Money*. Institute for Development Policy and Management, University of Manchester.

Skees, J., P. Varangis, D. Larson and P. Siegel (2004) 'Can Financial Markets be Tapped to Help Poor People Cope with Weather Risks?', in S. Dercon (ed.), *Insurance Against Poverty*, Oxford: Oxford University Press, pp. 422–437.

Tesliuc, E. and K. Lindert (2002) *Vulnerability: A Quantitative and Qualitative Assessment*, Guatemala Poverty Assessment Program, The World Bank.

Townsend, R. M. (1995) 'Consumption insurance: An evaluation of risk bearing systems in low-income economies', *Journal of Economic Perspectives*, 9 (Summer), 83–102.

World Bank (2000) World Development Report 2000/1. Attacking Poverty, Washington, DC: The World Bank.

World Bank (2003) *Guapa: The Guatemala Poverty Assessment*. Washington, DC: The World Bank.

Zaffaroni, C. (1999) 'Los recursos de las familias urbanas de bajos ingresos para enfrentar situaciones críticas', in R. Kaztman (ed.), *Activos y estructuras de oportunidades. Estudios sobre las raíces de la vulnerabilidad social en Uruguay*, ECLAC and UNDP.

4

Transformative Social Protection: The Currency of Social Justice

Rachel Sabates-Wheeler and Stephen Devereux

Introduction

Social protection emerged as a critical response to the 'safety nets' discourse of the late 1980s and early 1990s. In the *World Development Report 1990*, for example, safety nets were very much the third prong of the World Bank's three-pronged approach to 'attacking poverty' (World Bank, 1990), and were conceptualized as minimalist social assistance in countries too poor and too administratively weak to introduce comprehensive social welfare programmes. During the 1990s, as new thinking emerged in areas such as 'rights-based approaches', 'sustainable livelihoods', and the multidimensional nature of poverty and vulnerability, safety nets began to be criticized as residualist and paternalistic, and more sophisticated alternatives began to be proposed. As this agenda has evolved, the broader potential of social protection began to be recognized, and bigger claims are now being made for what social protection can and should strive to achieve.

There are two interconnected strands in this response, both linked to a concern for long-term and sustainable poverty reduction. The first links risk management explicitly with economic growth, and argues that reducing risk or protecting the poor against income and consumption variability will allow them to invest and accumulate – a 'trampoline' out of poverty (World Bank, 2000). Despite being promoted vigorously in international development publications, this link has not yet become a key component of anti-poverty programming in practice. In low-income countries, social protection continues to be perceived by governments and donors as comprising fiscally unsustainable 'consumption' transfers to the economically inactive or unproductive poor, which diverts scarce public resources from 'productive' investment for economic growth, and therefore deserves lower priority as a poverty reduction tool.

At the same time, most advocates of social protection do not make the second connection, which we argue is of fundamental importance to

64

long-term poverty reduction – namely, the positive relationship between livelihood security and enhanced autonomy or empowerment. While understandings of 'poverty' have moved to incorporate social dimensions of well-being together with rights-based approaches, social protection continues to be conceptualized by many development agencies mainly in terms of public responses to livelihood shocks – the conventional economic 'safety net' function. But this is 'economic protection', not 'social protection', and it is hardly socially transformative. Largely missing from the World Bank's 'social risk management' framework, for example, is a concern for equity and social rights. We argue that an appreciation of this second linkage can help to create the policy conditions for a virtuous cycle of pro-poor growth, governance systems that are accountable and responsive to poorer as well as wealthier citizens, and an approach to development that is grounded in concerns for social justice.

In an attempt to challenge the negative perceptions and narrow preconceptions that still surround social protection, this chapter addresses both conceptual and policy issues in the social protection literature. In the first part of this chapter we locate the conceptual origins of social protection as a response to risk and vulnerability, and argue for a broader conceptualization of vulnerability based on an appreciation of structural inequalities. Attempting to address structural vulnerabilities (together with other forms) requires taking a political approach to social protection, focusing on rights, duties, democracy and advocacy. We describe what we mean by the 'transformative' potential of social protection. The following section considers 'transformative social protection' in practice, by discussing several measures that highlight the economic growth and social transformation functions and linkages of social protection, drawing on experiences in mainstreaming social protection in Uganda's poverty reduction strategy. The chapter concludes by reasserting the case for social protection as supporting social as well as economic goals of development.

Social protection as a response to risk and vulnerability

People across the world face a wide range of risks and hazards that impact on their livelihoods, both directly and indirectly. In order to minimize the likelihood of downward livelihood trajectories, and institute effective and sustainable social protection strategies, we must understand how households, communities and countries attempt to manage potential impacts from hazards as well as the hazards themselves.

To be a useful concept, vulnerability must be defined in relation to some other phenomenon, such as poverty, malnutrition, exclusion or neglect. Vulnerability is thus a multidimensional concept and corresponds to the complexity of the phenomenon it is defined against. For example, if we are interested in measuring vulnerability to poverty and we know that poverty is multidimensional, then vulnerability to one aspect of poverty (say, malnutrition) may not mean vulnerability to another aspect (say, lack of access to education).

A common way of conceptualizing vulnerability is to view it as a product of two components: exposure to a hazard (a shock or process); and resilience, or the ability to manage the hazard (Chambers, 1989; Bankoff *et al.*, 2004). Understanding vulnerability in two-dimensional space is important as it illustrates the very different policy responses that need to be considered in relation to what constitutes the vulnerability of any one person, household, community or 'vulnerable group'. It is particularly useful for acute situations requiring an immediate response. That is, at any one time it is possible to construct a static vulnerability profile that indicates whether the hazard or the ability to cope is the main determinant of vulnerability. Policies appropriate to the composite nature of the vulnerability can then be designed. However, to understand vulnerability fully it is not enough simply to take a one-period view. Vulnerability needs to be forward-looking, as it makes a prediction about future poverty (or other outcomes). Vulnerability does not simply refer to those who are likely to become poor in the future as a result of an unexpected shock, but also to those who will remain poor, those who might fall deeper into poverty and those who may move in and out of poverty because of predicable fluctuations such as seasonality (Dercon, 2001). This disaggregation is important, as the appropriate policy responses are very different for each distinct group.

An understanding of vulnerability is further complicated by the notion of 'ability to manage'. How do we measure this, and what are the implications of different measurement approaches? If we do not unpack what 'ability to cope' means then we cannot determine whether we are dealing with transitory or chronic poverty, or vulnerabilities related to structural inequalities and lack of access to rights and opportunities. 'Ability to manage' is often proxied by income or consumption poverty measures. For example, if a household falls below a specified poverty line it may be considered unable to cope. Poverty-gap measures are also used to estimate the severity and depth of poverty, and these measures could also be used to infer (in)ability to cope. More recent work focuses on asset profiles, or asset bundles, as a way of understanding poverty. The problem with using any one of these measurements for looking at vulnerability is that each measurement will only provide a partial story. For example, using a consumption measurement, we may conclude that in a certain environment households are able to smooth consumption using a range of risk management strategies. However, it is not possible to see from this what households have been doing with their income or assets in order to smooth consumption. In other words, we are unable to understand the dynamic relationships between consumption and income smoothing, or income smoothing and asset depletion.

These income, consumption and asset-based understandings of vulnerability underpin the majority of government and donor approaches to vulnerability. For this reason we see many agencies taking an instrumentalist approach to social protection policies, as a collection of measures to manage risk and thus improve or protect livelihoods by stabilizing income and consumption or building up assets. Consider these definitions from the International Labour Office (ILO) and the World Bank: '[Social protection is] the provision of benefits to households and individuals through public or collective arrangements to protect against low or declining living standards' (van Ginneken, 1999); 'Social protection interventions assist individuals, households, and communities to better manage the income risks that leave people vulnerable' (World Bank, 2004).[1]

While we do not dispute the fact that income, consumption and assets are crucial in helping to overcome poverty and minimize livelihood shocks, we would argue that 'ability to manage' is rather more complex than a simple focus on household income and asset portfolios. It is instead a complex function of existing behaviour, reflected in livelihood profiles that themselves represent long-term or structural adaptation to predictable shocks and stresses; crisis response behaviour (such as the ability to rely on formal and informal insurance and networks in times of crisis); and external (policy) responses to a predicted and actual crisis. Provision of consumption, income and asset insurance is only a partial response to vulnerability. An expanded view of social protection must incorporate responses to both chronic and structural vulnerability.

Reconceptualizing vulnerability

Vulnerability can be conceptualized in a variety of ways, depending critically on the unit of analysis and the source of risk. Within the Social Risk Management framework of the World Bank (as in most literature on social protection) vulnerability is attributed to the characteristics of a person or group, an event affecting a person or group, or a point in a person's life-cycle. For example, in any given context, people living with disabilities can be characterized as being more or less vulnerable than people living without disabilities. This type of analysis tends to classify vulnerability according to a range of risks or shocks that affect one or more of a variety of livelihood assets (World Bank, 2000: 136–8). This is reflected in the range of policy instruments proposed, such as reception centres for orphans, shelters for women suffering domestic abuse, disability aids for farmers living with disabilities, foodgrain warehouses, and various social assistance programmes (World Bank, 2000: 141). However, if, rather than focusing on risk as an exogenously given factor to be managed, vulnerability is conceptualized as emerging from and embedded in the socio-political context, then our attention would no longer be focused on how to design a policy so that various groups face less risk in a given context, but on how to transform this context to minimize risk for a range of vulnerable groups.[2]

> Focusing on the vulnerabilities of the individuals or groups in any given space or at any given moment to enable them to better access and make use of that space is certainly important as a short-run agenda. However, if we re-focus our attention to include also the second conceptualization of vulnerability as presented above, space, context and time no longer bind, but instead become the crucial point of our understanding of constructions of vulnerability. The question no longer becomes how do we design a policy so that various groups face less risk in given spaces, but, how did this space, or context, emerge? Whose interests were served in the creation of the space and whose interests are served in maintaining the *status quo*? A focus on space and time necessarily leads to contextual socio-political analyses of vulnerability. (Sabates-Wheeler and Waite, 2003)

The dominant policy agenda around social protection is concerned almost exclusively with measures and programmes that stabilize expectations of risk, without affecting the fundamental causes of vulnerability that are embedded in social and political relations at all levels. For example, the social risk management (SRM) framework mainly addresses economic risks to household incomes and assets (World Bank, 2000: 138). Absent from this framework are 'social risks' that also contribute to poverty and the construction of vulnerability. This is evidenced by the way in which social inclusion, social cohesion and social stability are treated as being positive externalities of well-designed 'social risk management' interventions. Social risks may be categorized as 'structural' or 'contingent'. Structural risk refers to situations where groups or individuals are marginalized or discriminated against, and by its nature has longer-term implications for poverty and vulnerability than contingent risk, which is a function of environmental or economic factors, such as an earthquake, or hyper-inflation. Because the SRM framework is largely focused on *income variability*, with other (especially social) dimensions of vulnerability effectively being overlooked, we argue that the SRM approach does not incorporate a comprehensive understanding of vulnerability, and is therefore limited in its scope and purpose of social protection provisions.

Related to a limited conceptualization of vulnerability is the lack of attention paid to chronic poverty in standard approaches to social protection. The 'chronic poor' include people who have never recovered from a severe shock, such as a disabling illness or loss of assets. In their analysis of chronic poverty and social protection. Barrientos and Shepherd (2003: 7) state that: 'Although risk and vulnerability are key factors in explaining the descent into poverty, it is not clear ... how important they are in maintaining people in poverty, transmitting poverty from one generation to the next, and in preventing the interruption of poverty.' Importantly, Barrientos and Shepherd (2003: 3) highlight structural reasons related to 'social, political and economic structures and relationships, and processes of exclusion and adverse incorporation', that prevent some of the chronic poor from benefiting from development policies and market changes. The chronic poor 'have fewer options, less freedom to take up available options, and so remain stuck in patterns of life which give them low returns to whatever few assets they have maintained' (Hulme *et al.*, 2001: 8). Social, political and economic structures are typically the defining characteristics of livelihood risk, with the possible exception of some natural disasters – though even in these cases, the contribution of socio-political factors has persistently been underappreciated (Bankoff *et al.*, 2004).

Relocating an understanding of 'vulnerability' in socio-political space necessarily conjures up linkages to large literatures on social exclusion, rights-based approaches, citizenship and power (for example, Kabeer, 2002, 2005; Gaventa, 2004; Nyamu-Musembi and Cornwall, 2004). These literatures will not be reviewed here. However, in accordance with the general thrust of the literature, we would argue that, like the rights-based approach or an agenda for inclusive citizenship, a transformative approach holds little meaning if it is unable to achieve a positive change in power relations among various stakeholders – development actors, government agencies, differentiated socio-economic groups, different household members. Thus a vision of transformative social protection, 'must be interrogated for the extent to which it enables those whose lives are affected to articulate their priorities and claim genuine accountability' from different implementing and 'provisioning' stakeholders (Nyamu-Musembi and Cornwall, 2004).

Introducing the transformative element to social protection

If a person's needs for social protection are defined in a narrow 'safety net' sense, as mechanisms for smoothing consumption in response to declining or fluctuating incomes, then the focus of interventions will logically be on targeted income or consumption transfers to affected individuals. In our view, the range of social protection interventions should extend well beyond social transfers – and the resources transferred should be broader than cash or food, to include redistribution of assets that will reduce dependency on handouts and enable some of the poor to achieve sustainable livelihoods. Targeted social transfers provide 'economic protection' in response to economic risks and livelihood vulnerability. Other forms of 'social protection' would address distinct problems of 'social vulnerability', not necessarily through resource transfers, but by delivering appropriate social services and implementing measures to modify or regulate behaviour towards socially vulnerable groups.

Strategies to deal with problems of social vulnerability require a transformative element, where 'transformative' refers to the need to pursue policies that integrate individuals equally into society, allowing everyone to take advantage of the benefits of growth and enabling excluded or marginalized groups to claim their rights. For example, support to trade unions may enable socio-economically marginalized groups to claim their rights to decent working conditions; facilitation and creation of spaces for deliberative democratic processes can increase citizen participation; sensitization and awareness-raising campaigns can transform public attitudes and behaviour; and changes to the regulatory framework could protect vulnerable or minority groups against discrimination and abuse.

Another sphere where transformative social protection policies may be needed is the intra-household division of resource ownership, access and use. For example, many difficulties involved in the provision of social protection for women relate to socio-cultural values that leave women in particularly vulnerable positions. Clearly, social protection instruments designed for many categories of women must include a substantial 'transformative' element, in the sense that power relations between men and women become more balanced. Appropriate legislation is necessary, but this goes only a small way towards changing socio-cultural values. Efforts could focus on educating men and women about their rights, and how to access them. Other political and institutional constraints facing women relate to lack of access to the legal system; cultural resistance to changes in gender relations; and commonly held beliefs about women's role in land management and property ownership.

Bearing the above points in mind, we have devised our own conceptual and operational definitions of social protection. Our *conceptual definition* incorporates but goes beyond transfer-based responses to economic risk and vulnerability:

Social protection describes all initiatives that transfer income or assets to the poor, protect the vulnerable against livelihood risks, and enhance the social status and rights of the marginalized; with the overall objectives of extending the benefits of economic growth and reducing the economic or social vulnerability of poor, vulnerable and marginalized groups.

Our *working definition* adapts terminology first introduced by Guhan (1994), and elaborates on the mechanisms that deliver social protection. Social protection includes four categories of instruments: *'provision' measures*, which provide relief from deprivation; *preventive measures*, which attempt to prevent deprivation; *promotive measures*, which aim to enhance incomes and capabilities; and *transformative measures*, which seek to address concerns of social justice and exclusion.

'Provision' measures provide relief from deprivation. Provision measures are narrowly targeted safety net measures in the conventional sense – they aim to provide relief from poverty and deprivation to the extent that promotional

and preventive measures have failed to do so. Provision measures include *social assistance* for the chronic poor, especially those who are unable to work and earn their livelihood. This equates closely to mainstream 'social welfare'. Social assistance programmes include targeted resource transfers – disability benefit, single-parent grants, and social pensions that are financed publicly (out of the tax base, with donor support, or through NGOs). Other provision measures can be classified as *social services* for poor individuals and groups who need special care, including orphanages and reception centres for abandoned children, and the abolition of education and health charges to extend access to basic services to the very poor.

Preventive measures seek to prevent deprivation. Preventive measures deal directly with poverty alleviation. They include *social insurance* for 'economically vulnerable groups' – people who have fallen, or might fall, into poverty, and may need support to help them manage their livelihood shocks. This is similar to 'social safety nets'. Social insurance programmes refer to formalized systems of pensions, health insurance, maternity benefit and unemployment benefits, often with tripartite financing between employers, employees and the state. They also include informal mechanisms, such as savings clubs and funeral societies. Strategies of risk diversification – such as crop or income diversification – can also be considered as preventive measures.

Promotive measures aim to enhance real incomes and capabilities, achieved through a range of livelihood-enhancing programmes targeted at both households and individuals, such as microfinance and school feeding. The inclusion of promotive measures as a category here is open to the criticism that it takes social protection too far beyond its original conceptualization. However, the intention is not to broaden the scope to include (potentially) all development initiatives, but to focus on promotive measures that have income stabilization at least as one objective. Examples include micro-credit invested in small enterprises in order to fulfil income stabilizing and consumption smoothing functions, or public works projects that transfer food rations or cash wages while simultaneously building economic infrastructure such as roads or irrigation.

Transformative measures seek to address concerns of social justice and exclusion, such as the exploitation of workers, or discrimination against ethnic minorities. *Transformative* interventions include collective action for workers' rights, changes to the regulatory framework to protect 'socially vulnerable groups' (for example, people with disabilities, or victims of domestic violence) against abuse, as well as sensitization campaigns (such as the 'HIV/AIDS Anti-Stigma Campaign' discussed later in this chapter) and advocacy to enhance social equity.

These categories may, of course, overlap, and many social protection interventions aim to achieve more than one objective. Public works projects, school feeding schemes and micro-credit programmes all strive towards promoting incomes in the long term as well as preventing deprivation in the short term. Similarly, a 'transformative' measure such as eradicating labour market discrimination against HIV-positive people is not only a victory for social justice, it also enhances the employment prospects of people living with HIV and AIDS.

Figure 4.1 illustrates the relationship between these categories and presents our suggested conceptual framework for thinking about social protection. Reading from the bottom, 'provision' policies are essentially old-style 'safety nets'. However, if designed well these instruments can have positive effects on the prevention of deprivation, livelihood promotion and even social transformation. The solid black lines in Figure 4.1 indicate a strong and direct relationship. For example, 'preventive' interventions, such as crop diversification to reduce agricultural risk, may also have 'promotive' outcomes in the sense that a wider crop portfolio might lead to a competitive market advantage. In fact, most preventive mechanisms could be argued as having promotive effects, in the sense that risk reduction enables people to take advantage of opportunities that they would otherwise have been unable to do.

The top half of the diagram in Figure 4.1 corresponds with instruments and policies that facilitate movements out of poverty, or 'springboards'. Broadly speaking, the left-hand side of the diagram corresponds to social protection interventions that have economic outcomes and direct growth effects, whereas the right-hand side represents social outcomes – the 'transformative' aspect of social protection. At the top of the figure the economic and social dimensions come together and are interrelated. That is, by pursuing activities that overcome structural inequalities and injustice, people are better able to engage in both society and the economy, which will have positive spin-offs not only for their livelihoods but also for economic growth. The dashed line connecting 'promotion' and 'transformation' illustrates both the interconnectedness of economic and social vulnerabilities, and the potential for interventions in either sphere to reduce both sources of vulnerability. This is especially true of vulnerabilities that are structural and chronic, rather than contingent and acute.

The dashed lines indicate a less obvious or weaker relationship. For example, some preventive mechanisms can be transformative, and vice versa, but this relationship is neither strong nor inevitable. One example is microfinance schemes that provide both social insurance and economic opportunities, and often have positive knock-on effects by empowering individuals within their families, and households within their communities. Another weak relationship is illustrated by the dashed line from 'provision' to 'promotion', highlighting the possibility that certain safety net measures may build capabilities or assets, thereby enabling beneficiaries to grasp opportunities that otherwise would be denied to them. (In the next section of this chapter we draw on the example of school feeding schemes to illustrate this

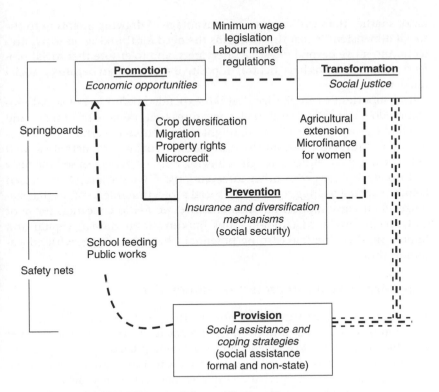

Figure 4.1 A conceptual framework for social protection

linkage.) Similarly, some social protection instruments, such as minimum wage legislation (also discussed below), can be both promotive and transformative. Paying workers a fair wage enhances their incomes and capabilities, while the very process of bargaining with employers to raise and enforce the minimum wage – through trade unions or public campaigns – can be politically empowering, especially when supported by government.

Finally, the very thick dashed line linking provision and transformation indicates a potential negative relationship between the humanitarian objective of delivering social assistance, and social objectives such as human dignity and autonomy. Some social protection measures can have the unintended consequence of reinforcing established power hierarchies, or of being stigmatizing and exacerbating social polarization and exclusion. Examples include certain targeting mechanisms that are applied to social assistance programmes for 'vulnerable groups' (for example, singling out 'AIDS orphans' from other vulnerable children, or requiring adults to declare their HIV status), or paying participants carrying out public works with food rations rather than cash wages. One advantage of drawing attention to the social dimensions is that this confirms the need for thinking on social protection to move beyond old-style safety nets, and to ensure that social protection interventions have neutral or positive – rather than negative – social impacts.

It is important to emphasize that our expanded definition of social protection does not extend to all policy measures that promote livelihoods and economic growth. Instead, we highlight the potential of certain social protection measures to contribute to economic growth and productivity as well as to social equity, either through achieving both objectives simultaneously or through linkages with other interventions. A good example (discussed below) is school feeding schemes – a social protection intervention that stabilizes food consumption but also enhances access to education for poor and socially excluded children, thus building their human capital and improving their lifetime earning potential, through linkages with education facilities.

Transformative social protection in practice

This section discusses three interventions that reflect a broader conceptualization of what social protection is, or what it can achieve. The selected case studies each relate to different parts of our conceptual diagram (Figure 4.1). The first intervention (school feeding) relates to the left-hand side of the diagram, and illustrates potential linkages between safety nets or social assistance programmes and economic growth. The second intervention (anti-discrimination campaigns) relates to the right-hand side of the diagram, and identifies how social protection can be mobilized for social justice ends. The third intervention (labour rights and minimum wages) relates to the top of the diagram, and illustrates how social protection can achieve growth-equity linkages. The actual case studies discussed in this section draw on work done by the authors with the Government of Uganda's Social Protection Task Force during 2002–2003 (Devereux and Sabates-Wheeler, 2003), as part of an effort by the Ministry of Gender, Labour and Social Development to 'mainstream' social protection across all sectors, in the process of revising the national Poverty Eradication Action Plan (PEAP).

Safety-net – growth linkages: school feeding

One example of a social protection intervention that can contribute to longer-term poverty reduction goals is school feeding schemes that provide learners with free meals at school. Because school meals serve two functions – providing an immediate consumption transfer to children who are often malnourished, and encouraging children from poor households to attend school even during difficult times – school feeding schemes can be characterized as serving both protective and promotive social protection objectives. However, making this case requires a demonstration that education generates higher incomes for school-leavers, that school feeding improves educational outcomes, and that school feeding is pro-poor. Education for all is not only a basic right, it is also an investment in the future. In Uganda, the right to education is enshrined in the Constitution of 1995, and the case for education as a driver of poverty reduction has been proved empirically (Appleton, 2001; Lawson et al., 2003). Poverty and lack of education are closely correlated, while returns to education are significant, and higher for primary than for secondary or tertiary education. Educated Ugandans benefited most from Uganda's strong recent growth and its poverty reduction performance. While the national poverty headcount fell by 39 per cent during the 1990s, it fell by only 28 per cent for Ugandans in households with uneducated heads (Appleton, 2001: 4). A large part of the explanation is that education enhances access to non-agricultural employment, and Uganda's agriculture sector grew more slowly than other sectors in the 1990s.

School feeding is controversial, and empirical evidence on its positive and negative impacts is limited and inconclusive. However, several case studies have confirmed that provision of free meals at school increases enrolment and attendance rates, and reduces drop-out rates, and that these effects are highest among the poorest families. School feeding even has 'safety net' effects: in difficult times such as during a drought or conflict, providing school meals (or take-home rations – 'food-for-education') encourages parents to leave their children in school, rather than withdrawing them to save costs and to assist with the search for food. Some school feeding and food-for-education projects have been found to reduce gender gaps in education access and attainment, and even to improve learners' concentration in class and their performance in examinations (Bennett, 2003; World Food Programme, 2006).

Uganda has implemented universal primary education (UPE) since 1997. Under UPE, fees were waived for state primary schools, which resulted in a doubling of primary enrolment. Given this success in terms of improved access to education, the case for introducing a school feeding scheme on top of UPE might seem rather weak. In fact, President Museveni declared in 2003 that there should be no free school meals in Uganda: the government's responsibility is to provide teachers, classrooms and textbooks; and it is the responsibility of parents to send their children to school and to ensure that they are adequately fed. On the other hand, large numbers of Ugandan children remain outside the formal education system, including several groups identified by the Ministry of Education as 'disadvantaged children': children who have never enrolled in school; those who have dropped out; orphans; refugees; geographically and culturally isolated children; street children; children who must work; children with disabilities; and abused children (MoES, 2002). UPE has not reached these vulnerable categories of children, partly because fees are not the only education cost facing parents and partly because the poorest families see no immediate benefit in educating their children or the orphans in their care. In these circumstances, providing a daily meal for a child from a food-insecure household can provide the incentive needed, and it enhances equity of access to education.

Taking these considerations into account, the Uganda Social Protection Study Team argued that targeted school feeding should be considered for specific vulnerable groups (such as orphans) and in areas where poverty is high and is recognized as a barrier to participation in education. This would include geographically inaccessible communities, areas with high concentrations of displaced or resettled people, and informal urban settlements where street children and destitute households are concentrated (Devereux and Sabates-Wheeler, 2003). This recommendation supported the second Participatory Poverty Appraisal (UPPAP2), which recommended providing orphans with meals at school, to improve both their nutritional and educational status (MFPED, 2002: 145).

Campaigning to transform:
anti-discrimination campaigns

One arena of social protection that attends directly to the 'social' needs of socially vulnerable groups is campaigning against various forms of discrimination – whether on the basis of ethnicity, gender, religion, disability or sexual orientation – as part of a broader emerging agenda around realizing economic, social and cultural rights. A good example is the Convention on the Elimination of All Forms of Discrimination Against Women (CEDAW), a United Nations campaign during the 1990s that raised awareness about gender discrimination in countries across the world.

Recently, concerns have been raised about the nature of formal and non-formal responses to HIV/AIDS, specifically its 'social impacts' in terms of the burden of caring and attitudes towards people living with AIDS (PLWA). In Uganda, which was the epicentre of HIV/AIDS in Africa during the 1980s, the pandemic has had a terrible impact, causing over 800,000 estimated deaths and creating over two million single – or double-parent orphans – almost one child in five. Approximately 25 per cent of Ugandan households now include one or more orphans. Many of these are elderly or widow-headed households, under traditional arrangements of caring for orphans through extended family and kinship relationships, which tends to place the burden of care on women. These informal social protection mechanisms are coming under severe strain, as the costs of caring for the sick and providing for the basic needs of large numbers of dependants is exceeding the limited resources of poor Ugandan families. Orphans who are not located in extended families or supportive communities, and are not taken into reception centres, often become street children, surviving by begging or petty crime.

In the late 1990s, the Government of Uganda launched a 'crusade' against HIV/AIDS, with donor support, under the umbrella of a five-year National Strategic Framework for reducing prevalence rates and strengthening national response capacity (UNDP, 2000: 16). HIV prevalence did in fact decline between 1996 and 2000, from 10 per cent to 8.3 per cent, largely because of changes in sexual behaviour among the Ugandan population (Republic of Uganda, 2001: 104). In this period, the government's response to AIDS focused on creating awareness about the causes of HIV transmission, encouraging behavioural change – including challenging cultural practices such as the remarrying of widows to a brother of the deceased – and promoting the use and availability of condoms.

A parallel set of interventions has also emerged in many high HIV-prevalence African countries since the 1980s, focusing more on the consequences of the disease than its prevention. Recognizing the costs that HIV/AIDS imposes on the livelihoods and coping capacity of poor households, these initiatives aim to provide various forms of support to PLWA, 'AIDS orphans' and carers. These initiatives are enormously important to the people they assist, but they are also patchy and limited in impact, with incomplete coverage across the country and variable provision of support – from food and cash transfers to nutritional advice for orphan carers, to reception centres for orphans without support, to vocational training and microcredit for older orphans.

Most of these measures can be characterized as standard social assistance to meet the subsistence and livelihood needs of PLWA and orphans. These provisions address the reality that HIV/AIDS has deepened poverty in Ugandan households, as affected families lose productive labour, sell off assets to care for terminally ill members, and pay burial costs after a death. In short, these measures address the economic costs of HIV and AIDS at the household level. Until recently, relatively little attention has been given to the 'social costs' of AIDS, such as the problems faced by PLWA in terms of securing or retaining employment, the stigma and social exclusion faced by bereaved relatives, the vulnerability of widows to losing property and being remarried against their will, and the risks faced by orphans of being abused or neglected.

In a special session on AIDS in June 2001, the United Nations General Assembly passed a declaration of commitment to fight AIDS, which included a global target for all UN member states to enact or strengthen anti-discrimination protection for people living with HIV/AIDS. In 2002, the International Federation of Red Cross and Red Crescent societies (IFRC) launched its own 'HIV/AIDS Anti-Stigma and Discrimination Campaign', in support of the United Nations declaration. Under this global initiative, the Uganda Red Cross Society launched a two-year campaign in July 2002, aimed at eliminating stigma and discrimination against Ugandans living with HIV/AIDS, in accordance with the commitment of the IFRC to 'making a difference in the lives of the vulnerable' (URCS, 2002). A key message of the campaign was: 'AIDS is a disease and not a disgrace'. The intention was to challenge attitudes and practices that discriminate against PLWA, such as employers insisting on job applicants taking pre-employment HIV tests, and rejecting all HIV-positive applicants. The overarching objective of the campaign was: 'to contribute to the change in perceptions, attitudes, policies and behaviour towards PLWA, in order to ensure that those people who are already HIV+ or have AIDS are able to receive the appropriate care, have access to affordable drugs and can live full and useful lives within their communities' (URCS, 2002).

This campaign can be characterized as a 'transformative social protection' measure. Unlike conventional social safety net or 'protective social protection' measures, anti-discrimination measures address the social rather than economic needs of a socially vulnerable group. Like minimum wages, this is an affordable intervention, since it has negligible implications for public spending or donor budgets. Anti-discrimination campaigns also have the potential to be 'protective' and 'promotive' as well as 'transformative'. It is well documented that discrimination reduces the livelihood opportunities of affected groups. Affirmative action campaigns to promote disadvantaged groups, such as black South Africans or low-caste Indians, recognize that social exclusion carries economic costs, and attempt to intervene in the labour market to correct for this socio-economic discrimination. Similarly, the anti-stigma campaign in Uganda attempts to ensure that hostility towards people living with HIV/AIDS does not undermine their ability to earn a living.

Growth – equity linkages: labour rights and minimum wages

Unskilled and semi-skilled workers are acutely vulnerable to exploitation by employers, especially in poor countries with widespread chronic poverty, limited employment opportunities and low levels of worker mobilization and unionization. In such conditions, it is often argued that low-paid workers need legal protection, through the introduction and enforcement of labour legislation that secures decent working conditions (reasonable working hours, maternity leave, job security and so on) and minimum wages. Labour market interventions are an attractive social protection policy arena, for several reasons: they reach people who live close to the poverty line, they cost government or donors very little to implement (since the costs are borne by private-sector employers), they have direct poverty-reducing impacts, and they are 'transformative' in that they empower categories of workers who are typically not unionized and have little bargaining power with their employers.

Despite these benefits, labour market interventions (especially mandated minimum wages) are controversial. The debate is often characterized as one between opponents of 'labour market rigidities' and supporters of 'fair labour standards'. Economists argue that legislation that raises wage rates and other employment costs above the market-clearing equilibrium will destroy jobs among the very group who were intended to gain. In a competitive labour market, employers faced with rising labour bills will respond by laying off some workers and shifting towards 'actualized labour' arrangements (daily or part-time contracts to which employment legislation does not apply) or mechanized forms of production. Those workers whose relative employment costs rise most – the lowest paid unskilled workers – are most vulnerable to these 'disemployment' and 'casualization' effects. A pragmatic argument against minimum wages is that many poor workers fall outside waged employment altogether, in 'uncovered' sectors such as subsistence agriculture and informal (self)-employment. Even if minimum wages are legislated for, compliance is difficult to enforce in these sectors, so the poorest segments of the working population are rarely reached (Alatas and Cameron, 2003).

The theoretical case against labour market interventions has been challenged by the '"new economics" of the minimum wage' (Lustig and McLeod, 1996), which argues that the critique is built on three 'textbook' assumptions – that labour markets are perfectly competitive, that workers are perfectly substitutable, and that perfect information exists in the economy – which do not hold in the real world. For example, where labour markets are monopsonistic – a realistic scenario in many developing countries – a higher wage rate can in fact *increase* aggregate employment. The reason is that monopsony employers pay workers less than their marginal value product (this is known as 'Pigovian exploitation') and hire to a point where the marginal cost of labour exceeds labour supply; hence, forcing the monopsonist to pay a competitive wage raises the supply of labour towards a market-clearing equilibrium (Jones, 1997: 3). Put another way, employers who are extracting excess profits by under-remunerating labour can afford to raise wage rates without laying off workers, and might even increase profitability by hiring more workers at these higher rates.

Empirical evidence can be found to support both sides of the debate. A cross-country regression analysis covering twenty-two countries found statistically significant evidence that minimum wage legislation can contribute to poverty reduction: 'minimum wages and poverty are inversely related: i.e., an increase (decline) in real minimum wages is accompanied by a fall (rise) in poverty' (Lustig and McLeod, 1996: 1). Another review of several

1990s studies found 'little, if any, disemployment effect' from minimum wage policies (Saget, 2001: 21). Conversely, a study of the impact of a mandated increase in Ghana's minimum wage in 1991 found that it had had the unintended effect of reducing manufacturing employment by 5–6 per cent, displacing workers who lost their jobs into the informal sector, and depressing informal wages (Jones, 1997). In South Africa, a simulation exercise found that legislating wage increases for domestic workers and farm workers would result in significant job losses in both sectors (Bhorat, 2000).

In Uganda, the debate about minimum wages is ongoing, and unresolved (Devereux, 2005). Although a Minimum Wages Board was established in 1935, the statutory minimum wage has not been raised since 1984, and its value has collapsed to such an extent that it has no real effect. In some sectors, such as the agricultural estates, wages and conditions of employment are so bad that workers are trapped in poverty and are at the mercy of employers who, *inter alia*, lay off pregnant women, who have to reapply for their jobs after giving birth; continuously rotate casual workers so as to avoid employing them on a permanent basis; and force their workers to work illegally long hours (MFPED, 2002). In the absence of effective trade unions, the Uganda Human Rights Commission has consistently called for government intervention to protect low-paid workers against exploitation and to raise the minimum wage to a 'living' level (UHRC, 1999).

During the process of revising Uganda's PEAP, the Social Protection Task Force recommended that the Government of Uganda intervene to provide social protection for vulnerable employees, not only by instituting a realistic minimum wage but also by insisting that working conditions are improved – that the laws on maximum working hours are not violated, that workers are provided with decent accommodation, that women are not dismissed for becoming pregnant, and that some form of job security is introduced for 'permanent casuals'. More effective labour inspections and enforcement mechanisms would be required to ensure compliance – the number of Labour Inspectors was cut drastically under Uganda's civil service reform programme – and adequate social assistance arrangements would need to be put in place to provide a transitional safety net for any adversely affected families (Devereux and Sabates-Wheeler, 2003: 35).

The PEAP Secretariat was initially sceptical about these proposals, arguing that 'it is difficult to design public interventions that improve the well-being of workers without simultaneously increasing the costs of employers and hence reducing employment'. However, the Secretariat did agree that labour market interventions such as a minimum wage might be appropriate in contexts of market failure. By the time the draft PEAP was published in March 2004, the Government of Uganda appeared to have accepted the case for introducing binding minimum wages, at least for specific sectors.

International evidence shows that blanket minimum wages tend to reduce employment opportunities. However, there is a case for some regulation of wages in sectors where employers have great market power, in which case the effects of a minimum wage on employment may not be harmful. Government, in consultation with the private sector will consider whether some regulation of wages or working conditions may be appropriate in certain sectors. (Government of Uganda, 2004: 103)

Conclusion

By arguing in this chapter for an approach to social protection that emphasizes social justice we are not arguing against the important 'safety net' role that social protection has conventionally played, in terms of safeguarding lives and livelihoods in contexts of chronic and acute economic risk and vulnerability. Instead, we are focusing attention on the relatively neglected area of *social* risk and vulnerability, and building a case for a stronger role for social protection in terms of empowering the poor and transforming the conditions in which they struggle to construct viable livelihoods.

In this chapter we have conceptualized vulnerability in social as well as economic terms, and argued for social protection as a comprehensive package of interventions that addresses both aspects. Although the socially vulnerable – orphans, people living with HIV/AIDS, ethnic minorities – often need income and consumption support, social protection, properly conceptualized, is not just 'economic protection'. Poverty and vulnerability are about social as well as economic deprivation, and our argument is for an elaborated understanding of social protection that concerns itself directly with addressing 'social risk' and non-economic vulnerability, such as social exclusion, discrimination and violations of minority rights.

Apart from establishing a more positive and proactive role for social protection that extends its scope beyond its roots in residualist and often stigmatizing social safety nets, there are other reasons for supporting the 'transformative' component of social protection. First, 'transformative social protection' is more fiscally affordable than 'economic social protection', which is unpopular with economists and governments because it implies expensive (and often recurrent) transfers of public resources to large numbers of people who are regarded as having low or zero productivity (McDonald *et al.*, 1999). In developing countries, policy-makers face binding fiscal constraints that limit their public spending choices, so the identification of low-cost interventions that can improve the livelihoods of the poor significantly – such as mandated minimum wages, whose cost is borne by employers rather than the state, or anti-discrimination campaigns that cost next to nothing – is doubly attractive.

Second, we have identified powerful synergies between the 'economic' (provision, prevention, promotion) and 'social' (transformation) functions performed by several social protection measures considered in this chapter. We have noted that income or consumption transfers such as school feeding schemes or public works projects have the dual aims of providing immediate protection against nutritional deprivation and investing in durable assets – human capital through education and physical capital through community-level infrastructure, respectively. By empowering low-paid workers to claim fairer wages, and challenging employers to provide better working conditions, labour legislation simultaneously raises incomes (which is 'promotive') and enhances workers' rights and bargaining power (which is 'transformative').

A transformative approach extends the definition of social protection beyond targeted income and consumption transfers that address chronic poverty and livelihood threats. Strategies to deal with social vulnerability must address the social injustice that arises from structural inequalities and abuses of power, and transformative social protection must aim to achieve empowerment, equity and the realization of economic, social and cultural rights. If carefully selected to match the nature of vulnerability, social protection mechanisms can be transformative and affordable, while contributing to the policy goals of pro-poor economic growth and improved social equity.

Notes

1. For other agency definitions of social protection, see Sabates-Wheeler and Haddad, 2005.
2. For a more detailed discussion, see Sabates-Wheeler and Waite 2003.

References

Alatas, V. and L. Cameron (2003) 'The Impact of Minimum Wages on Employment in a Low Income Country: An Evaluation Using the Difference-in-Differences Approach', *World Bank Policy Research Working Paper*, 2985. Washington, DC: World Bank.

Appleton, S. (2001) *Education, Incomes and Poverty in Uganda in the 1990s*, Mimeo. Nottingham: University of Nottingham.

Bankoff, G., G. Frerks and D. Hilhorst (eds) (2004) *Mapping Vulnerability: Disasters, Development and People.* London: Earthscan.

Barrientos, A. and A. Shepherd (2003) 'Chronic Poverty and Social Protection', paper prepared for the International Conference on *Staying Poor: Chronic Poverty and Development Policy.* IDPM, University of Manchester, 7–9 April 2003.

Bennett, J. (2003) *Review of School Feeding Projects.* London: Department for International Development.

Bhorat, H. (2000) 'Are Wage Adjustments an Effective Mechanism for Poverty Alleviation? Some Simulations for Domestic and Farm Workers', paper presented at the *Trade and Industrial Policy Secretariat (TIPS), 2000 Annual Forum.* Cape Town: Development Policy Research Unit, University of Cape Town.

Chambers, R. (1989) 'Editorial Introduction: Vulnerability, Coping, and Policy', *IDS Bulletin*, 20(2), 1–7.

Dercon, S. (2001) *Assessing Vulnerability*, Jesus College and CSAE, Department of Economics, Oxford University.

Devereux, S. (2005) 'Can Minimum Wages Contribute to Poverty Reduction in Poor Countries?', *Journal of International Development*, 17(7), 899–912.

Devereux, S. and R. Sabates-Wheeler (2003) *Social Protection in Uganda: Facilitating the Process of Mainstreaming Social Protection into the PEAP Revision (Phase II Report)*. Kampala: Ministry of Gender, Labour and Social Development.

Gaventa, J. (2004) 'Towards Participatory Governance: Assessing Transformative Possibilities', in S. Hickey and G. Mohan (eds), *From Tyranny to Transformation*. London: Zed Books.

Government of Uganda (2004) *Poverty Eradication Action Plan* (draft). Kampala: Ministry of Finance, Planning and Economic Development.

Guhan, S. (1994) 'Social Security Options for Developing Countries', *International Labour Review*, 133(1), 35–53.

Hulme, D., K. Moore and A. Shepherd (2001) 'Chronic Poverty: Meanings and Analytical Frameworks', *CPRC Working Paper 2*. Manchester: IDPM, University of Manchester.

International Labour Office and United Nations Development Programme (ILO/ UNDP) (1996) *Uganda: Report to the Government on the Development of Social Protection*. Geneva: ILO.

Jones, P. (1997) 'The Impact of Minimum Wage Legislation in Developing Countries where Coverage is Incomplete', *WPS/98-2*. Oxford: Centre for the Study of African Economies.

Kabeer, N. (2002) 'Citizenship, Affiliation and Exclusion: Perspectives from the South', *IDS Bulletin*, 33(2), 12.

Kabeer, N. (ed.) (2005) *Inclusive Citizenship: Meanings and Expressions*. London: Zed Book Ltd.

Lawson, D., A. McKay and J. Okidi (2003) *Factors Affecting Poverty Dynamics and Persistence in Uganda*, Mimeo. University of Nottingham.

Lustig, N. and D. McLeod (1996) 'Minimum Wages and Poverty in Developing Countries: Some Empirical Evidence', Brookings Discussion Papers in International Economics, No. 125. Washington, DC: Brookings Institution.

McDonald, C., C. Schiller and K. Ueda (1999) 'Income Distribution, Informal Safety Nets, and Social Expenditures in Uganda', *IMF Working Paper*, 99/163. Washington, DC: International Monetary Fund, Fiscal Affairs Department.

Ministry of Education and Sports (MoES), September (2002) *Basic Education Policy for Disadvantaged Children*. Kampala: MoES. Government of Uganda.

Ministry of Finance, Planning and Economic Development (MFPED), December (2002) *Uganda Participatory Poverty Assessment Report: Deepening the Understanding of Poverty*. Kampala: MFPED, Government of Uganda.

Nyamu-Musembi, C. and A. Cornwall (2004) 'What is the Rights Based Approach all about? Perspectives from International Development Agencies', *Working Paper 234*.

Republic of Uganda (2001) *Uganda Poverty Status Report: 2001*. Kampala: Ministry of Finance, Planning and Economic Development.

Sabates-Wheeler and L. Haddad (2005) Conceptualising Actions to Address Risk and Vulnerability in DAC Task Team Member Documents: Differences and Commonalities, prepared for OECD DAC PovNET Task Team, Brighton: Institute of Development Studies.

Sabates-Wheeler, R. and Waite (2003) *Migration and Social Protection*, Migration, Globalisation and Poverty Working Paper Series, Migration Centre, Sussex, December 2003.

Saget, C. (2001) 'Is the Minimum Wage an Effective Tool to Promote Decent Work and Reduce Poverty? The Experience of Selected Developing Countries', *ILO Employment Paper 2001/13*. Geneva: International Labour Office.

Uganda Human Rights Commission (UHRC) (1999) *Annual Report 1999*. Kampala : UHRC.

Uganda Red Cross Society (URCS) (2002) Launch of the 2002 World Disaster Report and HIV/AIDS Anti-Stigma Campaign. Kampala: Uganda Red Cross Society.

United Nations Development Programme (UNDP) (2000) *Uganda Human Development Report 2000*. Kampala: UNDP.

van Ginneken, W. (ed.) (1999) 'Social Security for the Excluded Majority: Case Studies of Developing Countries'. Geneva: International Labour Office (ILO).

World Bank (1990) *World Development Report 1990*. Washington, DC: World Bank.

World Bank (2000) *World Development Report 2000/2001*. Washington, DC: World Bank.

World Bank (2004) http://wbln0018.worldbank.org/HDNet/hddocs.nsf/c207c7f854-bd0a0985 25660b007a272d/fb93d792069e704e852568190058d7bc?OpenDocument, accessed 9 August 2004.

World Food Programme (2006) *Food For Education: Reviewing the Evidence,* Seminar Report. Rome: World Food Programme.

5
Poverty Traps and Natural Disasters in Ethiopia and Honduras

Michael R. Carter, Peter D. Little,
Tewodaj Mogues and Workneh Negatu*

Introduction

Ato Mohammed, 55 and illiterate, lives in the Bati district of South Wollo Zone (Ethiopia) and heads a household of nine. He has been chronically food insecure for more than ten years, when he lost his single ox because of drought. He sold the animal to buy food at the time and has not been able to acquire another. Currently, Mohammed holds one hectare of farmland and has no grazing land. Since he owns no oxen, he has been leasing out his land for share-cropping on a 50/50 sharing arrangement. Mohammed and his family members are engaged in various types of daily labour activities for cash and food, and the household is a regular recipient of food aid.

Mohammed asserts "oxen are the crucial productive asset that would liberate me from this insecurity trap." On the other hand, however, he does not want to take credit from a regional credit organization to buy an ox as he does not want to be indebted and fears that the debt may be passed on to his children if he fails to repay. He fears that the ox may die due to lack of adequate feed or animal diseases for which there is no dependable animal health service in the community. He also fears that he may not be able to pay back any loan, since crop failure is frequent because of insects and droughts.

The direct impacts of the droughts, hurricanes and other environmental shocks can be horrific, resulting in immediate increases in poverty and deprivation. But what are the longer-term effects of shocks on households and their livelihoods? Are households able to quickly re-establish their livelihoods and the assets needed to support them, or is recovery a slow, long-drawn-out process, especially for poorer households, who may be less able to leverage the resources needed to rebuild? Indeed, is there a "poverty trap" from which households can rarely recover, as Ato Mohammed's[1] story suggests? And, if there is such a trap – understood as a minimum asset threshold (for example, one ox), below which accumulation and livelihood growth are not feasible – do forward-looking households adopt asset protection strategies designed to avoid the trap, but which come at the very high cost of immediately reduced consumption, with perhaps irreversible losses in child health and education? Finally, to what extent does the existence of deep markets and/or social networks offset these longer-term consequences of disaster?

To explore these issues, this chapter examines data from two macabre, naturally-occurring experiments. The first is Hurricane Mitch, which struck Honduras and other parts of Central America in 1998. Through the vagaries of Mitch, some households lost nearly all their productive assets, while others were left unscathed. These changes in asset distribution[2] permit us to explore questions of resilience and the speed of longer-term recovery, and to examine whether there is any evidence of poverty traps.

The prolonged Ethiopian drought of 1998–2000 presents a second kind of disaster experiment. Direct destruction of assets was modest, but the income losses of repeated crop failures in some locations forced households to choose between preserving assets, or selling them to maintain current consumption and health. Examination of household asset holdings across the drought cycle provides insight into the longer-term effects of droughts, and into particular wealth-differentiated asset management strategies.

The work is part of a comparative project that addresses the interrelationships between climatic shocks, markets and asset recovery strategies among households in developing countries (see Little *et al.*, 2002). In Ethiopia, markets are relatively weak (especially for land, labour and capital), and non-market mechanisms are important. Factor markets are better-developed in Honduras, but its inegalitarian agrarian structure may limit the effectiveness and extent of the social assets that might aid recovery in Ethiopia.[3] Data on a sample of 416 rural Ethiopian households track household assets over a seven-year period of pre-drought (1996–7), drought (1998–2000), and recovery (2001–3). Data on a sample of 850 rural Honduran households capture the immediate impact of Hurricane Mitch in 1998 on assets and income, as well as these households' economic position in 2001, two and a half years after Mitch.

The remainder of this chapter is organized as follows. The second section proposes an anatomy of an environmental shock, tracing the evolution of assets through time in the face of a shock, and presents an empirical model of asset accumulation to investigate households' sensitivity to, and recovery from, shocks. The factors that influenced rural Honduran households' exposure to and recovery from the 1998 hurricane are examined in the third section. The fourth section describes the income losses households in north-eastern Ethiopia suffered as a result of the droughts of 1999/2000, and estimates the determinants of long-term asset recovery in the wake of these. Concluding remarks are offered in the final section.

Shocks, poverty traps and resilience

This section puts forward a conceptual framework for thinking about the longer-term economic impacts of environmental shocks. In their analysis of economic shocks and vulnerability, Calvo and Dercon (2005: 3) make the important observation that economic vulnerability is a "sense of insecurity, of potential harm people must feel wary of – *something bad can happen and 'spell ruin'*" (emphasis added). The notion that a random event (a flood, a drought, an illness, an unemployment spell) can have permanent effects, spelling ruin for a family, suggests that vulnerability (and perhaps poverty) can best be understood through the lens of poverty traps, as described by the quote at the beginning of the chapter. Here we follow Carter and Barrett (2006), and understand a poverty trap to be a critical minimum asset threshold below which families are unable to educate their children successfully, build up their productive assets, and move ahead economically over time. Below the threshold lie those who are ruined, who can do no better than hang on and who are offered no viable prospects for economic advance over time. Those above the threshold can be expected to invest productively, accumulate and advance.

The bifurcation of behaviour reflects the bifurcation of longer-term prospects, and thus of economic well-being. In the presence of poverty traps, temporary shocks have permanent adverse consequences for those pushed below the threshold, while others – those who do not cross between regimes – would be expected to recover fully and quickly from an objectively similar shock (Dercon, 2004). Anticipation of poverty traps would also be expected to shift coping behaviour, inducing those near the trap to protect or smooth their assets lest they fall below the critical minimum asset level and face ruin. In the remainder of this section, we explore further the empirical implication of poverty traps.

Asset shocks, sensitivity and poverty traps

Figure 5.1 presents a stylized anatomy of an natural disaster that destroys assets and reduces incomes. The x-axis measures time and the y-axis measures asset stocks and income shocks. Hypothetical asset trajectories are illustrated for an initially wealthier household, w (which begins with an initial asset level A_{bw}), and an initially poorer household, p (with pre-shock assets A_{bp}). The trajectories represented by the dashed lines illustrate the case of convergent asset dynamics in which the poorer household would eventually catch up with the wealthier household if it experienced no shocks and

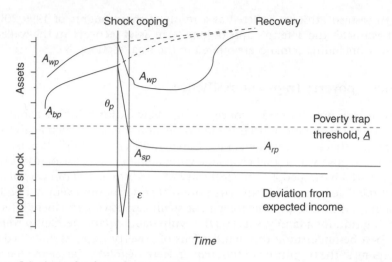

Figure 5.1   Asset shocks and poverty traps

stayed on the dashed asset accumulation path. The shock itself is displayed as a short-duration event (for example, a hurricane) that kills livestock, and washes away land and plantations, reducing assets by $\Theta_w(\Theta_p)$ for the wealthy (poor) household. In the wake of the shock, the rich and poor households are left, respectively, with asset stocks A_{sw} and A_{sp}. The shock may also reduce current income by an amount ε.

We are now in a position to consider the forces that shape the longer-run implications of an asset shock such as that illustrated in Figure 5.1. Two broad sets of forces will shape the asset level we would be able to observe at some future time when assets have recovered to their longer-term trajectory. The first set concerns coping strategies utilized in the immediate aftermath of the shock. The second set concerns the longer-run patterns of asset dynamics, namely the desired and achievable level of assets and the speed with which a household can approach this longer-term level.

Households' reactions to the direct income and asset losses during the coping phase are structured by the markets and other institutions to which they have access.[4] Households with financial market access might borrow against future earnings to sustain their consumption standard without further asset depletion. Informal finance and insurance arrangements can play the same role, as can receipt of disaster assistance. Another coping strategy is to redirect or increase work time (reduce leisure). The effectiveness of this strategy will depend on access to and the depth of labour markets.

Households without access to these markets may sustain their consumption by a further drawing down on their assets (households reluctant to draw down on their assets may also cope by reducing consumption, which will be discussed in the next section). While asset sales will help to smooth household consumption over time, it implies that assets will exhibit excess sensitivity to shocks (declining by more than the direct asset shock, Θ). Note that the severity of this secondary asset decline will also be shaped by changes in the prices of assets relative to the price of food and other necessities. Unfavourable asset price swings (as would be expected to happen if all households in an area respond to the shock by selling cattle) would threaten to further decapitalize households in the wake of a shock.

The market and social mechanisms that broker access to employment and financial services will also shape a household's resilience and the speed of its post-shock asset accumulation trajectory. A household with good access to capital (via markets, or via informal social arrangements) can borrow against future earnings to rebuild asset stocks immediately. Such a household might be expected to recover quickly, perhaps returning to the sort of convergent, long-term trajectory illustrated in Figure 5.1. However, a household without this access might face an even slower recovery process.

While there are thus multiple reasons why less well-positioned families may exhibit excess sensitivity to shocks and recover slowly from them, the story of Ato Mohammed, quoted above, suggests even deeper effects than those that would be signalled by slow recovery. His story suggests the existence of a poverty trap, understood as a minimum asset threshold below which it is not possible to engineer successful asset accumulation, barring positive shocks or interventions that would lift the household's wealth level above the threshold. The dashed horizontal line in Figure 5.1, drawn at a poverty trap threshold of $\underline{A}$, demonstrates the idea of such a threshold. As illustrated in the figure, a household falling below that threshold would be unable to accumulate assets and would be observed over time to follow a path from A_{sp} to $A_{rp'}$ rather than rejoining its convergent pre-shock trajectory.[5]

While households pushed below a critical threshold and into a poverty trap would be expected to exhibit slower post-shock growth, they would also be expected to remain permanently at a lower level than their more fortunate neighbours. Put differently, asset accumulation trajectories should bifurcate above and below a critical asset threshold if a poverty trap exists. Later sections of this chapter will test for the existence of such a threshold and bifurcated asset growth patterns.

Income shocks, asset smoothing and poverty traps

The sort of poverty trap described by Ato Mohammed has a second testable implication. Figure 5.2 illustrates hypothetical asset trajectories for households buffeted by income shocks that play out over an extended time (for example., a sequence of drought seasons). For simplicity's sake, we shall assume that there are no direct asset losses associated with these income shocks. An initially wealthier household that begins with assets A_{bw} might be expected to draw down assets in the face of income shocks in order to protect (or smooth) its consumption level. Following the drought period, the household might be expected to rebuild its asset stocks, returning towards its initial trajectory.

But will an initially poorer household, which begins with assets A_{bp}, pursue the same consumption-smoothing strategy? If there is indeed a poverty trap, denoted A in Figure 5.2, then the household might instead choose to reduce consumption and protect (or smooth) its assets in order to avoid the fate of Ato Mohammed. While this strategy might be a last resort for households that lack other options, it might also be pursued by households reluctant to increase their future vulnerability by further depleting their stock of assets.[6]

While the economics literature sometimes discusses consumption smoothing as if it were itself a primary behavioural objective, a few authors have noted the existence of constrained circumstances that might lead individuals towards asset smoothing, despite the fact that asset smoothing means that consumption becomes unstable and dips to painfully low levels. Drèze and Sen (1989), for example, note that very poor people are observed to "asset-smooth" in a way that necessarily destabilizes their consumption. At a theoretical level, Zimmerman and Carter (2003) show that optimal intertemporal consumption and saving can result in asset smoothing behaviour. Analysing data from a drought in Zimbabwe, Hoddinott (2006) finds that poorer households (defined as those with fewer than two oxen) tend to asset-smooth in the face of drought-induced income losses, while wealthier households above that threshold sell assets and smooth consumption.[7]

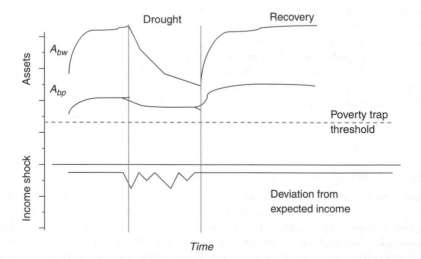

Figure 5.2 Income shocks and asset smoothing

Testing for asymmetric responses to random income shocks thus provides a second way to test for the existence of poverty traps.[8] In addition, as in the case of asset shocks, post-shock trajectories can be examined for direct evidence of poverty traps in the case of individuals who fall below the critical asset threshold.

Empirical strategy

This section puts forward an econometric approach for exploring the longer-run economic impacts of environmental shocks. With small modifications, this approach will be used to investigate the impact of environmental shocks in Ethiopia and Honduras. The data available for both countries includes measures of pre-shock (A_{bi}), post-shock (A_{si}) and post-recovery assets stocks (A_{ri}), measures of shocks received, and indicators of market access and social networks.

Consider first the following adaptation of a standard, single equilibrium growth model:

$$g_{bi} = A_{bi}\beta_A + \Theta_i\beta_\Theta(A_{bi}, L_i, K_i) + \varepsilon_i\beta_\varepsilon(A_{bi}, L_i, K_i) + \beta_z Z_i + v_i \qquad (5.1)$$

where g_{bi} is the asset growth for household i over the time stretching from the pre-shock period to the recovery period (several years after the shock). The household's initial asset level, A_{bi}, is included in the growth regression to capture the idea – common to neoclassical growth theory – that there is a single equilibrium asset level towards which households grow.[9] An estimate of $\beta_A < 0$ would signal a convergent accumulation process with lower-wealth households growing rapidly towards the equilibrium level, while the asset growth of wealthier households would slow down and approach zero as the equilibrium level was reached. The point at which the growth rate equals zero would be a long-term equilibrium or steady-state asset position. The hypothetical no-shock trajectories in Figure 5.1 illustrate such a convergent process.

The variables Θ_i and ε_i are, respectively, measures of asset and income shocks. Reflecting the preceding conceptual discussion, the coefficients that capture the impacts of asset (β_Θ) and income (β_ε) shocks on growth are written conditional on initial asset levels (A_{bi}) and on social and market access conditions, L_i and K_i (where L_i measures household i's access to off-farm labour markets, and K_i represents the household's access to financial and/or social capital). Finally, the regression specification in Equation (5.1) contains other control variables (geographical location, life-cycle age of the households, etc.) that are represented by the vector Z_i. The term v_i measures latent, random factors that have an impact on asset growth. Estimates of the parameters in Equation (5.1) would permit the investigation of many of the key questions put forward in this chapter.[10] Do poor households exhibit greater sensitivity to asset shocks, and recover more slowly in their wake?

Does factor market access mediate such excess sensitivity? Do poor households exhibit muted sensitivity to income shocks as they defend vulnerable asset bases?

While estimates of Equation (5.1) can thus permit us to see whether poor and rich households respond asymmetrically to randomly distributed damage, it does not permit us to identify directly the existence of a poverty trap. For example, a finding several years after a shock that poor households are more deeply affected than rich households may mean that poor households fell into a permanent poverty trap, or simply that they recovered more slowly than rich households and eventually returned to their pre-shock trajectory and long-run equilibrium destination. While the difference between these two scenarios is something of an academic point, a long enough time scale of observation (without further shocks) would in principle suffice to resolve this issue.

In the absence of this kind of very long-term data, the most compelling way to explore this issue with the available data is to examine post-shock asset accumulation to see if it is possible to identify long-run equilibrium positions of households with different wealth levels. Note that in the case of an asset shock such as a hurricane, the post-shock changes in a household's asset position is exogenous. In the case of a prolonged income shock, such as a drought, the change in asset position is endogenous to the household's coping strategy. Later analysis will examine this important difference.

Consider the following model of post-shock asset growth that is general enough to admit distinct long-run asset equilibrium for households of different wealth levels:

$$
g_{si} = \begin{cases} \beta_A^\ell A_{si} + \beta_Z^\ell Z_i + v_i^\ell, \ if \ A_{si} < \gamma, \\ \\ \beta_A^u A_{si} + \beta_Z^u Z_i + v_i^u, \ otherwise \end{cases} \tag{5.2}
$$

where g_{si} is household i's asset growth from the post-shock to the recovery period, A_{si} is the household's stock of assets in the immediate post-shock period, γ is the critical asset level around which bifurcation occurs, and the ℓ superscripts indicate the parameters that shape growth in the lower regime, while the u superscripts designate parameters that lead to the upper regime equilibrium. A poverty trap would exist if households below the threshold level ($A_{si} < \gamma$) moved towards a lower equilibrium asset level, at which growth became zero. Such a low level equilibrium would occur if the parameter β_A^ℓ was sharply negative, signalling that asset growth collapses quickly toward zero as assets increase. A low level equilibrium could also occur if the estimates of $\beta_Z^\ell Z$ were low.

While Equation (5.2) captures the basic notion of a poverty trap, a fundamental difficulty from a statistical perspective is that the threshold level is unknown, if it exists at all. One way to approach this problem has been to employ flexible, non-parametric methods to explore asset dynamics. As utilized by Lybbert *et al.* (2004) and later Adato *et al.* (2006) and Barrett *et al.* (2006), this method has been used to identify a critical asset threshold and corresponding high- and low-level equilibria. As used by these earlier studies, these methods have been limited to bivariate analysis (that is, asset dynamics are studied without controlling for shocks or other variables that might temper the accumulation relationship).

An alternative approach is to employ Hansen's (2000) methods and estimate directly the critical asset threshold around which asset growth dynamics bifurcate. In the empirical analysis to follow, we shall follow Hansen's proposed method and test explicitly for the existence of a critical threshold, examining the degree to which the parameters conform to the hypotheses explained earlier. A limitation of the Hansen estimator is that it assumes that the threshold is the same for all units (as well as the more conventional assumption that the error term, v_i, is orthogonal to the explanatory variables). While this latter assumption is somewhat troubling, for the usual reasons,[11] recent theoretical work (Buera, 2005; Barrett and Carter, 2006) indicates that the threshold itself should be a function of individual characteristics, including sill, entrepreneurial aptitude and so on.

While the econometric difficulties behind endogenizing the threshold have yet to be resolved, here we shall employ the standard Hansen estimator in order to obtain initial, tentative evidence on the possibility of asset thresholds. Our threshold results thus need to be treated with a degree of caution, as it is unclear whether an estimate of multiple stable asset positions reflects a true multiple equilibrium (in the sense that *any* agent would move to the low position if pushed below the threshold), or whether it simply identifies the distinctive asset positions towards which high- and low-type agents uniquely gravitate because of their intrinsic characteristics.

Gauging the longer-term impacts of asset shocks in Honduras

Hurricane Mitch carved a path of destruction across Honduras in 1998, and the direct impact of the hurricane was almost instantaneous. Drawing on data collected shortly after the event, Morris *et al.* (2001) report that poor rural households lost 30–40 per cent of their crop income and measured poverty immediately increased by 5.5 percentage points, rising from 69.2 per cent of households to 74.6 per cent. They also report that lower-wealth households lost 15–20 per cent of their productive assets (land, livestock and plantations), thus compromising their capacity to generate earnings and a livelihood. Unclear, however, from these early studies is whether households were able to recover from losses of this magnitude and rebuild their assets and livelihoods.

The data available for this study provide a window into these longer-term questions. Some thirty months after Mitch, a sample of 850 rural Honduran households (clustered in thirty municipalities spread across six provinces) was surveyed as part of a study on the impact of land market liberalization and asset accumulation. Included in the questionnaire were a number of retrospective questions that probed into the direct impacts of Mitch on household assets and income. The study also collected data on household assets in 2000/1, giving a window into the longer-term patterns of asset cycles and poverty traps.

Surveyed households included those located in mountainous and indigenous areas (in the Departments of Intibucá and Ocotepeque), as well as households in more commercial farming areas (including Comayagua and coffee-growing regions of the Department of Santa Bárbara) as well as the households located along the Caribbean coast, which is home to Afro-Caribbean Garifuna people (in the Department of Colón).[12] In addition to this cultural diversity, the sample also exhibits religious diversity, with some communities overwhelmingly Roman Catholic, others largely comprised of Evangelical Christians, and yet others a combination of the two. While these factors surely matter for how families and communities were able to cope with the impacts of Mitch, analysis of them is beyond the scope of this paper.

The impact of Hurricane Mitch on asset stocks and growth

Table 5.1 presents descriptive statistical indicators of the impact of Hurricane Mitch. Information is provided both for the overall sample and for households broken down into asset quartiles. Quartiles were defined based on households' pre-Mitch holdings of productive assets (A_b), where productive assets are defined as the value of land, plantations, machinery and livestock. Note that we do not have information on social capital or migration assets. Access to these assets may, of course, be very important for household coping strategies. All assets were valued using year 2000 price information and were converted to US$ using the market exchange rate. As can be seen, wealth varies substantially, averaging US$650 for the poorest quartile and just over US$75,000 for the wealthiest quartile. Annual household income in 2000/1 was six times higher for wealthier households than it was for poorer households (USUS$5,967). These low figures are consistent with the high poverty rates typical of rural Honduras. The variation in them is also a reflection of the sharp levels of inequality found across much of rural Honduras.

As can be seen, 44 per cent of households suffered a loss of productive assets from Hurricane Mitch. The percentage of households increases with household wealth (rising from 22 per cent to 68 per cent from the first to the fourth wealth quartile). This finding contradicts the notion that poorer households are more vulnerable to shocks, though it may be an artefact of the fact that poorer households had relatively little to lose. Indeed, as can be

Table 5.1 Losses caused by Hurricane Mitch – Honduras (mean values unless noted otherwise)

	All house-holds	Pre-Mitch asset quartiles			
		I	II	III	IV
Pre-Mitch productive assets (US$)	23,769	653	3,998	13,718	76,821
Annual household income 2000/1 (US$)	2,440	996	1,127	1,716	5,927
Loss of productive assets					
Households with losses (%)	44.3	21.8	31.7	55.6	68.3
Pre-Mitch assets lost (%)[a]	12.0	31.1	13.9	12.2	7.5
Structure of asset loss[a] (% of total assets lost)					
Land	29.6	22.6	16.5	25.1	31.4
Plantation loss	60.5	62.2	75.4	65.3	58.6
Livestock	8.6	13.8	8.1	9.6	8.3
Machinery	1.3	1.5	0.0	0.1	1.7
Households losing productive assets					
Income shock (US$)	428	144	164	328	722
Housing loss (US$)	442	58	310	481	596
Aid received (US$)	232	154	330	98	320
Median asset growth (%) (pre-Mitch to 2001)	–2.6	–5.0	–4.9	–2.1	–2.1
Households without loss of productive assets					
Income shock (US$)	93	101	70	95	121
Housing loss (US$)	119	187	96	53	89
Aid received (US$)	141	88	134	161	261
Median asset growth (%) (pre-Mitch to 2001)	5.4	8.8	5.4	4.6	3.0

Note: [a] Figures calculated only for those households that suffered asset losses.

seen, among those households suffering asset losses, that poorer households lost a greater percentage of their productive wealth (31 per cent) than did wealthier households (8 per cent).[13] Across all wealth quartiles, losses were comprised primarily of lost plantations and land (note that lost land literally means land rendered unusable because of soil loss, or in some cases, submersion by rivers that had changed course).

The second two panels of the table present additional descriptive data on households, based on whether or not they experienced a loss of productive assets from Mitch. Not surprisingly, households that suffered asset losses also experienced greater income losses (primarily crop income). For the lowest wealth quartile, these losses averaged 10–15 per cent of annual household income.[14] Loss of housing stock was also substantial for many households. Aid (typically in the form of food and building materials) averaged between US$50 and US$600 across the quartile groups, but in no case averaged more than 10 per cent of the value of lost productive assets.

Finally, Table 5.1 reports asset growth rates from mid-1998 (pre-Mitch) to early 2001.[15] Across all pre-Mitch wealth quartiles, households without assets losses show substantially higher growth than those that suffered losses. The gap is 13.8 per cent for the lowest quartile, where poor households with losses had showed –5 per cent net growth (loss) over the post-Mitch period, while poor households without losses had 8.8 per cent growth. The gap is a smaller 5.1 per cent for the wealthiest quartile (–2.1 per cent versus 3 per cent post-Mitch growth).

While these growth differences seem to signal that poor households are more sensitive to shocks (and less able to recover from them), at the same time, among those households that did not suffer any asset losses, poor households tended to grow faster (8.8 per cent) than did wealthier households (3.1 per cent), signalling a convergent accumulation process. We turn now to explore these patterns of vulnerability and resilience more thoroughly.

Regression analysis of asset loss and recovery

The standard growth model given by Equation (5.1) above permits us to explore the underlying pattern of asset accumulation as well as the impact of shocks. Table 5.2 displays the results of estimating two alternative specifications of Equation (5.1). The first, or basic, model includes initial assets (as a way to test for convergence), the shock variables, and basic demographic and regional control variables. The expanded model includes additional variables to see if the impacts of shocks are mediated by labour and capital market access. Asset shocks, income shocks and aid received are all normalized by the household's pre-Mitch asset level. Given this normalization, a coefficient of –1 on the asset shock variable would mean that the household had not recovered at all from the shock (for example, a 10 per cent loss of assets would reduce the growth rate by 10 percentage points). A coefficient of less than –1 would signal that households had further drawn down on their assets in the wake of the hurricane, while a coefficient greater than –1 would indicate at least partial recovery from the shock.

Table 5.2 OLS estimates of asset recovery and growth – Honduras

Explanatory variables	Basic model	Expanded model
Core growth & convergence		
Initial assets, A_b(log)	-0.55^a	-0.57^a
$(A_b)^2$	0.03^a	0.03^a
Sensitivity to asset losses, $\ominus$ (by initial asset quartile)		
$\ominus \times Q_b^1$	-1.78^a	-2.88^a
$\ominus \times Q_b^2$	-2.21^a	-2.85^a
$\ominus \times Q_b^3$	-1.17^a	-1.62^a
$\ominus \times Q_b^4$	-0.86^b	-1.22^a
Income & other shocks		
Income shock, ε	0.05	0.04
Housing loss	-0.14^a	-0.10^a
(equals 1 if housing loss)		
Mediating factors		
Labour market access, L $\times \ominus$	–	1.99^a
L $\times \ominus \times A_b$	–	-0.19^a
Capital market access, K $\times \ominus$	–	0.64^a
Aid received	–	-0.04^a
Demographic & other controls		
Age of household head	0.02^a	0.02^a
Squared age of head	-0.00^a	-0.00^a
Post-Mitch inheritance (equals 1 if received)	0.61^a	0.63^a
Constant	2.48^a	2.55^a
Provincial dummies	Included	Included
R^2	0.32	0.34

Notes
[a] Significant at the 5% level.
[b] Significant at the 10% level.

Two strong patterns emerge in both the basic and expanded models. First, the data signal a strong pattern of convergence, as expected: asset growth diminishes significantly with the level of initial assets. Second, households that were in the lower pre-hurricane wealth quartiles show much greater sensitivity to asset shocks (note that Q_b^1 is the lowest or poorest pre-Mitch quartile).

Both models permit the coefficient of the asset shock to vary with the pre-hurricane wealth quartile. As can be seen, the pattern of impact is non-linear across wealth levels. A Wald test for equality of the four coefficients is rejected easily for both models. For the basic model, the calculated F-statistic has a value of 3.31, while the 5 per cent critical value, $F(1,779)$, is 2.61. Efforts to capture this non-linearity with a parsimonious specification of the variables (for example, the asset shock interacted with pre-Mitch wealth) were unsuccessful. The results for the basic model indicate that a 10 per cent asset loss would be expected to reduce growth for quartile 1 households by about 18 percentage points and 22 percentage points for a second quartile household, but only 9 percentage points for a household in the top wealth quartile.[16] The asymmetric effects suggest that shocks will offset the tendency toward convergence, a finding consistent with the story told by the descriptive statistics in Table 5.1.

In addition to these core findings, both models give similar results with respect to income shocks and housing loss. Income shocks are counterintuitively estimated to have a positive but small and statistically insignificant impact on subsequent asset growth.[17] As a control for other losses suffered in the hurricane, a dummy variable was included in the regression, taking a value of one for households experiencing loss of housing. More intuitively, when households did experience housing loss, recovery of productive assets was significantly slowed by approximately 10 percentage points.

Given these average patterns of sensitivity to asset shocks, the expanded model in Table 5.2 permits us to see whether better access to factor markets mitigate the impacts of shocks. The labour market indicator for a household is defined as the average off-farm labour market earnings within its community (there are a total of thirty-one separate communities within the sample). The variable was scaled to lie between zero and one by dividing it by the highest community average earnings level within the sample. The data used to construct this variable was collected some two and a half years after the hurricane. This lag in the collection of the information should make it a more reliable indicator of labour market access rather than a measure of the endogenous exercise of labour supply in the wake of immediate needs created by the hurricane.

The capital access measure was also derived from a survey during the later time period and is based on a set of questions designed to probe whether or not a household was on its demand curve for credit (and hence price rationed in that market), or whether it had excess demand for credit and was therefore subject to some form of quantity rationing.[18] The capital access variable was defined as a binary variable taking the value of one when the household was price rationed.

As can be seen in Table 5.2, labour market access has a large mitigating effect on shocks, especially for low-wealth households (note that the mitigating effect of labour market access dissipates quickly as assets grow. Capital market access also strongly mitigates the impacts of shocks. While this mitigation effect is in principle wealth-neutral, Boucher et al. (2005) show that access to capital is highly skewed with respect to wealth (only 40 per cent of households in the lowest wealth quintile are price-rationed and do not have excess, unmet demand for formal-sector loans, while almost 90 per cent of households in the top quintile are able to satisfy their demand for capital in the formal credit market). Not surprisingly, when these mitigating factors are included in the regression, the average effects of asset shocks increase, indicating that households without access to labour and capital markets are affected more severely by the shocks than is indicated by the basic model.

In order to draw out the implications of the regression coefficients more clearly, we calculate predicted asset levels for a variety of stylized low- and high-wealth households that experienced different shocks in different market environments. Table 5.3 presents the results of these calculations. Initial asset levels are taken to be the mean for each quartile. For each asset level, the table contrasts the experience of a household that had no asset shock with the experience of a household that suffered a 31 per cent asset loss (which was the mean loss level for the lower-wealth quartile households that experienced losses). Other shocks were set to zero and all other household characteristics are set to mean levels for the sample.

For the "no shock case," the low-wealth households show higher growth (39 per cent over thirty months) than the high-wealth households (9 per cent), reflecting the convergence property discussed earlier. However, in the high-shock scenario, the excess sensitivity of poor households to asset shocks completely overturns this modest convergent process. In the absence of good market access, a low-wealth household that experienced an immediate 31 per cent asset loss is estimated to experience further declines and a net asset growth rate of –50 per cent from its pre-Mitch position to the time of the study thirty months later. A wealthier household that experienced an identical 31 per cent loss is estimated to have recovered partially from the loss and exhibit a net growth rate of –28 per cent. Were we also to take into account that wealthier households on average lost only 7.5 per cent of their assets (not 31 per cent), then the unequalizing effect of the shock would be further magnified. When poor households are compared to where they counterfactually would have been without a shock, the impacts of the shocks stand out even more sharply.

Finally, Table 5.3 shows that more buoyant labour and capital market access serves to offset the unequalizing effect of asset shocks. Under these circumstances, lower-wealth households would be able to offset the entire 31 per cent asset loss (climbing back to a net asset change of positive 5 per cent).

Wealthier households are also estimated to benefit slightly from better market access, though they still show a lingering effect of the asset shock on their asset accumulation.

These results are especially interesting in the context of a related study by Carter and Castillo (2005). In that study, Carter and Castillo found that recovery from Mitch was more rapid in communities characterized by high

Table 5.3   Sensitivity to and recovery from shocks – Honduras

	Lowest wealth quartile			Highest wealth quartile		
		31% asset loss			31% assset loss	
	No shock	Poor market access	Good market access	No shock	Poor market access	Good market access
Pre-shock assets (US$)	650	650	650	76,821	76,821	76,821
Post-recovery assets (US$)	902	321	686	83,905	54,951	64,537
30-month growth rate	39%	–50%	5.5%	9%	–28%	–15%

levels of pro-social norms of trust and altruism. Interestingly, further analysis by Carter and Castillo suggests that only a subset of households seems in fact to benefit from the pro-social environment, suggesting that there may be processes of exclusion that prevent all households from benefiting from socially mediated access to insurance and capital. If correct, when merged with the results presented here, we seem to see a situation in which local social mechanisms leave poor Honduran households quite vulnerable to asset shocks. In this environment, access to supporting capital, and in particular labour markets, seem to be especially important.

Testing for poverty traps

The analysis up to this point has shown that asset shocks in Honduras have the potential to derail an otherwise convergent accumulation process in which lower-wealth households accumulate more quickly than their richer neighbours. However, it is unclear whether or not these results signal an irreversible setback for low-wealth households who become mired in a poverty trap, or whether their recovery is simply slower. As discussed in the second section (entitled 'Shocks, poverty traps and resilience'), threshold estimation potentially offers additional insight into this question by permitting us to estimate the longer-run equilibrium towards which lower-wealth household are heading.

Table 5.4 displays the results of this analysis, based on the model in Equation (5.2). The dependent variable is asset growth over the 30-month period immediately following Mitch. Initial assets are defined as a household's post-shock asset level, A_s. Note that this definition is different from that used in the previous section's analysis. Growth in this section is defined from the base of the post-shock assets in order to test the notion of an asset poverty trap, which suggests that households that fall below a critical threshold level will become mired in a low-level equilibrium trap. Because this post-shock growth measure already nets out the direct effect of the shock, the regression specification does not include the shock itself (in contrast to the model in the previous section).

Using Hansen's (2000) threshold estimator, we can now estimate whether the data can be split into two groups – above and below a critical initial asset value – which exhibit significantly different growth dynamics. Note that any observations in a low group will include households that both randomly fell into this group based on the vagaries of Hurricane Mitch, as well as households that were already at low asset levels before the hurricane struck.[19]

Table 5.4   Threshold poverty trap estimates – Honduras

Explanatory variables	Low regime $A_s < 244$	High regime $A_s > 244$
Core growth & convergence		
Post-shock initial assets, A_s (log)	−0.65[a]	−0.04[a]
Asset loss		
Housing loss	−1.46[a]	−0.10
Mediating factors		
Labour market access, L	0.27	0.01
Capital market access, K	−1.19[a]	0.11[a]
Demographic & other controls		
Age of household head	−0.01	0.02
Squared age of head	0.00	−0.00
Post-Mitch inheritance (equals 1 if received)	1.95[a]	0.48
Constant	6.41[a]	0.23
Provincial dummies	Included	Included
Observations	43	727
R^2	0.62	0.22
Threshold interval estimate (95% interval)	235–249[a]	

Notes

[a] Significant at the 5% level.

As shown in Table 5.4, the data indeed suggest the presence of a threshold at an asset level of US$244. This estimate is quite precise, as the 95 per cent confidence interval estimate of the threshold ranges from only US$235 to US$249.[20] The explanatory variables are largely the same as those included in the Table 5.2 regression.[21]

The Table 5.4 regression results can perhaps be appreciated most easily by exploring them graphically. Figure 5.3 graphs the two regimes where all variables apart from initial assets are held at their mean levels for the full sample. The low regime displays a pattern in which growth drops off very quickly as assets increase, and signals the existence of a low-level equilibrium at about US$225 (where expected asset growth equals zero). The upper group displays a pattern of only very slowly diminishing growth and an upper-level equilibrium that is orders of magnitude greater than that for the low-level group.

While these results should be treated with caution (see the discussion in the section above entitled 'Shocks, poverty traps and resilience'), they are consistent with the sort of poverty trap described by Ato Mohammed in the quotation at the beginning of this chapter. While a full exploration of the poverty trap hypothesis will require further methodological developments (see Carter and Barrett, 2006), the Hurricane Mitch quasi-experiment does indicate unambiguously that asset shocks have long-lived, unequalizing effects.

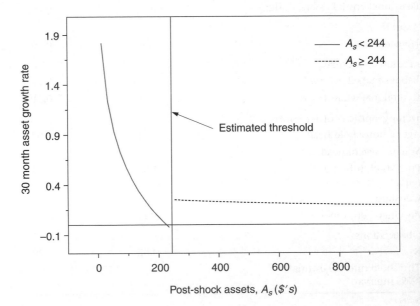

Figure 5.3   Post-Mitch poverty trap – Honduras

Asset smoothing and drought recovery in north-eastern Ethiopia

Unlike the swift destruction brought about by Mitch in Honduras, the drought of the late 1990s that afflicted our study area in north-eastern Ethiopia (the South Wollo and Oromiya Zones of the Amhara Region) was a prolonged event, with uneven consequences and a gradual onset. Indeed, the first signs of disaster can be traced to the poor short rains (January–April, called the Belg season) of 1998, where it is estimated that harvests were only 60 per cent of normal yields in the main Belg growing areas (Government of Ethiopia, 1997, 1998a, 1998b). That year, the long rainy season (June–September, called the Meher) was near normal for all areas except in the Belg growing zones, where there is also some dependence on the Meher season. Because the Meher rains of 1998 were near-normal in some locations, drought and relief agencies in Ethiopia failed to see the looming disaster until the Belg season of 1999 emerged as a massive failure, resulting in 90 per cent loss of crops (see Castro et al., 1999).

The 1999 Meher season was only a little better, yielding about 40 per cent of normal harvests in six of the eight kebeles[22] in which data for this study are available. Food aid distribution started in the region in June 1999, but was not widespread until August 1999. To make matters worse, the Belg season of 2000 was very poor (75 per cent reduction of normal yields). With massive imports of food aid and the recovery of the long rains in 2000, the nutritional status of the area's population had returned to near normal by early 2001. Thus the drought of the late 1990s was keyed by the failure or near failure of three successive short rainy seasons. The first of the crop failures was only 40 per cent, but with such widespread poverty it was enough to initiate the downward spiral of extensive food insecurity and distress sales of assets (mainly livestock) that characterized the region for the better part of thirty months.

The long-term possibilities of asset recovery from this series of shocks would be expected to be conditioned by several community and household characteristics. For example, in our study area 65 per cent of households participate in funeral clubs (called iddir or kire); 67 per cent in farm work groups (debo or wonfel), where members work on each other's farms during peak periods; and 18 per cent in religious organizations. The prevalence of certain social institutions varies by ethnic and religious affiliations. Individuals in the study area are either members of the Oromo (25 per cent) or Amhara (75 per cent) ethnic groups, and 86 per cent of the region's population are Muslims, with the remaining 14 per cent being Coptic Christians. The study region is characterized (as indeed are large parts of Ethiopia) by relatively weak labour markets and nearly absent credit markets. Land markets are severely restricted in that private ownership is prohibited, and legal constraints on land rentals were relaxed only recently. In part because insurance against crop loss is practically absent, and market-based coping mechanisms are limited, food aid makes up a relatively large portion of food consumption, as indicated above. Data are from a seven-round household survey conducted over three and a half years in eight *kebeles* in the South Wollo and Oromiya zones. The dataset also includes recall questions on livestock holdings from 1996 to 1999, which assess how households fared in terms of their assets prior to the onset of the drought.

From the data, 1999 was also the year of the heaviest livestock asset reductions, because of animal deaths as well as sales. Based on qualitative surveys in the study area (see Castro *et al.* 1999; Amare *et al.* 2000; Little *et al.* 2006), it is estimated that 25 per cent of livestock reductions in 1999 were distress sales at which the seller received less than 50 per cent of the normal price of the animal sold (cattle prices, for example, dropped from an average of 625 birr [US$74] in the pre-drought period to 291 birr [US$35]). Price swings of this magnitude constituted a huge capital loss for those forced to sell livestock during this period. Natural causes clearly precipitated the drought disaster of 1999, which resulted in a massive humanitarian effort, but the population's vulnerability to relatively small perturbations in climatic events is 'unnatural' and highlights the extreme poverty in the area.

Livestock losses and their recovery

Figure 5.4 gives a first indication of how the weather shocks discussed above impacted on households. The top panel shows the evolution of mean livestock by households in the four pre-drought wealth quartiles. Livestock assets are aggregated here in Tropical Livestock Units (TLUs).[23] Following the onset of the drought in 1998, the top two wealth quartiles appear to exhibit typical consumption smoothing behaviour, as livestock assets begin to dip sharply. In contrast, the two lowest quartiles appear to hold on to their livestock more stubbornly, showing on average only small decreases in livestock near the end of the drought period. This apparent asset smoothing behaviour is what we would predict if these lower-quartile households were in the vicinity of a critical poverty trap threshold (see Hoddinott, 2006 for an analysis of Zimbabwe).

Analogous to Honduras, one way to further probe the existence of poverty traps is to examine post-shock growth trajectories, to see if those households that were worst off at the end of the disaster show evidence of being unable to recover and move towards higher asset levels. The bottom panel of Figure 5.4 displays the livestock trajectories based on wealth quartiles defined according to animal holdings at the end of the drought. As can be seen from the chart, average holdings of the poorest quartile were essentially zero at that time. Interestingly, however, this group on average managed to add substantially to their livestock holdings over the following three years, especially in contrast to those households better positioned in the wake of the shocks. The latter also recovered, but at a slower rate. At this

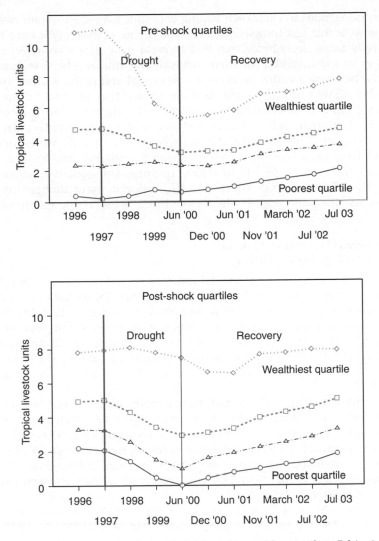

Figure 5.4 Evolution of mean livestock holdings by wealth quartiles – Ethiopia

descriptive level, these patterns are not consistent with what we would expect to see if the poorest households had indeed fallen into a poverty trap as did Ato Mohammed.

This pattern may be explained partially by the inclination of better-off households to continue to market animals after the drought, in order to benefit from the post-shock boom in livestock prices (Little *et al.*, 2006). It probably also reflects the fact that households' post-shock asset positions were endogenous to their own coping decisions over the drought period. Households that had completely stocked out by mid-2000 might have been precisely those households that had thought it necessary to invest thoroughly in social capital for their survival, and thus might have enjoyed relatively stronger endowments of social capital and perhaps other assets. Another study using the same data has shown that local social mechanisms assume considerably more importance for the poor during recovery periods (Little *et al.*, 2006: 220). Those households that apparently defended their livestock could be isolated households who – like Ato Mohammed – would have been trapped by low post-shock resilience and growth had they let their stocks deplete to almost nothing. Subsequent econometric analysis will take into consideration the endogeneity of drought coping strategies discussed above when examining recovery period livestock growth.

Econometric estimates of asset and consumption smoothing

Employing the asset growth model put forward before, we turn now to a more thorough analysis of the data using methods that permit us to control for these multiple factors that influence observed outcomes. In doing so, we shall estimate growth over the two distinct time periods. This section will examine coping strategies over the two-year drought period, using the asset growth model to study asset draw-down or negative growth. The following section will then turn to a separate examination of post-shock (positive) growth.

To explore coping and negative asset growth, we use a measure of the magnitude of the shock, ε_i, directly in the specification as well as letting the coefficient for ε_i depend on the pre-shock asset level of the household, A_{bi}. While the available data lack a measure of the severity of the shock received by each household, we approximate it with the share of households in the community of household i that suffered crop losses in the worst season – the 2000 Belg season.

The first column of Table 5.5 gives the results of the estimation of asset changes during the successive poor seasons. We see in the OLS estimation result that the shock coefficient is quite substantial in size (but not significant) across all estimations: for example, the model associates a 10 percentage point decrease in the share of households of the *kebele* that experienced weather-induced crop loss, with a 105.7 percentage point increase in the asset growth rate over the two-year time period of the drought. While this appears to be an enormous effect, it is not quite as huge when compared with the distribution of rates of livestock asset changes over this period. For example, for households that experienced positive growth (about 40 per cent of all households), the median two-year growth rates were 58 per cent,

Table 5.5 Estimates of asset changes during drought years – Ethiopia

Explanatory variables	OLS	Tobit
Shocks		
Income shock, ε	–11.80	–22.59
Income shock[b] Initial assets	–0.31[b]	–0.21[b]
Mediating factors		
Community social capital, *SK*	0.78	1.38
Labour market access, *L*	4.219[a]	3.17
Access to food aid, *F*	–5.98	–9.11
Demographic factors		
Household size	–0.15	0.09
Age of household head	–0.44	–0.48[a]
Squared age of head	0.004	0.004[a]
Gender of household head	1.64[a]	3.01[a]
Land assets (in timad = $1/4$ hectares)	0.41	0.63
Constant	19.62	25.79
Number of censored observations		60
R^2	0.07	
$LR \chi^2_{(11)}$		26.01
p-value		0.004

Note
[a] Significant at the 5% level.
[b] Significant at the 10% level.
Sample size: n = 416; Number of clusters: 8.

the third quartile 141 per cent, and the 90th percentile was 1025 per cent. The large effects of shocks can be seen as bringing growth rates back down from very high levels.

The estimates also show that having higher assets magnifies the detrimental impact of shocks on growth. This effect is significant at the 10 per cent level, though small in magnitude, and suggests that poor households seek to defend their assets in the face of successive droughts rather than to liquidate them and perhaps limit their subsequent chances of recovery. That is, it is consistent with asset smoothing behaviour by the lower-wealth households.

The estimated model also explores the degree to which social mechanisms, food aid and labour markets bolster asset growth. Access to social institutions is measured as community average membership in social organizations.[24] Food aid is measured as the percentage of a community participating in food for work programmes. This community level variable bypasses individual-level endogeneity problems created when more severely shocked households choose to participate in a programme. It may, however, still suffer from the fact that programmes are set up in communities where the drought was most severe. The labour market indicator is an average of off-farm earnings for all households within a *kebele*. This number was then normalized to vary between zero and one by dividing it by the highest level of average earnings among the eight *kebeles* in the sample.[25]

Community membership in social organizations (social capital) increases the rate of growth (or limits the rate of loss) of livestock over this period. There is even stronger evidence that labour market access has a positive effect on the rate of growth of livestock. Finally, availability of food aid in the community does not appear to protect households' future assets, and in fact seems to have the opposite effect.[26]

As indicated in Figure 5.4, after those in the lowest strata bottom out, they do not have the option to draw down further assets. This motivates the investigation of whether the results interpreted as evidence of asset smoothing by the poorer households (as suggested by the estimates in the first column of Table 5.5) are instead driven primarily by the inability of households in the lowest strata to liquidate assets, for lack of the latter. To check for this, Table 5.5 also includes a Tobit estimation with the asset growth rates censored from below at −100 per cent.[27] Indeed, the share of households that had some holdings at the beginning of the series of weather shocks but were stocked out by the end of this period is about 6 per cent, and 14 per cent of households had no livestock at the end of the shocks (irrespective of their initial assets).[28] Generally, in Table 5.5 the censored and OLS estimation do not differ from each other by much and, more specifically, the effects of asset smoothing are still present, suggesting that this was not merely driven by the potential growth censoring problem.[29]

Post-drought asset growth trajectories

This section focuses on the recovery period to explore the existence of long-run effects and poverty traps induced by the drought. Following the strategy outlined in the second sectionabove and Equation (5.2), we employ Hansen's (2000) threshold estimator to examine whether a critical asset threshold exists around which asset growth dynamics bifurcate. In assessing the determinants of the recovery period growth, including how households' starting position affects subsequent growth, it is important to account for how households' post-shock position is determined endogenously by the coping decisions they made during the drought period. Unlike the situation in Honduras, where the change in households' asset stocks immediately after Mitch was determined exogenously by the destruction caused by the hurricane, in Ethiopia the livestock assets people possessed post-drought depended on the coping strategies they employed during the drought period. In the following analysis of recovery period growth, we account for this endogeneity by basing our model on the predicted levels of post-shock assets, $\hat{A}_s$ (estimated using the results shown in Table 5.5), rather than the observed levels of post-shock assets, A_s.

The results employing Hansen's threshold estimator are given in Table 5.6. The dependent variable is the simply three-livestock growth rate (not annualized). The data indicate the presence of two distinct, statistically different regression regimes. Households with initial (predicted) assets in excess of 0.59 TLU fall into the upper regime, and those below into the lower regimes. Approximately half of the observations fall into each regime. The threshold dividing the two regimes is predicted quite precisely (the 95 per cent interval estimate of the threshold is 0.57 to 0.61). The Hansen joint-R^2, which indicates explanatory fit of the model given the estimated threshold, is 80.9 per cent, higher than the equivalent single equilibrium model (not reported here), which has an R^2 of 75.7 per cent.

Figure 5.5 graphs the two estimated regression functions, holding all variables apart from initial assets at their mean sample values. Within both the upper and the lower regimes livestock growth decelerates as initial assets increase. Access to off-farm opportunities is not only important for protecting assets during the poor seasons, as seen earlier, but also for the asset recovery period. However, there is stronger evidence that this is the case for the low-wealth regime. Similarly, the role of access to social institutions also

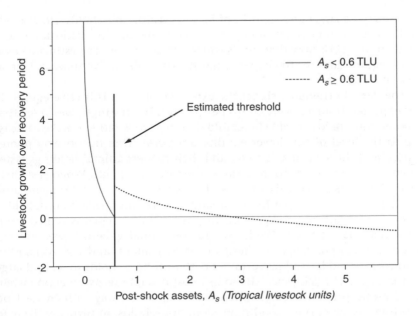

Figure 5.5 Growth equilibria of two asset regimes – Ethiopia

Table 5.6   Threshold poverty trap estimates – Ethiopia

Explanatory variables	Low regime $A_s \leq 0.65$ TLUs	High regime $A_s > 0.65$ TLUs
Convergence		
Initial assets, $\ln(A_s)$	–1.83**	–0.80**
Mediating factors		
Community social capital, SK	0.23**	0.05
Labour market access, L	1.11**	0.57
Access to food aid, F	–1.14**	–0.79
Demographic factors		
Household size	0.20**	0.14**
Age of household head	0.04	0.01
Squared age of head	–0.0004	–0.0001
Gender of household head	0.72**	0.67*
Land assets (in timad = $^1/_4$ hectares)	0.10	–0.01
Constant	–3.84**	–0.45
R^2	0.72	0.51
Number of observations	214	202

appears to be larger and significant for low-wealth households. Households in the lower regime show rapid initial growth that quickly dissipates to zero at about 0.5 TLU. Note that this is still less than one ox. The estimated livestock equilibrium for the upper group stands at about five times higher, at nearly 3 TLU.

The data do therefore signal the existence of two distinctive equilibria ,as expected from a poverty traps perspective. Interestingly, we do see that poorer households are able to rebuild their livestock rather quickly, at least up to the level of this lower equilibrium point. One reason why poorer households have been able to rebuild their modest animal holdings faster than others may relate to the land tenure system in South Wollo (see Little *et al.*, 2006). As explained earlier, land is controlled by the state and because of this there is an "upper limit" of land (2.5 hectares) that a household is allocated for farming and grazing purposes.[30] In a land-constrained economy like that of South Wollo, where communal grazing areas are few, there are real challenges (in terms of management, and the availability and costs of fodder and pastures) for better-off households to rebuild large herds quickly. This is especially so in a post-drought recovery period when land rental prices increase, which is an important way to increase land holdings under current conditions. Poor households, in turn, are likely to have adequate access to land and pastures, relative to their livestock asset endowments, to rebuild their small herds without the need to purchase fodder or rent additional land.

Finally, it is worth remarking that one feature of the estimated equilibria seems odd. Similar to the results obtained for Honduras, the asset equilibrium of the lower regime (that is, the initial asset level that is associated with zero growth) is just slightly below the threshold value of 0.59 TLUs. While there is nothing conceptually wrong with this proximity of the equilibrium to the threshold, we probably need additional experience with this class of estimator to better understand these kinds of results.

Concluding remarks

In the ideal world of full and complete markets, poor households could draw on loan and insurance contracts to cope with the often disastrous asset and income losses brought about by severe environmental shocks. Drawing on future earnings, households in this world could rebuild lost assets and sustain their level of current consumption without further depletion of their productive assets and future possibilities. The story of one Ethiopian household told at the start of this chapter is an example of how far the actually existing world can be from that ideal world. In the real world of Ato Mohammed, environmental shocks can decapitalize the poor, and trap them in an impoverished position from which they cannot escape. When this happens, a humanitarian problem of disaster relief becomes a long-term development problem.

In an effort to better understand the impacts of natural disaster, this chapter has employed longitudinal data on assets to understand the longer-term impacts of two shocks: the three-year drought of the late 1990s in Ethiopia, and the 1998 Hurricane Mitch in Honduras. Analysis of the Honduran data reveals that the medium-term effects of the shock differ by initial household wealth. Relatively wealthy households were able to (at least partially) rebuild their lost assets in the three years following the shock. In contrast, for the lowest wealth groups, the effects of the hurricane on assets were of longer duration and were felt much more acutely. This differential impact of the hurricane is especially striking because it seems to have derailed what would otherwise have been a convergent growth path in which poorer households accumulate productive assets more quickly than their richer neighbours. In an effort to determine whether these patterns signal the presence of a poverty trap, such that those poorer households who lost assets to the hurricane will never recover, we also estimated a threshold model of poverty traps. While the reliability of the estimates depend on several strong assumptions, they do indicate the presence of a poverty trap such that households that begin beneath (or fall below) an asset threshold of US$250 are expected to gravitate to a low-level equilibrium, orders of magnitude beneath that of their better-off or more fortunate neighbours. However, more work is clearly needed to generalize the estimation methods and improve the reliability of these estimates.

For Ethiopia we had the opportunity to examine asset changes over two distinct time ranges: a period of drought and coping, and a period of recovery. Analysis of this data reveals a weak pattern of asset smoothing among the lowest wealth households, meaning that the households at the bottom try to hold on to their few assets even as income and consumption possibilities dwindle during the period of severe losses in agricultural production. Such behaviour is consistent with what would be expected in the face of a poverty trap. Following the drought, low-wealth households are estimated to accumulate assets faster than non-poor households, controlling for other variables. But in a similar way to the Honduran case, the threshold estimates again signal the existence of a lower equilibrium at which these poor households settle down and stop growing. The possibility that shocks have different and more durable effects on the less well-off seems well established, though additional work is needed to increase the reliability of the threshold estimates that underlie the identification of a lower equilibrium for poor households.

In addition to these econometric issues, the analysis here has in other dimensions fallen short of fully resolving all the puzzles and complexities of the two disasters studied here. For example, an evaluation of the full welfare impacts of asset poverty traps would require a more complete set of assets and better information about asset values (in the Ethiopian case), as well as the consumption consequences of asset smoothing behaviour. Further research may also reveal other important facets of wealth-differentiated asset recovery experiences by exploring the asset composition of varied wealth categories of households. For example, do the poor in Ethiopia hold most of the animal assets in small stock and chickens, while the better-off own more cattle and plough oxen? These types of assets differ in their "lumpiness," their abilities to breed (hence recover) rapidly, their functions in income and wealth generation, and in the extent to which they are protected in the face of shocks. Future studies should address the likelihood that different asset portfolios of the rich and poor may constrain or facilitate post-disaster recovery paths.

While future research to solve remaining questions is always desirable, given the importance of natural disasters it seems worth speculating on the policy and development implications of our findings, especially since most disasters and their impacts are treated as humanitarian rather than development problems. Building "productive" safety nets that keep vulnerable households from losing their assets is one important policy intervention in disaster-prone areas. As Barrett and Carter (2006) analyse in detail, keeping households above critical asset thresholds can generate large social (and private) returns if poverty traps do, in fact, exist.

In addition to its implications for safety nets, the analysis here has shown that access to social and financial capital, and to off-farm earning opportunities, can be especially important for low-wealth assets as they cope with natural disasters. Policies that improve non-farm employment opportunities, rural market infrastructure and accessibility of credit – especially in the post-disaster period – are important ways that governments and development agencies can help to limit long-term asset depletion. Given the importance of social networks, especially for the poor, any form of development policy needs to be cognizant of the way in which such social networks operate so as to minimize any potential negative impact of programmes on the functional elements of social institutions.

Acknowledgements: We thank Elsevier for giving permission to republish Michael R. Carter, Peter D. Little, Tewodaj Mogues and Workneh Negatu's 'Poverty Traps and Natural Disasters in Ethiopia and Honduras', first published in *World Development*, 35 (5), 835–856.

Notes

* This publication was made possible by support provided in part by the World Bank and by the US Agency for International Development (USAID) Agreement No. LAG-A-00-96-90016-00 through BASIS Collaborative Research Support Program. Rob White and Francisco Galarza provided valuable research assistance. Helpful comments were received from anonymous referees of this journal, as well as by seminar participants at the 2005 ASSA meetings, the World Bank, the University of Manchester's Social Protection Conference and the University of Wisconsin. All views, interpretations, recommendations, and conclusions expressed in this paper are those of the authors and not necessarily those of the supporting or collaborating institutions.

1. Ato (which means Mr) Mohammed is the head of one of the households in one of the two country case studies of this chapter.
2. While the destruction wrought by the hurricane would seem to be random and unrelated to unobserved individual characteristics, we do not formally establish this point. We do show in the third section, entitled "Gauging the longer-term impacts of asset shocks in Honduras," that wealthier individuals probably suffered some losses, but among those affected, poorer households lost a larger percentage of their assets.
3. Mogues and Carter (2005) theoretically explore the idea that poor households will be less able to accumulate effective social capital in more polarized and inegalitarian economies.
4. While the discussion that follows lists coping strategies in a rough order of decreasing desirability for discursive purposes, any household's true preferences will depend on a number of factors.
5. The notion that some households might remain mired in a trap of persistent poverty is surprising from the perspective of some dynamic economic theory, which suggests that less-well-off households would be expected to have every

incentive to try to save, accumulate and catch up economically with their better-off fellow citizens. Carter and Barrett (2006) discuss the forces that could offset convergence, identifying lack of access to markets or socially mediated access as the key force.

6. Another possible motivation for retaining assets in a time of drought are adverse terms of trade for livestock *vis-à-vis* grain, as often occurs in drought periods (for example, see the discussion in Fafchamps *et al.*, 1998). The depreciation of the (relative) value of assets, however, would likely – all else being equal, including asset-smoothing motivations – exist for all households irrespective of wealth. Hence it is not expected that we would see asset retention for terms of trade reasons only among the poor. A similar comment applies to McPeak's (2004) observation that households may be expected to hold on to livestock if income losses were correlated with asset losses.

7. As Hoddinott stresses, the cost of an asset-smoothing strategy is not only immediate hunger. In the case of Zimbabwe, asset smoothing permanently reduced the growth and, presumably the future capacity, of young, nutritionally vulnerable children.

8. Fafchamps *et al.* (1998) find seemingly puzzling regression evidence that at least some households in their West African sample do not manage their livestock so as to smooth consumption over time in the face of shocks. One explanation of their finding is that a subset of their households is at a threshold where asset smoothing becomes a rational response to shocks, and hence their data is a mix of asset and consumption smoothers.

9. Note that this model is a microeconomic adaptation of the standard neoclassical growth model used in the literature studying convergence in living standards between nations. As in the case of this literature, one can raise the question about the potential endogeneity of initial wealth or income levels. While these initial levels are temporally predetermined, they may be correlated with household- (or nation-)specific characteristics not captured by the model. While we control for many household and community characteristics in our subsequent analysis of the model in Equation (5.1), we are in the end subject to the same criticisms that have been applied to the macroeconomic convergence literature.

10. The damaging events meted out by the natural disasters (for example, high winds; rain shortfalls) should be distributed randomly across households. These natural "experiments" thus gave us a random subsample of low-wealth households that experienced damage, and another subsample of low-wealth households that did not (the same, of course, holds for better-off households). Regression estimates of Equation (5.1) should thus permit us to reliably recover the impact of the shocks on those types of household found to be poor and those found to be rich.

11. Consistent estimation of Equation (5.2) will only result if the error term, v_i, is orthogonal to the explanatory variables. While it has been common to make this assumption in the macro growth literature which regularly regresses growth rates on initial conditions (see, for example, Hansen, 2000), it is a questionable assumption.

12. This sample comprises two distinct subsamples: panel and cross-section. The panel households (500) originate from a study conducted in 1994 (López and Valdés, 2000) in which 450 farm households were interviewed to analyse the impacts of the initial land titling programmes. The 2001 survey attempted to follow both these baseline households and the land they cultivated. Of the original

baseline households, 362 were resurveyed. In addition, 138 "new" panel households were added. In 2000, these households were cultivating land that had been worked by the original panel households in 1994. The remaining 350 cross-sectional households were added in regions that were not covered in the 1994 study. Households that were not operating their own farms in 1998 were eliminated from the sample for the purposes of this study, reducing the total number of households to 821.

13. This pattern is consistent with what would be expected if damage were random, in the sense that every hectare had an equal and independent probability of loss. In this case, fewer poorer households would experience loss (as each had fewer potential hectares on which a loss could potentially occur), but those who experience loss would lose a larger fraction of their total assets.

14. The percentages are approximate, as household income is measured only for the year 2000/1 and not for the year of the hurricane.

15. Median growth rates are reported in the table. Mean growth rates are higher in all cases, but follow the same qualitative pattern. Many of the high growth rates appear to be the result of inheritances received post-Mitch.

16. These differences are statistically different from a 10 per cent growth loss for the lowest two quartiles as we can reject the hypothesis at the 1 per cent level that the coefficient of the asset shock is –1. We cannot reject this hypothesis for the top two quartiles.

17. The insignificance of the income shock variable may be an artefact of a pattern in the data whereby highest income losses occurred for households involved in high-valued commercial activities that also gave them better access to market-based coping mechanisms. Interacting income shocks with the market access variables did not, however, uncover any systematic patterns.

18. Being price-rationed is not the same thing as having a loan. Price rationed includes both households that borrow as well as those that did not need or want to borrow, given the price of credit and their access to other sources of funds (see Boucher *et al.*, 2005 for further details).

19. We may worry that this latter group has intrinsic characteristics that lock them into a low equilibrium. It is thus unclear whether the equilibrium for this low group simply represents a low-level convergence club for "low-type" individuals, or whether it represents a genuine multiple equilibrium traps that would absorb high-type individuals were they to fall below the threshold. Efforts to estimate initial asset holding using data on parental characteristics were not successful.

20. The joint R-squared for the threshold model is 0.30, in contrast to an R-squared of only 0.17 for the pooled model, which assumes that there is only a single growth regression regime.

21. The squared initial asset term was tiny and insignificant, and was not included in the reported regression. Note that splitting the sample into two groups should reduce the need for additional terms to capture highly non-linear growth relationships.

22. A *kebele* is an administrative unit comprising four or five villages.

23. As used here, a TLU (Tropical Livestock Unit) is: 1 TLU = 1 head of cattle (ox, bull, cow, calf, heifer); 0.5 TLU = 1 horse/donkey/mule; 1.4 TLU = 1 camel; 0.1 TLU = 1 sheep/goat; 0.05 TLU = 1 chicken. The TLU factors the approximate weight, subsistence (food), and market value of different animals.

24. These include, for example, burial societies (kire), informal credit associations (iqqub), and religious groups (mehaber and senbete).

25. With "labour market" in this context we refer to the broader array of off-farm work opportunities including business income, rather than narrowly the wage labour market.

26. This result is somewhat surprising, especially since the direction of the impact cannot arise from endogeneity, as would be expected if household-level aid receipts were used (Quisumbing, 2003), since the measure used here is a community aggregate rather than individual participation in food-for-work. A study focusing on the impact on food aid on welfare in three regions in Ethiopia including South Wollo (Mathys, 1999) aims in a similar direction (though less pointedly), finding that while, in the short term, asset sales are somewhat reduced with food aid, months later households tend to return to elevated sales. Also, other work on South Wollo points to the limitations of food aid in enabling recovery from disasters in the long run (Little *et al.*, 2006). Furthermore, similar results are obtained in a study (Mogues, 2005) using the same dataset and dynamic panel data techniques to assess the determinants of the evolution of livestock assets in Ethiopia. Here, the endogneity is instrumented using GMM techniques. The negative coefficients in multiple studies and using multiple techniques remains a bit of a puzzle and may require further investigation in the future.

27. Households that entered the post-shock period with zero assets were censored to have growth no smaller than 0 per cent as they had nothing further to lose. To insure that the restricted choices of these households were properly treated by the programme, each was assumed to have one chicken (0.05 TLU) at the end of the shock period. If the household was registered as having zero TLU at the end of the recovery period, their growth rate thus became –100 per cent such that the Tobit regression properly reflected their censored behaviour.

28. Given that 16 per cent of the households started the drought period with no assets at all, we made an adjustment that would permit the obtaining of growth rates, namely to increase all livestock assets by the same small increment.

29. We also examined a specification including initial assets, in order to also see how these may change the results. Introducing a convergence effect indeed seems to obscure the asset smoothing effect identified in Table 5.5. This is perhaps not surprising: both the concept of convergence as well as asset smoothing have the same empirical implication in this context, at least for the time scale prior to the recovery period. They both suggest that the assets of the initially less-well-off households will grow at a faster rate (or decline at slower pace) than better-off households' assets. However, in examining the rate of change in assets over the drought period, we are not inherently interested in the question of convergence (discussed more fully in the next subsection), but in coping strategies implied by asset changes.

30. However, the legal bound on land size can be significantly smaller than that for any given household, as the maximum size is determined by the number of household members and other household characteristics.

References

Adato, M., M. R. Carter and J. May (2006) 'Exploring Poverty Traps and Social Exclusion in South Africa Using Qualitative and Quantitative Data', *Journal of Development Studies*, 42 (2), 226–247.

Amare, Y., Y. Adal, D. Tolossa, A. P. Castro and P. D. Little (2000) Food Security and Resource Access: a Final Report on the Community Assessments in South Wello and Oromiya Zones of Amhara Region, Ethiopia. Working Paper, Basis CRSP, University of Wisconsin.

Barrett, C., and M. R. Carter (2006) Social Protection Policy to Overcome Poverty Traps and Aid Traps. Paper Presented to Brookings Conference on Asset Based Approaches to Poverty Reduction in a Globalized Context. Washington, DC, 27–28 June 2006.

Barrett, C. B., P. P. Marenya, J. P. McPeak, B. Minten, F. Murithi, W. Oluoch-Kosura, F. Place, J. C. Randrianarisoa, J. Rasambainarivo and J. Wangila (2006) 'Welfare Dynamics in Rural Kenya and Madagascar', *Journal of Development Studies*, 42(2), 248–277.

Boucher, S., B. Barham and M. R. Carter (2005) 'The Impact of Market Friendly Reforms on Credit and Land Markets in Honduras and Nicaragua', *World Development*, 33(1), 107–128.

Buera, F. (2005) A Dynamic Model of Entrepreneurship with Borrowing Constraints. Working paper, Northwestern University.

Calvo, C. and S. Dercon (2005) Measuring Individual Vulnerability. Working paper, Oxford University.

Carter, M. R. and C. B. Barrett (2006) 'The Economics of Poverty Traps and Persistent Poverty: An Asset-Based Approach', *Journal of Development Studies*, 42(2), 178–199.

Carter, M. R. and M. Castillo (2005) 'Morals, Markets and Mutual Insurance: Using Economic Experiments to Study Recovery from Hurricane Mitch', in C. B. Barrett (ed.), *Exploring the Moral Dimensions of Economic Behavior*. Oxon, UK: Routledge, pp. 268–287.

Castro, A. P., Y. Amare, Y. Adal and D. Tolossa (1999) BASIS/IDR Community Assessments: Kebele Profiles. Working Paper, BASIS CRSP, University of Wisconsin.

Dercon, S. (2004) 'Growth and Shocks: Evidence from Rural Ethiopia', *Journal of Development Economics*, 74(2), 309–329.

Drèze, J. and A. K. Sen (1989) 'Famines and Social Response', in J. Drèze and A. Sen (eds), *Hunger and public action* 1st ed. Oxford, UK: Clarendon Press, pp. 65–81.

Fafchamps, M., C. Udry and K. Czukas (1998) 'Drought and Saving in West Africa: Are Livestock a Buffer Stock?', *Journal of Development Economics*, 55(2), 273–305.

Government of Ethiopia (1997) *Food Supply Prospect 1998: Early Warning System Report*. Addis Ababa, Ethiopia: Disaster Prevention and Preparedness Commission.

Government of Ethiopia (1998a) *Food Supply Prospect 1999: Early Warning System Report*. Addis Ababa, Ethiopia: Disaster Prevention and Preparedness Commission.

Government of Ethiopia (1998b) *Food Situation in 1998 and Assistance Requirement*. Addis Ababa, Ethiopia: Disaster Prevention and Preparedness Commission.

Hansen, B. (2000) 'Sample Splitting and Threshold Estimation', *Econometrica*, 68(3), 575–604.

Hoddinott, J. (2006) 'Shocks and Their Consequences across and within Households in Rural Zimbabwe', *Journal of Development Studies*, 42(2), 301–321.

Little, P. D., with assistance from A. G. M. Ahmed, M. R. Carter and W. Negatu (2002) *Building Assets for Sustainable Recovery and Food Security*. BASIS Brief, No. 5. Madison, WI: BASIS Research Program, Department of Agricultural and Applied Economics, University of Wisconsin-Madison.

Little, P. D., M. P. Stone, T. Mogues, P. Castro and W. Negatu (2006) '"Moving in Place": Drought and Poverty Dynamics in South Wollo, Ethiopia', *Journal of Development Studies*, 42(2), 200–225.

López, R. and A. Valdés (2000) 'Fighting Rural Poverty in Latin America: New Evidence of the Effects of Education, Demographics, and Access to Land', *Economic Development and Cultural Change*, 49(1), 197–211.

Lybbert, T., C. Barrett, S. Desta and L. Coppock (2004) 'Stochastic Wealth Dynamics and Risk Management among a Poor Population', *Economic Journal*, 114(498), 750–777.

Mathys, E. (1999) Assessment of the Impact of Food Aid on Household Economies of North Wollo, South Wollo and East Hararghe, Ethiopia. Food Security Unit, Save the Children Fund (UK).

McPeak, J. (2004) 'Contrasting Income Shocks with Asset Shocks: Livestock Sales in Northern Kenya', *Oxford Economic Papers*, 56(2), 263–284.

Mogues, T. (2005) Shocks, Livestock Asset Dynamics, and Social Capital in Ethiopia. Working paper.

Mogues, T. and M. R. Carter (2005) 'Social Capital and the Reproduction of Inequality in Polarized Societies', *Journal of Economic Inequality*, 3, 193–219.

Morris, S., O. Neidecker-Gonzales, C. Carletto, M. Munguia, J. M. Medina and Q. Wodon (2001) 'Hurricane Mitch and Livelihoods of the Rural Poor in Honduras', *World Development*, 30(1), 39–60.

Quisumbing, A. (2003) 'Food Aid and Child Nutrition in Rural Ethiopia', *World Development*, 31(7), 1309–1324.

Zimmerman, F. and M. R. Carter (2003) 'Asset Smoothing, Consumption Smoothing and the Reproduction of Inequality under Risk and Subsistence Constraints', *Journal of Development Economics*, 71, 233–260.

Part III

What Policies Work for the Poorest?

6

Indonesia's Social Protection during and after the Crisis

Sudarno Sumarto, Asep Suryahadi and Sami Bazzi[1]

From pro-poor growth to economic crisis

Before the onset of the economic crisis in mid-1997, Indonesia was one of the most rapidly growing economies in the world. This rapid growth had generated an unprecedented reduction in poverty within a remarkably short period of time.[2] Between 1970 and 1996, absolute poverty fell by around 50 percentage points, accompanied by substantial gains in education and health standards. In the first half of the 1990s, GDP grew at an average annual rate of 7 per cent, and the poverty rate fell dramatically from 32.7 per cent in 1990 to 17.4 per cent by 1996 (Suryadarma *et al.*, 2005).

In mid-1997, after nearly a quarter of century of dramatic growth and welfare gains, a currency crisis struck Indonesia, and by early 1998 the country was suffering from the combined effects of financial, economic and political crises. Within one year, the value of the Rupiah (Rp) fell by 85 per cent, domestic prices rocketed by 78 per cent, nominal food prices increased threefold, and the economy contracted by almost 14 per cent. As the crisis worsened, mass rioting occurred in the capital, Jakarta, and a few other major cities, culminating in May 1998 with the fall of the Suharto government, which had been in power for three decades.

The social impact of the crisis was enormous. The national poverty rate increased from 15 per cent in mid-1997 to 33 per cent by the end of 1998, implying that an additional 36 million people were pushed into absolute poverty because of the crisis.[3] More than half of the increase in poverty between 1996 and 1999 was caused by an increase in chronic poverty, as the proportion of chronic poor within the total population increased from 3.2 per cent to 9.5 per cent during this period.[4] Meanwhile, the proportion of non-poor Indonesian households facing a high probability of falling below the poverty line had increased dramatically, from 6.8 per cent in 1996 to 18.4 per cent in 1999.   The crisis primarily affected the poor and vulnerable non-poor through falling real wages[5] and a drastic increase in the price of basic commodities.[6] (Figure 6.1)

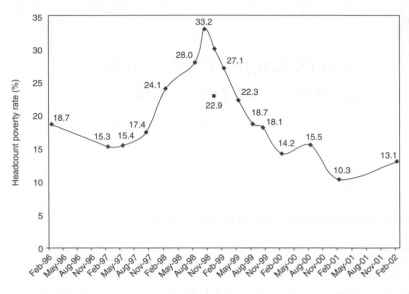

Figure 6.1   The evolution of poverty, 1996–2002
Source: Suryahadi, Sumarto, Pritchett (2003b).

While a general improvement in the macroeconomic environment is *necessary* to reduce vulnerability among the non-poor, it is not always *sufficient*. However, macroeconomic upturns are in most circumstances altogether insufficient to lift the chronic poor from the depths of poverty. To mitigate the adverse social impact of the crisis, the government of Indonesia (GOI) introduced public safety-net programmes aimed at protecting the chronic poor from falling deeper into poverty, and reducing vulnerable households' exposure to risk. The social safety net (SSN) had a four-pronged purpose: (i) to ensure the availability of affordable food; (ii) to improve household purchasing power through employment creation; (iii) to preserve access to critical social services, particularly health and education; and (iv) to sustain local economic activity through regional block grants and the extension of small-scale credit. It was hoped that the implementation of these programmes, widely known as JPS,[7] would prevent or at least significantly reduce the worst effects of the crisis.

Without a clear institutional antecedent, policy-makers faced the daunting task of undertaking these social interventions amid severe political instability and an increasingly inhospitable fiscal environment. In July 1998, with financial support from international donors including the World Bank and Asian Development Bank, the government allocated Rp3.9 trillion directly to JPS programmes out of a total development budget of Rp14.2 trillion. JPS programmes covered education, health, community empowerment and employment creation, in addition to the rice subsidy programme known as OPK. The scope and magnitude of this social protection initiative was simply unprecedented in Indonesian history. In the turbulent years after Suharto's fall, incumbent administrations strongly emphasized poverty reduction.[8] While maintaining some JPS programmes in the years after the crisis, the government also aimed to restructure the grossly regressive fuel subsidies (BBM)[9] and to channel budgetary savings into targeted social protection and poverty alleviation programmes. On several occasions after 2000, the government reduced BBM subsidies and subsequently reallocated a portion of the savings to social programmes, known as PKPS-BBM.[10] Alongside dramatic cutbacks in March and October 2005, the government implemented a substantial compensation package including unconditional cash transfers, health support, educational assistance and infrastructure development programmes. In drawing lessons from the JPS and PKPS-BBM programmes, policy-makers and researchers today are striving to create a more efficient, equitable and coherent social protection policy. The goal is not merely to provide risk-coping mechanisms in response to crises but also to institute sustainable programmes that support intergenerational pathways out of poverty. While the targeting of the SSN programmes has been called into question by numerous authors, without such programmes social welfare would not have recovered in such a relatively short time. Several JPS programmes generated clear welfare improvements at the household and aggregate level, and by 2002 many of the worst welfare losses had been reversed as the poverty rate fell to 12.2 per cent, even below pre-crisis levels. The PKPS-BBM programmes have since helped to maintain these post-crisis gains despite periodic bouts of economic volatility and, more importantly, have enabled the central government to move gradually into a more progressive public spending regime. Today, however, Indonesia's budgetary allocations to social and human development priorities still remain among the lowest in South East Asia as a proportion of GDP, and its policy-makers face a critical trade-off between further repairing the state budget and making necessary social investments.

This chapter draws on the work of several studies that have analysed carefully Indonesia's experience with social protection during and after the financial crisis. The chapter is organized as follows. The second section addresses the role of informal social protection in Indonesia. The third section assesses the policies and programmes implemented during and immediately after the crisis years. The fourth section highlights the policies and programmes of the post-crisis period, focusing on the efforts since 2000 to replace generalized fuel subsidies with targeted social programmes. In the third and fourth sections we also assess the impact of the various programmes. The fifth section concludes with a set of insights on the lessons learnt and the way forward for social protection in Indonesia.

Informal social protection

During the pre-crisis high-growth period, government-run SSN programmes were almost non-existent in Indonesia. The general anti-poverty strategy at that time included (i) general social spending on health, family planning and education; (ii) development programmes aimed at increasing productivity among the poor; and (iii) some small programmes for disadvantaged groups such as disabled people and orphans. There were also mandatory social security and health insurance schemes for employees in medium-sized and large enterprises, the civil service and the military. However, these schemes proved to be largely ineffective during the crisis because they excluded most of the population, and in particular the poor, as 65 per cent of Indonesian workers are to be found in the informal sector, where compulsory social security schemes do not apply.[11]

It is important to understand that the Indonesian people were not merely passive victims of the crisis. Given that citizens had never relied to any significant extent on public safety net programmes in the past, they set up many of their own private coping measures. Household surveys conducted during the crisis revealed three main coping strategies: reducing expenditure; borrowing; and/or attempting to increase income. Clothing and recreation expenditures were cut most frequently, followed by transportation; not to mention reductions in the quality or, in some instances, even the quantity of food. Some households maintained expenditures by borrowing or selling assets. Meanwhile, households were able to increase their income by taking additional jobs, working longer hours, or increasing the number of family members who were working. In fact, children often augmented family income by engaging in labour activities *in addition to* attending school.[12]

Several researchers have found evidence in Indonesia of what Ravallion and Dearden (1988) initially identified as a moral economy in which the distributional outcomes of traditional government-run social programmes might be achieved through private giving between families and within communities. The progressiveness of private transfers can be discerned in 1999 SUSENAS data with nearly 75 per cent of households in the poorest quintile having received transfers that comprise as much 20 per cent of household expenditures (Sumarto *et al.*, 2005). Drawing on Townsend's (1994) hypothesis that the presence of insurance mechanisms cushioning the impact of idiosyncratic shocks on household consumption can be inferred from observing that changes in consumption among rural households are largely determined by what happens to the rest of the village, Sumarto *et al.* (2005) found a partial insurance effect among Indonesian households during the crisis. In contrast to Townsend's findings for India, their estimates suggest that village-level income shocks were associated with only partial reductions in household consumption, pointing to some inter- and/or intra-household insurance or redistributive mechanism at work.[13] Undoubtedly this "moral economy" complemented official JPS programmes in limiting the worst effects of the crisis.

Social policy objectives and programme implementation during the crisis

The JPS programmes operated in five major sectors: food security; employment creation; education; health; and community empowerment. While different sectoral ministries and agencies designed and implemented each of the programmes, the government also established a team tasked specifically with monitoring overall implementation. The team was headed by the National Development Planning Agency (BAPPENAS) at the central level, and by the provincial and district development planning boards at the local level. Table 6.1 summarizes the objectives, intended magnitude, geographical coverage, benefits provided, eligibility, source of funding, and targeting of the major SSN programmes.

Table 6.1 Social safety net programmes in Indonesia during the economic crisis

Programme	Description of benefits	FY 1998/9 budget (Rp billions)	Planned coverage	Targeting in fiscal year 1998/9
OPK (subsidized rice)	Sales of subsidized rice to targeted households	5,450	12.8 million KPS and KSI households	Geographic: BKKBN pre-prosperous rates Household: BKKBN list
Padat karya programmes (employment creation)	A loose, uncoordinated collection of several "labour-intensive" programmes in a variety of government departments	2,066	12.7 million man-days	Geographic: None Household: Weak self-selection by wage rate
SBG (scholarships and block grants to schools)	Providing scholarships directly to elementary, lower secondary, and upper secondary students and block grants to selected schools	1,138	6% of primary, 17% of lower secondary, 10% of upper secondary school students 60% of schools	Geographic: Data on enrolment in 1997 Household: By school committees

Continued

Table 6.1   Continued

Programme	Description of benefits	FY 1998/9 budget (Rp billions)	Planned coverage	Targeting in fiscal year 1998/9
SSN-BK (health cards)	Providing subsidies for medical services, operational support for health centres, medicine and imported medical equipment, family planning services, supplemental food, midwife services	1,043	7.4 million KPS households	**Geographic:** BKKBN pre-prosperous rates **Household:** BKKBN list
PDM-DKE (community empowerment)	Block grants for villages for public works, or revolving funds for credit	1,701	Almost all villages in the country	**Geographic:** 1997 data on district poverty rate **Household:** Local decision-making

Food security

The government initially introduced the rice subsidy programme (OPK) in July 1998 to ensure continued access among the poor to affordable rice, the basic staple food for the majority of Indonesians. After a successful pilot programme in Jakarta, the programme was expanded to the rest of the country. Programme guidelines initially allowed eligible households to purchase ten kilograms of rice per month at a highly subsidized price of Rp1,000/kg, compared to an average market price of Rp3,000/kg for medium-quality rice.[14] In April 1999, officials increased the benefit to 20kg and then revised it downward again to between 10kg and 20kg a year later.

The OPK programme was the largest and arguably the most critical component of the SSN programmes during the crisis. The initial target population included around 7.4 million households, or roughly 15 per cent of all households in the country. By far the most important commodity for poor households, rice comprises nearly a quarter of average monthly expenditure in poor households, contributing 34 per cent and 26 per cent to the official rural and urban poverty lines, respectively. Initially, only households in the lowest category of the official poverty classification of the National Family Planning Agency (BKKBN) were eligible to participate in the programme, but coverage was expanded to include the second-lowest category during the course of the year.[15] Geographical targeting was conducted according to regional poverty rates derived from aggregate BKKBN data.

At the community level, however, where village governments were responsible for implementation, administrative guidelines often proved to be socially unacceptable. In distributing the benefits, local village leaders generally did not adhere to the list of eligible households, which they argued were an inaccurate reflection of village welfare distribution. By mid-1999, over 50 per cent of households in all but the richest quintile reported receiving OPK rice.

Mistargeting or elite capture do not fully explain leakages. Village officials locally corrected the official eligibility criteria, but it is also possible that local social pressures led to uniform distribution as the only fair, and hence politically acceptable, allocation. The danger was that the poor received fewer benefits than were intended. Some researchers suggest that this outcome (i) might have been necessary to achieve the requisite socio-political equilibrium[16]; or (ii) might have protected those vulnerable near-poor in villages where the official distinction between poor and non-poor, as reflected in the eligibility roster, proved to be rather arbitrary.

Although poor households were targeted explicitly, the programme also admitted an element of implicit self-selection by restricting the quality of OPK rice to medium-quality rather than the higher quality traditionally purchased by wealthier households. However, as Figure 6.2 suggests, neither explicit nor implicit targeting were effective in limiting programme participation to the poor. In 2001, 20.2 million households received subsidized rice, nearly double the target population, and yet only 52.6 per cent of the poor participated.[17] To account for mounting criticism and perhaps the de facto distributional incidence, the official eligibility criteria were expanded to include both the lowest and the second-lowest BKKBN welfare categories. In mid-2001, programme planners also introduced a set of primarily cosmetic changes, including the new, ambitious programme title of *Raskin*, or "rice for the poor." The *Raskin* programme remained the most extensive SSN programme to mid-2005. Many experts and policy-makers have questioned the wisdom of continuing the programme without substantial reforms to Indonesia's rice production and import policies – a persistent source of consumption volatility for poor households.

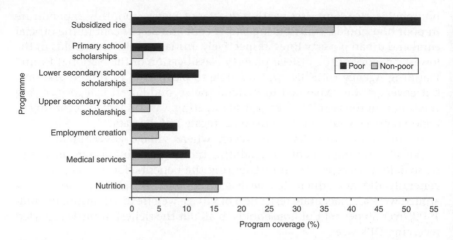

Figure 6.2   JPS programme coverage rates among the poor and non-poor population
Source: Sumarto, Suryahadi, and Widyanti (2005).

Employment creation

A large component of the JPS was the employment creation programme, known as *padat karya*, launched in late 1997 and funded primarily through the state budget to the tune of Rp2.1 billion. By FY1998/9, sixteen different programmes were operating under the "employment creation" category. Under severe budget pressure, the only avenue for securing continued funding for labour programmes was to reclassify these programmes as "labour creating" in the hope of qualifying for JPS funding (Pritchett *et al.*, 2002: 20). By FY1999/2000 the *padat karya* programmes were reduced to two: a public works programme; and a special initiative for unemployed women. The dynamic benefit incidence of the labour programmes fared better than other JPS programmes in health and education, largely as a result of the self-selection mechanism, which naturally responds to welfare changes more effectively than do administratively assigned benefits.[18] In this regard, the labour programmes may have reached effectively not only the chronic poor but also vulnerable near-poor households facing transitory shocks.

Health sector

Anticipating a deterioration in public and family health as a result of the crisis, the government established SSN programmes in the health sector, known as JPS-BK programmes.[19] The programmes consisted of a targeted consumer price subsidy, nutritional supplements, and operational support for public health facilities and village midwives. These programmes were aimed at enabling public health providers to maintain the quality and availability of services, and poor households to afford the higher costs of medical care. Based on BKKBN criteria, irrespective of health status, eligible poor households received health cards, which could be used to obtain medical services free of charge at public health clinics.[20] By February 1999, approximately 22 million Indonesian households had at least one health card. Programme planners in Jakarta allocated operational grants to providers based on the *predicted* number of poor in the area served by the respective facility or midwife organization. The bulk of these funds went towards the procurement of medical supplies (Sparrow, 2006: 44).

Impact evaluations of the health programme produced mixed findings. First, targeting was progressive, as the poorest two quintiles received nearly 60 per cent of the health cards. Roughly 18.5 per cent of the poorest quintile received health cards compared to only 3.7 per cent of households in the richest quintile.[21] Despite the pro-poor distribution of the cards, the actual utilization of them for outpatient care paled in comparison with the quantity of cards distributed. The low utilization rates among recipients were probably attributable to the same constraints the poor face in non-crisis times, including high time and travel costs to reach health facilities as well as limited access to information regarding health service quality and availability.[22] The high rate of underutilization also reflected the weak linkage between the disbursement of health cards and the allocation of operational grants.

PDM-DKE community empowerment

The PDM-DKE programme, an acronym for "regional empowerment in order to overcome the impact of the crisis," provided funds to villages across Indonesia. The size of disbursements ranged from Rp10 million for relatively well-off villages to Rp1 billion for the poorest villages. The programme permitted maximum discretion at the local level with regard to the use of funds. The decisions about who benefited were left entirely in the hands of the lowest-level village governing body known as the Village Community Resilience Institution (LKMD).[23] Since the official guidelines on targeting were sufficiently general, almost any decision could have been justified as being consistent with the programme.

Officially, the programme had three goals: (i) to improve the purchasing power of the poor through employment creation; (ii) to jump-start economic production and distribution systems through the development of socioeconomic infrastructure; and (iii) to preserve the physical environment. In practice, the majority of communities, by way of consensus, utilized the funds for physical infrastructure development and maintenance, and for employment generation through subsidized credit schemes.

Since the PDM-DKE programme was implemented as a "crisis programme," local officials often made decisions without adequate time for a proper public information campaign, training of programme administrators, or community consensus-building. In some communities, PDM-DKE appears to have reached the poor reasonably effectively, while in other locations the local community had never heard of the programme, suggesting poor socialization and/or local capture.

Education

In the early stages of the crisis, there was a concern that parents might be pressured to withdraw their children from schools as a way of coping with falling income and rising costs, hence triggering a large increase in dropout rates.[24] This rightly alarmed the government, which responded by establishing an educational funding programme in the academic year 1998/9.

The JPS education programme included scholarships for students from poor families, and block grants for schools to facilitate continued operations. Not unlike the *Progresa* programme in Mexico, the JPS scholarships provided cash to students from poor households as an increasing function of enrolment level, with Rp10,000, Rp20,000 and Rp30,000 per month for primary (SD), junior secondary (SMP), and upper secondary (SMA) school students, respectively. Monthly expenditure on education per student was Rp4,900, Rp16,100, and Rp30,400 for primary, junior secondary and senior secondary students respectively in the 1997/8 school year.[25] The scholarships covered nearly 8 per cent of average monthly per capita expenditure among recipient households in the poorest quintile.[26] The programme aimed to reach at most 6 per cent of primary school students, 17 per cent of lower secondary school students, and 10 per cent of upper secondary school students nationwide. This particular targeting distribution is consistent with new research demonstrating that the probability of dropping out is highest among students at the cusp of primary and junior secondary school, and particularly in the early years of junior secondary enrolment in Indonesia (Suryadarma *et al.*, 2006). Meanwhile, 60 per cent of schools in each district were to receive operational grants (DBO), which could be used to purchase school materials, make physical repairs and cover other operational costs.

The official targeting mechanism consisted of three stages. The scholarship recipients were selected using a range of criteria, including household data from school records, family BKKBN status, household size, and the likelihood of the student to drop out. In the first stage, scholarships were allocated to districts based on a poverty index constructed from 1996 SUSENAS. Subsequently, district committees decided on the amount of scholarship funds to allocate to schools, based on three criteria: (i) the number of poor students according to BKKBN household status; (ii) percentage of IDT-eligible villages; and (iii) average school fees. In the final stage, JPS committees at each school[27] allocated scholarships to students based on BKKBN status, household structure, distance from school, and gender. Half of the scholarships were to be distributed to girls, and in fact, girls received more scholarships than boys at all three levels of schooling (Sparrow, 2006: 35). Given that primary school attendance in grades 1–3 is relatively income inelastic in Indonesia, students in these grades were deemed to be ineligible for the scholarships. Allocation committees were also permitted to target students who had already dropped out of school. To all intents and purposes, the programme operated as a quasi-conditional cash transfer. Although monitored very loosely, receipt of the scholarships did require continuing enrolment and a passing grade, but there were no formal conditions on school attendance or how the funds could be used.

Although programme coverage of the poor was rather limited, the scholarship programme generated welfare improvements at both household and aggregate levels. Household recipients of JPS scholarships experienced a substantial increase in consumption almost 10 per cent higher than similar non-recipient households (Sumarto *et al.*, 2005). Despite the severity of the impact of the crisis on household welfare, large-scale drop-outs were prevented. Although the JPS scholarships only reached 4.96 per cent of all students in primary, junior and senior secondary schools in the first year, strong econometric evidence suggests that the programme succeeded in returning enrolment to pre-crisis levels, especially for primary school-age children in rural areas. Approximately 13 per cent of JPS recipients would have dropped out of school if they had not received the scholarship, yielding an increase in overall enrolment of 0.6 per cent.[28] Unlike the JPS health programmes, though, the demand-side (scholarships) had a larger impact on enrolment than did the supply-side (DBO operational grants) (Sparrow, 2006, Appendix 5B: 122–3). By raising the reservation wage of poor students, a reservation wage is the minimum wage that would induce some people/ groups to work, the JPS programme reduced the use of child labour as a consumption-smoothing mechanism in recipient households.[29]

Social protection after the crisis: replacing a regressive commodity subsidy with an anti-poverty programme

In mid-2000, policy-makers launched the first phase in a long-drawn-out process of fuel (BBM) subsidy cutbacks. Increased in May 1998, the fuel subsidy drastically reduced the cost of fuel products relative to international prices. The subsidy was highly regressive in absolute terms in that the majority of cumulative benefits accrued to non-poor households. The subsidy was only mildly progressive in relative terms in that BBM, particularly kerosene, comprised a slightly larger proportion of total expenditures among poorer households. It was primarily a result of political expediency, though, that governments did not reduce the subsidy on kerosene substantially until several years later in the context of more dramatic overall price adjustments.

After cutting the fuel subsidy by roughly 12 per cent in October 2000, the government reallocated Rp800 billion in savings to a package of short-term compensatory programmes (PDPSE),[30] including cash transfers, revolving funds, and community empowerment programmes aimed at employment generation.

Over the next several years, successive governments gradually increased the price of BBM and began to experiment with new compensation packages (PKPS-BBM).[31] During this period, policy-makers implemented new programmes in health and education.[32] Despite gradual cutbacks, though, no government was willing to make adjustments on the required order of magnitude.

After nearly a year in office, President Susilo Bambang Yudhoyono (SBY) had amassed sufficient political legitimacy to launch the first massive reduction of the fuel subsidy since the crisis had begun eight years prior. By 2006, spending on fuel subsidies absorbed nearly 2.9 per cent of GDP (or Rp76.5 trillion) in the revised budget for 2005. In March 2005, the government raised the price of fuel products by a weighted average of 29 per cent and promised to reallocate half of the expected savings to a compensation fund worth Rp11 trillion comprising health, education and infrastructure programmes (World Bank, 2005: 19). Five months later, the government boldly slashed the BBM subsidy again, extending the cutbacks to premium gasoline, automotive diesel and household kerosene. The subsequent potential shocks to the economy in general, and to household purchasing power in particular, were clear to policy-makers.[33] The pressing challenge for the government was to reallocate resources swiftly to social programmes so as to mitigate the impact of the price shock on welfare.

On 1 October 2005, the government launched its most ambitious social protection programme to date, an unconditional direct cash transfer programme (BLT).[34] Prior to the October price hike, the government had already allocated Rp5 trillion to education, Rp3 trillion to health and Rp3 trillion to infrastructure. Initial estimates placed the expected savings from the October subsidy cut at Rp25 trillion, and the government planned to allocate Rp4.7 trillion to the first of four quarterly tranches of the BLT programme. The first tranche aimed to reach 15.5 million households, or approximately 62 million people, making the transfer programme the largest of its kind in the world.

In the remainder of this chapter, we shall address the implementation of the primary PKPS-BBM programmes, namely the BLT, health and education.

Health

In August 2003, the government launched the JPK-Gakin[35] programme in the health sector. Financing for the programme came primarily from two sources: PKPS-BBM compensation and special regional budgetary allocations (DAU). General programme guidelines stipulated that poor households receive guarantees (in the form of health cards) for free health services at public health clinics and hospitals. While evidence suggests that hospital utilization among beneficiaries has been low,[36] this was the first time that a safety net programme in the health sector guaranteed hospital services for the poor. In early 2005, the government allocated approximately Rp3.87 trillion of PKPS-BBM funds to expand and strengthen the JPK-Gakin programme. The programme initially aimed to provide 12 million households with health service guarantees worth Rp5,000 per person per month.

Two unique aspects of the JPS-Gakin programme set it apart from the previous JPS health card programme. First, district governments had the flexibility to design targeting and benefits schemes. In Tabanan district, Bali, for example, officials undertook their own data collection on poor households, drawing up a different list of recipients from BPS, which they viewed as being too subjective. In Purbalinnga district, East Java, officials designed separate insurance schemes for poor, previously poor and non-poor, with the co-payment increasing with welfare status. Second, the programme planners in Jakarta established Management Units (Bapel) tasked with overseeing local design and implementation in each district, and in late 2004 the government also authorized PT Askes, a for-profit public health insurance corporation with little experience in implementing safety net programmes, to provide JPK-Gakin benefits alongside the Bapel. This created a competitive process among service providers with two rather different modus operandi. At the end of 2005, regional governments were asked to evaluate the two institutions and determine whether to continue using only one of the providers or both simultaneously.

Education

In the 2001/2 academic year, the government utilized PKPS-BBM funds to implement a new scholarship programme (BKM)[37] for students in primary, junior and senior secondary schools. Operating alongside the JPS scholarships programme, the BKM programme provided scholarships to far more students and stipulated how scholarship funds could be spent. Nearly 20 per cent of SD students and 26 per cent of SMP students received scholarships in 2004 (Hastuti *et al.*, 2006). School committees were asked to designate eligibility based on flexible criteria similar to JPS. School administrators could direct scholarship funds towards any of the following: (i) monthly tuition; (ii) purchase of schoolbooks or other supplies; (iii) transportation costs; and (iv) daily living costs.

After the March 2005 subsidy cutbacks, the government developed a new educational assistance programme, known as the school operational assistance programme (BOS) for the 2005/6 academic year. As part of a government initiative to achieve nine years of compulsory education for all children, the Ministry of Education (MOE) had calculated that Rp50 trillion would be required annually to provide free primary and junior secondary schooling. The BOS programme targeted SD and SMP schools, and unlike the DBO-JPS operational grants that went to the poorest 60 per cent of schools in each district, the BOS programme provided funds to all schools across the archipelago. Alongside BOS, education planners refocused the BKM programme on SMA schools, increasing the scholarship size to Rp60,000/month for nearly 700,000 senior secondary school students. BOS planners allocated approximately Rp5.136 trillion to all public and private schools based on the total enrolment at each school. SD schools received Rp23,5000 per student, and SMP schools received Rp324,500 per student per year for approximately 39.6 million total students.

In contrast to the BKM/JPS programmes, which provided scholarship funds directly to poor students, BOS funds were provided to schools to be managed in accordance with requirements laid down by Jakarta. In practice, the BOS programme functioned as a generalized education subsidy targeting both supply- and demand-side outcomes. While Indonesia has ensured significant achievements in maintaining high primary and junior secondary enrolment rates since the crisis, many have questioned whether there have been quantity–quality trade-offs. The BOS programme addressed supply-side weaknesses directly by advancing the quality and quantity of educational resources, particularly in the form of better-paid teachers and more abundant school supplies available to students.

Field research by SMERU indicates that poor students benefited – but not substantially – from the BOS programme.[38] In the SMERU study of forty-three schools across five provinces, only 23 per cent of students received special assistance by way of BOS funds. Ultimately, the BOS programme generated clear benefits to schools with extremely limited sources of revenue. In some primary schools, BOS funds led to a near tripling of school revenue, allowing schools to purchase writing utensils, supplementary teaching tools and textbooks, as well as to pay the salaries of temporary teachers.

Unconditional cash transfer

The widely publicized unconditional cash transfer programme provided nearly a quarter of Indonesian households with Rp300,000 per household every three months from October 2005 to October 2006. Given the time and administrative constraints facing policy-makers, the programme unfolded rather smoothly. Crude simulations initially suggested that the proposed subsidy cuts would induce a 5.5 per cent increase in poverty in the absence of a transfer programme.[39] Although the magnitude of real income shocks varied widely across regions, according to BPS figures, the poverty headcount rate only increased by roughly 2 per cent (to 18.2 per cent) in 2005. In general, the BLT programme was an effective and equity-enhancing means of reallocating savings from the BBM subsidy cutbacks.

Targeting took place in four stages. First, BPS officials met with village leaders and cross-checked other data sources to establish an initial roster. Second, BPS enumerators interviewed the individual households on the roster to determine final eligibility according to fourteen qualitative household variables correlated with welfare status.[40] Third, the government generated household welfare rankings based on the outcomes of a proxy means test. In the final stage, budgetary quotas for total BLT recipients in each sub-district were set according to regional welfare rankings and the BPS Poverty Map of 2000. Targeting at the sub-district level was quite accurate, while the most significant mistargeting took place at the household level.[41] The primary causes of mistargeting were (i) local capture by relatively well-off households tied to local officials; and (ii) weak proxy indicators in the household survey. This was the first time in Indonesian history that proxy means tests had been used to target poor households in a national SSN programme. Although the fourteen proxies used by official enumerators moved beyond the limitations of previous BKKBN targeting criteria, they ultimately failed to capture sufficient variation between poor and non-poor households, particularly in areas where there was a concentration of households around the poverty line.

In subsequent tranches, the government expanded the number of eligible households significantly, from 15.5 million to approximately 19.2 million households, partly as a response to the overwhelming number of supplementary eligibility requests. Drawing on continued savings flows from the subsidy cutbacks, the government was able to diffuse these social and political pressures directly by expanding outreach. The swift implementation of the BLT programme ensured the irreversibility of the October 2005 subsidy cutbacks despite the high potential for popular backlash. A basic political economy model suggests that the post-crisis Indonesian approach of gradual subsidy reductions coupled with compensation programmes reduced the likelihood of the policy reversals that took place in several countries of the Middle East and North Africa, where governments attempted drastic subsidy cuts in one fell swoop.[42]

By most accounts, the BLT programme prevented the drastic increase in poverty many had predicted in the period leading up to October 2005. Nearly 27.1 per cent of Indonesian households received BLT funds in late 2005, and the programme was relatively well targeted to the poor. However, targeting was more pro-poor in urban areas, where 28.2 per cent of programme benefits reached the poorest decile, compared to only 17.5 per cent in rural areas.[43] This differential reflects the relative ease of targeting in urban areas, where the distinction between poor and non-poor is more striking than in rural areas, where the majority of poor Indonesians reside. The programme reached 55.6 per cent of households in the poorest decile and 39.4 per cent in the second-poorest decile.

The government has subsequently justified the targeting outcomes on the grounds that the programme aimed to reach not only poor households but also those vulnerable to poverty. Between February 2005 and March 2006 – the period during which the BBM subsidy was slashed on two occasions and PKPS-BBM programmes were introduced – 56.5 per cent of initially poor households remained poor, 19.4 per cent moved to near-poor, 17.7 per cent to near-non-poor, and 6.5 escaped poverty altogether, moving to non-poor.[44] Meanwhile, only 6 per cent of non-poor households in February 2005 became poor or near-poor a year later. The BLT funds constituted a significant proportion of monthly expenditure for the poorest households, covering 24 per cent of average monthly household expenditures in rural areas and 17 per cent in urban areas among households in the poorest decile. Furthermore, survey evidence suggests that, for certain households, the funds were sufficient to cover not only consumption goods but also some health and education expenditure.[45]

In retrospect, the BLT programme addressed three fundamental concerns of any social planner: (i) to ensure poor households do not fall deeper into poverty as a result of income/purchasing power shocks; (ii) to protect near- and non-poor households from slipping into poverty; and, most ambitiously, (iii) to promote welfare improvements among poor households, pushing them to higher expenditure gradients. Today, the challenge is to integrate an incentive structure into the transfer programme in order to generate and maintain the human capital investments vital for sustained growth and poverty reduction. Careful restructuring of existing targeting and transfer arrangements will be required to secure the potential gains of a more equitable and efficient cash transfer programme.

Lessons learned and the way forward for social protection in Indonesia

As policy-makers and researchers in Indonesia look to the future of social planning, careful stocktaking of past programmes has yielded a number of revealing findings. Social protection is always a dynamic and complex challenge, but the Indonesian experience since the financial crisis has demonstrated the central importance of careful planning and learning-by-doing. As the BLT programme neared its final stages in mid-2006, policy-makers were busy formulating a new approach to social protection *and* poverty reduction in the form of a conditional cash transfer (CCT) programme uniting the disparate health, education and cash transfer components of the PKPS-BBM programme. At the time of writing, the pilot programme was scheduled for launch in early to mid-2007. Table 6.2 compares major social protection programmes in Indonesia during and after the crisis. What are the primary lessons to be drawn?

On balance, the JPS programmes prevented the crisis from generating the full sweep of welfare losses that would have been expected under such rapid erosion of purchasing power and widespread unemployment. With limited prior institutional grounding for formal social protection programmes, the government utilized existing village-level institutions including BKKBN cadre, health clinic administrators, school committees

Table 6.2 Areas and major programmes of Indonesia's social safety net during and after the crisis

Safety net area	Crisis 1997–9	Post-crisis 2000–6
Food security	Special Market Operation (OPK) programme: sales of 10–20kg of subsidized rice to targeted households	Rice for the Poor (*Raskin*) programme: continuation of OPK with expanded eligibility rosters
Employment creation	*Padat karya*: a loose, uncoordinated collection of several "labour intensive" programmes in a variety of government departments	
Education	JPS scholarships and school block grants (DBO) providing • Scholarships directly to elementary (SD), junior secondary (SMP), and senior secondary (SMA) students • Block grants to selected schools	BKM scholarships and school operational assistance (BOS) programme providing • Scholarships directly to SD, SMA and SMP students • Block grants supporting operational costs and massive tuition reductions for students
Health	Health sector SSN (JPS-BK): a programme providing subsidies for • Medical services • Operational support for health centres • Medicine and imported medical equipment • Family planning services • Nutrition (supplemental food) • Midwife services	Health service guarantees for poor families (JPS-*Gakin*): subsidized health services for poor families at primary and tertiary care facilities
Community empowerment	Regional Empowerment to Overcome the Impact of Economic Crisis (PDM-DKE): a 'community fund' programme providing block grants directly to villages for either public works or a revolving fund for subsidized credit	PDPSE community empowerment and revolving funds support programmes Infrastructure development programme, PKPS-BBM 2005
Cash transfer		Direct cash transfer programme (BLT): unconditional cash transfers of Rp300,000 every three months to targeted households

and local government officials to implement the education, health, community empowerment and rice subsidy programmes. Meanwhile, existing public works programmes expanded in scope and readjusted hiring policies to reach some of the newly unemployed. Participation in all of the JPS programmes, apart from the small nutrition component of the health programmes and subsidized credit programmes, helped to increase household consumption (Sumarto *et al.*, 2005). The OPK programme was particularly effective in ensuring staple food intake among poor households. Despite considerable under-coverage, the JPS scholarship and block grant programme helped to sustain enrolment at pre-crisis levels and may have even reduced the time allocated to child labour by school-age children.

A notable feature of the initial SSN programmes in Indonesia was the heterogeneity of targeting performance across programmes and regions. The major factors contributing to variation in programme outcomes include differences in (i) programme design; (ii) the scale of budget allocations across regions; and (iii) local institutional capacity. In the OPK programme's early stages, more than half of all poor households in Indonesia reported receiving benefit from it,[46] while more than a third of non-poor households also reported receiving some benefit.

When designing targeting mechanisms, it is necessary to consider that the vulnerable and chronic poor may respond differently to different types of welfare-enhancing interventions. The actual sources of vulnerability ultimately matter most when designing effective interventions. Vulnerability related to low mean consumption prospects, which tends to predominate in rural areas, might best be addressed through cash transfer programmes. On the other hand, vulnerability caused by consumption volatility, a relatively more common finding among the urban population, might best be addressed through *ex ante* interventions aimed at consumption smoothing (Chaudhuri *et al.*, 2001). In the final analysis, improvements in targeting will require not only finer methodological innovations but also strong political will and public institutional support.

The PKPS-BBM programmes launched in 2003 built on the lessons of previous programmes. Given the large and flexible budget funded primarily by flows of savings because of BBM subsidy cutbacks, the PKPS programmes achieved a degree of national coverage that was not possible for the JPS programmes. This established credibility among stakeholders at all levels of government. In terms of management and implementation, programme outcomes depend centrally on whether (i) the distribution of funds is timely; (ii) the programmes are well co-ordinated both horizontally and vertically; and (iii) the programmes are sufficiently and properly socialized.

The success of the CCT in improving household welfare and sustaining human capital investments will depend on getting the incentives "right."[47]

The JPS scholarships programme concentrated resources on junior secondary schools, because this education level is where the likelihood of attrition is highest. Also, the variable size of scholarships in both the JPS and BKM programmes reflected the higher opportunity costs of post-primary education. Arguably, the CCT could set variable transfer sizes according to individual household scores on a range of proxy welfare indicators. In North Sulawesi province, several schools actually applied a targeting design along these lines by calibrating the amount of BOS funds allocated to poor students based on the distance each student lived from school. With sufficiently rich data and administrative capacity, planners can improve programme efficiency by determining eligibility and transfer size simultaneously. Policy-makers should target households with the highest likelihood of responding to the induced conditionality. It is these households for which marginal income improvements enable greater investments in health and education.

Indonesia's social protection policy since the late 1990s reflects a clear progression towards greater equity and efficiency. The JPS programmes set the stage for the institutionalization of an SSN framework at all levels of governance. In subsequent years, policy-makers utilized the *Raskin* programme and introduced new safety net programmes to manage a gradual transition away from regressive fuel subsidies. Throughout this process, we have seen a steady growth in progressive public spending. Certainly, the government of Indonesia has an obligation to intervene in protecting the most vulnerable members of Indonesian society against the pernicious effects of market failures, many of which are driven by the inability of poor households to articulate demand for social services through formal market mechanisms. In the final analysis, though, the fate of the poor hinges on factors other than improved targeting and an appropriately calibrated conditionality. A truly sustainable reduction in poverty requires deeper investment in rural areas where the majority of the poor live, a reduction in the instability of food commodity (in particular, rice) prices, serious labour market reforms *and* a secure financing scheme for a permanent social safety net for poor households. An equitable and efficient social safety net is one of the vital mechanisms to halting the intergenerational transmission of poverty. Sustainable social protection is no easy task, but Indonesia's policy-makers undoubtedly have both the tools and the experience to emerge as a leader among developing countries in an increasingly crisis-prone global economy.

Notes

1. This chapter is based on several papers co-authored with Lant Pritchett, Emmanuel Skoufias and Wenefrida Widyanti. We are grateful to BPS and UNICEF for the use of data. Sudarno would like to thank Edward Anderson for

his constructive suggestions, and participants at the workshop in Addis Ababa on "Addressing Inequalities: Policies for Inclusive Development" made helpful comments. The authors retain responsibility for errors. A full listing of publications by SMERU researchers and co-authors can be found on the SMERU Research Institute website: www.smeru.or.id

2. See Timmer (2004) for a detailed history of Indonesia's pro-poor growth.

3. The poverty rate increased by 164 per cent from the onset of the crisis in mid-1997 to the end of 1998. Suryahadi *et al.* (2003) produced poverty figures consistent throughout the duration of the crisis. These figures differ from official figures published by BPS based on annual SUSENAS data, which generated poverty lines based on incomparable consumption baskets across the crisis years.

4. Generally, the chronic poor include those households whose expected future consumption levels fall below the poverty line, while the transient poor have expected consumption above the poverty line. See Suryahadi and Sumarto (2003) for a detailed technical exploration.

5. Real wages were estimated to have fallen by around a third between August 1997 and August 1998. See Manning (2000) and Feridhanusetyawan (1999).

6. According to World Bank estimates, the price of rice rose by 180 per cent, while prices of non-food items rose by 80 per cent between February 1996 and February 1999.

7. *Jaring pengaman social* (social safety net).

8. In December 2001 under the leadership of the Co-ordinating Ministers for Social Welfare and the Economy, the government established the inter-ministerial Committee for Poverty Alleviation, to steer national development policy in a pro-poor direction.

9. In Indonesia, *bahan bakar minyak (BBM)* refers primarily to three fuel products: kerosene, automotive diesel and gasoline.

10. Program Kompensasi Pengurangan Subsidi Bahan Bakar Minyak, Fuel Subsidy Reduction Compensation Programme.

11. Authors' calculations using the National Labor Force Survey, *Sakernas*.

12. See Suryahadi *et al.* (2005) on the determinants of child labour in Indonesia during the crisis.

13. Estimations indicate that a 10 per cent change in household income results in a 3 per cent change in consumption, while a 10 per cent change in the village cluster mean income results in only a 1.5 per cent change in consumption.

14. In the period October–November 1998, the market price for medium-quality rice was Rp2,500/kg.

15. The official classification was created by the national family planning agency (BKKBN), which groups households into five welfare status: "pre-prosperous households" ("*keluarga pra-sejahtera*" or KPS), "prosperous I households" ("*keluarga sejahtera* I" or KS I), KS II, KSIII and KS III+. Every year, BKKBN conducts a census on households all over the country and, based on the data collected, classifies households into the five welfare categories using 23 indicators. For example, a household is defined as a KPS household if it fails to satisfy the first five indicators: (i) all household members are able to practice their religious principles; (ii) all household members are able to eat at least twice a day; (iii) all household members have different sets of clothing for home, work, school and visits; (iv) the largest floor area of house is not made of earth; and (v) the household is able to seek modern medical assistance for sick children, and family planning services for contraceptive users.

16. See Gelbach and Pritchett (1997) and Pritchett (2005) for an articulation of this hypothesis.
17. Hastuti and Maxwell (2002) provide a detailed account of the evolution of the OPK and *Raskin* programmes.
18. See Suryahadi *et al.* (2003a) on the dynamic benefit incidence of the *padat karya* and OPK programmes.
19. JPS *bidang kesehatan* (JPS health sector).
20. Soelaksano *et al.* (1999) find that,, in many cases, poor non-recipients were also able to obtain a health card directly from service providers after seeking medical care.
21. Using the 100 Villages Survey, we found greater leakage in the health card programme during 1999 than did Sparrow (2006) using the SUSENAS JPS Module.
22. There are two other potential explanations for low utilization rates. The first is that households refrained from using the health cards when obtaining medical service because they perceived such services to be inferior. Another straightforward explanation is that the SUSENAS survey was conducted only a few months after the majority of the health cards had been distributed, leaving a only short time window in which households could utilize health services, the expenditure on which is generally more sporadic than on education or food. The fact that health cards were to be distributed to the poor irrespective of health status supports this hypothesis.
23. These institutions consisted of basically unelected representatives at the village level.
24. Sparrow (2006) cites the following findings on the educational response to the crisis: Cameron and Worswick (2001) find that households smoothed consumption by reducing expenditure on education, particularly for girls in rural households, in response to crop loss, while Frankenberg *et al.* (2003) found that households smoothed consumption by reducing expenditure on education and health during the crisis by as much as 37 per cent. Thomas *et al.* (2004) found that household spending on education declined by 19 per cent per enrolled household member from 1997 to 1999.
25. According to Sparrow (2006: 32), the scholarships covered 7–18 per cent of average per capita consumption in recipient households.
26. Authors' calculation based on SUSENAS 1999.
27. School committees consisted of the principal, a teacher representative, a student representative, the head of the parents' association, and the village head.
28. See Sparrow (2006: 94). Additionally, Cameron (2002) found that the JPS scholarships reduced dropouts at the junior secondary level by 3 per cent.
29. See Sparrow (2006: 109–17) on the effect of the JPS scholarship programme on the joint decision regarding school attendance and work activities among enrolled children. Suryahadi *et al.* (2005) show that labour and schooling are not mutually exclusive activities among children in poor Indonesian households.
30. *Penanggulangan Dampak Pengurangan Subsidi Energi,* Programme to Reduce the Impact of the Fuel Subsidy.
31. Since 2002, the various programmes have been referred to as PKPS-BBM programmes.
32. The original JPS health cards programme was discontinued in most areas by the end of 2001, and the JPS scholarships programme ended in 2003.
33. Simulations of the proposed subsidy cuts using household data from SUSENAS 2004 show that the poverty rate would have risen dramatically, from 16.66 per cent

in 2004 to 22.5 per cent in the absence of a cash compensation package, while a transfer programme with perfect targeting (that is, one that exhausts transfer budget resources on a random subset of poor households) would still have yielded an increase in poverty to 17.85 per cent. Remarkably, the latter estimate proved to be close to the actual poverty estimates for 2005/6 (BPS Circular, September 2006).

34. The programme was referred to officially as either *bantuan langsung tunai* (BLT, direct cash assistance) or *subsidi langsung tunai* (SLT, direct cash subsidy).
35. *Jaminan pelayanan kesehatan untuk keluarga miskin*, health service guarantees for poor families.
36. SMERU has produced in-depth studies of the programme in three provinces.
37. *Bantuan khusus murid* (special assistance for students).
38. In a five-province study by SMERU researchers, 40 schools were surveyed across rural and urban districts providing detailed insights into programme mechanics and short-term impact. See Widjajanti *et al.* (2006).
39. See note no. 36 above.
40. The 14 variables include: floor width per capita, type of floor, types of walls, toilet facilities, source of drinking water, source of lighting, cooking materials, purchase of meat/chicken/milk, frequency of meals per day, purchase of clothes, ability to purchase medicine, household head field of work, household head education level, assets owned by household.
41. See Hastuti *et al.* (2006: 13–17).
42. Most notable are the cases of Jordan in the early 1990s and Egypt in the late 1970s. Another factor to consider is that the SBY government made it very clear from the outset that the decision to reduce subsidies was a wholly Indonesian initiative. The information management strategy here was crucial in an environment where the World Bank and IMF were still routinely vilified for their meddling in national economic policy making during the crisis.
43. Based on calculations using SUSENAS 2006.
44. Using the SUSENAS panel, BPS has begun to disaggregate welfare into four categories: (i) *poor* = below the poverty line; (ii) *near-poor* = within 1.25 times of the poverty line; (iii) *near-non-poor* = within 1.5 times of the poverty line; and (iv) *non-poor* = 1.5 times greater than the poverty line. See BPS (September 2006).
45. See Table 4.10 in Hastuti *et al.* (2006).
46. The other half of the poor did not receive benefits because they were not classified as KPS households, the allocation of rice did not reach their villages, or they did not have cash to buy the rice in bulk, even at subsidized prices.
47. Several researchers have produced interesting proposals for the design of optimal transfer schemes based on lessons from *Progresa* in Mexico. De Janvry and Sadoulet (2006) is most indicative of this innovative approach, which essentially argues for more rigorous yet practical proxy means tests.

References

Arifianto, A., R. Marianti, S. Budiyati and E. Tan (2005) "Making Services Work for the Poor in Indonesia: A Report on Health Financing Mechanisms Scheme (JPK-Gakin) in Kabupaten Purbalingga, East Sumba and Tabanan," *Working Paper*, SMERU Research Institute, Jakarta (September).
Badan Pusat Statistik (2006) "Tingkat Kemiskinan di Indonesia Tahun 2005–2006," *Berita Resmi Statistik*, No. 47/IX/1 September.

Cameron, L. A. (2002) "Did Social Safety Net Scholarships Reduce Dropout Rates During the Indonesian Economic Crisis?," *Policy Research Working Paper No. 2800*, The World Bank, Washington, DC.

Cameron L. A. and C. Worswick (2001) "Education Expenditure Response to Crop Loss in Indonesia: A Gender Bias," *Economic Development and Cultural Change*, 49, 351–363.

Chaudhuri, S., J. Jalan and A. Suryahadi (2001) Assessing household vulnerability to poverty: A methodology and estimates for Indonesia, Mimeo. Washington, DC: World Bank.

Daly A. and G. Fane (2002) "Anti-Poverty Programs in Indonesia," *Bulletin of Indonesian Economic Studies*, 38, 309–329.

de Janvry A. and E. Sadoulet (2006) "Making Conditional Cash Transfers More Efficient: Designing for Maximum Effect of the Conditionality," *World Bank Economic Review*, 20, 1–29.

Feridhanusetyawan, T. (1999) "The Impact of the Crisis on the Labor Market in Indonesia," *Report prepared for the Asian Development Bank*, Centre for Strategic and International Studies, Jakarta.

Frankenberg, E., J. P. Smith and D. Thomas (2003) "Economic Shocks, Wealth, and Welfare," *Journal of Human Resources*, 38, 280–321.

Gelbach, J. and L. Pritchett (1997) Redistribution in a Political Economy: Leakier Can be Better, Mimeo. Washington, DC: The World Bank.

Hastuti A. and J. Maxwell (2002) "Rice for Poor Families (*Raskin*): Was the 2002 Program Operating Effectively?," *Working Paper*, SMERU Research Institute, Jakarta.

Hastuti, S. Usman, N. Toyamah, B. Sulaksono, S. Budiyati, W. Widyanti, M. Rosfadhila, H. Sadaly, S. Erlita, R. J. Sodo, S. Bazzi and S. Sumarto (2006) "A Rapid Appraisal of the Implementation of the 2005 Direct Cash Transfer Program in Indonesia: A Case Study in Five Kabupaten/Kota," *Research Report*, SMERU Research Institute (July).

Lanjouw, P., M. Pradhan, F. Saadah, H. Sayed and R. A. Sparrow (2002) "Poverty, Education and Health in Indonesia: Who Benefits from Public Spending," in C. Morrisson (ed.), *Education and Health Expenditures and Development: The Cases of Indonesia and Peru*. Paris: OECD Development Centre, pp. 17–78.

Manning, C. (2000) "Labour Market Adjustment to Indonesia's Economic Crisis: Context, Trends and Implications," *Bulletin of Indonesian Economic Studies*, 36, 105–136.

Maxwell J. and A. Perdana (2004) "Poverty Targeting in Indonesia: Programs, Problems and Lessons Learned," *Working Paper 083*, Centre for Strategic and International Studies, Jakarta (March).

Olivia, S. (2003) "Is There Still a Moral Economy in Java, Indonesia," *Working Paper*, University of Waikato.

Olken, B. (2006) "Corruption and the Costs of Redistribution: Micro Evidence from Indonesia," *Journal of Public Economics*, 90, 853–870.

Pradhan, M., A. Suryahadi, S. Sumarto and L. Pritchett (2000) "Measurements of Poverty in Indonesia: 1996, 1999, and Beyond," *Working Paper*, SMERU Research Institute, Jakarta.

Pritchett, L. (2005) "A Lecture on the Political Economy of Targeted Safety Nets," *Social Protection Discussion Series No. 0501*, The World Bank, Washington, DC (January).

Pritchett, L., S. Sumarto and A. Suryahadi (2002) "Targeted Programs in an Economic Crisis: Empirical Findings from the Experience of Indonesia," *Working Paper*, SMERU Research Institute, Jakarta (October).

Ravallion M. and L. Dearden (1988) "Social Security in a 'Moral Economy': An Empirical Analysis for Java," *Review of Economic and Statistics*, 70, 36–44.

SMERU (2001) "Pelaksanaan Reorientasi Kebijakan Subsidi BBM di Kab. Jember, Jatim, Kab. Kapuas, Kalteng, Kab. Barito Kuala, Kalsel," *Working Paper*, SMERU Research Institute, Jakarta (July).

SMERU (1999) "Hasil Pengamatan Lapangan Kilat Tim SMERU pada Persiapan Pelaksanaan Program PDM-DKE," *Research Report*, SMERU Research Institute, Jakarta (May).

Soelaksano, B., S. Budiyati, Hastuti, M. Nabiu, Akhmadi, P. Wibowo, S. K. Rahayu and J. Maxwell (1999) "The Impact of the Crisis on the People's Behavior and Perceptions of the Use and Effectiveness of *Puskesmas*, *Posyandu*, and the Role of Midwives," *Research Report*, SMERU Research Institute, Jakarta.

Sparrow, R. A. (2006) *Health, Education and Economic Crisis: Protecting the Poor in Indonesia*, Research Series No. 373. Amsterdam: Tinbergen Research Institute-Vrije Universiteit.

Sumarto, S., D. Suryadarma and A. Suryahadi (2006) "Predicting Consumption Poverty Using Non-consumption Indicators: Experiments Using Indonesian Data," *Working Paper*, SMERU Research Institute (February).

Sumarto, S., A. Suryahadi and W. Widyanti (2004) "Assessing the Impact of Indonesian Social Safety Net Programs on Household Welfare and Poverty Dynamics," *Working Paper*, SMERU Research Institute, Jakarta (August).

Sumarto, S., A. Suryahadi and W. Widyanti (2005) "Assessing the Impact of Indonesian Social Safety Net Programmes on Household Welfare and Poverty Dynamics," *European Journal of Development Research*, 17, 155–177.

Suryadarma, D., Akhmadi, Hastuti and N. Toyamah (2005) "Objective Measures of Family Welfare for Individual Targeting: Results from Pilot Project on Community Based Monitoring System in Indonesia," *Working Paper*, SMERU Research Institute, Jakarta (December).

Suryadarma, D., R. P. Artha, A. Suryahadi and S. Sumarto (2005) "A Reassessment of Inequality and Its Role in Poverty Reduction in Indonesia," *Working Paper*, SMERU Research Institute, Jakarta (January).

Suryadarma, D., A. Suryahadi and S. Sumarto (2006) "Causes of Low Secondary School Enrollment in Indonesia," *Working Paper*, SMERU Research Institute, Jakarta (August).

Suryahadi, A., A. Priyambada and S. Sumarto (2005) "Poverty, School, and Work: Children during the Economic Crisis in Indonesia," *Development and Change*, 36, 351–373.

Suryahadi A. and S. Sumarto (2001) "The Chronic Poor, the Transient Poor, and the Vulnerable in Indonesia Before and After the Crisis," *Working Paper*, SMERU Research Institute, Jakarta (May).

Suryahadi A. and S. Sumarto (2003) "Poverty and Vulnerability in Indonesia Before and After the Economic Crisis," *Asian Economic Journal*, 17, 47–54.

Suryahadi, A., S. Sumarto and L. Pritchett (2003) "The Evolution of Poverty during the Crisis in Indonesia," *Working Paper*, SMERU Research Institute, Jakarta (March).

Suryahadi, A., S. Sumarto and L. Pritchett (2003a) "Safety Nets or Safety Ropes? Dynamic Benefit Incidence of Two Crisis Programs in Indonesia," *World Development*, 31, 1257–1277.

Suryahadi, A., S. Sumarto and L. Pritchett (2003b) "Evolution of Poverty during the Crisis in Indonesia," *Asian Economic Journal*, 17, 221–241.

Suryahadi, A., S. Sumarto, Y. Suharso and L. Pritchett (2000) "The Evolution of Poverty during the Crisis in Indonesia, 1996–99," *Policy Research Working Paper No. 2435*, The World Bank, Washington, DC (September).

Sumarto, S., A. Wetterberg and L. Pritchett (1998) "The Social Impact of the Crisis in Indonesia: Results from a Nationwide Kecamatan Survey," *Working Paper*, SMERU Research Institute, Jakarta.

Thomas, D., K. Beegle, E. Frankenberg, B. Sikoki, J. Strauss and G. Terruel (2004) "Education in a Crisis," *Journal of Development Economics*, 74, 53–85.

Timmer, P. (2004) "The Road to Pro-Poor Growth: The Indonesian Experience in Regional Perspective," *Working Paper No. 38*, Center for Global Development (April).

Townsend, R. M. (1994) "Risk and Insurance in Village India," *Econometrica*, 62, 539–591.

Widjajanti, I. S., Hastuti, S. Sumarto, N. Toyamah, S. Usman, B. Sulaksono, S. Budiyati, W. Widyanti, M. Rosfadhila, R. J. Sodo and S. Bazzi (2006) "A Rapid Appraisal of The PKPS-BBM Education Sector School Operational Assistance Program 2005/2006," *Research Report*, SMERU Research Institute, Jakarta.

World Bank (2005) "Indonesia: Socioeconomic Update 2005," The World Bank, Jakarta.

7
HIV/AIDS, Social Protection and Chronic Poverty

Rachel Slater

Introduction

The implications of the HIV/AIDS pandemic for global poverty are stark. In the absence of appropriate measures, which include social protection, the pandemic will result in a rise in chronic or persistent poverty. Rising morbidity and mortality associated with HIV/AIDS stress the urgent need to think about the ways in which different kinds of social protection interventions might be used to prevent HIV/AIDS from undermining poverty reduction and development progress. The main focus of this chapter is to identify the most effective social protection instruments for helping HIV/AIDS-affected households, assess whether there is a strong, or special, case for promoting social protection measures exclusively for HIV/AIDS-affected households, and review the issues and lessons learned around targeting HIV/AIDS-affected households.

The impacts of HIV/AIDS are manifold, with varying permutations in different social, economic, political and geographical contexts. In rural contexts, where the impact of HIV/AIDS is greatest, households that are affected show a diminishing asset base over time and become less able to produce enough through agriculture to meet their subsistence needs or income requirements. Declining capacity to work is reflected in labour shortages, either through loss of labour (when people become unable to work through illness and, ultimately, die) or through the displacement of labour (as household members look after those who are sick in the household rather than working in their fields). At the same time, productivity falls because of a lack of investment, as money that would otherwise be spent on fertilizers and other inputs is allocated to paying for medicines and funerals. When people die from AIDS, the local knowledge and skills that are crucial for successful agricultural production are not passed down to the next generation (Barnett and Blaikie, 1992; Barnett *et al.*, 1995; Gillespie and Loevinsohn, 2003).

HIV/AIDS also has implications for food security. Proponents of the 'New Variant Famine' (NVF) thesis (FANTA, 2001; de Waal, 2003; WHO, 2003) posit the emergence of a new type of famine as HIV/AIDS increases vulnerability to shocks and risk. There is also evidence of a link between HIV/AIDS and nutrition: infection is highest among people with poor diets; undernourished HIV-positive people develop AIDS more quickly; and people with AIDS have increased nutritional requirements (Gillespie and Haddad, 2002). Anti-retrovirals (ARVs) are ineffective and have serious side effects if they are not combined with a good diet.

HIV/AIDS also affects social development and reflects inequitable gender relations (Baylies, 2002). Women are more likely to be infected, both because of physiology and because they are less able to protect themselves through abstinence or condom use, and take on greater burdens of caring for the chronically ill. Men tend to die before women, increasing the number of female-headed households. There are many published references to the susceptibility of widows to property-grabbing by in-laws (Baylies, 2002; FAO, 2003; FAO, 2004). Increasing numbers of orphaned children represent another outcome of the HIV/AIDS epidemic. In 2001, there were 13.4 million AIDS orphans, and this figure is expected to reach 25 million by 2010 (UNICEF, 2002). Many orphans and vulnerable children (OVCs), especially girls, drop out of school because there is no money to pay for school fees, uniforms and books, and because the opportunity cost of lost labour in agriculture or in domestic work, including caring for the sick, is high.

In parallel with the growing literature describing the impacts of HIV/AIDS, there has been a return to concerns with options for supporting households that are in danger of becoming destitute. Social protection is defined here, as in Shepherd *et al.* (2004), as a 'range of processes, policies and interventions to enable people to reduce, mitigate, cope with and recover from risk in order that they become less insecure and can participate in economic growth' (p. 14). Thus, rather than focusing solely on safety nets, there has been a shift towards identifying potential linkages between the protection of people's livelihoods and the promotion of livelihoods through economic growth (Devereux, 2001; Conway and Norton, 2002; Farrington *et al.*, 2004).

Blending these debates about social protection and HIV/AIDS raises two sets of questions for policy-makers. The first question asks how implementation of social protection is affected by HIV/AIDS. The second question asks about the ways in which different kinds of social protection interventions might be used to help people reduce, mitigate or cope with the impacts of HIV/AIDS. While it is recognized that financial and human resources for social protection in government and in civil society are severely constrained as a result of the HIV/AIDS epidemic (Slater, 2004), in this chapter the principal concern is with how to support the poorest people, often rural smallholders or the landless, rather than how to protect human resources among civil service and civil society workers, who have stable, albeit small, incomes.

The chapter is organized in three sections. The next section assesses the potential effectiveness of social protection interventions in reducing the impact of HIV/AIDS on poverty and chronic poverty. The third section outlines issues of sequencing and prioritization associated with social protection for HIV/AIDS affected households. A final section discusses the policy implications and concludes.

Assessing social protection interventions for HIV/AIDS

Before considering various different social protection interventions, it is important to sketch out the main elements of an analytical framework for exploring the interventions.[1] A framework is required that distinguishes between the different stages of the disease and the impact at different levels on individuals, households and communities. The following are key elements of this framework:

- The social protection needs of people who are HIV-positive but asymptomatic are different from those of people who have AIDS and increasingly debilitating diseases. HIV-positive people are not all unproductive and unable to work, so interventions need not be restricted to handouts.
- It is often difficult to identify (and therefore to target) those who are either HIV-negative or HIV-positive but asymptomatic, and those who have AIDS, so in assessing interventions it is critical to be mindful of the differential impacts on each of these groups.
- People who do not have AIDS but live in households with people who are HIV positive and/or in households where people have died from AIDS are important too. The household impacts of morbidity are different from those of mortality.
- Beyond households, we need also to include those in the broader community who are affected indirectly by the disease through disruptions to local labour supply and community-based safety nets.

Assessment of the relative effectiveness of social protection to address the impacts of HIV/AIDS focuses on four main types of intervention: transfers (such as food, cash and inputs); public works programmes (food for work and cash for work); education and training (particularly around prevention, nutrition and life skills for orphans); and financial resources (micro-credit, savings and insurance) (see Slater, 2004).

Transfers for HIV/AIDS infected and affected people

The main advantage of transfers is that they can safeguard existing productive assets that otherwise might be drawn down to meet basic households needs. Drawing down on productive assets is a coping strategy that can lead households into a vicious cycle of impoverishment.

Food aid

The most common type of transfer in many of the countries with high HIV prevalence rates is that of food. In some circumstances, food may be the most appropriate form of transfer, particularly in remote areas where there is a limited supply and where cash transfers are likely to cause inflation because of increased demand without an accompanying increase in supply (Devereux, 2002). Food distribution can also address nutrition issues – in Southern Africa between 2002 and 2004, estimates of calorific requirements and protein requirements were increased to take into account the greater nutritional needs of people with AIDS. Targeting additional food to individuals within households is unlikely to be effective, as any additional food supplies are likely to be shared among household members. Furthermore, adult household members (who are much more likely to have HIV or AIDS, and therefore to require more food), especially women, often give the additional food to their children. FANTA (2002) identify various examples of situations where food aid may not be appropriate, but all but one of these examples (regarding stigma) is about food aid in general rather than food aid in relation to HIV/AIDS.

There is a long-standing debate and a large amount of literature about the possible negative impacts of food aid, particularly when delivered over the long term, from Clay and Stokke (1991) to Barrett and Maxwell (2005). Negative impacts include local production disincentives, market distortion and dependency. While these debates are not new, the development of the NVF thesis and annual humanitarian appeals in Southern Africa since 2002 question the role of food distribution as a long-term developmental response. For example, Harvey (2004) notes that, in Southern Africa, World Food Programme (WFP) referred to food in its second appeal as a component in wider service delivery programmes that aim to 'deploy food, technical advice and advocacy measures to encourage and support government efforts to create or strengthen safety nets that provide minimum protection to populations facing food insecurity and the risks of living in an HIV/AIDS affected environment' (WFP, 2003: 8).

HIV/AIDS certainly reinforces the need for a shift in perspective in which a degree of reliance on long-term welfare is increasingly accepted for destitute households. Thus, de Waal suggests that 'we must face the distinct possibility that we can no longer talk about food aid and other forms of welfare assistance as short-term measures until "normal" development is "resumed"' (WFP, 2003: 21). However, the costs and benefits of food aid over the medium to long term need to be compared with other ways of providing long-term welfare and safety nets. It should not be assumed that, even where people with HIV/AIDS are hungry and have inadequate diets, food aid is the only (or the best) way of addressing their needs.

Cash transfers

With reference to emergencies rather than HIV/AIDS, Peppiatt *et al.* (2001: 1) argue that, in comparison with food distribution,

> cash is more cost-effective because its transaction costs are lower, it is more easily convertible, allows for greater beneficiary choice and can stimulate local markets. On the other hand, cash can be used in ways not intended by the donor, can contribute to local inflation and poses security risks not normally associated with food aid.

Where cash is used in ways not intended by the donor, this may indicate misappropriation, but also possibly that the donor has not fully understood people's needs. Cash transfers can be used to buy food or household goods, and can be invested in income-generating activities. For women, some of these activities can easily be combined with household work and caring roles, while others force them to travel long distances from their homes. Giving cash rather than food can, in some cases, also enable the avoidance of complex targeting mechanisms. Where interventions are attempting to differentiate between people who require relief, rehabilitation or recovery support, households can tailor their use of the cash transfer to their own specific relief , rehabilitation or recovery needs, without the involvement of donor or government institutions.

A growing body of evidence from countries with starkly contrasting HIV prevalence rates demonstrates the importance of social pensions paid to elderly people, particularly those who are supporting orphans. Pension payments are often used to pay for the education costs of grandchildren or to buy food for the rest of the household (IDPM and HelpAge International, 2003). It is often assumed that pensions are unaffordable in all except middle-income countries such as Brazil, South Africa and India. Large recurrent costs associated with pensions need to be balanced with the growing numbers of orphans and vulnerable children, particularly in Africa, but Devereux (2003) claims that pensions are a policy choice competing with other (fixed-term) investments that are intended to alleviate poverty by driving economic growth. Similarly, Farrington *et al.* (2003) argue that 'cash transfers paid through certain channels (e.g. the Post Office) for specific purposes such as pensions and allowances are less corruptible than many "in kind" transfers. They may help in reducing under-nutrition and stimulating the local economy by reducing "demand deficits" and merit increased funding' (p. 1). In the context of the growing prevalence of HIV/AIDS in India (which now has the second-largest number of infected individuals after South Africa) and the likelihood of a growing number of orphans being supported by the elderly, pensions could play an important role in mitigating and coping with the effects of HIV/AIDS. There are signs that, among governments that have prioritized dealing with HIV/AIDS in, for example, their Poverty

Reduction Strategy Papers (PRSPs), there has been a rethink about the afford-ability of long-term cash transfers. In Lesotho, for example, the government has just introduced a pension for people over 70 years old. The size of the cash transfer is small – 150 maloti (about US$21) – but this can buy a 50kg bag of maize meal.

In contrast to pensions, cash transfers to or for orphans have been the subject of much more limited research. Cash transfers to orphans may be inappropriate if not accompanied by training or support to help them make sensible purchasing and budgeting decisions. It is also possible that people in the surrounding community may take advantage of orphans as they attempt to manage household resources. However, it may also be the case that orphan allowances, paid either to orphans or their guardians, encourage other house-holds to take in double orphans. There has been increased demand for child-benefit allowances in South Africa and Thailand; these 'demands may, how-ever, compete with other claims on the budget, with the risk that the support to families with orphans, foster families, poor relief and so on, may stagnate in the face of mounting needs' (Cornia and Zagonari, 2002: 11).

Inputs programmes

These have traditionally been focused on agricultural production and, while their stated aim is usually to increase agricultural productivity, they also have important risk-reducing effects. Examples include the distribution of different (drought-resistant) seed varieties to help households extend the length of the cropping season and so smooth income, and the distribution of free fertilizer, which reduces the risk associated with spending money on it only to see crops fail. Given that poor households are very risk adverse, inputs are seen as an important risk-reduction strategy. However, for house-holds that are severely labour constrained, agricultural inputs may be inap-propriate, although options for adapting inputs programmes to provide labour-saving technologies should be explored.

School feeding

Another intervention in which there is renewed interest in the context of HIV/AIDS is that of school feeding. In the past, school feeding schemes have aimed to promote nutrition among children, to improve enrolment rates and reduce numbers dropping out. The nutritional impact on children remains as yet unproven, partly because the children eat at school instead of at home. However, there is evidence that school feeding improves enrol-ment and reduces numbers of dropouts, particularly among girls (Devereux, 2002; Farrington *et al.*, 2004). HIV/AIDS threatens to undermine school enrolments, as children take on increased labour and caring responsibili-ties. The long-term impacts will be a generation of adults who, even if they are able to avoid HIV infection, will not have the skills gained through edu-cation to lift themselves out of poverty. It is unclear whether school feeding is enough of an incentive to keep OVCs in school, particularly in the case of child-headed households.

Public works programmes

Public works programmes focus largely on food for work (FFW) and cash for work (CFW) but can also include inputs for work. They provide payment in cash or in kind, in return for labour. The efficacy of these programmes, in general and in comparison with other forms of transfers, has been discussed elsewhere (see, for example, McCord in Chapter 9 in this volume). Central to assessing the appropriateness of these programmes to HIV/AIDS-infected and affected households is the labour constraint they involve. Excessive work requirements may be inappropriate for HIV-positive people at risk of developing AIDS. Others suggest that asymptomatic HIV-positive people can participate in FFW or CFW schemes, and it is wrong to assume that households with chronic illness are 'not viable'. Harvey (2004: 35) thus argues that we must improve monitoring and evaluation of HIV/AIDS labour constraints to see whether they really are restricting effective participation in programmes. Furthermore, the Zimbabwe Red Cross argues that excluding people from programmes that require labour risks increased stigmatization (in Harvey, 2004: 35).

In the case of FFW, self-targeting is used frequently to ensure that only poor households participate. However, self-targeting is usually achieved either by offering non-preferred foods (for example, yellow maize in Eastern and Southern Africa, or broken rice in Asia) or by paying low wage rates relative to the market wage. This could be counter-productive for people who are HIV-positive, since a full diet is essential to delay the onset of AIDS. Self-targeting processes that force households to reduce consumption because of low wages, or undertake physically demanding work without an increase in calorific intake, are likely to induce a more rapid onset of AIDS. For households where one or more people are chronically ill, and other household members are under increasing pressure as carers, FFW and CFW are less appropriate. FFW and CFW programmes must also be designed alongside support for orphans and vulnerable children in order to avoid encouraging children to take on responsibilities of work associated with adulthood.

Financial services and financial capital

Community-based financial services, especially savings, micro-credit and insurance, can play an important role, particularly in *ex ante* risk mitigation for households affected by HIV/AIDS. However, HIV/AIDS makes many of these services unsustainable and so they are unlikely to be effective in areas that already have high prevalence rates. Thus financial services may be more appropriate in Asia, where they are already better established and where prevalence of HIV and AIDS is fairly low, than in Sub-Saharan Africa, where prevalence rates are high and financial services much more rudimentary in both scope and coverage.

Savings

Drawing down on savings is an important risk-mitigating strategy on the part of households affected by HIV/AIDS. In the case of social risk management, it has been argued that 'financial saving as well as the accumulation of other assets that can be sold at fair market prices is perhaps the most important asset management instrument used to address income variability' (Holzmann and Jørgensen, 1999: 1015). In the case of HIV/AIDS, though, the disposal of savings is recognized as one of the first coping strategies that households draw on in times of stress. Encouraging savings *ex ante* is one way to help households prepare in advance for the effects of AIDS-related poverty. Since households are usually unaware of their HIV-status, encouraging savings needs to take the form of *ex ante* preparation for various kinds of poverty or vulnerability, not solely HIV/AIDS.

For poor people (particularly women), formal savings accounts with banks are often not available, either because people do not have the required documentation to open accounts or because they live in areas that are too remote. Instead, savings can be held in other forms, such as cash, jewellery, trees and livestock. Given the unpredictability of the impacts of HIV/AIDS, and the risks and costs associated with maintaining livestock, especially cattle and buffalo, smaller stock units – for example,goats or chickens – can be a very important and flexible source of savings for poor households.

Private and community-based informal savings clubs are important throughout Asia and Africa, and offer savings opportunities to poor people who cannot access bank accounts or who face high transaction costs with formal banking. Savings clubs can be flexible and enable households to draw down small amounts of money to pay for medicines. Many donors are considering ways to support community-based savings as a risk mitigation strategy for households affected by HIV/AIDS. In exploring options for mitigating the impact of HIV/AIDS through savings, it is important to remember that, for households that are already poor, *ex ante* savings are not possible. For the poorest households, other options should be explored. Similarly, many countries with higher prevalence rates have already passed the window of opportunity where savings might provide one form of *ex ante* preparation for HIV/AIDS. In countries with lower prevalence rates, savings may be more appropriate.

Micro-credit

Parker (2000) argues that there is a need to raise awareness about the impacts of HIV/AIDS on microfinance, given that, as the disease progresses, HIV/AIDS-affected clients of microfinance institutions are likely to need access to a wider range of financial services. She argues that, 'even in its most basic form, access to microfinance services gives households a way to both prepare for and cope with crisis' (Parker, 2000: 2). However, households are likely to have a reduced ability to make repayments on loans. Baylies (2002) is critical of the implied assumption in work on microfinance and HIV/AIDS that the sustainability of HIV/AIDS-affected households will depend, in part, on their fuller integration into the market economy. She suggests instead that micro-credit has clear limits 'where high levels of morbidity and mortality undermine the economic arena within which the logic of microfinance schemes is nested' (Parker, 2000: 625). Poor people, including those affected by HIV/AIDS, are often risk adverse: they are unwilling (and unable) to take out loans that allow them to access more (risky) remunerative markets or activities, and tend to be limited to subsistence activities. They may also be more susceptible to debt, so that the provision of micro-finance can become a further burden rather than a means of recovery (Parker, 2002: 625). Microfinance programmes need to be more sensitive to the changing demography of rural poverty and the needs of older people and orphans if they are to be useful to HIV/AIDS-affected households.

Insurance

Formal contributory insurance schemes with large commercial companies are out of the reach of most of the rural poor. However, there are various informal and semi-formal insurance mechanisms that people draw on, and concern about the sustainability of these in communities affected by HIV/AIDS. Burial societies in South Africa are becoming less viable under the pressure of AIDS-related deaths and the failure of households to make regular contributions. However, there are also arguments that community-based informal insurance mechanisms may be more adaptable and flexible, and thus more able to accommodate the changing circumstances of households. In Ethiopia, members of community groups to which people pay subscriptions to meet funeral and mourning costs are being trained for HIV/AIDS-related work (UNOCHA, 2004). Barnett and Blaikie (1992) argue that modifications in customary practice regarding funerals are one community-based response to the HIV/AIDS epidemic. Holzmann and Jørgensen (1999) argue that traditional structures combine insurance functions with other activities, and the insurance depends on the trust that arises from other functions. Thus 'while insurance mechanisms provide insurance, they are guided more by a principle of balanced reciprocity' (Holzmann and Jørgensen, 1999: 1015). In the context of stigma, discrimination and growing vulnerability among many households in the community, it is easy to see how informal insurance mechanisms and reciprocity can break down.

Sequencing and prioritising social protection for HIV/AIDS

It is not just the type of social protection instrument that is important in responding to HIV/AIDS; time lines are also critically important. While it is often assumed that responses should be tailored to prevalence rates, Topouzis (2003) argues that HIV/AIDS prevalence rates do not alone capture or reflect epidemic impact. High prevalence does not always entail high impact, and declining prevalence does not necessarily result in a lessening of impacts. The lesson is that social protection interventions should be designed around actual impact rather than estimated prevalence rates. Appropriate indicators will vary, but include the percentage of single and double orphans, of households fostering orphans, of household income spent on health-related expenditure, of households with access to healthcare, the age and gender of household heads, and the dependency ratio adjusted for adult morbidity (Topouzis, 2003). The implications for the timing of different protection priorities are shown in Table 7.1. Given that most countries are in Phases 1 or 2 of the epidemic, it is important to note that the worst of HIV/AIDS-related impact is yet to come.

Table 7.1 also highlights a weakness in the categorization of instruments in the social risk management framework, and a gap in analysis presented here, namely that there is a lack of explicit focus on instruments that enable people to recover from HIV/AIDS (Phase 4). Few countries have reached the phase of declining prevalence/high impact, and in those countries there is little evidence of recovery interventions (see Shepherd, 2003, on Uganda, where a lack of recovery options may be contributing to re-emerging high prevalence rates) but challenges for recovery will emerge in various countries within the next few decades.

Table 7.1 Prevalence rates, impact levels and priorities for social protection

Level of Impact	HIV/AIDS adult prevalence rates	
	Low	High
Low	*Phase 1: Low prevalence, very low impact level* Focus on: Reduction of vulnerability to HIV infection	*Phase 2: High prevalence, still low impact* Focus on: Reduction of vulnerability to AIDS impact and preparedness
High	*Phase 4: Declining prevalence, high impact level* Focus on: Rehabilitation	*Phase 3: High prevalence, high impact level* Focus on: Impact alleviation

Source: Topouzis (2003).

Policy implications

HIV/AIDS presents huge challenges to policy-makers developing programmes to address chronic poverty. But is HIV/AIDS a special or unique type of crisis that requires a special and unique response? There are some features that are unique to HIV/AIDS – for example, the fact that it affects mainly economically active members of the population. As a result it is important to ensure that HIV-negative people remain negative; recognize the needs of people who are positive but asymptomatic, versus those that are positive and ill; and recognize the wider needs of orphans and other household members who are left behind when people die of HIV/AIDS.

However, treating HIV/AIDS as a special case and targeting interventions accordingly can have serious implications for equity and social justice. There are compelling ethical reasons to prioritize people with high levels of poverty or vulnerability, which may or may not be HIV/AIDS-induced. For example, those who are ill with AIDS should not be treated preferentially over those with malaria, and AIDS orphans are no more or less deserving than those orphaned as a result of road accidents or conflict. There are also practical considerations. First, it is difficult, if not impossible, to identify the HIV/AIDS-infected or affected. Proxy indicators are not always reliable (de Waal, 2003). Second, operating a large number of discrete social protection programmes is economically inefficient (Farrington *et al.*, 2003) and introducing a parallel stream of programmes for HIV/AIDS may have created an impenetrable maze of programmes for poor people to negotiate. Third, keeping the range of mechanisms simple but flexible also enables interventions to respond to the changing needs of beneficiaries, especially given that our understanding of the future impact of HIV/AIDS remains patchy (Anderson *et al.*, 2004).

Community-based targeting is one option for targeting that can respond more flexibly to changes in HIV/AIDS-induced poverty and vulnerability. While this is cost-efficient, there is a danger that the notion of community is being romanticized (Levine, 2001). In communities, processes of stigmatization, discrimination and denial are important. Attempts to incorporate community-based targeting should be mindful of how patronage relationships and divisions within communities may lead to the exclusion of certain vulnerable people, and how the stigma of AIDS may exacerbate exclusion.

Social protection for the HIV/AIDS affected should form part of broader social protection mechanisms. The focus should be on reducing vulnerability and increases the capacity of households to respond to HIV/AIDS-induced shocks and stresses. Social protection should seek to overcome the gender inequalities that are reinforced through HIV/AIDS – for example, by supporting labour-saving domestic and agricultural technologies or providing water sources closer to homes. Financial services programmes that target women should also beware of increasing their financial, labour and budgetary responsibilities because of the additional burdens they face as a result of HIV/AIDS. Support aimed at empowering women can inadvertently have the effect of overburdening them with additional responsibilities. Various institutions have a role to play in contributing to or implementing safety nets (for a detailed discussion of institutional arrangements, see Slater 2004). Ultimately, the challenge for all stakeholders lies in going beyond the rhetorical commitment about doing something to reduce, mitigate and enable households to cope with the impacts of HIV/AIDS, and translating rhetoric into action. Achieving this will mean that governments and donors must acknowledge the synergies and trade-offs between their preferred approaches to development – especially investments to drive economic growth – and alternative long-term commitments to recurrent spending on social protection.

Note

1. An expanded analytical framework drawing on social risk management and mechanisms for reducing, mitigating and enabling households to cope with risk is developed further in Slater (2004).

References

Anderson, E., H. Chaplin and S. Wiggins (2004) 'Can Africa feed itself in 2025 under the impact of HIV/AIDS? A report to UNAIDS'. London: ODI.

Barnett, T. and P. Blaikie (1992) *AIDS in Africa: Its Present and Future Impact*. London: Bellhaven Press.

Barnett, T., A. Whiteside and C. Desmond (1995) 'The social and economic impact of HIV/AIDS in poor countries: a review of studies and lessons', *Progress in Development Studies*, 1(2), 151–170.

Barrett, C. B. and D. G. Maxwell (2005) *Food Aid after Fifty Years: Recasting Its Role*. Routledge: London.

Baylies, C. (2002) 'The impact of AIDS on rural households in Africa: A shock like any other?', *Development and Change*, 33(4), 611–632.

Clay, E. and O. Stokke (eds) (1991) *Food Aid and Human Security*. London: Frank Cass.

Conway, T. and A. Norton (2002) 'Nets, ropes, ladders and trampolines: the place of social protection within current debates on poverty reduction', *Development Policy Review*, 20(5), 533–540.

Cornia, G. and F. Zagonari (2002) 'The HIV/AIDS impact on the rural and urban economy', in Cornia, G. (ed.), *AIDS, Public Policy and Child Well-Being*, online at http://www.unicef-icdc.org/research/ESP/aids/, accessed March 2004.

Devereux, S. (2001) 'Livelihood insecurity and social protection: A re-emerging issue in rural development', *Development Policy Review*, 19(4), 507–519.

Devereux, S. (2002) Social protection for the poor: lessons from recent international experience, IDS Working Paper No. 142. Brighton: IDS.

Devereux, S. (2003) *Policy options for increasing the contribution of social protection to food security*, Forum for Food Security in Southern Africa Theme Paper No. 4. London: ODI.

FANTA (2001) *HIV/AIDS: a Guide for Nutrition, Care and Support*. Washington, DC: FANTA.

FANTA (2002) *Potential Uses of Food Aid to Support HIV/AIDS Mitigation Activities in Sub-Saharan Africa*. Washington, DC: FANTA.

FAO (2003) *HIV/AIDS and Agriculture: Impacts and Responses: Case Studies from Namibia, Uganda and Zambia*. Rome: FAO.

Farrington, J., N. C. Saxena, T. Barton and R. Nayak (2003) 'Post offices, pensions and computers: New opportunities for combining growth and social protection in weakly integrated rural areas?', *Natural Resource Perspectives*, No. 87, June. London: ODI.

Farrington, J., R. Slater and R. Holmes (2004) The search for synergies between social protection and the productive sectors: the agriculture case, ODI Working Paper No. 232. London: ODI.

Food and Agriculture Organization (FAO) (2004) *Impact of HIV/AIDS on the Agricultural Sector and FAO's Response*, FAO contribution to *HIV/AIDS and work: global estimates, impact and response 2004*. Rome: FAO, Population and Development Service (SDWP) (March).

Gillespie, S. and L. Haddad (2002) 'Food security as a response to AIDS', in *AIDS and Food Security: Essays by Peter Piot and Per Pinstrup-Andersen and by Stuart Gillespie and Lawrence Haddad*. Washington, DC: IFPRI.

Gillespie, S. and M. Loevinsohn (2003) *HIV/AIDS, Food Security and Rural Livelihoods: Understanding and Responding*, Renewal Working Paper No. 3. Washington, DC: IFPRI.

Harvey, P. (2004) *HIV/AIDS And Humanitarian Action*, HPG Report No. 16, April. London: ODI.

Holzmann, R. and S. Jørgensen (1999) 'Social protection as social risk management: conceptual underpinnings for the social protection sector strategy paper', *Journal of International Development*, 11(7), 1005–1027.

IDPM and HelpAge International (2003) 'Non-contributory pensions and poverty prevention: a comparative study of Brazil and South Africa', IDPM, Manchester.

Levine, A. (2001) *Orphans and Other Vulnerable Children: What Role for Social Protection?*, Social Protection Discussion Paper No. 0126, World Bank Human Development Network. Washington, DC: World Bank.

Parker, J. (2000) *Microfinance and HIV/AIDS*, Discussion Paper, USAID Microenterprise Best Practices Project.

Peppiatt, D., J. Mitchell and P. Holzmann (2001) *Cash Transfers in Emergencies: Evaluating Benefits and Assessing Risks*, Humanitarian Practice Network Paper No. 35. London: ODI.

Shepherd, A., R. Marcus and A. Barrientos (2004) 'Policy paper on social protection'. London: ODI.

Shepherd, A. with N. Kyegombe and M. Mulumba (2003) 'HIV/AIDS, socio-economic mobility and chronic poverty: Case study results from a small panel in Rakai, Uganda' International Conference on Chronic Poverty and Development Policy, University of Manchester, 7–9 April.

Slater, R. (2004) 'The implications of HIV/AIDS for social protection', Paper produced for the UK Department for International Development, London.

Topouzis, D. (2003) 'Mitigating the impact of HIV/AIDS: a review of response and concepts', Workshop on Mitigating of HIV/AIDS: Impacts through Agriculture and Rural Development, Human Sciences Research Council, Pretoria, 27–29 May, Available online: http://www.sarpn.org.za/mitigation_of_HIV_AIDS/m0023/Daphne_Topouzis.ppt, accessed February 2007.

UNAIDS/UNICEF (2002) *Children on the Brink 2002: A Joint Report on Orphan Estimates and Program Strategies*. New York: UNAIDS.

UNICEF (2002) 'Orphans and other children affected by HIV/AIDS', UNICEF Fact Sheet, New York. Online at: http://www.unicef.org/publications/pub_factsheet_orphan_en.pdf, accessed February 2007.

UNOCHA (2004) 'Ethiopia: traditional burial societies help people living with HIV/AIDS': http://www.irinnews.org/AIDSreport.asp?ReportID=2909&SelectRegion=Horn_of_Africa, accessed February 2007.

de Waal, A. (2003) '"New variant famine": hypothesis, evidence and implications', *Humanitarian Exchange*, 23, March, 20–22.

WFP (2004) 'Front-line defence against HIV/AIDS', Online at: http://www.wfp.org/aboutwfp/introduction/hiv.html, accessed February 2007.

WHO (2003) 'Nutrition requirements for people living with HIV/AID', Report of a technical consultation, Geneva, 13–15 May.

8
The Social Protection Function of Short-Term Public Works Programmes in the Context of Chronic Poverty

Anna McCord

This chapter examines the role of public works programmes offering one-off, short-term episodes of employment, as a social protection instrument in the context of chronic poverty. Such programmes are characterised as 'short-term public works programmes' to differentiate them from public works programmes offering sustained or repeated employment. The chapter does not question the appropriateness of public works as a tool to deal with problems of acute conjunctural poverty, such as the 1997 crisis in East Asia, but is concerned with the use of short-term public works in situations of chronic poverty.[1] From a wide range of possible social assistance options,[2] public works are experiencing continued popularity and policy prominence, in Asia, Latin America and Africa, often with funding from international donor agencies. This is based on the assumption that they offer a 'win–win' social protection option, providing employment while also creating assets, and offering a welfare payment that is also a tangible economic investment. The efficacy of public works in situations of chronic poverty is, however. challenged in a growing body of literature from a range of critical commentators, as well as within the World Bank and the International Labour Organization (ILO). Even so, such programmes continue to be implemented, and this chapter examines the assumptions underlying their popularity, and some of the challenges to these assumptions, drawing on experiences from South Africa and Malawi.

Public works are a somewhat anomalous and conceptually problematic social protection instrument. Whereas social protection programmes are conventionally divided into social assistance and social insurance, public works programmes do not conform to either category. While social assistance offers transfers in the form of grants, which are unrequited, and social insurance is dependent on prior contributions, public works programmes require that work is performed in exchange for the social assistance payment, with the result that public works are a special form of conditional transfer, in which the transfer is, in fact, a wage. In addition, in the case of the short-term public works programmes, the duration of the 'transfer' is limited to the period of employment, rather than being extended to match the duration of need (on the basis of meeting criteria of poverty, illness, disability, old age and so on), as are alternative forms of social assistance. There is frequently an a priori assumption that public works have a positive impact on the accumulation of productive assets required to move out of chronic poverty, which operates through three vectors: the wage payment; improved labour market attachment (as a result of both workplace experience and training); and benefits accruing from the assets created. While there is a growing body of literature that is critical of the efficacy of public works in terms of poverty reduction through each of these vectors (see, for example, McCord, 2004a; and Pellissery's Chapter 12 in this volume), this issue is not dealt with in this chapter, which focuses instead on the key factors that lead to the dominance of public works over alternative interventions.

Setting aside the assumed poverty-reducing impact of public works programmes, such programmes are attractive, both to donors and to governments, for a number of reasons. These fall into four main groups: (i) they are consistent with the dominant development ideology that eschews 'dependency' and the perceived 'welfarism' of direct transfers; (ii) they involve the production of assets, thereby avoiding the perceived trade-off between productive investment and expenditure on welfare; (iii) in the popular political discourse they are perceived as creating 'jobs' rather than offering welfare; and (iv) they are perceived as offering the benefit of self-targeting by the poor, by means of a low wage rate, rendering alternative targeting mechanisms unnecessary. For these reasons, public works programmes are currently a popular social protection instrument in situations of chronic as well as acute poverty, seeming to offer a 'win–win' policy option for both policy-makers and donors. But this chapter argues that the assumptions underlying the reasons for selecting public works over alternative interventions are in many cases illusory, or based on false expectations. In the light of this, a fundamental question emerges: are public works an appropriate policy instrument in the context of chronic poverty?

The paper explores this question by drawing on case studies from South Africa and Malawi. In both countries, public-works-based responses to poverty and unemployment play a central role in both national social protection policy, and equally, if not more importantly, the popular political discourse.

Before examining the assumptions underlying the selection of public works, it is useful to review the key components of public works programmes and their implementation. There are many different kinds of public works interventions, but the key components are the provision of employment by the state at a prescribed wage for those unable to find alternative employment, in order to provide a form of social safety net and simultaneously create public goods. This chapter focuses exclusively on public works interventions offering single, short-term episodes of employment, rather than employment guarantee schemes, or programmes intended to offer repeated or ongoing public works employment.[3] The dominant rationale for public works is that they function as an instrument for responding to acute or transient shocks (see, for example, the *World Development Report 2000/2001* or the World Bank PovertyNet website). In this context, the economic and labour market function of public works is to promote consumption smoothing during periods of disrupted access to income, particularly where the problem is covariate (that is, affecting a whole community),[4] and in this way prevent or reduce distress selling of assets. Hence programmes offer a risk insurance function, responding to acute or transient shocks that may occur as single, one-off shocks, resulting from some exogenous event, or may be cyclical – relating, for example, to annual shortfalls in labour demand at a given point in the agricultural cycle, while at the same time producing output assets that will reduce vulnerability to future shocks. In these circumstances, the World Bank argues that the use of a public works instrument offering temporary employment may be appropriate, in terms of cost and impact, particularly where the output of the programme is an asset that will reduce the vulnerability of the community to future shocks.[5]

The key insight offered in the literature is that public works function as responses to acute or transient poverty. This is summarized by Subbarao *et al.* (1997) who, drawing on cross-country experience, assert that, 'public works have been an important *countercyclical* intervention in industrial and developing countries' (Subbarao *et al.*, 1997: 67) (emphasis added).

In the context of chronic poverty, however, it is not apparent that public works interventions offering a short episode of employment will have a significant or sustained impact. The key factor inhibiting the poverty reduction performance of public works in situations of structural unemployment is that public works employment is short-term and wages are low. As a consequence, the potential for accumulation is low and the intervention therefore cannot address the reproduction of chronic poverty. In this context, workers remain asset poor and public works income functions primarily as a positive wage shock (see, for example, McCord (2004a) with reference to South Africa). Drawing on cross-country experience, Subbarao *et al.* stress that the appropriateness of short-term public works is limited to situations of transient rather than chronic poverty, arguing that, 'public works are essentially a temporary safety net and should never be used as a permanent escape route from poverty' (ibid.: 168).

Yet, despite these insights reflected in donor literature,[6] short-term public works programmes are repeatedly developed, funded and implemented in situations of chronic mass un(der)employment, with the objective of providing social protection. Moreover, governments and donors frequently also anticipate sustained improvements in livelihoods and poverty reduction as the outcome of such interventions.[7] These programmes are developed with support from the same donors, whose own research teams have argued that the effective sphere of public works is limited to temporary or cyclical crises. The fact that such programmes continue to be implemented suggests that, for donors and governments, the attractiveness of the 'public works concept' is sufficient to override appraisals of the limited potential of public works, and scepticism regarding the performance of public works programmes in addressing chronic poverty. To understand the apparently contrary selection of public works as an instrument of social assistance in the context of chronic poverty, the key assumptions made by policy-makers and donors underlying the selection of public works in preference to alternative instruments are examined below.

Ideological concerns: the work ethic and dependency

One reason for the popularity of public works programmes is their consistency with the dominant development and social protection ideology.[8] The work requirement is consistent with an assumption that the work ethic may be weak among those in poverty, and a belief in the intrinsic benefit of having the poor work in return for social protection to prevent 'laziness' or a diminution of the work ethic. This assertion is particularly problematic given the extremely low value of most public works wages and the short episode of employment offered.[9] Similarly, public works programmes are consistent with the dominant development ideology, which eschews the perceived 'dependency' effect of direct transfers. Within this discourse it has been argued that public works represent a significantly different intervention from direct transfers in terms of their dependency effect. Both the concept of dependency itself, and the differential dependency impact of public works compared to other interventions, have been challenged.[10] Even if the 'dependency' argument were to be accepted, it is not clear that a distinction can be drawn between public works and other forms of social assistance intervention. In situations of mass unemployment/underemployment and chronic poverty, public works employees come to depend on public works employment, representing a form of 'dependence' arising from absolute reliance on the state to provide employment, which is as strong as the dependence on the state for direct grant transfers. Where the programmes do differ significantly is in terms of the dignity often conferred on public works participants by virtue of employment. It is also the case that, in some instances, the possibility of acquiring skills may lead to improved employment opportunities. Neither of these benefits are liable to accrue to those simply receiving transfers.[11] However, while the 'self respect and independence' ascribed to employment by Sen (1995) is an important component of the benefits reported to ensue from some programmes (see, for example, McCord, 2004a), public works employment may in other instances primarily be stigmatizing rather than empowering (see, for example, ILO, 2004: 372).

The work requirement can also have negative impacts in terms of the opportunity cost it implies. For households without access to sufficient resources to meet current consumption needs, the work requirement may lead to the diversion of labour away from their own production activities (agricultural or small-scale household production) into public works employment in order to gain immediate cash income, reflecting the time preference for immediate rather than deferred income resulting, for example, from agricultural production, or the sale of the results of their own production. In the case of a diversion of labour out of agricultural production, there are potentially negative medium- to long-term livelihood consequences, which would not arise in the case of a simple transfer. This is particularly problematic when programme implementation coincides with periods of high agricultural activity. Prompting a direct trade-off between the two activities offering short- and longer-term income/consumption benefits may have negative consequences in terms of medium- to long-term production – for example, through the loss of individuals' own production and seed for the next season. Programme data suggests that the work requirement frequently leads to the forgoing of alternative income-generating or subsistence activities (see, for example, Datt and Ravallion 1994, or McCord 2004a), because of the desire to generate cash incomes, and to optimize predictable household income in the short term, in the context of irregular and unpredictable employment opportunities outside the public works programme.

The reality of income forgone by public works employees is recognized by the World Bank, who note that: 'Since poor people can rarely afford to be totally idle, they often give up some form of income to join a workfare scheme' (World Bank, 2001: 156).[12]

This claim is supported by the finding from a range of programmes that mean income forgone by public works employees represents a significant proportion of the value of the public works wage transfer.[13] Van de Walle argues that the discrepancy between the gross and net value of a transfer through public works is given insufficient recognition in the evaluation of public works as a form of social assistance (Van de Walle, 1998). Once income forgone is taken into account, the net value of a transfer through public works may be significantly lower than its gross value, and as a result the net transfer may not necessarily have the anticipated welfare impact. So it is not clear that the work requirement has the function of either preventing 'dependency' or supporting the 'work ethic'. In addition, the use of the work requirement represents a significant opportunity cost, particularly for labour-constrained poor households. The work requirement may even lead to the exclusion of labour-constrained households from public works programmes, unless programmes are designed sensitively to reduce the opportunity cost of participation – for example, through flexible working practices.[14]

Given the preoccupation within the social protection debate of avoiding dependency while at the same time preserving the work ethic, public works programmes may be perceived within the dominant discourse as a more ideologically acceptable form of social protection than cash transfers (Meth, 2004), despite the potentially negative impact of the work requirement outlined above.

Asset creation

The creation of assets is generally cited as a key rationale for the selection of public works interventions over alternative social assistance measures. Public works offer the potential to kill two birds with one stone, combining social protection and asset creation, as Smith recommends in relation to Malawi: 'as far as possible safety nets in Malawi need to be productivity-enhancing (for example in the form of public works...rather than pure transfers...), to maximize long-term income growth among the poor' (Smith, 2001: 13)

However, the beneficial economic and developmental value of the assets created through public works is frequently assumed rather than being established empirically. In some instances, such as the flood and drought-related assets created in Bangladesh and India, which have a direct impact on mitigating future risk and promoting land productivity, the economic benefit of the infrastructure created is readily apparent, in terms of a reduction in flooding and improved water harvesting. Where the assets created are intended to promote economic growth, rather than mitigate known environmental threats, the value of those assets is less apparent. Under these conditions, evaluation is critical, yet it is rarely carried out. An example of the conflation of asset construction with poverty alleviation is to be found in South Africa's *Towards a Ten Year Review, Synthesis Report on Implementation of Government Programmes 1994–2004*, which justifies the claim of poverty alleviation by stating the number of assets constructed under public works programmes, rather than assessing their impact on poverty: 'these [public works] programmes have been successful in alleviating the asset poverty of communities. Over R6.5 billion of expenditure on infrastructure has provided 2,182 community assets' (The South African Presidency, 2003: 19).

In South Africa and Malawi, there is little evidence of a positive economic or livelihood impact arising as the result of the creation of assets through public works programmes (or, for that matter, evidence to the contrary), since data is not gathered on this aspect of public works programmes.

The objective of one Department for International Development (DFID)-funded public works programme in Malawi is 'to contribute to a sustained improvement in the livelihoods of the poor and to longer-term economic growth in Malawi' (DFID, 2003), and the World Bank and DFID funded public works component of the Malawi Social Action Fund (MASAF, 2004) describes itself as a 'safety net operation' (Government of Malawi, 2003). Since both programmes offer only temporary employment, the wage transfer is unlikely to function as a safety net or instrument for sustained livelihood improvement, and hence the potential of the programmes to achieve their anticipated outcomes is dependent on the ability of the assets created to deliver significant medium- to long-term benefits to participants. The failure to evaluate the impact of the assets created is problematic. This failure is partly attributable to the methodological difficulties in measuring the impact of assets on communities over time, as acknowledged in the *World Development Report 2004* (ch. 11),[15] but is primarily a result of an implicit and frequently unsubstantiated assumption within the public works discourse that the creation of assets, such as roads or community structures, is de facto of significant economic or livelihood benefit, either to participants, or to the broader community.

In some instances, the construction of a road may have positive direct and indirect effects for a community. This cannot, however, be assumed a priori; it is critical that this assumption is evaluated. A recent study in South Africa highlighted the potential for discrepancies between the aspirational objectives and actual outcomes in a rural road construction programme (Mashiri and Mahapa, 2002). This study challenges the assumption underlying the creation of assets through public works, and places public works asset performance within its institutional setting. This setting is noticeably absent from the public works debate. Subbarao and Smith noted a similar problem with public works programmes in Ethiopia, observing that:

> Workfare programs are not integrated with activities at various levels of government ... because there has been no integration of aid-funded projects with the broader developmental activity ... the program suffered from ... low productivity [did not lead to assets of the type found in India's Maharashtra Employment Guarantee Scheme]. The program is driven by the consideration of labour use ... rather than the creation

of assets consistent with regional (community) needs and priorities .... As a result [the] aim to use food aid as a 'dual purpose instrument of relief and development' did not materialize. (Subbarao and Smith, 2003: 21–22)

Questions also arise as to which segments of the population benefit from the creation of various assets, and over what time horizon. There is a tension between the creation of assets that may promote national growth, but do not have a significant impact on the livelihoods of the poor in the short to medium term, on the one hand (such as road infrastructure), and those that may promote development and sustainable livelihoods for the poor in the short term, but may not contribute significantly to national growth, such as improved irrigation. The quality and sustainability of assets created through public works is also open to question, because of the limited attention paid to accountability, oversight and ownership in the implementation of such programmes.

These issues are particularly important if policy-makers anticipate long-term benefits accruing from assets created through public works interventions. The wage benefits of public works participation will be limited to the duration of the programme, and are unlikely to confer long-term benefits themselves. The ability of a public works programme to deliver a sustained reduction in poverty is then dependent on whether the assets created confer long-term benefits on the poor. For this to occur, the assets would need to be instrumental in promoting productive asset accumulation by the poor, expanding sets of livelihoods opportunities in a sustained manner (for example, by improving road access, or rehabilitating irrigation facilities), benefits that can only be identified and realized through developmental, as well as technical (engineering) engagement with affected communities. Such positive impacts are also contingent on public works programmes (or complementary programmes) providing a sufficient asset base and risk insurance to enable beneficiaries to engage in new or diversified economic activities. The situation is frequently exacerbated by lack of planning or budget allocations for asset maintenance, which further undermines the potential benefit of the productive component of public works, by shortening the lifespan of any assets created.

The ability of assets to promote accumulation is of critical importance given the high non-wage component in Public Works Programmes budgets, with wages typically comprising between 30 per cent and 60 per cent of the total programme cost (Subbarao *et al.*, 1997: 80). The remaining budget is consumed in material and management costs, rendering the net cost of a unit transferred through public works significantly higher than alternative measures,[16] an insight accepted by the World Bank, who concede that: 'Workfare [*sic*] programs are not necessarily an inexpensive way of delivering benefits to poor people' (World Bank, 2001: 155).[17]

The paucity of interest in monitoring and evaluating this aspect of public works programmes is problematic. Evaluation of the economic value of the assets created has not been part of either the World Bank and DFID supported Social Action Fund public works programmes in Malawi (MASAF), or the South African government's current or past public works programmes (the Community Based Public Works Programme (CBPWP) and Expanded Public Works Programme (EPWP), respectively). In both countries, programmes are based on the assumption that public-works-produced assets will promote local and national growth through the provision of public services (see Government of Malawi, 2003; and Phillips 2004, respectively). The failure to evaluate this assumption is problematic in terms of justifying any premium arising from the relatively high cost of adopting public works, rather than alternative social protection instruments.

The fallacy of job creation

Public works are popular with politicians as they offer the opportunity for a government to claim to be 'creating jobs' in a far more direct and observable way than the opaque medium- to long-term processes that deliver genuine economic growth and employment.[18] Since they are presented as offering 'jobs not grants', they reinforce the impression of avoiding dependence on social assistance.[19] The reality of public works employment, however, frequently belies these impressions, with the majority of public works employment in Africa comprising short-term and temporary work opportunities (Subbarao *et al.*, 1997). In South Africa and Malawi, government public works programmes tend to offer employment for between two and four months, and while such programmes may be presented as 'employment creation' programmes, in reality they represent only short-term employment opportunities that are not an appropriate response to a situation of chronic poverty and un(der)employment. Offering a temporary consumption-smoothing intervention, in the context of chronic mass un(der)employment and poverty represents a serious mismatch between problem and policy response.

While participants work in return for payment, thereby qualifying technically as employees, the value of the work they are carrying out is in many instances open to question, and, as noted above, the quality and economic or developmental relevance of the asset being created is frequently omitted from project monitoring and evaluation criteria. A consequence is that much work carried out under the aegis of public works may in fact be 'make-work' rather than genuinely contributing to the livelihoods either of those employed on the programme, or the wider community (see, for example, Subbarao *et al.*, 1997).

If the scale of employment in public works programmes was sufficiently large relative to the scale of unemployment, and the duration of employment sufficiently extended,[20] then it would be appropriate to speak of employment creation and attendant poverty reduction, as the direct link between employment and poverty reduction would have been well established; see, for example, Bhorat*et al.* (2001). It is, however, important to place public works programmes in perspective, recognizing that the effectiveness of small-scale, temporary public works programmes in the context of chronic poverty and mass under- or unemployment is trivial.

Self targeting through the wage

The fourth assumed benefit of public works programmes is in terms of their simplicity of targeting, using self-targeting through a low wage rate to reach the poor, rather than using alternative targeting criteria that are often complex and costly to administer. This self-targeting aspect of public works programmes is based on the premise that the work requirement and low wages, conventionally set at or below the prevailing wage, lead to an outcome in which the poor self-select themselves into the programme. As the World Bank confidently asserts: 'They [the public works programmes] can easily be self-targeting by paying wages below market rates' (World Bank, 2001: 155).

This assumption is prevalent in the public works literature; see, for example, Subbarao *et al.* (1997: 77–8), who cite evidence from Kenya that when the wage is increased, non-poor inclusion errors also increase (Teklu, 1994). Similar arguments have also been made on the basis of findings from the Maharashtra Employment Guarantee Scheme (MEGS) in India, where non-poor participation increased significantly after the upward revision of the public works wage (Ravallion *et al.*, 1991).[21] The received wisdom is then that by the adoption of a low wage rate, the poor will select themselves into programmes, while the less poor will find them unattractive and not seek to participate.[22] It is argued that this obviates the need for the administration of more complex poverty targeting mechanisms, based on some form of community-based selection or means testing.[23] The supposed ease of targeting is therefore a major factor in the selection of public works as a social protection instrument. The implementation of explicit targeting criteria is costly in terms of both budget and skills, and is problematic if the programme is to be implemented by the private sector.

A number of studies, however, challenge this assumption, suggesting a degree of leakage to the non-poor, even in the context of 'sub-market' wage rates (see, for example, Barrett and Clay, 2003; McCord, 2004b). As Barrett and Clay (2003) argue, this premise is conditional on a perfectly functioning labour market, which is frequently absent in the settings where public works programmes are implemented. They suggest that the marginal value of labour varies considerably within and between households, depending on the amount of labour available in the household, and access to productive assets such as land. This variation in the marginal value of labour renders public works employment at a given wage attractive to surplus labour in less-poor households in some cases, as a form of supplementary income, yet unattractive to poorer households with limited access to labour, *even with public works wage levels at or below the prevailing wage.*[24] When the imperfection of labour markets is taken into consideration, Barrett and Clay argue that economic theory supports the empirical finding that self-targeting through a low wage may not be an adequate mechanism to target employment to the poorest.

Barrett and Clay also argue that a wage set at an extremely low level may be contrary to the social protection objectives that were the initial rationale for programme implementation. This analysis is particularly relevant in a segmented labour market where the prevailing wage in the most poorly paid sector is extremely low, as in the *ganyu* (informal agricultural contract labour) system in Malawi, where the daily *ganyu* wage is approximately MK33/day (£0.16) (Government of Malawi, 2004). This wage is used to guide remuneration in the Social Action Fund public works programme. Replicating this wage level in a public works programme is unlikely to have a significant impact on chronic poverty (McCord, 2004b), and creates a tension within a programme with the objective of providing social assistance and addressing chronic poverty.

The assumptions underlying the self-targeting function of a low wage in public works programmes are currently coming under attack from a range of theoretical perspectives. For example Scandizzo *et al.* (2004) and Pellisery (Chapter 12 in this volume) draw similar conclusions on the basis of the theory of real options and public choice theory, and with a focus on institutional 'process deficits' (respectively), regarding the illusory nature of effective self-targeting in the context of imperfect labour markets with fluctuating wages, and high public works entry and exit costs.

In this context, Subbarao's assertion that a wage rate no higher than the prevailing market wage is an ideal public works programme design feature (Subbarao, 2003: 14), is problematic, as is his response to his own question, 'How low should the program wage be?' Subbarao argues that the wage 'should not be set at such a low level that it stigmatizes the work, thus leading the "poor but proud" to go hungry' (ibid., : 10), irrespective of the fact that the social protection impact of public works programmes is a function of the value of the wage, or that a low wage may serve as a barrier to participation by the labour-constrained poor.[25] Barrett and Clay present a fundamental challenge to this popular but problematic argument. They conclude that higher wages, together with alternative targeting mechanisms, would be the appropriate response if social protection outcomes were the goal, since low wages in public works are neither sufficient to ensure adequate poverty targeting, nor are they consistent with programme objectives relating to the sustained reduction of poverty.

In situations of chronic poverty and mass unemployment/underemployment where the scale of public works employment offered is trivial in relation to the scale of the unemployment and poverty problem, it is likely that competition for public works employment will further erode any putative poverty-based self-targeting. In South Africa, for example, with the national public works programme aiming to offer 200,000 employment opportunities per annum in the context of unemployment of more than four million using the narrow definition (and rising to over eight million if the broad definition is used),[26] such targeting problems are likely to occur (McCord, 2003). Given that demand for public works employment tends to exceed the supply of employment opportunities, and given the leakage of employment opportunities to the non-poor, inherent within a segmented labour market when wages are set low, Barrett and Clay's argument for the adoption of an increased wage rate, together with the use of explicit targeting mechanisms, is strong. It offers a serious alternative to the conventional public works theoretical canon.[27]

Overview of assumptions informing policy choice

It is not evident that public works constitute a social protection instrument that can simultaneously (i) create work: (ii) avoid dependency; (iii) create assets that will promote livelihoods and/or growth; and (iv) through self-targeting spontaneously deliver resources to the poor, in the context of chronic poverty. This insight offers a major challenge to the assumptions and prejudices that continue to inform policy choice, in the absence of adequate supporting evidence, and it undermines the dominant position of public works in the current social protection debate.

Can public works perform a social protection function in the context of chronic poverty?

Having questioned the assumptions underlying the selection of public works programmes as a social protection policy choice, we now turn to the question of whether public works programmes actually deliver on their social protection function of alleviating or, better still, eradicating poverty? As discussed above, public works are characterized repeatedly as *counter-cyclical* interventions.[28] Subbarao *et al.* (1997) argue that, while public works have an important consumption-smoothing impact in the context of crises, they are not, as generally conceptualized, instruments for delivering sustained poverty reduction (Subbarao *et al.*, 1997: 70).

The clear message is that short-term public works are appropriate only where poverty is transient or cyclical (in which case, the intervention must be repeated), and that if poverty is chronic, there is a need to offer ongoing rather than temporary employment, for public works to perform a social protection function. Datt and Ravallion argue that: 'failure to obtain this work [public works employment] whenever needed will tend to undermine the social insurance function of public-works schemes' (Datt and Ravallion, 1994: 1358). Subbarao et al. concur, suggesting that: 'in countries where poverty-gap ratios are high, the need to run the program year-round (and thus raise transfer benefits to the poor) assumes greater importance' (Subbarao *et al.*, 1997: 84).

This indicates that sustained, rather than short-term, employment opportunities are required if public works are to address chronic poverty. Some programmes, such as the Zibambele road maintenance programme in KwaZulu-Natal, South Africa, have responded to this challenge by offering year-round public works employment, It is notable, however, that this programme is not donor designed or funded, and operates outside the international ideological norms and constraints that tend to limit such programmes. It uses explicit poverty rather than wage-based targeting, and pays above the prevailing wage. This has resulted in an extremely low inclusion error, consistent with Barrett and Clay's thesis outlined above.[29] This programme is, however, the exception rather than the rule in Sub-Saharan Africa, where a common assumption or pretence remains among policy-makers that the implementation of a public works programme offering short-term employment will have a meaningful impact on poverty.

Voice and beneficiary perceptions

While public works continue to be a popular policy choice with governments and donors, this enthusiasm is not necessarily shared by participants, who recognize the extremely limited social protection impact of such programmes. It is notable that participants have very little voice in the public works discourse. Where their perceptions of the value of public works employment and its impact on livelihoods have been solicited, most participants do not consider that programmes will have a sustained impact on their livelihood.[30] Some poor participants in a DFID-funded programme in Malawi (the Improving Livelihoods Through Public Works Programme (ILTPWP))[31] voted with their feet by leaving the programme because of the low wage rate, which was sufficient only to meet the subsistence requirements of one household member, and hence was unlikely to contribute significantly to the broader social protection objectives of the programme. These workers chose to seek casual employment in the bottom segment of the open labour market, rather than to continue to engage in public works employment (McCord, 2004b). This offers a critical insight into the impact of public works at the household level. However, since the poor have little, if any, voice in the process of social protection programme selection and implementation, their experience is of little significance in policy choice. There is little evidence that household-level programme impact, or lack thereof, is a key determinant of continued public works programme selection. This issue of lack of voice among participants, and imperfect feedback loops, which is recognized more generally in the *World Development Report 2004* (World Bank, 2004), applies egregiously in the case of many public works programmes.

Critical public works design features in the context of chronic poverty

Given the wide range of potential public works programme design options, it is not useful to dismiss all public works interventions as a means of addressing chronic poverty. This chapter has primarily been concerned with programmes offering short-term employment in isolation from other developmental initiatives. The literature suggests that the provision of short-term, consumption-smoothing wage transfers will not significantly impact on either poverty or livelihoods. Hence, if public works are to be used constructively in situations of chronic poverty, it is necessary to address this limitation in programme design. The literature is broadly consistent in terms of the key considerations that should be taken into account in this situation, highlighting the need for:

- Sustained public works employment;
- Integration of public works programmes with other developmental initiatives;
- Linkages with micro-finance, and micro-enterprise activities;
- Creation of assets which directly impact on reducing vulnerability and promoting livelihoods;
- Flexible or piece-based employment, enabling participants to combine public works employment with other responsibilities and income earning opportunities;
- Higher wages; and
- Poverty targeting measures.

Implemented in this way, public works could play a significant role in situations of chronic poverty. If the public works model adopted however is simply a replication of the model used in situations of transient poverty, the developmental impact is likely to remain negligible.

Conclusion

On the basis of cross-country experience, Subbarao *et al.* are confident to assert that: 'public works are essentially a temporary safety net and should never be used as a permanent escape route from poverty' (Subbarao *et al.*, 1997: 168).

Also, the ILO is forthright in its criticism of the reality, as opposed to the 'presentation package' offered by public works, confirming the critique set out in this ILO paper:

> Unfortunately there are reasons for scepticism about the wilder positive claims made for public works. One is that that they use up a lot of scarce resources, and result in low productivity work being done. Another is that they are not very good at 'targeting'. The poorest and most insecure are likely to be at the end of the queue for these casual jobs... And perhaps above all, they have to be massive schemes if they are to have much effect on the incidence of poverty and economic insecurity. (ILO, 2004: 372)

Despite this, short-term public works programmes with social protection and long-term developmental objectives continue to be implemented, with donor funding and support. The limitations of such interventions are documented, yet donors are still willing to endorse them in preference to alternatives. It is not possible to explain this policy dominance in situations of chronic poverty in terms of either empirical evidence or theory, but it is possible to explain it in terms of the ideological attractiveness of public works, their apparent ease of self-targeting, and the fact that, in theory at least, they involve the creation of productive assets. These ideological interests and assumptions appear in some contexts to dominate theoretical and empirical arguments, representing a victory of political over 'technical' considerations in the sphere of social protection.[32]

This chapter has argued that public works programmes appear to be protected from the scrutiny and criticism to which other social protection instruments are subject, and to dominate alternative options as the result of a number of ideological preferences and assumptions. The problem is that, while public works programmes offering short-term employment – a one-off social assistance response – may function well in terms of consumption smoothing in the context of cyclical problems of varying degrees of severity, they are unlikely to succeed in achieving social protection objectives in the context of chronic poverty. Programmes of this sort tend to offer only palliative inputs of limited significance, rather than facilitating the accumulation of productive assets required for participants to move out of chronic poverty. If the objective is social protection in situations of chronic poverty, then public works programmes, as frequently implemented, are not the most appropriate policy choice, and do not offer the apparent 'win–win' outcome widely anticipated by politicians and policy-makers.

Notes

1. Following Hulme *et al.* (2001) chronic poverty is defined as a situation in which a significant proportion of the population remain in poverty between one period and the next, because of their inability to accumulate the productive assets required to exit poverty. Chronic labour market failure is a situation in which high levels of involuntary unemployment persist over a prolonged period, and are a consequence of the structure of the economy rather than an exogenous shock.
2. Social security programmes are conventionally divided into social insurance and social assistance. In this chapter, public works programmes are considered as a form of social assistance. Whereas the social grants that form the bulk of social assistance are transfers (i.e. unrequited payments), public works programmes require that work is performed in exchange for the social assistance transfer.
3. Examples of programmes with the objective of offering sustained or repeated episodes of employment are the Indian National Rural Employment Guarantee Scheme, and the Ethiopian Productive Safety Nets Programme.
4. The term covariate is used to describe a shock that is experienced across a community and cannot be mitigated by risk-sharing within a specific social group or network (see Cafiero and Vakis 2006).
5. See Subbarao *et al.* (1997) for a full discussion of this question.
6. See, for example, World Bank 2001, ILO 2004 and Subbarao 1997 (cited above).
7. An example is one short-term DFID-supported public works programme in Malawi, which has as its goal 'enhanced livelihoods for poor people in Malawi', (DFID, 2004).
8. See Culpitt (1999) for a discussion of the neo-liberal theoretical basis of the dominant social protection ideology.
9. It is interesting to note that the concept of 'benefit scroungers' implied by this concern has spread along with the ideology of dependency from developed to developing economies, despite the fact that the value of many public works transfers still leave participating households well below the poverty line. For example, the gross public works wage in South Africa vary between R350 and R600 per month (approximately £30–£55), leaving over 90 per cent of participating households below the poverty line (McCord, 2004a). In Malawi, the World Bank and DFID-funded Social Action Fund public works programme offers remuneration of MK792 per month (approximately £4), again leaving participating households well below the poverty line (McCord, 2004b).
10. See Meth, 2004 for an overview of this debate, with particular reference to public works.

11. It should be noted, however, that the impact of skills acquisition through public works may be limited by both the short duration of employment (and hence the short period available for skills transfer), and by constrained demand for semi-skilled workers, particularly in situations of slow economic growth and mass unemployment.

12. It should be noted that while the terms 'workfare' and 'public works' are sometimes used interchangeably in the literature, the two concepts are quite distinct and should not be used synonymously. The concept of 'workfare' demands that participants take up available employment opportunities as a condition of receipt of welfare. This concept has been imported from the first world literature on social protection and unemployment, but is not readily applicable in the context of the elevated levels of unemployment currently experienced in many developing countries, where the fundamental problem is the net lack of employment opportunities rather than a reluctance on the part of the unemployed to take up vacant positions (see Meth, 2003).

13. Studies have found a range of estimates of income forgone; for example, McCord found that 30 per cent of participants in two programmes in South Africa had given up alternative paid employment to participate in the public works programme, and that for these workers, the net value of the public works employment was between 30 and 50 of the gross transfer (McCord, 2004a: 38–41). Similarly, the World Bank estimates that forgone income could represent up to 50 per cent of the wages paid by 'workfare' schemes (World Bank, 2001: 156), and Datt and Ravallion (1994) report a wide range in income forgone, contingent on both the characteristics of the worker, the size of the programme, and demand for employment.

14. An example of this is the Zibambele road maintenance programme in South Africa, which offers flexibility in working hours enabling workers to combine public works employment with domestic responsibilities and other income-generating activities. The programme also allows other members of the household to substitute for workers if temporary alternative remunerative employment opportunities occur (McCord, 2004a).

15. Despite their positive conclusions regarding the impact of rural road construction in China, Gannon and Liu concede 'knowledge of the transport conditions of the poor and especially how these interact with other factors ...is modest' (Gannon and Liu, 2000: 8).

16. Smith calculated a per unit cost of 13.9 to transfer a unit to the poorest in Malawi through public works, compared to 1.73 through cash transfers (Smith, 2001: 39).

17. This insight is also conceded in the South African *Towards A Ten Year Review* (The South African Presidency, 2003).

18. It is no coincidence that Subbarao *et al.* (1997) note the frequency of the initiation of public works programmes in the run-up to elections.

19. This is illustrated in a statement by President Mbeki of South Africa at the launch of a new public works initiative: 'a million unemployed people will get jobs over the next five years because of a dramatically expanded government public works programme [which would] *help to move people off social grants and into public employment*' (my emphasis) (Presidential address to the National Council of Provinces, 11 November 2003).

20. Subbarao *et al.* (1997: 84) argue that, in the context of chronic poverty, public works employment must be offered year-round, as do Datt and Ravallion, who state that failure to obtain this work whenever needed will tend to undermine the social insurance function of public-works schemes' (Datt and Ravallion, 1994: 1358).

21. Leakage to the non-poor increased significantly after the minimum wage that guided MEGS remuneration levels was increased to *above* the 'prevailing wage' in the 1980s.

22. The terms 'poor' and 'less poor' will not be further defined in this chapter. The purpose here is to explore participation in public works programmes using a relational concept of poverty, based on the depth of poverty, since the majority of the population in many developing countries may be defined as poor, depending on which poverty line is adopted. In the light of this, it may be most useful to differentiate within the category of the poor rather than seek to define those who fall within or outside this category.

23. The issue of self-targeting through the wage is discussed in Subbarao *et al.* (1997).

24. This theoretical analysis confirms empirical programme evaluation findings, such as the review of the DFID funded Sustainable Livelihoods Through Inputs for Assets (SPLIFA) public works programme in Malawi, which found non-poor participants from labour-rich households self-selecting into the programme despite extremely low wage levels (DFID, 2004).

25. While Subbarao recognises that 'a low wage rate will also result in low transfer earnings to each [poor] participant' (Subbarao, 2003: 4), he does not explore the consequences of this statement in terms of the efficacy of public works as a form of social assistance.

26. Under the narrow definition, unemployment in South Africa stood at 25 per cent in 2006, rising to 39 per cent if the broad definition, including discouraged workers, is used.

27. One example of such practice is the Zibambele programme in South Africa, which has adopted a higher wage rate than most public works programmes in South Africa and includes explicit poverty targeting using community selection methods, in which 99 per cent of the workers' households fall below the poverty line.

28. The characterization of public works as a counter-cyclical instrument is repeated throughout World Bank literature; see, for example, the 2001 World Development Report, 'public works are a useful countercyclical instrument for reaching poor unemployed workers' World Bank (2001: 155), and the PovertyNet website (2005).

29. For a full discussion of the programme, see McCord (2004a).

30. See, for example, McCord (2004a), McCord *et al.* (2006), and Ndoto and Macun (2005).

31. This programme is a sub-component of a World Bank-funded Malawi Social Action Fund public works intervention, in which the wage rate was influenced by the World Bank, which set the wage at 20 per cent *below* the prevailing wage. This is more draconian than even the conventional World Bank principles of successful workfare programming would dictate, according to which, 'programs should pay *no more than* the average wage for unskilled labour' (World Bank, 2001: 156). A theoretical justification for this uniquely punitive choice of wage

level, in the context of the extremely low unskilled wages prevailing in Malawi, when the purpose of the intervention is 'raising incomes for poor households through cash transfers' (Government of Malawi, 2003) is not included in the programme documentation.

32. For a discussion of the inherent tension between political and 'technical' considerations in the South African policy environment, with reference to the issue of poverty, see Everatt (2003: 89–90).

References

Barrett, B. and D. C. Clay (2003) 'Self-targeting accuracy in the presence of imperfect factor markets: Evidence from food-for-work in Ethiopia', *Journal of Development Studies*, 39(5), 152–180.

Bhorat, H., M. Leibbrandt, M. Maziya, S. van der Berg, and I. Woolard (2001) *Fighting Poverty, Labour Markets and Inequality in South Africa*. Cape Town: UCT Press.

Cafiero, C. and R. Vakis (2006) *Risk and Vulnerability Considerations in Poverty Analysis: Recent Advances and Future Directions*, Social Protection Discussion Paper No 0610. Washington: World Bank.

Culpitt, I. (1999) *Social Policy and Risk*. London: Sage Publications.

Datt, G. and M. Ravallion (1994) 'Transfer benefits from public-works employment: Evidence for rural India', *The Economic Journal*, 104(427), 1346–1369.

Department for International Development (DFID) (2003) Learning from DFID's investment in MASAF to date and linking support through ILTPWP [Improving Livelihoods Through Public Works Programmes] with MASAF III, DFID Malawi, unpublished.

Department for International Development (DFID) (2004) *Sustainable Livelihoods Through Inputs for Assets Output to Purpose Review*, DFID Malawi, unpublished.

Everatt, D. (2003) 'The politics of poverty', in D. Everatt and V. Maphai (eds), The Real State of the Nation, South Africa After 1990, *Development Update Special Edition*, 4(3), 75–99.

Expanded Public Works Programme, EPWP Website (2004), http://www.epwp.gov.za – accessed on 01/05.

Gannon, C. and Z. Liu (2000) 'Transport: Infrastructure and services', in *Poverty Reduction Strategy Paper – A Source Book*. Washington, DC: The World Bank.

Government of Malawi (2003) *MASAF III/ECEDP Operational Manual*, 12 September.

Government of Malawi (2004) Study to Inform the Selection of an Appropriate Wage Rate for Public Works Programmes in Malawi, unpublished.

Hulme, D., K. Moore and A. Shepherd (2001) 'Chronic poverty: Meanings and analytical frameworks', *Chronic Poverty Research Centre Working Paper 2*, University of Manchester: Institute for Development Policy and Management.

International Labour Office (ILO) (2004) Economic Security for a Better World. Geneva: ILO Socio-Economic Security Programme.

Malawi Social Action Fund (MASAF) (2004) The Evaluation of the Improving Livelihoods Through Public Works Programme (ILTPWP), unpublished.

Mashiri, M. and S. Mahapa (2002) 'Social exclusion and rural transport: A road improvement project', in P. Fernando and G. Porter (eds), *Balancing the Load: Women, Gender and Transport*. London: Zed Books.

McCord, A. (2003) 'An overview of the performance and potential of public works programmes in South Africa', *CSSR Working Paper no.49*. South Africa: University of Cape Town.

McCord, A. (2004a) 'Policy expectations and programme reality: The poverty reduction and employment performance of two public works programmes in South Africa'. Economics and Statistics Analysis Unit & Public Works Research Project, SALDRU, School of Economics, University of Cape Town. *ESAU Working Paper*. London: Overseas Development Institute.

McCord, A. (2004b) 'Setting the public works wage in Malawi: The challenges and contradictions of social protection, self targeting and market distortion in the context of an imperfect labour market', CARE *Malawi Working Paper,* unpublished.

McCord, A., K. Adonis, G. McDermott, and L. van Dongen (2006) *The Labour Market Impact of the EPWP in the Western Cape,* unpublished, Public Works Research Project. SALDRU, University of Cape Town.

Meth, C. (2003) 'What to do until the doctor comes: relief for the unemployed and for poorly-paid workers', Unpublished Monograph, School of Development Studies, University of KwaZulu Natal.

Meth, C. (2004) 'Ideology and social policy: "handouts", and the spectre of "dependency"', *Transformation,* 56, 1–30.

Ndoto, M. and I. Macun (2005) *World Wide Fund for Nature Rapid Socio-economic Survey of Working for Wetlands.* Community Agency for Social Enquiry (CASE), Johannesburg, unpublished.

Phillips, S. (2004) *The Expanded Public Works Programme (EPWP).* Presentation to the UNDP, HSRC & DBSA Conference on Overcoming Under-development in South Africa's Second Economy, Pretoria, South Africa, 29 October.

Ravallion, M., G. Datt, and S. Chaudhuri (1991) 'Higher wages for relief work can make many of the poor worse off', *Working Paper, WPS 568.* Agricultural and Rural Development Department. Washington, DC: The World Bank.

Scandizzo, P., R. Gaiha and K. Imai (2005) *Option Values, Switches and Wages – An Analysis of the Employment Guarantee Scheme in India.* Paper prepared for presentation at the Manchester Conference on Social Protection for Chronic Poverty, IDPM, University of Manchester, 23–4 February (originally written in 2004).

Sen, A. (1995) 'The political economy of targeting', in D. Van de Walle and K. Nead (eds), *Public Spending and the Poor.* Baltimore: Johns Hopkins University Press.

Smith, W. J. (2001) Spending on Safety Nets for the Poor: How Much, For How Many? The Case of Malawi. Africa Region Working Paper Series, Number 11. Washington, DC: The World Bank.

South African Presidency (2003) Towards a Ten Year Review: Synthesis Report on Implementation of Government Programmes; Policy Co-ordination and Advisory Services Discussion Document, Pretoria: The South African Presidency.

Subbarao, K. (2003) *Systemic Shocks and Social Protection: Role and Effectiveness of Public Works Programs.* Social Protection Unit. Human Development Network. Washington, DC: The World Bank.

Subbarao, K., A. Bonnerjee, J. Braithwaite, S. Carvalho, K. Ezemenari, C. Graham, and A. Thompson (1997) *Safety Net Programs and Poverty Reduction, Lessons from Cross Country Experience.* Directions in Development. Washington, DC: The World Bank.

Subbarao, K., W. J. Smith (2003) Safety Nets Versus Relief Nets: Towards a Medium-term Safety Net Strategy for Ethiopia. Draft. http://www1.worldbank.org/sp/risk_management/Training/Ethiopia%20Safety%20Nets.pdf – accessed on 11/04.

Teklu, T. (1994) Minor Roads Program in Kenya: Potential for Short-Term Poverty Eradication Through Asset Creation. Washington, DC: International Food Policy Research Institute.

Van de Walle, D. (1998) 'Assessing the welfare impacts of public spending', *World Development,* 26(3), March, 365–379.

World Bank (2001) World Development Report 2001: Attacking Poverty. Washington, DC: World Bank.

World Bank (2004) World Development Report 2004: Making Services Work For Poor People. Washington, DC: The World Bank.

World Bank, Poverty Nets Web Site (2005) http://www1.worldbank.org/sp/safetynets/ Public%20Works.asp – accessed on 01/05.

9
The Emergence and Popularity of Conditional Cash Transfers in Latin America

Tatiana Feitosa de Britto

Since the mid-1990s a new trend in social policies has appeared in Latin America: the provision of grants to targeted poor households on condition that they engage in human capital investments, such as sending children to school and making periodic visits to health centres. These programmes, known as conditional cash transfers (CCTs), address demand-side constraints for structural poverty reduction, through an incentive scheme that combines the short-term objectives of safety nets with long-term goals of breaking intergenerational poverty traps.

Although initiated with domestic funding, CCTs have received substantial support from the international community, as one of the 'best practices' for social protection in Latin America. This support is not only theoretical, but also practical: considerable funding has been provided for the exchange and dissemination of experience, expansion of existing initiatives, and replication of similar programmes elsewhere. In Latin America alone, there are records of at least ten countries implementing CCTs, not to mention more recent experiences in other developing regions.

The primary objective of this chapter is to make a contribution to understanding how and why these programmes came about, what they can deliver, and what are the main challenges that have arisen. Based on a discussion of two pioneer CCTs within a policy analysis framework, I focus on particular characteristics, selected implementation aspects and contextual factors that help to explain the reasons behind the emergence and popularity of these programmes among both governments and donors.

Policy options and choices

There are a myriad of criteria that can be used to study policy options. This chapter uses a framework adapted from Patton and Sawicki (1996) and

Grosh (1995) to develop a critical assessment of the design and implementation of CCTs, taking into account the following elements:

- political feasibility (the distribution of costs and benefits and the motivations and values of stakeholders);
- targeting accuracy and mechanisms;
- administrative operability and capacity requirements;
- adequacy (the extent to which a particular policy is in line with the problem addressed); collateral effects (indirect impacts and externalities).

Additionally, it discusses the factors that explain the popularity of CCTs in Latin America in the late 1990s through the framework proposed by Grindle and Thomas (1991). This analyses the political economy of policy choices and decision-making with respect to: political stability and support; bureaucratic implications; technical advice; and international pressure and leverage.

The elements of these two sets of analytical tools are related in mutual reinforcements and overlaps. For example, the criterion of political feasibility is closely connected to the lenses of political stability and support. Underlying both concepts are the notions of constituencies and stakeholders. Administrative operability, in turn, is linked to bureaucratic implications, as organizational capacity and institutional commitment permeate them. Adequacy is primarily a function of technical advice, since the fit between problem and response depends on precise diagnostics for policy formulation. Targeting is simultaneously related to bureaucratic implications (in the sense of capacity), technical advice (in terms of accuracy) and international leverage (as donors are enthusiastic advocates of targeting).

CCT pioneers

Mexico's *Progresa*[1]

Progresa was launched by President Ernesto Zedillo in 1997. Zedillo had taken office in December 1994, amid political and economic turmoil, which included political assassinations and kidnappings, corruption scandals, the Chiapas uprising and the crash of the Mexican peso. His initial concerns were not related to poverty or social programmes, but to the very survival of the regime. He took a series of decentralizing reforms at all levels, with the aim of dissociating his administration from the widely condemned practices of corruption and patronage of the Institutional Revolutionary Party (PRI), which had been ruling the country since the 1920s. Dismantling the highly politicized PRONASOL, PRI's main poverty-reduction programme, was part of this strategy (Menocal, 2001).

In his second year in office, Zedillo launched *Progresa* as an innovative programme, replacing highly regressive and urban-biased general food subsidies (Scott, 1999). It consisted of cash and in-kind transfers to beneficiary households, conditional on school attendance by the children of those families up to the age of eighteen, and regular visits to health centres by all household members. Progresa claimed to be non-political in terms of its targeting and transfer mechanisms.

The targeting of beneficiary households was carried out in three steps (Skoufias *et al.*, 2001). First, demographic data was used to target the most deprived communities (but to be included in the programme these communities had to have access to the education and health services inherent to Progresa's conditionalities). The second step consisted of the selection of beneficiary households within the targeted communities, on the basis of household surveys that used income and other socioeconomic characteristics to identify the most vulnerable families. The final step involved an element of community participation: the list of selected households was presented in a community meeting to review the accuracy of the selection. The transfers were directly addressed from the national co-ordinating body to recipients, without intermediation through state or municipal budgets. Beneficiaries would collect their transfers every other month from post office branches or banks.

The claims of innovation were related to Progresa's integrated approach to poverty (combining education, health and nutrition in a single intervention); to a positive gender bias (addressing the transfers to female members of the household and granting higher subsidies for girls than for boys); and to the emphasis on the participation of beneficiaries (not only in the targeting review, but also by having a beneficiary liaison, the local *promotora*). A remarkable aspect of the programme was the inclusion of an experimental evaluation at the design stage, carried out by an independent organization of renowned researchers, which provided early evidence of positive impacts and boosted international recognition for the programme.

Progresa was implemented gradually. In 1997, it reached eleven states and 300,000 families in rural areas. By 2004, under the framework of *Oportunidades*, the programme reached more than five million households in all thirty-one Mexican states, including urban areas.

As Progresa became the centrepiece of Mexico's targeted poverty reduction strategy, and contrary to the usual policy discontinuities that occur with political change in Latin America, the programme continued and expanded after Zedillo's PRI stepped down from the presidency.

Brazil's *Bolsa Escola*[2]

The roots of *Bolsa Escola* lie in relatively successful programmes at the local level. From the mid-1990s, Brazilian municipalities had introduced cash transfers, conditional on school attendance. These achieved good results and high visibility in the media (Sedlacek *et al.*, 2000). In 2001, President Fernando Henrique Cardoso was responsible for the introduction of *Bolsa Escola* nationally, building on the original programme, which transferred resources from central government to municipalities to implement their own CCTs. The programme was financed through a tax increase and introduced through a presidential measure, approved in Congress.

At the time *Bolsa Escola* was launched, the Brazilian economical and political context was not as difficult as 1997 in Mexico, but the country's macroeconomic stabilization package (in place since 1994) was being challenged by the effects of external financial crises. Also, presidential elections were scheduled for 2002, and the political scenario for the governing party was unclear. At the time of *Bolsa Escola*'s introduction, the minister in charge of its implementation (the Minister of Education) was viewed as a potential presidential candidate. The Minister of Health also intended to run for this position and he instigated another large-scale CCT programme focused on health and nutrition (*Bolsa Alimentação*).[3] The proximity of the electoral race seems to explain the speed with which *Bolsa Escola* was implemented. Launched in February 2001, by the beginning of 2002 the programme had reached more than five million beneficiary households in almost all of Brazil's 5,565 municipalities.

Bolsa Escola granted monthly transfers to poor households with children aged six to fifteen enrolled at school in grades one to eight, on the condition that they had at least 85 per cent school attendance. As in *Progresa*, the transfers were paid to the female head of the household, with no intermediation through sub-national budgets. But, in contrast to the Mexican case, whose transfers could add up to US$60 per month, *Bolsa Escola*'s transfers were only US$15 per family per month. There were no variations in the transfers based on age, gender or geographical location, but the decentralized fiscal arrangements in place in Brazil allowed the national programme to be combined with local ones. Thus, richer states and municipalities were permitted to top up the transfers or to expand coverage.

The government established a poverty line for the selection of beneficiaries and calculated estimates of the target population in each municipality from demographic data. This created a form of quota for each municipality, which was then in charge of implementing targeting at the household level. Local practices for targeting have shown considerable variation. Repeated cases of exclusion of potential beneficiaries, because the municipality had reached its coverage quota, have been identified (MEC, 2002). This could be related either to failures in the estimates, or in the targeting methods themselves.

The programme was initiated with domestic resources, but by the end of 2003 *Bolsa Escola*'s successor, *Bolsa Família*, had attracted a number of positive comments in international reports as well as significant loans from multilateral donors.

Understanding CCTs

The techniques and politics of CCTs

Based on a purely rational analysis, CCTs appear to be attractive social programmes, which should have scored better than possible alternatives considered by the governments of Brazil and Mexico at the time of their appraisal and approval. Hypothetically, at least one clear alternative was at hand for policy-makers: not introducing any new social programme. Governments could have chosen simply to boost existing education or health interventions with the funding that was available to start up the new CCT programmes. While this option would be easier than designing whole new programmes, it would be much less visible and was likely to focus only on supply-side issues.

To understand why these programmes were introduced and replicated across the region, it is important to bear in mind that the appeal of CCTs has much to do with their potential to tackle one key determinant of chronic poverty in Latin America: low educational attainment. They also had a good fit into the current mainstream discourse on poverty reduction. Contemporary concerns, such as gender, human capital, community participation, empowerment and targeting are all included, to varying degrees, in CCT programmes. But there are high administrative requirements associated with the setting up of conditional cash transfers. There can also be significant political economy issues involved in these programmes, with accusations that grants can be perceived as entitlements and thus create negative incentives for beneficiaries to work.

In terms of results, initial evaluations have shown positive effects on school enrolment and nutrition patterns (Sedlacek *et al.*, 2000; Morley and Coady, 2003; Rawlings and Rubio, 2004). The evidence regarding the impact on child labour is not conclusive, since school attendance can frequently be combined with work, indicating the need for broader interventions (Bourguignon *et al.*, 2002). The impact on poverty reduction is still not known precisely. In the short run, the magnitude of effects on poverty rates might vary by programme,[4] but in the long run, the translation of higher educational attainment into higher earnings cannot be taken for granted, as it is mediated by the quality of the education received, rates of employment, absorption of skilled labour in the economic structure, and general rates of return to education (Bourguignon *et al.*, 2002; CEPAL, 2002).

All in all, the popularity of CCTs is not only related to their basic characteristics but also to implementation aspects and contextual factors that enhanced their visibility among policy elites and donors.

Political support and feasibility

CCTs appeared at a time of economic crisis in Latin America, when the need for social safety nets was widespread. Although in the late 1990s the situation was nowhere near as devastating as the crisis of the 1980s, the whole of Latin America was trapped in a repetitive cycle of small economic recoveries followed by downturns.

In this context, what are the factors that encouraged decision-makers to select CCTs? Electoral concerns seem to have been important in both Brazil and Mexico. Cash transfers establish a direct and regular link between the national governments and beneficiaries. *Bolsa Escola* made this very visible, through a magnetic card that reached five million households one year before the presidential elections. Thus the logic of the programme seems to have been to retain or win votes for the governing party through the maximization of the number of beneficiaries, even if the amount of the transfer was kept rather low. As for *Progresa*, its greatest expansion in coverage took place in the two years preceding the presidential elections. While the programme's implementation showed some positive changes in relation to the clientelistic practices of previous interventions, its expansion did not follow only poverty indices; it had a political rationale behind it, with greater expansions in PRI-dominated states (Menocal, 2001).

It seems that the lenses of political stability and support played a key role in the creation of CCTs. The stakes involved were not the survival of a regime per se, but the continuation of the government parties in power, within the constraints set by the democratic game. Interestingly, in both Brazil and Mexico, the government candidates lost the electoral races, but this did not compromise the continuity of both CCT programmes. After the changes in the Mexican and Brazilian administrations, *Progresa* and *Bolsa Escola* were renamed and experienced considerable improvements, though their basic features and rationale were maintained.

The political feasibility of this type of programme seems to be high. Linking cash transfers to a specific and desirable change in behaviour highlights the co-responsibility of beneficiaries for their own well-being, and is a move away from more paternalistic forms of social assistance (Coady, 2003).

At the same time, there appears to be a broad consensus on the 'public' nature of goods, such as education or health in the region (Graham, 2002). In this sense, the fact that CCTs are related both to the present living conditions of poor children, and future human capital (with presumably positive effects in competitiveness) make them acceptable to middle-class voters and elites. They are seen as a way of helping the 'deserving poor' to escape poverty and, simultaneously, boosting the elusive phenomenon of sustained national economic growth.

The importance attributed to this 'co-responsibility' component was experienced by the Brazilian government in late 2004. When *Bolsa Família* replaced *Bolsa Escola* and other sectoral CCTs in Brazil, it began an accelerated expansion in coverage to reach its goal of 11.2 million families by 2006. The initial position adopted by the government agency in charge was that monitoring whether beneficiaries were complying with the programme's conditionalities was not a priority: the cash transfer provided by *Bolsa Família* was to be seen as a citizenship right, in the context of a basic income approach, and the conditionalities were simply a reinforcement of basic universal rights.[5] Nevertheless, the media and the general public do not appear to have accepted this perspective. When the news that the federal government did not in fact check whether beneficiary families were ensuring their children's attendance at school and or visiting health centres reached the newspapers, opponents from both the left and the right united to accuse the government of transforming a genuinely innovative scheme into an old-fashioned and paternalistic handout. Urgent measures had to be taken by programme managers to create a system to monitor these conditionalities and, if they were not met, to put in place corresponding sanctions (eventually leading to the suspension of benefits).

As well as the public benefits associated with the accumulation of human capital among poor children, one can speculate that the growing rates of urban violence in Latin America, and the widespread notion that they are associated with poverty and inequality, contribute to the political feasibility of CCTs. Fear encourages the elites to favour public policies that tackle poverty directly and, in particular, that keep poor children and adolescents in school. This helps to explain why the successors of *Progresa* and *Bolsa Escola* promoted a considerable expansion of coverage towards urban and metropolitan areas.

Thus, despite originally being created through redistributive reforms (tax increases or the reduction of subsidies) CCTs were congruent with other personal interests of policy elites and their constituencies.

In the particular case of Brazil, two other elements of political feasibility should be noted. The successes of local CCT programmes had been disseminated widely by the media, which contributed to an increasing degree of support from public policy and economic elites to this kind of intervention. Additionally, the decentralized operation of *Bolsa Escola* allowed municipalities to share the credit for it and manage a crucial political instrument: the identification of beneficiaries at the local level.

Targeting

In theory, CCTs have striven for the most accurate targeting of the poor. From the start, however, both programmes incurred an under-coverage of poor households, as *Progresa* did not serve areas lacking health and education services (usually the remotest communities), and *Bolsa Escola* excluded families without school-age children as well as marginal groups outside conventional households.

In practice, the targeting mechanisms employed presented flaws. Although studies showed that *Progresa*'s methodology outperformed other targeting methods (Coady *et al.*, 2002; Skoufias *et al.*, 2001), community reviews did not take place as originally envisaged (Adato, 2000). These functioned more as legitimation exercises for the 'scientific' steps of targeting procedure. The general perception on *Progresa* at the grassroots level was of an unfair targeting system, where 'needy' households were excluded and, to a lesser extent, less 'needy' ones were included.

In *Bolsa Escola*, the problems were even more serious, as there was significant room for political patronage and leakage of benefits, in particular because of the speed with which the programme was implemented. As *Bolsa Escola*'s decentralized targeting practices were continued by *Bolsa Família*, there have been numerous accusations of deliberate inclusion and exclusion errors, despite recent survey results that show fairly accurate targeting indexes (Soares *et al.*, 2006). The initial view adopted by the government on *Bolsa Família* was close to a basic income approach that eventually would move towards becoming universal. Thus targeting was not considered a priority element of the programme, but rather a necessary mechanism to implement it under budgetary constraints. Narrow targeting and means-testing were not valued by the agency in charge of the programme. In fact, the word 'targeting' itself was not commonly used by the implementing ministry of *Bolsa Família*. The social assistance programmes it implemented were described as universal rights, available to all who need them, and *Bolsa Familia* was legally set under the framework of a national policy on citizens' basic income. However, public opinion repeatedly demanded that tighter and more transparent procedures be used to screen potential beneficiaries. Notions that the programme's implementation suffered from 'unfairness' and patronage seemed to be the driver behind these claims. Moreover, there was an implicit and unresolved tension between two distinct notions of the programme: as a basic right, or as a response to a need.

Bureaucratic implications and administrative operability

Regarding administrative operability, CCTs entail considerable costs and capability requirements, especially in their setting-up stage. Such programmes involve relatively complex mechanisms for targeting and logistics for the delivery of transfers, as well as good co-ordination with service providers in health and education, for monitoring and supervision. As they expand, however, there are economies of scale, which can contribute to keeping overall administrative costs low (Morley and Coady, 2003).

Both *Progresa* and *Bolsa Escola* were integrated into existing line ministries, as regular government programmes. The capacity levels of central ministries in middle-income countries might be related to this, since later CCT initiatives implemented in different settings were placed in departments directly linked to the top executive office (Ayala, 2003). While integration into line ministries might increase the prospects of sustainability and institutionalization of these programmes, important administrative challenges remain.

For example, cost-effective mechanisms for monitoring the compliance of conditionalities, which are both timely and accurate, still need to be designed (and, as discussed above, are crucial for political acceptability). Also, no clear formula seems to be in place to calculate the optimal amount of the transfers. In Mexico, the differentiated size of transfers by age and gender signalled an attempt to cover the opportunity costs of children's education; but in Brazil, the flat-rate, low-value transfer indicated an attempt to maximize the number of beneficiaries across the country. Relatedly, there were no consistent rules and procedures about the inclusion of new beneficiaries in already-served communities or for the exclusion of recipients after a certain period of time in the programme and/or as a result of improvements in their socioeconomic status. Although these issues reveal administrative issues, they are also closely connected to political economy considerations, which shape the programme's political feasibility. Re-certification of beneficiaries might create tensions with current recipients, highlighting the potential conflicts between the counter-cyclical nature of safety nets and a natural trend of transfers to be perceived as permanent entitlements. It might also lead to considerable budgetary redistribution across states, a particularly sensitive issue for federal governments (Morley and Coady, 2003).

Adequacy and collateral effects

In terms of adequacy, CCTs have the great advantage of tackling several problems in a single policy. They can provide additional income to poor households, and have significant impacts on human capital. Also, since they are handed out in cash, CCTs entail lower transaction costs than in-kind transfers. Additionally, the direct transfer of cash to mothers may bring considerable efficiency gains if, as many claim, the mothers are better managers of family budgets.

Nevertheless, as much as these programmes try to bridge important gaps in social provisioning for poor households, they can only be an adequate solution if they overcome supply biases and geographic barriers. In this sense, CCTs can only be a complement to broader social provisioning, and never substitutes. They can only work where social services exist and are delivered to an acceptable level of quality.

A crucial question concerns the need for conditionalities in the first place. The assumption behind CCTs is that poor households do not automatically choose to invest in human capital, but this cannot be taken as given. In particular, could the same impact of CCTs be obtained through uncondi-tional transfers combined with significant improvements in the delivery of social services? While this might be a logical question from the viewpoint of adequacy, the criteria of political feasibility (acceptability to the general population) and administrative operability (introducing a new programme, even if complex, might still be easier than reforming existing supply-side policies) help to explain the inclusion of conditionalities in their design.

As a safety-net mechanism, CCTs may not be adequate to shield the poor from temporary macroeconomic shocks or natural disasters, as cyclical contractions or expansions have complex effects – temporarily, geographically and socially. Rather, they appear to be an effective mechanism to boost social development by tackling one major structural cause of poverty. Other emergency safety nets are needed to deal with short-run shocks causing deprivation, as well as different structural factors (Morley and Coady, 2003).

In relation to collateral effects, one can identify the general positive impacts of CCTs on women, and multiplier impacts on the local economies of the areas covered (Adato *et al.*, 2000).

But CCTs also entail costs to beneficiaries and their communities. At the individual level, there are private costs in terms of time and money for households to meet conditionalities and collect transfers, which affect women in particular. At the community level, there can be adverse impacts of household targeting on social relations, undermining community cohesion and solidarity, especially in rural areas (Adato, 2000).

Technical advice and international leverage

Besides political considerations, technical advice seems to have played an important role in shaping the decisions that led to the creation of CCTs. Their complex operational design, especially *Progresa's*, resulted from a careful process of trial and error and pilot tests, as well as a thorough experimental evaluation (Yaschine, 1999).

International pressure and leverage, in turn, appear to have had a smaller role in the original creation of CCTs than other social safety nets established in Latin America, such as social investment funds (Tendler, 2000). The design of *Progresa* and *Bolsa Escola* was 'home-grown', and international funding was only introduced at later stages of both programmes.

However, international leverage seems to be the key factor explaining the replication of these initiatives in other countries in a relatively short time-span. If the innovative characteristics of CCTs matched many of the concerns of the international agenda on poverty, the visibility of these programmes to international donors was enhanced by scientifically 'proven' results (made possible by the experimental evaluation of *Progresa*) and close links with some of the programme's designers. This visibility, in turn, accounts for the high popularity of these programmes elsewhere, as additional loans and funds were made available for policy transfer and governments willing to implement them. Moreover, it has translated into considerable efforts of dissemination, as donor agencies progressively adopt the approach of intermediaries for policy transfer, the diffusion of 'best practices' and the sharing of experiences among developing countries.

This illustrates the way in which international organizations are increasingly shaping the discourse and practice of social policy around the developing world (Deacon *et al.*, 1997), but it does not lead to a narrow conclusion that governments have no choice or room for manoeuvre in their poverty-reduction agenda. The home-grown experiences of *Progresa* and *Bolsa Escola* show how this phenomenon can also work in reverse: they were national 'inventions' that were 'bought' by donors and 'sold' as innovative solutions elsewhere.

Conclusion

As much as CCTs have an important role in structural poverty reduction, there are clear limits to what these interventions can achieve. Low levels of human capital are a central reason for the low incomes of the poor in Latin America, but this is only one part of the story. Complementary macroeconomic policies, which take into account the balance between social protection and macroeconomic stabilization, are essential for long-term sustainable poverty reduction (Cornia, 2002). Also crucial are interventions to alter deeply rooted and reproduced inequalities (often based on ethnic or cultural discrimination), as well as to foster the accumulation of other assets by the poor (such as finance and access to natural resources) (Székely, 2001).

From this perspective, the increasing prominence of CCTs in the development agenda and discourse of Latin America should be regarded with caution. They can be a step forward from conventional safety nets in the direction of 'enabling springboards' that promise win–win alternatives for donors and recipients. But they just cannot do it all: to achieve the ambitious goals of poverty reduction or eradication, CCTs have to be integrated into a broader development strategy.

Notes

1. In 2002, the Mexican government transformed *Progresa* into a new programme called *Oportunidades*. The basic features of Progresa were maintained, but its coverage and scope were expanded so as to reach urban areas, achieve greater coordination with other initiatives, and include transfers and a savings component for upper secondary students.
2. In 2003, *Bolsa Escola* was unified with other federal CCTs, in a programme called *Bolsa Família*, which by 2006 reached more than 11 million families.
3. The Minister of Health finally became Cardoso's party candidate, but ended up losing the elections to the left-wing Luis Inacio Lula da Silva.
4. Recent studies have shown significant aggregate poverty impacts in the cases of Brazil and Mexico, linked to the magnitude of these programmes and their relatively good targeting results (Soares *et al.*, 2006; Zepeda, 2006).
5. Basic education and health care for all are enshrined rights in the Brazilian constitution. Moreover, at the beginning of 2004 the country passed legislation that assured all Brazilians of the right to a guaranteed basic income to cover basic citizenship rights (food, education and health). The legislation establishes that this basic income is to be introduced gradually, giving priority to the neediest population. This law had been under discussion in Congress for over ten years and it was only after Lula became President that it was finally approved and sanctioned. The understanding of the main supporters of the law was that *Bolsa Família*, although targeted at the poor, was a first step in the direction of this national basic income that would later become universal (Suplicy, 2006).

References

Adato, M. (2000) *The Impact of PROGRESA on Community Social Relationships.* Washington, DC: International Food Policy Research Institute.

Adato, M., B. de la Brière, D. Mindek and A. Quisumbing (2000) 'El Impacto de Progresa en la Condición de la Mujer y en las Relaciones al Interior del Hogar', in SEDESOL, *Más Oportunidades para las Famílias Pobres – Impacto en el Trabajo y las Relaciones Familiares.* Mexico City, Mexico: SEDESOL, pp. 65–211.

Ayala Consulting (2003) Workshop on Conditional Cash Transfer Programs (CCTs): Operational Experiences. Final Report (Quito, Ecuador, 29 April–1 May, 2003).

Bourguignon, F., F. Ferreira and P. Leite (2002) *Ex-ante Evaluation of Conditional Cash Transfer Programs: The Case of* Bolsa Escola. Washington, DC: The World Bank.

CEPAL–UN Economic Comission for Latin America and the Caribbean (2002) *Panorama Social de América Latina 2001–2002.* Santiago, Chile: CEPAL.

Coady, D. (2003) *Alleviating Structural Poverty in Developing Countries: The Approach of Progresa in Mexico.* Background paper for the World Development Report 2004. Washington, DC: The World Bank.

Coady, D., M. Grosh and J. Hoddinott (2002) 'The Targeting of Transfers in Developing Countries: Review of Experiences and Lessons'. *Social Safety Net Primer Series.* Washington, DC: The World Bank.

Cornia, G. A. (2002) 'Social Funds in Stabilization and Adjustment Programs: A Critique', *Working Paper ChilD 13/2002.* Turin, Italy: Center for Household, Income, Labour and Demographic Economics.

Deacon, B., M. Hulse and P. Stubbs (1997) *Global Social Policy: International Organizations and the Future of Welfare.* London, UK: Sage Publications.

Graham, C. (2002) 'Public Attitudes Matter: A Conceptual Frame for Accounting for Political Economy in Safety Nets and Social Assistance Policies', *Social Protection Discussion Paper Series No. 0233.* Washington, DC: The World Bank.

Grindle, M. S. and J. W. Thomas (1991) *Public Choices and Policy Change: The Political Economy of Reform in Developing Countries.* Baltimore, MA: Johns Hopkins University Press.

Grosh, M. E. (1995) 'Five Criteria for Choosing among Poverty Programs', in N. Lustig (ed.), *Coping with Austerity: Poverty and Inequality in Latin America.* Washington, DC: The Brookings Institution, pp. 146–186.

MEC – Ministério da Educação (2002) *Identificação e Inclusão de Famílias no Bolsa Escola Federal.* Brasilia, Brazil: MEC.

Menocal, A. R. (2001) 'Do Old Habits Die Hard? A Statistical Exploration of the Politicisation of Progresa, Mexico's Latest Federal Poverty-Alleviation Programme, under the Zedillo Administration', *Journal of Latin American Studies*, 3(33), 513–538.

Morley, S. A. and D. Coady (2003) *From Social Assistance to Social Development: Targeted Education Subsidies in Developing Countries.* Washington, DC: International Food Policy Research Institute.

Patton, C. V. and D. S. Sawicki (1996) *Basic Methods of Policy Analysis and Planning*, pp. 207–219. Englewood Cliffs, NJ: Prentice Hall.

Rawlings, L. B. and G. M. Rubio (2004) *Evaluating the Impact of Conditional Cash Transfer Programs: Lessons from Latin America.* Washington, DC: The World Bank.

Scott, J. (1999) *Análisis del Programa de Educación, Salud y Alimentación (PROGRESA): México.* Mexico City, Mexico: CIDE.

Sedlacek, G., N. Ilahi and E. Gustafsson-Wright (2000) *Targeted Conditional Transfer Programs in Latin America: An Early Survey.* Washington, DC: The World Bank.

Skoufias, E., B. Davis and S. de la Vega (2001) 'Targeting the Poor: An Evaluation of the Selection of Households into PROGRESA', *World Development*, 29(10), 1769–1784.

Soares, F., S. Soares, M. Medeiros and R. Guerreiro (2006) 'Cash Transfers Programmes in Brazil: Impacts on Inequality and Poverty', *Working Paper # 21*. Brasília, Brazil: International Poverty Centre.

Suplicy, E. (2006) *Renda Básica de Cidadania: a resposta dada pelo vento*. Porto Alegre, Brazil: L&PM.

Székely, M. (2001) 'Where to from here? Generating capabilities and creating opportunities for the poor', *Research Network Working Papers, R-431*. Washington, DC: IDB.

Tendler, J. (2000) 'Why are social funds so popular?', in Y. Shahid, W. Wu, and S. Evenett (eds), *Local Dynamics in the Era of Globalization*. Oxford: Oxford University Press for the World Bank, pp. 114–129.

Yaschine, I. (1999) 'The changing anti-poverty agenda: What can the Mexican case tell us?', *IDS Bulletin*, 2(30), 47–60.

Zepeda, E. (2006) 'Do CCTs reduce poverty?' *One Pager # 21*. Brasília, Brazil: International Poverty Centre.

10
Assisting the Poorest in Bangladesh: Learning from BRAC's 'Targeting the Ultra-poor' Programme

David Hulme and Karen Moore

> The poorest are not like the poor but 'a little bit poorer'. They may benefit from policies to help the poor, but need other policies as well.
>
> Sen and Hulme (2006: 8)

Introduction

Social protection seeks to reduce the deprivation and improve the future prospects of poor and vulnerable people and households. However, even when such policies and programmes are working well, assisting the poorest and most socially marginalised people can be very difficult. This is a particularly important issue in countries with mass poverty, where a large minority, or sometimes a majority, of the population live below the poverty line. In such contexts, effective social protection policies may benefit millions of poor people but do little or nothing for the very poorest (CPRC, 2004).

This chapter commences with an examination of the evolution of a programme designed to reach the poorest people in Bangladesh, to improve their immediate situation and to give them the assets and other skills to move out of poverty and dramatically reduce their vulnerability – BRAC's Challenging the Frontiers of Poverty Reduction/Targeting the ultra-poor Programme (TUP). It then reviews what is known about the impacts of TUP, and finds evidence that the programme is both reaching significant numbers of Bangladesh's poorest people and improving their economic and social conditions. The concluding sections draw lessons from the TUP about the types of programme design features and the processes required to develop such ambitious initiatives.

The context of the Targeting the ultra-poor (TUP) Programme

Bangladesh has been doing well in recent times (Drèze, 2004), with reasonable rates of economic growth, improving social indicator levels and strengthened resilience to environmental shocks (floods, storm surges and drought). The headcount poverty index dropped from 52 per cent in 1983/4 to 40 per cent in 2000, although the fall in extreme poverty has been more modest (Hossain *et al.*, 2000). The UN's Human Poverty Index (HPI), based on income poverty, illiteracy and health deprivation measures, fell from 61 per cent in 1981/2 to 36 per cent in 2004. Despite these improvements, life for many remains characterised by severe deprivation and vulnerability, with around 31 per cent of the rural population trapped in chronic poverty and 24 per cent of the entire population experiencing extreme income poverty (that is, with consumption expenditure at less than 60 per cent of the government's official poverty line). Between 25 and 30 million Bangladeshis have seen little or no benefit from democracy or the country's significant and consistent economic growth.[1]

Chronically and extremely poor people – the 'ultra-poor' to use BRAC's terminology – 'face a complex structure of constraints that mainstream development approaches [including the country's social protection policies][2] have found difficult to address' (Hossain and Matin, 2007: 381). ultra-poor people have not been able to improve their lives through (i) accessing employment opportunities created by the growth of the formal sector (for example, the garment industry, fisheries, services); (ii) benefiting from the 'green revolution' that filtered across the country in the 1980s and 1990s; or (iii) participating in the self-employment and casual employment opportunities of the dynamic informal economy that has been supported by Bangladesh's much-praised microfinance industry (Hulme and Moore, 2007). Market-related opportunities, governmental social policies, and non-governmental organisation (NGO) programmes miss out the ultra-poor because they lack the material, human, financial and social assets to engage, and/or they live in areas or belong to ethnic/social groups that are bypassed or excluded.

In particular, rural people living in remote areas or difficult environments (for example, the seasonally eroded *chars* or seasonally flooded *haors*), and disadvantaged women are likely to be ultra-poor. The ultra poor are not a distinct group, but a heterogeneous assemblage of different people usually experiencing multiple deprivations. Commonly they are casual labourers (in agriculture or services), migrants or displaced people, ethnic or indigenous minorities, older people and those with severe disabilities or ill-health.

For analytical purposes we can recognise both the economically active ultra-poor, commonly surviving through their precarious, multiple livelihoods, and the economically inactive or dependent ultra-poor (frail old people, the physically or cognitively impaired, chronically sick or destitute).[3] BRAC's TUP has chosen to focus on the economically active ultra-poor. The inactive ultra-poor remain dependent on ultra marginal economic activities and support from family, relatives, neighbours, NGOs and community-based organisations and, sometimes, government social policies such as old age pensions.

BRAC was established in 1972 to provide humanitarian relief to the tens of millions of Bangladeshis suffering after the war of independence and later environmental disasters.[4] Subsequently it moved on to development work, and has evolved into the world's largest service delivery NGO. As of June 2006, BRAC was working in over 65,000 villages and more than 4,300 urban slums, in all districts of Bangladesh. It claimed to have over 5 million members, almost entirely women, and an annual expenditure of over US$250 million. Nearly 1 million children were enrolled in a BRAC school, and almost 3.5 million have graduated. The NGO employs more than 37,000 full-time staff, over 53,000 community school teachers, and tens of thousands of poultry and community health and nutrition workers and volunteers. There are now international programmes in Afghanistan, Sri Lanka, East Africa and the United Kingdom (BRAC, 2006). In Bangladesh, BRAC's major programmatic foci are the promotion of self-employment (microfinance, and technical support) and human development (non-formal education and health services). BRAC, the NGO, is at the centre of a corporate network including BRAC University, BRAC Bank, BRAC Printers, the country's largest cold-store company, and several other businesses.

Three key points must be noted:

1. BRAC has the capacity to manage operations across Bangladesh thatrival the business sector and often outperform the government;
2. BRAC has substantial experience in programme experimentation and learning; and
3. BRAC's economic programmes are heavily loan-driven and envision poor people as micro entrepreneurs.

The evolution of the TUP programme

BRAC launched the TUP programme in January 2002 as an experimental initiative that recognised two key findings from BRAC field experience and research:

BRAC's highly regarded microfinance programme rarely reached the poorest women.[5] This was partly because of self exclusion – the poorest women report being very worried about the consequences of not being able to make weekly loan repayments (*kisti*) and so do not join BRAC's village organisations (VOs). Partly it was a result of social exclusion – many VO members do not want to associate with the very poor, for both economic and social reasons. And partly it was because BRAC's loan-driven approach to microfinance does not match the needs or preferences of the poorest. BRAC has been aware of this issue since the mid-1980s, when it began to experiment with new programmes to reach the poorest (see the next section). For many years, the World Food Programme (WFP) operated a Vulnerable Group Feeding (VGF) scheme that provided poor women with 31.25kg of wheat per month for two years. In 1985, BRAC began working with WFP to create a 'laddered strategic linkage', the Income Generation for Vulnerable Group Development (IGVGD) programme, that would allow food aid recipients to climb out of poverty by graduating to BRAC's microfinance groups and self-employment initiatives. WFP's food aid would be complemented by BRAC-provided savings programmes, social development, income-generation training and, eventually, microcredit. The IGVGD has received favourable evaluations and continues to operate,[6] but at least 30 per cent of IGVGD participants do not progress to microfinance programmes, and these are usually from the poorest and most vulnerable households (Webb et al., 2001). In addition, a significant minority of 'new' IGVGD participants have taken part in the programme previously but have failed to improve their livelihood security (Matin, 2002).[7]

These two experiences indicated that BRAC's programmes were experiencing problems in assisting the poorest. TUP was launched to build on existing knowledge and the organisation's commitment to the very poor. TUP was overseen by BRAC's founder-director, Fazle Abed, and monitored systematically by BRAC's Research and Evaluation Division (RED).[8]

The programme used the concept of a 'laddered strategic linkage'; however, its approach was 'more systematic, intensive and comprehensive, covering economic, social and health aspects' (Hossain and Matin, 2007: 382). The idea behind the TUP approach is to enable the ultra-poor to develop new and better options for sustainable livelihoods. This requires a combination of approaches – both promotional (for example, asset grants, skills training) and protective (for example, stipends, health services) – as well as addressing socio-political constraints at various levels. TUP employs two broad strategies: 'pushing down', and 'pushing out' (Matin, 2005a):

'Pushing down': TUP seeks to 'push down' the reach of development programmes through specific targeting of the ultra-poor, using a careful methodology combining participatory approaches with simple survey-based tools. Within geographically selected areas, certain exclusion and inclusion conditions must be met. The selected households are then brought under a special two-year investment programme involving asset transfer, intensive social awareness and enterprise training, and health services.

'Pushing out': TUP also seeks to 'push out' the domain within which existing poverty alleviation programmes operate by addressing dimensions of poverty that many conventional approaches do not. This involves a shift away from conventional service delivery modes of development programming to a focus on social-political relations that disempower the poor, especially women, and constrain their livelihoods. Building links and support networks with other groups and organisations is key to 'pushing out'.

By late 2003, after experimentation and redesign, the programme had nine main components (see Table 10.1) that were carefully sequenced and linked. It carefully targets the poorest (see Table 10.2),[9] gives them a monthly stipend and health services to provide basic security, provides social development and income generation training,[10] transfers assets to participants (for example, poultry and cages, milch cows and stables), and provides technical support, inputs and advice.

The initial TUP plans envisioned that TUP members would graduate to joining BRAC VOs, but a number of problems in the field led to a redesign (Hossain and Matin, 2007: 383). In particular,

- TUP members became heavily dependent on BRAC staff for assistance and advice, rather than on VOs, effectively treating BRAC as a patron;
- many VO members resented TUP beneficiaries, as they had not received 'gifts' but had to repay BRAC for assets and services; and
- the assets transferred to poor women experienced relatively high levels of theft or damage, sometimes because of jealousy.

Table 10.1 TUP programme components and their purpose

Component	Purpose
Integrated targeting methodologies	Identify and target ultra poor
Monthly stipends	Consumption smoothing, reduce vulnerability, and reduce opportunity costs of asset operations
Social development (functional literacy)	Confidence building, and raise knowledge and awareness of rights
Health support	Reduce morbidity and vulnerability
Income generation training and regular refreshers	Ensure good return from asset transferred
Income generating asset transfer (e.g. poultry, milch cows, horticulture)	Significantly increase the household's asset base for income generation
Enterprise input and support	Ensure good returns from the asset transferred
Technical follow-up and support of enterprise	Ensure good returns from the asset transferred
Establishment of village assistance committee and mobilisation of local elites for support	Create a supportive and enabling environment

Source: Adapted from Hossain and Matin (2007: 383).

Table 10.2 TUP programme targeting indicators

Exclusion conditions (all selected households must satisfy all conditions)	Not borrowing from a microcredit-providing NGO
	Not receiving benefits from government programmes
	At least one adult woman physically able to put in labour towards the asset transferred
Inclusion conditions (all selected households must satisfy at least two conditions)	Total land owned less than 10 decimals
	Adult women in the household selling labour
	Main male income earner is disabled or unable to work
	School-aged children selling labour
	No productive assets

Source: Matin (2005a).

This led to the design of Village Assistance Committees (VACs),[11] to enlist the energies of local elites to support TUP participants, and the poorest more generally, in villages. The VACs have seven voluntary members – a BRAC fieldworker, a TUP participant, two VO members, and three members of the village elite.[12] The contribution of these committees to TUP performance, and more broadly to local level social and political change, are complex and difficult to assess. However, Hossain and Matin (2007: 390) judge them to be a 'modest success' and a challenge to those who automatically assume that the involvement of local elites in development programmes will always be negative.[13]

The present status of the TUP

The TUP aims 'to build a more sustainable livelihood for the extremely poor, by providing a solid economic, social, and humanitarian foundation, which would enable this group to overcome extreme poverty' (Hossain and Matin, 2007: 382). By mid-2006 the TUP was operating in fifteen of Bangladesh's sixty-four districts, with a geographical focus on the north of the country and in particular in areas experiencing seasonal hunger (*monga*) on an annual basis. At that time the cumulative number of TUP participants was 100,000, and there are plans to scale up the programme over the next five-year phase. The programme is funded by a donor consortium.[14] The high initial costs of the TUP, at US$460 per household, was reduced to US$268 by 2006 as the programme scaled-up and found ways of reducing expenditure.

TUP already receives a flow of international visitors, usually funded by aid agencies, who are keen to learn from it. Interestingly, the TUP has already begun to influence other programmes in Bangladesh, with DFID's Chars Livelihood Programme redesigning itself from being a broad-based capacity building initiative to become an asset transfer programme.

The achievements of the TUP

The large majority of data collection and assessment of TUP performance is undertaken by BRAC-RED. This includes the maintenance of a panel dataset that tracks key indicators for a sample of selected ultra-poor households (SUPs) who have participated in the TUP since 2002, and non-selected ultra-poor households (NSUPs) who have not participated in the TUP. At the pre-programme baseline study stage, both SUPs and NSUPs were ranked objectively in the 'poorest' group in the villages. However, NSUPs were not selected for the programme, because their household scores were close to the cut-off line between the 'poorest' and 'poor' categories – that is, NSUPs had higher welfare scores than SUPs. In addition to the panel dataset of objective indicators, BRAC-RED also conducts regular subjective assessments of SUP and NSUP poverty and welfare indicators and change.

Rabbani *et al.*'s (2006) analysis of the TUP panel dataset provides evidence of TUP recipients (that is, SUPs) improving their livelihoods more rapidly than the NSUP control group.

Asset accumulation: Over the period 2002 to 2005, TUP participants had a greater rate of asset accumulation than non-participants in all asset domains – financial assets (savings and credit), physical assets (a range of livestock, household and productive assets), natural assets (access to cultivable and homestead land), social assets (social and legal awareness), and human capital (household demographic structure, education, health and sanitation). Figure 10.1 provides a diagrammatic comparison of SUP and NSUP asset pentagon dynamics. Although the human capital picture is relatively complex and overall improvements are very small for both groups, as many of these changes can take longer to emerge, nutritional improvements are already apparent. Figures 10.2 and 10.3 illustrate the dynamics for human capital in terms of food and calorie intake; SUP households have also improved the quality of their food intake to a greater extent than NSUPs (see also Haseen, 2007). It is also notable that a greater proportion of SUP households have been able to improve their situation in terms of combinations of multiple types of assets than have NSUP households, suggesting that improvements may be more sustainable over time.

Vulnerability: In 2002, SUP households self-reported higher levels of food insecurity (occasional and chronic deficit) than NSUP households. In 2005, both groups reported improvements in food security. But the food security of

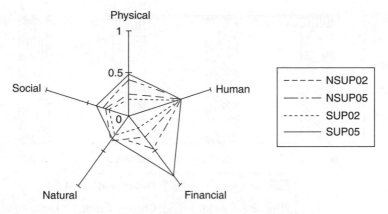

Figure 10.1 Asset pentagon dynamics – comparing SUPs and NSUPs over time
Source: Rabbani *et al.* (2006: 16).

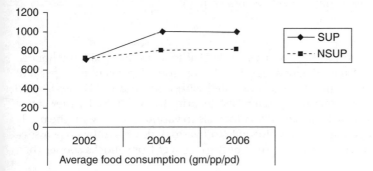

Figure 10.2 Changes in food consumption – comparing SUPs and NSUPs over time
Source: Matin (2006).

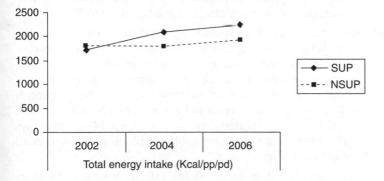

Figure 10.3 Changes in energy intake – comparing SUPs and NSUPs over time
Source: Matin (2006).

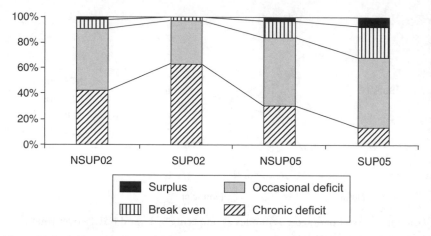

Figure 10.4 Self-perception of food security – comparing SUPs and NSUPs in terms of changes in availability of food over one year

Source: Rabbani *et al.* (2006: 24).

NSUPs had improved only a little, while SUP food security had ameliorated significantly, with food deficit reports reducing from 98 per cent to 70 per cent (see Figure 10.4). The TUP was associated with a reversal of SUP and NSUP status – SUPs now reported greater food security than NSUPs. Further, while both SUPs and NSUPs are equally vulnerable to various crises – with the newly asseted SUPs perhaps more vulnerable to livestock death – subjective assessments suggest that the SUPs can expect to recover from shocks sooner than the NSUPs.

Subjective poverty dynamics: Community-level assessments of changes in household poverty status reported SUPs as having experienced significant improvements in their welfare. This contrasted with NSUPs, who were reported to have experienced a downturn in their circumstances (see Figure 10.5).[15]

Graduation to mainstream BRAC microfinance: By 2004, the first TUP participants had completed the two-year special investment phase and were organised into separate village organisations. They were being offered a full range of BRAC's development services, including microfinance. Based on previous experience, BRAC takes a flexible, experimental and member-driven approach to credit provision, and it generally seems to be working – about 70 per cent of these women had taken and regularly repaid a first loan. BRAC continues to strive to assist the 30 per cent who were unable or unwilling to take a small loan, or had trouble in repaying.

Child development: Not all of the indicators for TUP have shown improvements, and there has been particular concern about the lack of progress for children in TUP households. Nutrition status among the under-fives and

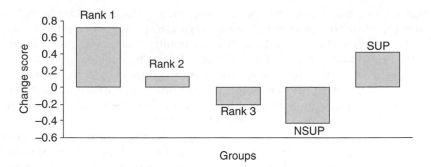

Figure 10.5 Average change score over period 2002–5 of households in different wealth rankings, as assessed by community meetings

Source: Sulaiman and Matin (2006: 8).

primary school enrolment rates have changed little, or not at all. This may be because of time lags associated with changes in such indicators, or patterns of intra-household resource allocation. These findings have led to deep debates in BRAC, concerned about the interruption of intergenerational poverty, and about modifications to the TUP approach.

Independent verification: An independent review of the TUP in 2004 concluded that the programme had resulted in extremely poor women improving their livelihoods, had been relatively cost effective, and had been more effective than comparable initiatives targeting the poorest (Posgate *et al.*, 2004, in Hossain and Matin, 2007). In addition, our limited fieldwork and interviews with TUP participants provides support for these generally positive assessments and has not yielded any data to challenge such conclusions.

Learning from the TUP

The most obvious lesson from the TUP is that the very poor can be reached and supported through carefully designed and targeted programmes. Moreover, with appropriate support, the poorest households can develop the capacity to engage with the economy in ways that permit them to sustain their improved welfare position without further subsidies or transfers. The poorest are not a residual group to be ignored or put on permanent social assistance until the growth process 'trickles down' to them: with a strategic 'hand up' they can engage in the economy and share in the benefits of growth.

However, one needs to be cautious about drawing wide-ranging conclusions from the TUP, as it is a highly context-specific initiative. It is very dependent on the capacity of BRAC to experiment, innovate, learn and develop service delivery systems that can operate across the country. This demands high-level analytical and management skills, alongside the ability to 'win' substantial financial resources to run the programme. In particular, BRAC's technical capacity to advise on poultry, dairy and horticultural activities should not be taken for granted. The broader environment in Bangladesh has also been supportive – steady economic growth, improving physical infrastructure (for example, the Jamuna Bridge, easing access to the north for people and goods, as well as local roads and electrification), high population density, and socio-political stability.[16]

For analytical purposes we can divide the potential lessons into two main types – the design features that are TUP's 'context', and the 'process' features that describe how the TUP evolved. In practice, successful programmes need to integrate both of these elements – an effective process has to generate content that can develop into a standardised package for delivery at scale.[17]

Design features

Laddered, strategic linkages: At the heart of TUP is the idea that the poorest people cannot benefit from a single 'magic bullet' (microcredit, bed nets, women's groups). Rather, they need a carefully sequenced set of supports that provides livelihood security; confidence building and business/technical skill development; an asset transfer; and support for and institutionalisation of their improved position within the local economy and society. BRAC's experience suggests that programmes for the poorest need to be relatively complex, involving several different elements of social protection, income generation and local organisation-building, which are carefully related to each other.

Asset transfer: One of the highly innovative features of the programme is that it involves the transfer of what is, in local economic terms, a substantial asset grant to each poor household. The relatively low level of initial assets of the poorest, allied to their ability to accumulate assets because of the frequency of adverse shocks that they experience, requires that they be given a 'hand up'. In effect, this means a 'one-off' gift of a micro-business so that they have both the material (for example, poultry, cages, veterinary support) and non-material (technical skills and social standing) resources to engage with the economy.[18] Organisations learning from TUP will need the ability to identify and support such micro-businesses, and the financial capacity to meet the costs involved.

Financial costs and impact assessment: The unit costs of TUP – running at US$280 in 2005, 84 per cent of which is asset transfer (Matin, 2005b) – are relatively high. For an aid donor or charity, that works out at 3,571 households assisted per US$1 million. To encourage donors and sponsors to meet such costs, organisations maintaining such programmes will need to be able to demonstrate that there are substantial benefits accruing and that, to a high degree, these are sustained after the initial investment. Similar programmes will only be feasible: (i) in contexts where there is substantial donor commitment; and (ii) for organisations that have the capacity, or can contract the capacity, for high-quality programme monitoring and evaluation that can be externally validated.

Local institutional development: Perhaps the most challenging aspect of TUP, and the one that demands the most 'acting out' in the field, is the institutionalisation at the local level. This is not about the service delivery agency, but about the 'new' village level organisations and the modified social norms and practices that are needed to ensure that short-term programme gains continue into the future. BRAC's early design – TUP participants would join existing BRAC village organisations (VOs) after two years, access services through these and have an enhanced social position because of VO membership – proved to be problematic. Their revised approach – developing the TUP VOs that can work directly with BRAC, and establishing local committees that enlist the support of the local elite to assist TUP participants both economically and socially – shows substantial promise, but success is by no means guaranteed. It is highly original in challenging the entrenched idea that, in Bangladesh, local elites are always exploitative and must be bypassed and/or disempowered (Hossain and Matin, 2007). In effect, the TUP assumes that local elites are segmented, and that while some may mirror the well-substantiated, rapacious stereotype of academic and popular literature, others are more humane and socially-minded. Further, this second group can be developed by promoting the pre-existing social norms of co-operation and the better-off helping the less well-off (Uphoff, 1992).

This local institutional development component is perhaps the most context specific and least transferable aspect of TUP design. It is highly dependent on the programme 'process'.

The TUP process

A process approach: The processes out of which the TUP has evolved is akin to the idealised notions of adoptive management and learning process approaches that have been written up in the development management and rural development literature over many years (Korten, 1980; Johnston and Clark, 1982; Rondinelli, 1993; Bond and Hulme, 1999). BRAC diagnosed a problem with its existing programmes, systematically reviewed its own experience and that of others, and moved into a carefully monitored experiment with a new programme. This experiment was 'learnt from' by encouraging field staff to voice concerns and propose ideas about what might be done, through both process documentation and baseline studies by RED and the guiding hand of Fazle Abed. Uncomfortable 'errors' were embraced – such as the admission that existing VOs were not keen to admit the ultra-poor to their organisations – and the programme modified. From a strong knowledge base the TUP was expanded (from 5,000 to 50,000 new households per annum) and cost-reduction measures made to permit increased staff caseloads and reduced financial costs. The programme continues to experiment with the frank admission at head office that the VACS are by no means a proven social technology.

The main difference between the TUP experience and the idealised process approaches relates to the balance between technical analysis and beneficiary participation. The TUP has been driven by the technical analyses of BRAC's directors and field managers. BRAC listens carefully to TUP participants and documents their experiences; indeed, they are encouraged to use their 'voice'. But this is not a participatory approach as envisioned by Robert Chambers (1997) and others. It is much more akin to the private-sector model of having a 'customer orientation'. BRAC also listens carefully to field staff and elicits their ideas about how the TUP could be improved. However, data analysis is a task for the head office, and decision-making for a small handful of staff.

A service delivery approach: The TUP is managed by a standardised business-type approach, with clear organisational structures, lines of responsibility, financial controls, and input, output and outcome monitoring. As knowledge is gained, it is routinised in the programme through documentation, training and supervision. BRAC operates a tight administrative 'machine' which seeks to reward performance (especially through promotions within expanding programmes), reduce costs and encourage poorly performing staff to move on. This is not a worker co-operative, it is an effective business with a strong social goal.

Partnerships: 'Partnerships' is such an all-embracing term that it can become meaningless. However, BRAC has built on a set of strategic partnerships that allow it both to pursue its goals and to acquire support where it lacks capacity. Its partnership with donors, and in particular with DFID and CIDA through its AKF-C partnership, provides the finance it needs, but also permits the flexibility and learning for TUP that is essential. A whole set of other donors, who would want a blueprint and would engage in micro-management, are strategically avoided by BRAC – they have the money but lack other qualities.

The most adventurous partnership of TUP is its engagement with local elites. Conceptually this is an extraordinary step; it is hoped that, as the experiment unfolds, the news will continue to be positive.

Conclusion

BRAC's TUP programme started out from earlier attempts to combine social protection programmes (food aid) with economic promotion schemes (microcredit, and business and technical services). Its recent performance demonstrates that the poorest people can be reached and, with a carefully sequenced set of programme components, supported to a position in which they have a high probability of sustaining their enhanced levels of welfare and assets.

There are many potential lessons that might be drawn from TUP, including its design features and the process from which it has evolved and continues to evolve. On the 'content' side, its major innovations are (i) the transfer of a substantial set of assets to very poor households – in effect, a redistribution of assets from the taxpayers of aid donor countries to the ultra-poor in Bangladesh; and (ii) the recruitment of village-level elites to local committees to support TUP participants and other very poor people. The latter is a radical idea in terms of the social engineering of a more 'pro-poorest' context in rural Bangladesh.

In terms of 'process', the TUP, like most of BRAC's other programmes, has benefited from many of the elements idealised in 'learning process approaches' and 'learning organisations'. It has built on experience, mounted carefully monitored experiments, standardised and scaled up its delivery systems, and gradually reduced the programme's unit costs. While this process has listened carefully to TUP participants and field staff, it is far from the 'participatory' approach lauded by some development theorists. The experiment is closely controlled by BRAC's upper echelons.

In the future it will be important for other agencies – NGOs, donors, governments, pro-poor elites – to learn from the TUP experience, but two notes of caution must be sounded. First, the TUP is a very complex programme and only organisations, or partnerships of organisations, with high levels of analytical and management capacity are likely to be able to mount such large-scale initiatives. Second, the TUP cannot reach all types of ultra-poor people. The economically 'inactive' ultra-poor (frail older people, AIDS orphans, people in chronic ill-heath) and socially excluded or adversely incorporated people (bonded labourers, refugees, indigenous people in remote areas) will need more conventional forms of social protection – old age provisions, humanitarian aid, 'free' health services, and child grants.

Acknowledgements: Our thanks to Bangladesh's poor people and to BRAC's staff for helping us to learn from their experiments and experiences. Particular thanks to Fazle Abed, Founder-Director of BRAC; Imran Matin and the entire BRAC-RED team involved in research on CFPR-TUP; and Rabeya Yasmin, CFPR-TUP Programme Co-ordinator.

Notes

1. For more detail on economic, social and poverty indicators in Bangladesh, see Sen and Hulme (2006).
2. For an inventory, see World Bank (2005).
3. When this division is operationalised empirically then it is often found that the 'economically inactive' are in fact heavily involved in low-paid or unpaid work such as gleaning, caring for children or older people, and begging.
4. Formerly known as the Bangladesh Rural Advancement Committee.

5. This is true for most of the country's microfinance institutions (Zaman, 2005) and may be the situation internationally (Hulme and Mosley, 1996).
6. In its 2003/4 annual cycle, the IGVGD model took on 44,000 new beneficiaries (Hashemi, 2006: 5).
7. For detailed discussions of BRAC's learning from the IGVGD, see Matin and Hulme (2003) and Matin (2005a).
8. This 'Learning Partnership' is supported by the Canadian International Development Agency (CIDA) via the Aga Khan Foundation-Canada (AKF-C). Working papers can be downloaded from www.bracresearch.org.
9. The 2002 baseline survey found that, of the ultra-poor, 54% were totally landless, 50% ate two meals or fewer a day, 70% were dependent on irregular, casual labour, and 95% lived without sanitation facilities (BRAC-RED, 2004).
10. The social development component focuses on functional literacy, but BRAC fieldworkers believe its main contribution is to build the confidence of TUP participants.
11. In Bangladesh these are known as *Gram Shahayak Committees* (GSCs). For a detailed description and analysis of these, see Hossain and Matin (2007).
12. These are described as 'respected individuals in the local community [chosen] through a process of guided selection' (Hossain and Matin, 2007: 384–385). Often they have strong religious beliefs and reputations for being publicly-minded.
13. We must confess to being rather cynical about this innovation when we heard of it in 2003 – 'Is this an act of desperation?' we wondered. However, fieldwork in 2004 revealed its potential – in effect, empowering some local elites to pursue a social mission that for religious and other reasons they valued.
14. Made up of the UK's Department for International Development (DFID), the Canadian International Development Agency (CIDA), the European Commission, Novib (Oxfam Netherlands), and the World Food Programme (WFP), and recently joined by AusAid.
15. It should be noted that while the objective assessment of assets (Figure 10.1) and subjective assessment of poverty dynamics (Figure 10.5) are consistent for SUPs, with both showing an improvement, there is inconsistency for NSUPs.
16. Many might challenge this latter point, but compared to many other countries with high levels of ultra-poverty – Afghanistan, Nepal, Democratic Republic of Congo, Sierra Leone, Somalia – Bangladesh's recent political problems and violence are enviable.
17. See Korten (1980), who recognised BRAC's capacity for innovation and service delivery at an early stage; and Johnston and Clark (1985), who eloquently explain the need for effective programme development both to 'think through' and to 'act out' its components.
18. One of the design features of the TUP that is not yet clearly specified is how it deals with women whose TUP projects fail (for example, their milch cow dies or their horticultural products cannot be marketed). Our own fieldwork indicates that such women are usually given a 'second chance', but this seems to be at the discretion of field level staff rather than as a formal programme component.

References

Bond, R. and D. Hulme (1999) 'Process Approaches to Development: Theory and Sri Lankan Practice', *World Development*, 27(8), 1339–1358.
BRAC (2006) BRAC At A Glance June 2006. Available at: www.brac.net/downloads_files/June_06_AAG_BW.pdf.

BRAC-RED (2004) *Towards a Profile of the Ultra Poor in Bangladesh: Findings from CFPR/ TUP Baseline Survey*. Dhaka: Brac-Research and Evaluation Division/Aga Khan Foundation Canada. Available at: www.bracresearch.org/highlights/cfpr_tup_baseline_survey.pdf. Accessed March 2007.

Chambers, R. (1997) *Whose Reality Counts? Putting the Last First*. London: ITDG.

CPRC (2004) *The Chronic Poverty Report 2004–05*. Manchester: Chronic Poverty Research Centre. Available at: www.chronicpoverty.org/resources/cprc_report_2004-2005_contents.html. Accessed March 2007.

Drèze, J. (2004) Bangladesh shows the way. *The Hindu*, September 17.

Haseen, F. (2006) Change in Food and Nutrient Consumption among the Ultra Poor: Is the CFPR/TUP Programme Making a Difference? CFPR/TUP Working Paper Series No. 11. Dhaka: BRAC Research and Evaluation Division/Aga Khan Foundation Canada. Available at: www.bracresearch.org/workingpapers/changeinfnconsumption.pdf. Accessed March 2007.

Haseen, F. (2007) 'Change in Food and Energy Consumption among the Ultra Poor: Is the Poverty Reduction Programme Making a Difference?', *Asia Pacific Journal of Clinical Nutrition*, 16(Suppl. 1), 58–64.

Hashemi, S. (2006) Graduating the Poorest into Microfinance: Linking Safety Nets and Financial Services. *CGAP Focus Note 34*. Available at: www.cgap.org/portal/binary/com.epicentric.contentmanagement.servlet.ContentDeliveryServlet/Documents/FocusNote_34.pdf. Accessed March 2007.

Hossain, M. and I. Matin (2007) 'Engaging Elite Support for the Poorest? BRAC's Targeted Ultra Poor Programme for Rural Women in Bangladesh', *Development in Practice*, 17(3), 380–392.

Hossain, M., B. Sen and H. Z. Rahman (2000) 'Growth and Distribution of Rural Income in Bangladesh: Analysis Based on Panel Survey Data', *Economic and Political Weekly*, December, 4630–4637.

Hulme, D. and K. Moore (2007) 'Why Has Microfinance Been a Policy Success? Bangladesh (and beyond)', in A. Bebbington and W. McCourt (eds), *Statecraft In The South: Public Policy Success In Developing Countries*. London: Palgrave MacMillan.

Hulme, D. and P. Mosely (1996) *Finance against Poverty*, Volumes I and II. London/New York: Routledge.

Johnston, B. F. and W. C. Clark (1982) *Redesigning Rural Development: A Strategic Perspective*. Baltimore: Johns Hopkins University Press.

Korten, D. (1980) 'Community Organisation and Rural Development: a Learning Process Approach', *Public Administration Review*, 40, 480–511.

Matin, I. (2002) Targeted Development Programmes for the Extreme Poor: Experiences from BRAC Experiments. CPRC Working Paper 20. Manchester: IDPM/Chronic Poverty Research Centre. Available at: www.chronicpoverty.org/resources/cp20.htm. Accessed March 2007.

Matin, I. (2005a) Addressing Vulnerabilities of the Poorest: a Micro Perspective from BRAC. Paper Presented to the Annual Bank Conference in Development Economics (Amsterdam, May 2005). Available at: www.BRACresearch.org/publications/addressing_vulnerability_of_the_poorest.pdf. Accessed March 2007.

Matin, I. (2005b) Delivering the 'fashionable' [inclusive microfinance] with an 'unfashionable' [poverty] focus: Experiences of BRAC. Presentation to ADB Microfinance Week, Manila, 14–18 March 2005. Available at: http://www.adb.org/Documents/Events/2005/ADB-microfinance-week/presentation-day1-03-matin.pdf. Accessed March 2007.

Matin, I. (2006) Towards a bolder microfinance vision for attacking poverty: The BRAC case. Presentation at DFID, London, October 2006.

Matin, I. and D. Hulme (2003) 'Programs for the Poorest: Learning from the IGVGD Program in Bangladesh', *World Development*, 31(3), 647–665.

Posgate, D., P. Craviolatti, N. Hossain, P. Osinski, T. Parker and P. Sultana (2004) Review of the BRAC/CFPR specially targeted ultra poor (STUP) programme: mission report. Dhaka: BRAC Donor Liaison Office. (Unpublished report.)

Rabbani, M., V. A. Prakash and M. Sulaiman (2006) Impact Assessment of CFPR/TUP: A Descriptive Analysis Based on 2002–2005 Panel Data. CFPR/TUP Working Paper Series No. 12. Dhaka: BRAC Research and Evaluation Division/Aga Khan Foundation Canada. Available at: www.bracresearch.org/workingpapers/impact_tup.pdf. Accessed March 2007.

Rondinelli, D. (1993) *Development Projects as Policy Experiments: an Adaptive Approach to Development Administration*. London: Routledge.

Sen, B. and D. Hulme (eds) (2006) *Chronic Poverty in Bangladesh: Tales of Ascent, Descent, Marginality and Persistence*. Dhaka/Manchester: Bangladesh Institute of Development Studies/Chronic Poverty Research Centre. Overview available at: www.chronicpoverty.org/resources/cp43.htm. Accessed March 2007.

Sulaiman, M. and Matin, I. (2006) Understand Poverty Dynamics: Examining the Impact of CFPR/TUP from Community Perspective. CFPR/TUP Working Paper Series No. 14. Dhaka: BRAC Research and Evaluation Division/Aga Khan Foundation Canada. Available at: www.bracresearch.org/workingpapers/TUP per cent20Working per cent20Paper_14.pdf. Accessed March 2007.

Uphoff, N. (1992) *Learning from Gal Oya*. Ithaca: Cornell University Press.

Webb, P., J. Coates, R. Houser, Z. Hassan and M. Zobaid (2001) Expectations of Success and Constraints to Participation among IGVGD Women. *Report to WFP Bangladesh*. (Mimeo) Dhaka: School of Nutrition Science and Policy/DATA Bangladesh.

World Bank (2005) *Social Safety Nets in Bangladesh: An Assessment*. Report No. 33411-BD. Washington, DC: Human Development Unit, South Asia Region, World Bank. Available at: http://siteresources.worldbank.org/BANGLADESHEXTN/Resources/FINAL-printversion_PAPER_9.pdf. Accessed March 2007.

Zaman, H. (2005) *The Economics and Governance of NGOs in Bangladesh*. Consultation draft. Washington, DC: Human Development Unit, South Asia Region, World Bank. Available at: http://www.lcgbangladesh.org/NGOs/reports/NGO_Report_clientversion.pdf. Accessed March 2007.

11
Protecting the Poorest with Cash Transfers in Low Income Countries

Bernd Schubert

Is it feasible to assist the poorest in low-income countries? Is it practicable to use cash transfers in rural areas with only the most basic administrative and financial infrastructure? Can we rely on community organizations to manage social protection for the poorest among them? These questions, and the issues they raise for the scope and effectiveness of social protection, are of great significance for poverty reduction in Africa. This chapter outlines and assesses a pilot social transfer scheme implemented in the Kalomo district of Zambia in 2004, with a view to providing answers to the questions above.

The motivation of the pilot scheme emerged from applied research at the national, district, village and household levels in Zambia, conducted in March/ April 2003 by the Deutsche Gesellschaft für Technische Zusammenarbeit (GTZ)-assisted Social Safety Net Project of the Ministry of Community Development and Social Services of the Republic of Zambia (MCDSS). The main objective of the project was to assess the effectiveness of existing interventions and to identify potential areas for improvement. Primary data collection concentrated on six villages in Choma District, Southern Province.[1]

The main findings from this research indicated some priorities for poverty reduction. First, 10 per cent of all households were found to be in need of urgent assistance. They are critically poor (surviving on just one meal a day) and at the same time labour-constrained. The children living in these households lack their most basic needs in terms of nutrition, medical services, clothing and basic education, regardless of whether or not they are orphans. The main, though not the only, factor behind their destitution is AIDS. Second, organizations at the village, sub-district and district level were preoccupied with relief food operations, AIDS prevention, health-care-related activities and development activities targeting households with the capacity to work. Assistance for households with limited capacity to work was found to be insignificant. Third, the Public Welfare Assistance Scheme (PWAS) of the MCDSS had a structure of welfare assistance committees at the district, sub-district and village level. This structure had been established in most districts to distribute transfers in kind to needy households, but partly as a result of extreme under-funding, PWAS has had no significant impact on the welfare of households urgently needing social welfare interventions. However, PWAS seems to have the potential to implement a scheme that targets critically poor and labour-constrained households. Fourth, it was found that nearly all transfer programmes in Zambia focused exclusively on food aid, but critically poor households pleaded for transfers in cash, which they could use flexibly according to their own priorities. Further research revealed that the administrative and logistical costs of cash transfers would be substantially lower compared to transfers in kind, such as food aid. Considering also that additional purchasing power of poor households would result in economic multiplier effects for the local economy, it was concluded that social cash transfers were the most effective tool to reduce the suffering and to ensure the survival of the most needy and incapacitated households.

The decision to design and implement a pilot social cash transfer scheme in 2004 was intended as an experiment to establish whether using cash transfers to assist the poorest 10 per cent of households provided a feasible and effective way of reducing poverty and vulnerability in Zambia. This chapter describes and assesses this ground-breaking experiment. The chapter is organized as follows. The next section considers the rationale for the focus on the poorest households. The following section discusses the main design features of the pilot. The section after that assesses the operation of the scheme. A final section discusses the financial sustainability of the scheme beyond its pilot phase.

Why focus on the poorest?

According to the Food and Agriculture Organization (FAO), 50 per cent of the Zambian population falls under the food poverty line (FAO, 2004). This means that 5.3 million people, or around one million households, are food poor. The food poverty line is defined by the cost of a basket of food providing a minimum energy requirement, which according to FAO in Zambia is 1,800 Kcal per person (adult equivalent) per day. In order to better understand the extent and the nature of the vulnerability of the different types of households affected by poverty, it is important to disaggregate the one million food-poor households into homogenous sub-groups. The depth of poverty and the main causes of the persistence of poverty can be used to distinguish between different sub-groups. For the purpose of identifying the poorest, a consumption-based food poverty line is more appropriate because (i) actual consumption is related more closely to a person's well-being than is income; (ii) consumption better reflects a household's ability to meet basic needs; and (iii) consumption can be measured with greater accuracy than income. In most low-income countries, food poverty is a good indicator of acute poverty as well as persistent poverty.

With regard to the degree of hunger, it is useful to distinguish between moderate poverty, understood as average energy consumption of between 1,400 and 1,800 Kcal per person per day, and critical poverty, defined as average energy consumption of less than 1,400 Kcal. This distinction is important, because people suffering extreme hunger over a period of time become physically weak, tend to sell or consume their productive assets (for example, livestock, tools, seed), give up investing in their future (for example, sending children to school), and die from infections that other people might survive. It is likely that their situation persists and even deepens. It is estimated that, in Zambia, approximately 400,000 households (or two million people) suffer from moderate food poverty, and about 600,000 households (or three million people) live in critical poverty.

The proximate causes of food poverty provide another criterion for distinguishing sub-groups among the poor. Out of the one million households suffering from food poverty in Zambia, approximately 700,000 are poor because of conjunctural factors. Conjunctural poverty is caused by unemployment or underemployment. It involves households with able-bodied adults who have no access to productive employment. If these households gain access to credit, to employment, to programmes such as food for work or cash for work, they are able to escape from their poverty, and are then considered to be poor but viable. The remaining 300,000 are labour-constrained households.

Poverty among the labour-constrained households is structural. These households have few or no able-bodied adult household members. In statistical terms, they have a high dependency ratio – that is, the relationship between the number of dependent household members who are not able to perform productive work, and the number of household members able to perform productive work. AIDS affects many of the households suffering from structural poverty. The breadwinners have died, leaving grandparents, who are too old to work, and orphans, who are too young. These households cannot respond to self-help-orientated or labour-based projects or programmes. Figure 11.1 summarizes the four categories of poverty described above, and provides estimates of the numbers of households in each category.

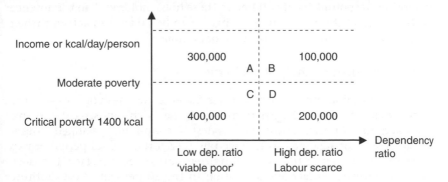

Figure 11.1 Number of households suffering from different categories of poverty, Zambia

The 300,000 households in Category A are in a relatively favourable situation. They are just moderately poor and include household members able to do productive work. They can respond to self-help-orientated projects and programmes in order to overcome their poverty and hunger. The 100,000 Category B households are labour-constrained and are therefore unable to respond to labour-based interventions. However, in a very poor country such as Zambia, they are not eligible for social welfare interventions because they are only moderately poor. Households headed by a pensioner, who receives only a small pension, or households regularly supported by the extended family are typical for this group.

The 400,000 Category C households suffer from critical poverty in spite of the fact that they have household members able to perform productive work. Many small-scale farmers and fishermen fall into this category. To improve the economic situation of these households they have to be targeted by programmes tailored specifically to vulnerable but viable households.

The 200,000 households in Category D are in the most unfavourable situation. They suffer from critical poverty. At the same time, they cannot take advantage of development projects or programmes because they have no household members able to perform productive work. They have very little, or no, self-help capacity. This group, estimated to be the 10 per cent worst-off households in Zambia, are in the most urgent need of social protection interventions. Among category D households, 60 per cent are children, so the returns from these interventions are potentially very large.

With economic growth and development, which will be accompanied by increasing opportunities for employment and self-employment, it is to be expected that a number of households in Categories A and C will be able to escape from food poverty. Category B and D households will, however, not benefit automatically from economic development, because they lack employable adults who can make use of such opportunities. Demographic trends and the impact of AIDS will increase the number of incapacitated households considerably over the next decade. And the lifetime opportunities for the vast numbers of children in these households will, in the absence of these interventions, be limited. This has to be taken into account when designing social protection strategies for Zambia.

Design features of the pilot scheme

The Kalomo Pilot Social Cash Transfer Scheme was designed to test the hypothesis that a social cash transfer scheme is the most cost-effective approach to empower economically destitute and incapacitated households.[2] The pilot scheme was financed by GTZ for an initial period of two years and implemented by PWAS, with three main objectives. First, to reduce extreme poverty, hunger and starvation in the 10 per cent most destitute and incapacitated (labour-constrained) households in the pilot region (approximately 1,000 households). Second, to focus mainly – but not exclusively – on households that are headed by the elderly and are caring for orphans and other vulnerable children (OVC) because breadwinners are chronically sick, or have died because of HIV/AIDS or other reasons. Third, to generate information on the feasibility, costs and benefits, and all positive and negative impacts of a social cash transfer scheme as a component of a social protection strategy for Zambia.

Based on a draft manual of operations, the scheme started with a test phase, conducted from November 2003 to April 2004. In April 2004, the test phase was evaluated and the manual improved (Schubert, 2004). The Honourable Minister of Community Development and Social Services, Marina Nsingo, officially launched the scheme on 4 May 2004.

During the period May to November 2004, the Scheme was rolled out to cover the whole pilot area, consisting of two agricultural blocks (Kalomo Central and Kanchele) with 143 villages, 5 township sections, 11,349 households, and a population of 85,624. At the time of writing, the scheme includes six Area Co-ordinating Committees (ACCs), 36 Community Welfare Assistance Committees (CWACs), nineteen pay points and the Kalomo Branch of the Finance Bank, and is paying monthly cash transfers to 1,027 households with a population of 3,856 people.

Information on the structure of the beneficiary households is given in Table 11.1. The Table shows that 66 per cent of the beneficiary households are headed by females, 54 per cent are headed by elderly people, and 54 per cent are affected by AIDS (it is not known whether the remaining 46 per cent are AIDS-affected or not). Of the household members, 61 per cent are children, and of them, 71 per cent are orphans.

Targeting and transfers

The scheme targets households, not individuals, meeting the following two criteria:

- they are critically poor – that is, suffering from chronic hunger, malnutrition, in danger of starvation, or reliant on begging; and
- they are incapacitated – that is, breadwinners are sick or have died, no person in the household of working age is able-bodied, or the household has a high dependency ratio.

Each household approved by the Scheme receives ZMK30,000 (US$7.5) monthly in cash. If the household has children, the monthly transfer increases to ZMK40,000 (US$10). ZMK30,000 is the equivalent of the average price of a 50kg bag of maize. According to FAO (FAO, 2003), the poorest 10 per cent of rural households in Southern Province consume on average one meal a day. If the beneficiary households spend the transfer on buying maize, this will enable them to have a second meal. The transfer does not

Table 11.1 Number and structure of beneficiary households

ACC Name	Total no. of households	Total no. of households, by gender of HHH		No. of households headed by elderly (over 64 years old), by gender of HHH		No. of AIDS-affected households		No. of household members including HHH, by gender of HHH		No. of household members fit for work	No. of children (below 19 years old), by gender of child		Of them: no. of orphans, by gender of child	
		M	F	M	F	Yes	Not sure	M	F		M	F	M	F
Choonga	169	73	96	36	38	105	64	263	307	10	176	162	147	134
Inkumbi	167	57	110	35	69	81	86	322	425	57	221	219	133	135
Siambala	201	65	136	34	86	92	109	352	393	26	266	197	186	129
Kanchele	185	42	143	22	82	98	87	247	361	7	191	195	136	135
Mukwela	95	45	50	26	21	47	48	151	185	10	107	107	71	80
Bekilumasi	210	67	145	31	71	127	83	371	479	13	255	266	206	193
Subtotal (proportion of Grand Total)	1027 (100%)	349 (34%)	680 (66%)	184 (33%)	367 (67%)	550 (54%)	477 (46%)	1706 (44%)	2150 (56%)	123	1216 (51%)	1146 (49%)	879 (52%)	806 (48%)
Grand Total for Scheme (proportion of relevant total)	1027 (100%)	1027 (100%)		551 (54% of all households)		1027 (100%)		3856 (100%)		123 (3% of all household members)	2362 (61% of all household members)		1685 (71% of all children, 44% of all household members)	

lift the beneficiary households out of poverty, but it is expected to lift them from critical poverty. The beneficiary households are, however, free to spend the transfers in any way they want. The scheme applies no conditions on how to use the monthly transfers.

At the same time, the scheme assumes that the beneficiary households will spend the money wisely: that, even though they are poor, people are not stupid or irresponsible, and they know best how precarious their situation is, and what they need most in order to survive. It is also assumed that the heads of the beneficiary households (mainly older women) will spend most of the transfers on the OVC living in their households. All these assumptions are closely monitored and have so far proved to be realistic.

Selection, approval and payment processes

The targeting and approval process is carried out entirely by the Public Welfare Assistance Scheme (PWAS) structures, which were in existence before the Social Cash Transfer Scheme started. The PWAS structures are a hierarchy of committees that work on a voluntary basis. At the village level, there are CWACs, each of which covers 200 to 400 households. The members of the CWACs are elected or approved by the community. The CWACs network with other village-level committees working in the social sector. The next higher level is the Area Co-ordinating Committees (ACCs) which co-ordinate between five and ten CWACs. The ACCs are in turn co-ordinated by the District Welfare Assistance Committee (DWAC).

Each CWAC receives one day of training, based on the manual of operations and conducted by the District Social Welfare Officer (DSWO). The CWACs then use a multi-stage participatory process to identify the 10 per cent of households who are the most needy and incapacitated in their area.[3]

They first interview all potential candidates for the scheme and document the household structure and the degree of poverty. Then they rank the interviewed households according to the severity of their destitution, giving the worst-off household Rank One, the second worst off Rank Two, and so on. The ranking is presented to a community meeting and discussed with the community until consensus is reached. Finally, applications for the 10 per cent worst-off households are sent to the ACC, which passes them on to the DSWO. The DSWO scrutinizes the applications submitted by the CWACs and presents them to the DWAC, who finally approves or rejects the applications.

Payments to approved beneficiary households are channelled through the Kalomo Branch of the Finance Bank. Beneficiaries living within 15km of Kalomo town are required to open savings accounts, into which their monies are transferred. For payments to beneficiaries living further away from the town, nineteen pay points have been established at rural health centres and schools. The co-operation of these organizations is formalized by standardized agreements signed by the DWAC chairperson and the pay point manager. All financial transactions are closely monitored and

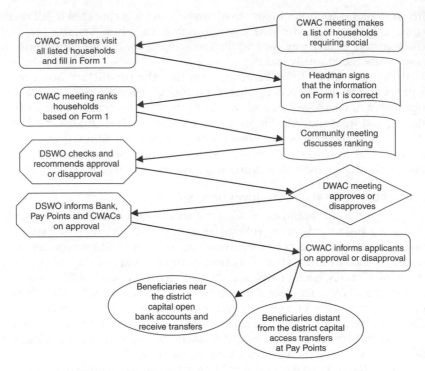

Figure 11.2   Simplified flow chart of the participative targeting, approval and payment process

controlled by the DSWO. A flow chart of the entire targeting, approval and payment process is given in Figure 11.2.

Performance and impact of the scheme

In addition to the internal monitoring performed by the DSWO as a part of the management tasks, the scheme has an external monitoring and evaluation (M + E) system, implemented by an independent consultant. The M + E system has been designed to provide information on:

- effectiveness of targeting;
- reliability, timeliness and costs of the scheme;
- how households use the transfers, and who in the household benefits;
- the impact of the transfers on household-level welfare indicators (for example, under-nutrition, child mortality, school attendance, self-esteem);
- impact on the community; and
- other positive and negative impacts.

Baseline surveys and the first rounds of focus group discussions and interviews were conducted in September and December 2004 before the beneficiaries started to receive transfers. The data collection for the evaluation was done in September and December 2005. The randomized sample included 304 of the approximately 1,000 beneficiary households.

Effectiveness of targeting and delivery

The vertical effectiveness of targeting is high. This means that the CWACs have been effective in selecting those households that fulfil the criteria 'critically poor' and 'incapacitated', but the horizontal effectiveness of targeting is not as good. This means that not all critically poor and incapacitated households in the pilot area have been included in the scheme. This is not the fault of the CWACs but is a result of the 10 per cent ceiling applied to each village. As noted above, the scheme approves only a maximum of 10 per cent of all households in the catchment area of a CWAC. In some villages, more than 10 per cent of the households fulfil the eligibility criteria but not all of the applications could be approved. The CWACs try to link these households to other social intervention programmes if they are available.

Reliability and timeliness of the payments to beneficiaries has been perfect for those with bank accounts. For those living further away and having to rely on pay points, the reliability and timeliness was also good once the pay points were established and functioning. However, in some cases, it took two to three months to establish pay points, causing a delay in starting payments. The biggest problem with regard to the payment system is the distance that the heads of the beneficiary households have to travel to access the transfers. Especially for the very old, and disabled or sick persons, this distance is a matter of concern. The scheme has reacted by establishing as many pay points as possible. But in a very sparsely populated rural area, Kalomo District has a population density of less than 10 people per square kilometre, there is a limit to the capacity of the scheme to reduce travel distances. In order to mitigate this problem, the scheme has introduced a procedure by which another household member or a trusted neighbour can become a signatory and access the transfers.

Client satisfaction with the performance of the delivery system has been rated as 'very happy' by 48.9 per cent of the interviewed beneficiaries; as 'happy' by 40.4 per cent; as 'unhappy' by 7 per cent; and 2.9 per cent have registered as 'don't know'.

Operational costs

Once the scheme had reached 1,000 households, the total costs per month amounted to ZMK39 million (US$10,000) on average for the period January to July 2005, of which 5.8 million were operational costs and 34.2 million paid to beneficiaries. Thus the operational costs for targeting, delivery and administration amount to 13 per cent of total costs.

Impact of the transfers on target group level

Heads of beneficiary households have understood the purpose of the transfers and make rational use of them. They buy basic necessities such as food, soap and blankets. Some invest part of the transfer in seed, getting a field ploughed by neighbours, or buying chickens or a goat to raise and resell. Some of those beneficiaries with savings accounts left part of the transfers in the account in order to be able to use the money later in the year when food would become scarce. The beneficiary households say that the transfers have improved their well-being and given them new hope. Head men report that the incidence of begging has been significantly reduced by the scheme.

Many of those beneficiaries with bank accounts save part of their transfers in order to invest them later in assets such as chickens, goats or blankets. A number of beneficiaries using pay points have also started saving by using a traditional 'Chilimba' system. They form groups of five beneficiaries. Each time they collect their transfers, they all pay ZMK5,000 to one member, who in this way gets her/his own ZMK30,000 plus ZMK20,000 from the other group members. The next month, another group member receives the 'jackpot' and can use it for an investment. So far, only women have been involved in Chilimba.

Sixty-one per cent of the members of beneficiary households are children under 19 years of age (see Table 11.1). These children do not only benefit in terms of better nutrition but also in terms of meeting their school requirements such as books, pencils, clothing and soap. The headmasters of Mabuyu Basic School and Matondo Community School, in the catchment area of which beneficiary households have been receiving transfers for more than two years, report that the attendance and appearance of children from beneficiary households has improved substantially.

The fact that the transfers are in cash, which is fungible and can be used flexibly in accordance with the individual needs and priorities of the beneficiaries, and the transfers are regular and reliable (unlike most other assistance reaching the villages) are regarded by the beneficiaries and the other stakeholders as the most important features of the scheme. Another highly praised feature is the systematic, participative and transparent selection and approval processes.

Quantitative data on the impact of the scheme with regard to changes in the number of meals consumed, the nutritional status of children, school attendance, and the health, self-esteem and social position of different categories of household members differentiated by gender are being collected by the M + E system but are not yet available.

The role of the community

Community members who are not beneficiaries, especially the CWAC members including head men and teachers, are welcoming and supportive of the scheme. More than 90 per cent of the CWACs that have been integrated into the scheme have performed effectively all the functions laid down in the manual of operations and explained to them during training. The concept of voluntarism seems to be well-established and accepted in the PWAS structures, which is remarkable when one takes into account that most committee members are themselves poor, albeit not destitute. They take pride in their role and are satisfied with the impact of their work on the well-being of beneficiary households.

The decision to integrate head men into the CWAC training had positive effects. Most head men play a constructive role in assisting the CWACs, in particular with regard to holding community meetings. One reason why head men are interested in the success of the scheme is that they are traditionally the first to be approached for help by destitute households. They realized that the scheme results in a reduction in begging. In cases where head men tried to exert undue influence, this was contained in the approval process.

Roles and tasks of co-operating partners

PWAS structures at national, provincial, district, sub-district and village level manage the scheme and perform the implementation tasks, including the internal monitoring. The CWACs, the ACCs and the DWAC, constituted by members who all work without any payment, are responsible for effective targeting and for counselling the beneficiaries. In order to facilitate a smooth functioning of all these committees, the DSWO and her staff of three officers have to undertake capacity building for all voluntary PWAS structures, including training, motivating, supervising and guiding them. The DSWO and her staff also supervise the delivery of the transfers through the Finance Bank and the nineteen pay points.

For the district level officers of the MCDSS, the scheme involves a substantial amount of additional work, in terms of both quality and quantity. Mastering the additional tasks requires skills in leadership, communication, administration and problem-solving. Compared to the working routine of most district-level MCDSS officers, the scheme demands higher standards with regard to professional management and discipline. In order to achieve these standards, close supervision and guidance of the district level officers by the Provincial Social Welfare Officer (PSWO) is required. Efforts of the MCDSS to strengthen district offices are supplemented by capacity-building assistance provided by GTZ in the form of day-to-day advisory services and training, and by supplying equipment, materials and monthly administrative budgets to be managed by the DSWO. The success of the scheme depends to a large extent on the performance of the district officers.

Beyond the pilot? Lessons and financial sustainability

With regard to ensuring financial sustainability of the scheme beyond the three-year pilot phase and beyond the pilot area, some progress has been made since the beginning of 2005. The Department for International Development (DFID) has signed a Programme Partnership Agreement (PPA) with CARE International that includes a social cash transfer component. The first districts where social cash transfer schemes financed by the PPA have been established are Kazungula and Chipata. PWAS is the implementing structure for both PPA-financed schemes.

The Government of Zambia has established a Social Protection Sector Advisory Group (SP/SAG) chaired by the Permanent Secretary of the MCDSS. The main task of SP/SAG is to integrate social protection into the Poverty Reduction Strategy Paper (PRSP) 2006–2008. After completion of this task, the SP/SAG will be involved in co-ordinating and monitoring the social protection programmes and will eventually advise GRZ on establishing the 2009–2011 PRSP. With regard to financial sustainability, SP/SAG provides the institutional platform to integrate successively the Social Cash Transfer Scheme into the GRZ budget process. There is evidence that policy-makers and donor agencies have begun to realize the potential of social cash transfers as a means of coping with the impact of AIDS on the livelihood of the affected households, and to contribute to achieving the Millennium Development Goals.

There is momentum for the scaling-up of the scheme: CARE is now working on pilots in several districts in Zambia, and GTZ and DFID are assisting the MCDSS to scale-up the scheme in the districts of Kalomo and Monze. If the Social Cash Transfer Scheme is eventually extended to all the 200,000 destitute households in Zambia (the Category D households in Figure 11.1), the annual costs will amount to US$26 million – the equivalent of 5 per cent of the annual foreign aid inflow, or 0.5 per cent of Zambian GDP. This means that social cash transfers are affordable, particularly if GRZ and donors share the costs.

In conclusion, the Kalomo pilot social cash transfer scheme provides a unique example of evidence-based poverty reduction policy in Africa. The chapter traced the design of the scheme to the research undertaken under the social safety nets project, which identified the need for cash transfers focused on the poorest. The implementation of the pilot and the assessment of its operational effectiveness to date demonstrate that it is feasible to focus assistance on the poorest, that cash transfers are practicable and effective even in conditions where administrative and financial infrastructure are very limited, and that it is possible to rely on community organizations to manage social protection interventions for the poorest among them. The Kalomo Social Cash Transfer Scheme has successfully enlarged the options available to address chronic poverty in low-income countries.

Acknowledgements: This chapter has been produced as a result of a consultancy for the GTZ-assisted Social Safety Net Project of the Ministry of Community Development and Social Services of the Republic of Zambia. I am indebted to the GTZ Adviser to the project, Dr Jörg Goldberg, for his detailed review of an earlier version of the chapter; to Chalo Mwimba (GTZ Zambia) for contributing Table 11.1; and to Karen Moore (CPRC) and the editors for suggestions and comments on the chapter. The author is, however, entirely responsible for the contents.

Notes

1. Research results have been published in a report which can be accessed via the website of the GTZ-assisted Social Safety Net Project of the MCDSS (Schubert, 2003a).
2. Details of the design are documented in two separate reports: see Schubert, 2003b and 2003c.
3. The 10 per cent limit is based on results of the National Household Survey carried out by PWAS in September/October 2003, and on a number of smaller surveys carried out before the scheme was designed.

References

FAO (2003) Baseline Report on Inter-linkages between HIV/AIDS, Agricultural Production and Food Security, Southern Province, Zambia, June.

FAO (2004) The State of Food Insecurity in the World, Rome.

Schubert, Bernd (2004) *Test Phase Results of the Pilot Social Cash Transfer Scheme*, Kalomo District, May (www.socialcashtransfers-zambia.org).

Schubert, Bernd (2003a) *Social Welfare Interventions for AIDS Affected Households in Zambia*, Lusaka, March. http://www.socialcashtransfers-zambia.org

Schubert, Bernd (2003b) Social Cash Transfers for AIDS Affected and Other Incapacitated and Destitute Households in Zambia, Lusaka, August.

Schubert, Bernd (2003c) *The Pilot Social Cash Transfer Scheme, Kalomo*, November (www.socialcashtransfers-zambia.org).

Part IV

The Politics and Financing of Social Protection

12
Process Deficits in the Provision of Social Protection in Rural Maharashtra

Sony Pellissery[1]

Introduction

In response to donor concerns that funds reach the neediest, evaluations of anti-poverty programmes are increasingly focused on identifying targeting failures: 'F-mistakes', where some of the target group (for example, the 'poor') are excluded from benefits, and 'E-mistakes', where benefits are provided to the non-poor as well as the poor (Cornia and Stewart, 1995). Yet the identification of F- and E-mistakes in itself does little to help us understand *why* targeting failures occur – and what can be done to address the problem. There is a dearth of studies of this kind, including in the context of social protection[2] interventions, an emerging set of targeted programmes in developing countries.

This chapter aims to begin to fill this gap, by presenting empirical evidence tracing the processes of provision of one form of social protection in rural Maharashtra, India, arguing that there are significant *process deficits* in this provision, with significant and negative effects on people in persistent poverty. The chapter demonstrates how the aims of social protection schemes are undermined when the public authorities responsible for implementing programmes are insufficiently independent from the interests of local elites. Following a brief introduction to social protection schemes in rural India, and an overview of research methodology, the chapter turns to a detailed description of the problematic set of processes through which poor, rural Maharashtrians who are old, disabled or separated/widowed with dependent children, can avail themselves of non-contributory income maintenance.

Social protection in rural India

Structures of state provision
Since the late 1960s, both national and state governments have implemented a wide range of targeted 'protective' and 'promotive'[3] anti-poverty

227

programmes – from free and compulsory primary education and child nutrition programmes, to infrastructure development in rural and slum areas, to the Public Distribution Scheme intended to ensure food security for the poor, and Maharashtra's famous Employment Guarantee Scheme. While various protective social security programmes existed before 1995 at the state level – for example, Maharashtra began to provide protective social security in 1980 – it was only in 1995 that the Government of India started a nationwide, comprehensive, protective, social security plan, the National Social Assistance Programme (NSAP).[4]

NSAP is financed completely by central government, although state governments provide additional benefits. The beneficiary eligibility is narrowly defined and means-tested, and benefits are provided through cash transfer. The programme consists of three different schemes:

1. The National Old Age Pension Scheme (NOAPS) is for men and women above the age of 65 years, in households living below the poverty line, who are destitute in the sense of having no regular means of subsistence from their own sources of income or through financial support from family members or other sources. It provides Rs.75 per month per beneficiary.[5]
2. The National Family Benefit Scheme (NFBS) is for households living below the poverty line following the death of the primary breadwinner. The benefit is a one-off payment of Rs.10,000 to the bereaved household.
3. The National Maternity Benefit Scheme (NMBS) is for pregnant women in households living below the poverty line, for her first two live births. The benefit is a one-off payment of Rs.500 per pregnancy.

There are three committees involved in the implementation of the NSAP: the state-level committee, headed by the chief secretary of the state; the district-level committee, headed by the district collector; and the *panchayat* (village council), which is responsible for identifying the beneficiaries. Central government disburses the fund on a quarterly basis to state headquarters, and the beneficiaries are paid either through a bank account, the post office, a money order, or direct cash disbursement at a village meeting. Publicity for the programme is the responsibility of all three committees. This division of labour is intended to make the programme both cost-effective and responsive.

A numerical ceiling for each state is calculated by central government, taking into account population, poverty rate, and proportion of the eligible group in terms of age, birth rate or mortality rate, depending on the programme. It is expected that 50 per cent of eligible people below the poverty line will be covered within this numerical ceiling. Thus the *panchayat*s are able to choose only some of the many eligible candidates.

State government provisions are in addition to these benefits. For example, the Government of Maharashtra (GoM) provides Rs.175 to older poor people in rural areas, in addition to the Rs.75 given by the NOAPS. Thus, a total of Rs.250 per month is the actual income support from the old age pension in Maharashtra. There are also those who, while they do not fall within the eligibility criteria of NSAP, are vulnerable to destitution – for example, young widows with dependent children. The GoM has created two different schemes for such groups, and pays a monthly benefit of Rs.250. However, even including these additional state-level benefits, Many poor people are not covered and the extremely low levels of benefits rates are crucial issues.

There is increasing evidence that there are problems with the implementation of NSAP and its associated state-level programmes in Maharashtra and elsewhere. First, take-up rates are often low: Prabhu's (2001) study showed that, while the overall take-up rate for NOAPS was 81.6 per cent in 1996/7, the rates for NFBS and NMBS were only 28.9 per cent and 27.6 per cent, respectively. Other evidence suggests that the availability of benefits is crucially linked to local-level political institutions and systems of governance. For example, Harriss-White's (2004) study of the Government of Tamil Nadu's social security schemes revealed the inclusion of many ineligible cases, resulting in resource wastage; and Banik's (2002) study of Orissa revealed that many people eligible for the NSAP schemes were turned down by the village council despite repeated attempts. Cases of misrepresentation of income, age and place of residence, as well as lax administrative scrutiny and political interference, are reported by Subrahmanya and Jhabvala (2000). Scheme publicity has also been shown to be problematic. A study of availability and awareness of NSAP in Orissa, Uttar Pradesh and Gujarat revealed that most people came to know about the scheme either through the *sarpanch* (village head) – 53 per cent – or through friends or relatives who happened to work in the Block Development Office – 38 per cent. The role of government officials was minimal, with only 5 per cent of people learning about the programme through them (Sankaran, 1998). This points to the possible importance of linkages to elites in obtaining welfare benefits.

Overlap between state and non-state social protection sources

How do poor people survive despite mistargeted benefits and seriously insufficient funds? Here we must turn to the different sources of social protection available to poor people. Harriss-White (1999b) and Jutting (2000) identify four: state, market, non-governmental organizations and civil society institutions, and households. The ideological orientation, resource availability, decision-making process, provisioning methods and eligibility criteria differ significantly between these sources. It is a combination of benefits from different mixes of these agencies that allow a poor person to survive in the context of insufficient state provision. Yet for many poor people, state programmes remain the main source of benefit, since the state is the only institution accountable for the welfare rights of its citizens (Harriss-White, 1995, 1999b).

Although this fourfold categorization is useful for analytical purposes, it is important to note that, in close-knit communities like those of rural India, the resources, roles, power structures, norms and legitimacy all overlap in multi-plerelations between individuals and formal and informal organizations. For example, a poor household may relate to an elite in his/her roles as political leader, landlord and co-participant in a religious event, all at the same time (Kabeer, 1994). The ways in which networks between individuals in organizations function, and how decision-makers involved in the organizations, in their different roles, act differently in different relationships, become very important. It is in this tension between state, market and societal forces that policy formulation and implementation takes place. Where these intersect there is the potential to impede or facilitate the public policy process.

Therefore, it is important to investigate the impact of redistributive policies and provision within a framework of the institutions and public authorities responsible for implementation. The role of the elite is of crucial concern for three reasons:

1. the elite are often placed at critical state–society intersection points, and thus become important actors in public programme implementation;
2. the nexus of wealth and power also makes the elite crucial actors in the market provision of social security; and
3. the elite as formal or informal leaders are likely to take the initiative in, and exercise control over, any collective action.

Thus, elite members of a given community may have access to and control over more than one institution, allowing them to use social security provision as a mechanism to expand their power in the community through patronage. This can also allow the creation and consolidation of intra-elite networks, strengthening their position. For example, a member of the 'market elite' may, by drawing upon his/her network with other elites, prevent public provision or collective action, such that a poor household is pushed to serve the market 'interest' instead – for example, to provide labour on a landlord's farm at a lower wage than an unemployed person with access to public provision would accept. On the other hand, a member of the 'political elite' may encourage collective effort by a self-help group, as long as it is in his/her favour and has the potential to reduce the power of rival 'market elites' on poor community members.

Research sites and methodology

In order to examine the processes behind social protection provision, two villages from two different *tehsils* (a group of about 100 villages) of the Marathwada region of central Maharashtra were selected, controlling for socio-economic factors.

Marathwada is one of the poorest regions in India (Mehta and Shah, 2001), and all eight districts in the region appear in the list of 100 'most backward' districts (GoI, 1997). The economy is predominantly agrarian, with 84.5 per cent of the rural population dependent on agriculture, and 40.5 per cent of these are landless agricultural labourers (NCAER, 2002). *Marathas* constitute the chief landholding and majority caste. *Mahars*, comprising 15 per cent of the population are, though landless, a politically conscious lower-caste community. *Marwaris* constitute the trading caste and moneylenders of villages. Around 25 per cent of the population are Muslim. Communal tensions between Hindus and Muslims have been common since the 1990s, when the Hindu-nationalist political parties Bharatiya Janatha Party and Shiv Sena gained significant popular bases in the region, drawing on traditional supporters of the Congress Party.

The purposive selection was guided by the criterion of having a large number of persons eligible for social protection, so the number of below poverty line (BPL) households was considered. Also, in order to understand the overall rural situation, it was important to study both a village with a relatively large population and a weekly market, and a village with a smaller population and no weekly market. This difference is typical of the demographic composition of villages in rural India. Thus, Bajgaon and Saralgaon were selected. In Bajgaon, a market village with a population of about 7,255, 20 per cent of households (n = 235) were BPL; in Saralgaon, a non-market village with about 2,825 residents, 28 per cent of households (n = 138) were BPL.

In total, five months of fieldwork were undertaken in Bajgaon, and three in Saralgaon. These two villages were, however, only focus areas. The entire district was considered as a unit of study, and visits to other villages were undertaken and interviews with different levels of officials conducted. Four phases of fieldwork, conducted in the following order, can be distinguished in each community:

1. familiarization with the community – meeting people, introducing ourselves, making strategic friends and identifying key informants;
2. identifying community elites through the reputation technique;[6]
3. in-depth interviews with elites and other stakeholders in social protection provision from state, market and civil society institutions; and
4. surveys of beneficiaries and potential beneficiaries of social protection.

Here, only those benefits that can be received on a continual basis are examined, as there is a large difference between one-off benefits (for example, NFBS and NMBS) and continuing benefits (for example, NOAPS), both in terms of management and public awareness. Thus the discussion below pertains to the provision of non-contributory income maintenance, available when a poor person becomes old, disabled, or separated/widowed with dependent children.

The process of obtaining income maintenance

Unlike universal systems of income maintenance provision, where everyone in a particular situation is eligible for the benefit irrespective of their income level, means-tested systems are based on a process of making an application, application approval, and delivery of the benefit. Each part of the process involves the applicant relating to other people. Since the applicant is a very poor person, these relationships tend to be unequal. Therefore, it is important to unravel the processes involved in order to understand the mechanisms that may facilitate or prevent individuals from obtaining benefits.

Preparing the application – 'various locks, just one key'

Making an application for income maintenance involves a substantial amount of effort, and is very time-consuming. It starts with the process of obtaining an application form. This should be available in both the village and *tehsil* offices, but this is usually not the case. Instead, they are usually available in photocopying shops near the *tehsil* office or with 'writers' (*karkhoon*). The photocopying shopkeepers obtain the application form from the *tehsil* office and make copies to sell for Rs.15. The *tehsil* office generally does not admit that application forms are unavailable there; a *tehsil* office was even observed to be making official announcements that people should not buy the application form from private agencies, as the forms are available without charge from the *tehsil* office. This 'trumpeting' of the official procedure while practising an unofficial procedure is typical of all the provisioning processes.

In practice, the application form *is* available from the *tehsil* office – to those 'who know how to get things done'. To understand what is meant by this we need to understand further how *tehsil* and other government officials deal with poor people. When a villager wants to obtain an application form, he/she goes to the *tehsil* office where he/she would straight away be told that the application form is obtainable from a photocopying shop. If the applicant insists on an application form from the *tehsil* office, he/she may be asked a few questions informally. First, the name of the applicant would be requested, and the answer would reveal the person's caste and religion. Next, the office would need to know the name of the village he/she comes from. Outwardly, these two questions sound like a neutral, preliminary administrative mechanism to establish a personal identity. However, with the answers to both questions, the official will be able to place the person within a particular community and understand his/her social status and power linkages. The official knows who is important and how each caste/religion is connected to powerful people in each of the hundred or so villages of the *tehsil*. Officials also take the applicant's style of dress and mode of speech into account to decide their economic class, and then makes a decision whether or not to provide the application form.

Most of the fifteen pages of a typical application form contain statements to be certified by village-level government officers. Poor people, particularly those who are illiterate, but even some with an average level of education, have to depend on someone else to fill the application out correctly. There is no one in the *tehsil* office to assist in this process. When asked about the lack of this facility to assist poor people, one official said that people get help from relatives or village leaders in order to fill out applications. However, officials are aware that often such help is not available to poor people without paying a fee.[7]

There are two sources of help at this stage: 'writers', with small offices near the *tehsil* office; and brokers (also called 'agents'), operating at the village level. 'Writers' are often educated youths acting as paralegal professionals involved in a variety of paperwork ranging from land transactions to civil and criminal case preparation. There are generally about forty such 'writers' near a typical *tehsil* office, some operating with a single table under a tree, others with a single-room office. They have most of the necessary forms required for government purposes available for purchase, including the application forms for income maintenance. They charge an additional fee for filling these application forms in 'appropriately'. This fee can vary from Rs.50 to Rs.250, depending on the writer's fame, the applicant, and his/her ability to pay. Based on their experience, the 'writers' are able to recommend how an applicant should complete the application. For example, to obtain an old age pension, it is advisable to present oneself as having 'no children, no land and no income', even though the case may be otherwise. However, the 'writer' does not take responsibility for obtaining certification from village officers of the facts he records; this responsibility remains with the applicant.

In contrast, village-level brokers not only sell application forms and complete them appropriately, but they also take on the responsibility of acquiring certificates from village officers. Brokers do not operate everywhere, however – usually only in market villages that act as administrative hubs for both the large village population and for people from smaller surrounding villages. Brokers are generally linked to, and have an understanding with, the main village elite.

A broker bargains and strikes a deal with a potential applicant regarding the fee, which varies from Rs.250 to Rs.1,000. A critical point of bargaining is the extent of the broker's responsibilities: if the applicant is only able to pay a small amount, the broker will simply act as a writer, and leave the responsibility for obtaining certificates from village officials to the applicant him/herself. The fee also depends on the difficulty of the case, or the ineligibility of the applicant. On certain occasions, an extraordinarily high fee will be quoted in order to discourage any applicant not on good terms with the elite with whom the broker works in tandem, as there is no point in the broker undertaking responsibility for the applicant if ultimately the elite will not grant the application. If a deal is struck, it becomes the responsibility of the broker to see that the application is successful, and as such the broker does everything possible, including exerting influence on local elites, to ensure the application is granted. If an applicant is unable to pay the fee immediately, he or she will pay a small initial amount, with the balance payable after the successful application, normally from the first instalment of his/her income maintenance.[8]

When asked why he is engaged in this kind of work, one broker portrayed himself as a 'social worker', helping the people. On further probing, he explained that during the process of helping people he incurs significant expenses for travel, photocopying and bribes. By charging a fee to the applicant, he is able to make a living for himself. In response to a question on why people approached him for this service in increasing numbers, he quoted a Marathi phrase: 'Various locks, but just one key': going through a broker to submit an application avoids the delay and expense of meeting the various personnel involved in the process. Significantly, the emergence of brokers has largely ruled out help being available from other villagers. Where people used to go to a village official or another educated person, now they are directed to a broker, who is perceived as being a more competent completer of forms.

A broker's main job is to obtain certificates from village officers. Three certificates are mandatory for all applications:

1. *Age certificate*: The applicant needs to submit either a school leaving certificate or an attested extract of the *gram panchayat* birth register. Often these do not exist, or are very difficult to obtain. When a poor person approaches the village office to obtain such a certificate, village officers take it as an occasion to make the person pay any outstanding taxes. As these taxes are generally not paid regularly, poor households may have large arrears of Rs.500 or more. The officer makes payment of arrears a precondition to providing certificates unless a small bribe of about Rs.20 is paid, resulting in both an accumulation of an individual's arrears and a resource loss to the village government.

Because of these difficulties, applicants and brokers usually turn to a third option – an age certificate from a government medical officer – to provide proof of age. A medical officer is expected to examine the person's appearance to determine age. In practice, medical officers will often certify any age if given a small amount of money (about Rs.20). The village broker knows the medical officer, and the medical officer knows the broker and the broker's relationship to the village elite. Therefore, under pressure, a medical officer may even give certificates without seeing the applicant or taking any money.

2. *Income/property certificate*: The *talathi* (village revenue officer) is the competent authority to give this certificate. Often the *talathi* or his assistant[9] will examine the land records and state whether a person owns land, and

what the income from the land is. There is little room for making a wrong statement in this case. A *talathi* will give the certification for a fee of about Rs.20. However, it is not easy for an applicant to find and meet with the *talathi*, as the *talathi* usually has responsibility for five or six villages. Here, the broker's proximity to the *talathi* is helpful, and he can obtain the certification without any further expense.

3. *Certificate of residency*: A person has to prove that he has been living in Maharashtra for at least fifteen years. The *talathi* or *sarpanch* are competent persons to certify this. The difficulty here is the same as with the income certificates – to locate and arrange a meeting with the *talathi* or *sarpanch* – but a broker is able to get things done quickly without paying any bribes.

Applications for disability benefits require additional certificates, which are much harder to obtain, so brokers charge much more. A respondent explained to us that she was asked by a broker to pay Rs.3,000 to obtain a benefit on behalf of her mentally impaired daughter.

Poor people use a broker for three reasons: time, money, and a chance of success. First, it can take several days to obtain one certificate if an applicant tries him/herself, but casual agricultural wage labourers cannot afford to miss even a day's labour. Second, obtaining certificates from the officers means paying bribes to them individually.[10] Third, there is a higher chance of obtaining the benefit when applying through a broker, since he works in tandem with the elite of the village.

Submitting the application

It is not sufficient merely to deliver the application to the *tehsil* office – the completed application must reach the appropriate official, and these officials usually do not accept an application without a meeting and a small bribe (at least Rs.10) from the applicant. The official understands whether an application is coming through a broker, directly from the applicant, or even via a political elite. Brokers are very tactful and are able to handle the officials efficiently. A *tehsil* official said of the brokers:

> they know when the official is happy, when the official is angry, when it is a good time and when it is a bad time. The agents approach the officials looking at the situation and mood of the official, while the people bluntly go to the officials, and if the official is in bad mood, their application will go in the dustbin.

Indeed, a good number of applicants who applied a second time were told that their first application was unsuccessful because the official could not find it, and that they needed to make a new application. For example, a woman named Taramati applied for income maintenance for her young children after her husband died in an accident. Her first application was not successful. She started working regularly on a daily wage basis on an elite villager's farm. The elite told her to apply for income maintenance but she explained that she had applied some six years previously but had not heard from the officials. The elite asked Taramati to pursue the matter, and said he would ask the officials to grant her application. She went repeatedly to the *tehsil* office, where she was directed from one official to another. After four trips, officials told her that her application could not be found, and she was asked to submit a new one. She again collected the required certificates, and submitted her application a second time. She said:

> I would not move from the office even after submitting the application. I kept looking at the application, and the place where the official had kept it. The official was casual with my application. I had made the application with much difficulty. He kept my application among a heap of files. What certainty is there that he would find my application at the right time, when some decision has to be made?

Sometimes officials refuse to accept applications on the basis of a small mistake or a missing document, although the government directive to *tehsil* officials is that applications should be accepted and any missing supporting documents should be requested in writing from the applicants. Especially if an applicant is submitting the application directly, the official may glance through the form, point out a mistake, and ask the applicant to bring back the corrected form.

Gangubai, a woman of great determination, is illiterate, yet after her husband died of tuberculosis, she decided to have the income maintenance application completed without the assistance of a writer or broker. It took seven months for Gangubai to get the necessary documents signed as she was dependent on daily wage labour to feed her four young children and found taking time off to chase officials very difficult. Finally, when she took the application form to the *tehsil*, the official told her, 'Look, I can't take this application, because where the *talathi* is supposed to sign, the village-level worker has signed.' She took the application back, hoping that she may be able to submit it again another time.

By refusing to accept an application, an official is making a double gain. First, he reduces the likelihood of having to face the applicant again, as those who are refused are often disappointed and give up, especially considering the difficulty of filing supporting documents with the original application. Attempts by bureaucrats to reduce their workloads, with effects on people's rights, have been well-documented in the literature on 'street level bureaucrats' (Lipsky, 1980; Blalock, 1991). Second, by refusing to accept applications, records show that there are few rejected applications, and therefore that the *tehsil* office is meeting demand. This also has implications for funding: when demand for a scheme is perceived to be low, there is little reason to allocate more funds to it. Finally, at the policy level, there will only ever be changes made to eligibility criteria if rejected applications can be scrutinized. Therefore, by refusing to accept application forms, the possibility of any policy change is being blocked.

Decision-making

Officials are expected to scrutinize all applications received, remind the applicants to present any missing documents, and present the applications to the Social Security Committee (SSC), which is expected to meet bi-monthly. Ideally. the SSC should verify whether the applications presented to them meet the eligibility criteria, and inform the applicants about its decision. Actual SSC practice tends to differ from this ideal. The composition of a typical SSC can help to explain why.

The state government, in active consultation with the respective District Guardian Minister, appoints members of the SSC. Guardian Ministers come from the ruling party, and consult local party workers regarding the appointment of sub-committees at *tehsil* level. Ideally, this consultation should result in the appointment of a group of active members of civil society capable of checking the *tehsil* officials, to ensure the quality of service provision to poor people. In practice, nominations to the SSC are made up primarily of party workers, with a minority of civil society representatives. At the same time, whatever the committee's composition, its powers can be controlled through the enforcement of guidelines.

Asked whether there is a maximum threshold for the number of applications to be granted in an SSC meeting, officials at all levels – *tehsil*, district and state – said that there is no restriction: any number of applications that meet the eligibility criteria can be granted. However, this differs from actual practice at SSC meetings. The observed committees granted about thirty applications every time they met, from the 100–150 applications received. SSC members recognize that scrutinizing a large number of highly standardized applications is problematic. The applications that reach the SSC tend to look much the same, because most are submitted through writers or brokers. These 'experienced hands' ensure that each application has been completed appropriately, with the correct documents attached. If a document does not support the application, it is not attached. Further, as *tehsil* officials do not record the date when the application was received, it is impossible for a 'first come, first served' principle to be followed. So how are these thirty applications selected? Do they all meet the eligibility criteria? Are there other applications that meet the criteria? Observing an SSC meeting can help to answer these important questions.

During one such a meeting, it was noticed that the SSC chairman had a small piece of paper on which certain names were scribbled. He picked applications using the names on this list. Other members of the committee also picked one or two of the applications each. They asked the chairman, 'How about granting this one?' The chairman glanced at each application and put it aside. Two brokers were present as informal observers, one of whom was linked with the vice-chairman. This broker had a list of twelve people, and he asked the vice-chairman to select these applications for consideration. Thus, of the 150 applications, only those in which at least one committee member had a personal interest were granted.

It is interesting to note that the chairman held the list of pre-identified names entirely openly. On the one hand, it was probably difficult for him to remember all the names of those whose applications had to be granted, as the list was quite long, and probably not many of the names were familiar to him since they had been recommended by brokers. But on the other, the chairman's capacity to exercise power with the confidence that no one would challenge him is significant.

Over the course of the meeting, only one application was granted in another way. Towards the end of the meeting an official pleaded with the chairman on behalf of a disabled person applying for benefits. The official may have taken an interest in the case because the applicant had frequented his office, so that he was convinced that the applicant met the eligibility criteria. The chairman was irritated by this, and asked to see the application. After committee members laughed about the applicant's photograph, the chairman said, 'This application cannot be granted. Where is this person?' The official, perhaps foreseeing such a situation, had asked the applicant and a relative to wait nearby during the meeting. The official brought the applicant into the meeting room. The applicant – who was blind, found it difficult to walk and has twisted arms – demonstrated his impairments to the committee, after which they changed their minds. A committee members said 'Yes, he should be given the benefit and we don't need any other proof', and the chairman assented. This episode illustrates that a person's need has to be directly perceived by an elite/committee member for that person to be seen as deserving of the state benefit.

About twenty applicants also attended the meeting; they sat on the floor, while SSC members were seated on chairs, and the brokers stood near their respective elites. By the end of the meeting it had become clear which applications were being granted and which rejected, and there was some unrest among the applicants present. A committee member explained why applicants were allowed into the meeting: 'If the *tehsil* officials conduct a meeting, they do not allow the people to come... We are the people's representatives. We want to be close to the people.'

This suggests that the political body desires a certain visibility in front of the applicants. However, this visibility does not relate to the transparency of the process. Rather, the committee members want to assert their power and present themselves as decision-makers. The process signals to people that they do not have a right to the benefits but need to bargain directly with committee members. During the meeting, the chairman frequently scolded and shouted at the officials in front of all present, further underlining the fact that the success of applications does not depend on officials but on the committee, which may 'grant' benefits. Thus, the committee systematically demanded people's loyalty through its proceedings, not only to the SSC members but indirectly to the ruling party, thus making welfare access conditional on party affiliation.

Delivery of benefits – 'like a bee on a sweet'?

There are also deficits in the process of communicating with applicants about the success of their applications and how to avail themselves of the benefit. *Tehsil* officials claim that they inform, by post, both the selected applicants and those whose applications have been denied. This is a very important step, but one that is not often done. Most applicants come to know the SSC's decision informally through the broker or the delivery mechanism. Applicants ask the postman repeatedly whether any money has come. This puts the applicant in a bargaining position with yet another person.

From the beginning of the scheme in 1980, benefits have been delivered to beneficiaries through the post. At a central place in the village, the postman shouts out the names of beneficiaries for whom money orders have come. He hands over the money, taking a thumb impression or signature from each beneficiary.[11] It is a normal practice to take Rs.20 from each person, and the beneficiaries do not protest. One of them said, 'We all decided amongst ourselves that Rs.20 should be given to the postman by beneficiaries.' While this sounds as if people collectively have decided to accept a corrupt system, it can also be considered a mechanism through which the people have decided its limits, rather than being forced to enter into a bargaining process with the postman every time.

Earlier, there were such serious levels of irregularities in the postal delivery system that the government made changes, and now many *tehsils* deliver the benefit through banks. This is a relatively new system that deserves further study, but it is clear that delivering through banks brings new issues, and two problems have been noted so far. First, as most beneficiaries open their first bank account to receive welfare benefits and are inexperienced account holders with a limited knowledge of withdrawal procedures, bank officials are able to keep some of the money in the account. Bank officials argue that this is their way of encouraging savings among the poor. Thus it is possible for recipients to sign for and receive an amount different from the benefit, which is not possible through postal money orders. Second, banks are not located in or near small villages, like Saralgaon, making access to their benefits especially difficult for infirm beneficiaries. Under the older system, postmen would bring benefit payments to even the most remote villages.

Why do poor people put up with such irregularities? Because of two interrelated factors, it is not easy for people to identify whether they have been given the correct amount. First, illiteracy and innumeracy are widespread. However, this can be overcome with the help of more educated community or household members. Second, most beneficiaries do not know how much money they are entitled to receive. This is largely because of the different timings of state and national benefit disbursements. While the Government of India disburses money annually, state governments disburse every three months. People often find it difficult to calculate and understand their entitlement, so most beneficiaries 'trust' that the money given to them is the entire amount sent. This 'trust' emerges from the fact that it is difficult to counter-check and argue over actual amounts due. Often beneficiaries would compare the amount of money received with that of another beneficiary, and if it were a similar amount, they would be content.

Given these limitations to identifying irregularities, people are willing to part with a small amount of money because they know that if they insisted on the payment of the full amount, they might stand to lose it all. Therefore, complaints and collective protests are only heard if a postman steals the whole amount. A beneficiary explained: 'You are getting something. Why ask for the full amount of money? Is this money from our home or ancestor's home? The government is giving something and you should be thankful rather than fighting.'

Community elites and officials perpetuate this view. According to a head *tehsil* official, 'It is so difficult to manage this office. All kinds of people come ... People are getting some free money so everyone gathers there like a bee on a sweet.' The response from the official and that of the beneficiary complement each other, suggesting that the official is doing a tedious task of distributing free money, not a welfare right, and the beneficiary should be grateful for whatever he or she is given.

Reasons for differential allocations

The theoretical basis of this study is that a policy choice, resulting in differential allocations of state provision, is a residual from the kind of transactions that exist in private and civil society spheres. Therefore it is important to study private-sector and civil society transactions in the village, and the transaction stakeholders. Thus the reasons why a particular application is picked out by a particular committee member lie in the community in which the applicant lives, and the nature of his/her relationships with a hierarchy of elites.

Among the elites in both communities, people with a political power base and a large amount of agricultural land occupy the uppermost positions, irrespective of caste. Credit providers and shopkeepers are among the ranks of the community elite, but they appear at the bottom of the ranking. It was expected that village-level government employees would appear on the 'elite list', but neither these, nor any other institutional employees (apart from those of NGOs in Saralgaon) were considered to be elite by the community. It is likely that these institutions have been co-opted by community elites so that people do not see the institutions themselves as centres of power.

Applicants for social security benefits, who are landless or own very small farms, tend to be involved in intensive transactions within the daily wage agricultural labour market. Many community elites, who are landlords, engage in bargaining with the daily wage labourers. While there is no significant bargaining on issues of wages or jobs, bargaining about social security issues is significant. Bargaining for wages or demanding more jobs is seen as a threat to the landlord's power, and one labourer can easily be replaced by another, since a large supply of labour is readily available. The labourer is aware of this situation, so tries to gain benefits by making demands in non-threatening ways. This can be through requesting assistance from the landlord when a member of the labourer's household falls ill, or there is a marriage or pregnancy and delivery, or when the labourer becomes old. These are non-threatening requests when the labourer communicates, non-verbally, to the landlord that he or she is at their mercy in such a situation. The labourer also tells the landlord that the requested amount would be paid back at a later point in time, or that the amount could be deducted from his/her wages.

These requests are not, however, granted to every labourer. Broadly speaking, across India there are two types of agricultural labourers: the *ghadi* ('the landlord's man'), and the daily wage labourer.[12] Financial requests at a time of household need will often be granted to *ghadi*, but rarely to a daily wage labourer.

Only males are appointed to the post of *ghadi*, a job much in demand. The landlord handpicks them annually at the beginning of the agricultural season. They are given half of the contractual amount when selected (Rs.20,000 per year, partly in the form of grain). The *ghadi* is expected to carry out various kinds of work on the farm, as determined by the landlord. He also organizes daily wage labour when additional workers are needed. He may be asked to do additional non-farm jobs if there is less work to do on the farm. The landlord often chooses to stay with the same *ghadi* if the person is a reliable and cautious worker. This in turn increases loyalty on the part of *ghadi* to both the farm and the landlord. Daily wage workers, on the other hand, are employed on a day-to-day basis, and paid weekly. It is the responsibility of the *ghadi* to bring enough daily wage labourers to the farm. However, the landlord interacts with the daily wage labourers and supervises the work.

Most *ghadis*, when they stop working with the landlord, are able to gain a state pension through the landlord's influence. This becomes easier when the landlord himself is a member of the political elite. Indeed, one *ghadi*, aged 46, was working on the farm of a political elite *and* benefiting from the state pension (for which one should be aged 60 or above). Therefore, people are more prepared to work as *ghadis* on land owned by political elite, although these employers pay about Rs.2,000 less per year than other landlords. Working as a *ghadi* with a non-political elite landlord makes the chances of receiving benefits much more remote, and depends on the extent of the landlord's personal network links. When a *ghadi* working for a non-political elite, or a daily wage labourer, fulfils in general all the criteria for receiving a benefit, he would tend to approach a broker directly rather than approach his employer. On such occasions, it is the leniency on the part of the elite's political party that is crucial.

Introduction of protective measures by the state seems to be having a reverse influence on 'informal pensions' from the landowners to those labourers who have worked on the landlord's land over their entire lifetime. The landowner feels that the state, rather than him, needs to take care of the labourers , so now the responsibility of the landowner is to help the labourer obtain benefits from the state system. This becomes easier if the landowner has political connections. Political elite landlords benefit by being able to get cheaper labourers to work on their farms. In other words, loyalty from workers can be drawn upon at the local level through distributing benefits according to the discretion of local elites.

Preventing receipt of benefits

In some cases, the elite–official nexus can have the serious implication of benefits that have been granted not reaching the beneficiary. There is, in fact, a provision to stop benefits if circumstances change; for example, a young widow's income maintenance benefit can be revoked when her children become adults. However, this research suggests that the most important reason for prevention is not that a previously eligible person falls out of the eligibility criteria, but that political reasons in the community lead to the beneficiary not receiving a granted benefit.[13] In one case, the disgruntled neighbour of a benefit recipient pointed out to an official that the woman had a son older than 18 years of age, but did not mention that there were other younger children for whom the woman remains eligible for benefit. The neighbour, an elite, asked the official directly to stop the benefit. Under law, the *talathi* should then conduct an investigation and report to the *tehsil* official. But as the *talathi*'s first point of inquiry is the elite, the elite's decision prevails.

When a change of government occurs, or when the SSC or the village *sarpanch* changes, the people belonging to the opposition parties are vulnerable to deletion from the list of welfare beneficiaries. The easiest way of doing this is for an elite to tell the official that the particular beneficiary is dead. It is an almost impossible task for a 'dead person' to prove that he or she is alive (Debroy, 2003). In such cases, officials have proved to be extremely subservient to elites, and not demanded any death certificates to protect the rights of beneficiaries.

Conclusions

A range of ways in which policy objectives have been translated through programmes, with negative effects on the welfare rights of poor people, have been identified in this chapter. Table 12.1 summarizes these process deficits and their effects. What emerges most strongly is the importance

Table 12.1 Process deficits and their effects

Process deficits	Possible effects
Obtain application form from informal sources	• Additional expense
	• Easier to obtain than from government sources
Complex application form	• Dependence on middlemen to complete application
Demands for proof of identity and other certificates	• Excludes the poorest people, who are unlikely to have documents, or the money to secure them
The official, rather than the office, accepting application	• The individual and his affiliations increase in importance
	• No objective treatment of the applications.
Non-acceptance of partially completed applications	• Administration is able to show that supply meets demand, since there are few applications
	• Reduces chances of rethinking the criteria for benefits or methods of application
Receipt of application not acknowledged	• Results in officials being able to discard applications from those who have not paid kickbacks
Political body controls officials	• Exclusion of eligible persons who are loyal to opposition parties
Visibility of meeting to the applicants	• Mechanism for drawing loyalty to political elites, so that they can further exercise power over officials
Political backing for the success of application	• Increases clientelistic politics in the community: the poor may be exploited to do favours or labour for political elite
Lack of review of the applications at district level	• Complete discretion is given to the local authority, favouring local elites
Not informing applicant of result of application	• Power of informal stakeholders further strengthened
Lack of review mechanism when benefit stopped	• Possible for political elite to prevent a benefit through an official, in order to settle scores of personal rivalry

that must be placed on the concept of 'informality' while designing a programme of social protection in a rural setting. Both officials and claimants choose to handle the processes in an informal manner, creating serious effects on the welfare rights of claimants.

The role of local elites is instrumental in creating and perpetuating process deficits, through overshadowing the local officer and presenting the view that without the wishes of the elite, obtaining social protection benefits is impossible. On the other hand, these process deficits do not impinge on the state's necessity to justify that social protection is being provided, since performance indicators are designed in ways that do not make the weaknesses of the schemes transparent. In Maharstra, and indeed much of India, the performance of social protection policies depends not so much on policy design as on policy implementation.

Notes

1. This chapter is based on data collected by the author in October 2003 and June 2004 as part of his D.Phil. at Oxford University. It is drawn from a longer paper presented to the Social Protection for Chronic Poverty Conference, and subsequently published as a CPRC Working Paper (Pellissery, 2005). The author is grateful to the participants of this conference for their useful comments, and offers special thanks to George Smith and Barbara Harriss-White for suggestions during the design of the study. Karen Moore and David Hulme provided insightful thoughts and revision of the final manuscripts. Any errors remain the author's.

2. There is an emerging consensus on using 'social protection' as an umbrella term to include the concepts of social security, safety nets and social insurance (Barrientos and Hulme, Chapter 1 in this volume). In this chapter, 'social security' and 'social protection' are used interchangeably. For a broader discussion of social protection, see Pellissery (2005) and the other chapters in this volume.

3. While protection is 'the task of preventing a decline in living standards or the basic conditions of living' (Drèze and Sen, 1991: 1), promotion is about the enhancement of general living standards and the expansion of basic capabilities. See Barrientos and Hulme (Chapter 1 in this volume) and Sabates-Wheeler and Devereux (Chapter 4 in this volume) for further discussion.

4. Social security is placed in the concurrent list of the Constitution of India, whereby both central and state governments share responsibility for providing social security to citizens. See Dev (1998) for a list of state-level protective programmes.

5. Rs.45 was approximately equal to US$1 in 2006.

6. See Singh (1988) for details of this and other techniques to identify community elites.

7. The GoM has recognised the need to help poor people deal with government offices. A project called SETU (Bridge) has started at *tehsil* offices specifically for this purpose, but applicants for income maintenance grants rarely use the facility. Although the SETU office is run by an NGO, the space to run the service is provided by the government and these function in a similar fashion to government offices. SETU's services are mainly used to obtain birth, death and land record certificates.

8. There have been cases where the broker has returned the initial token fee to the applicant after an unsuccessful application. In order to build confidence among community members, brokers need to be seen as not to be acting as cut-throat businessmen who cheat poor people.
9. Land records are huge log-books and it is tedious to examine them. (However, Maharashtra is currently computerising all land records). Usually *talathis* pay an assistant a meagre salary to do the routine jobs. The assistant has to collect bribes to make a decent salary for himself.
10. The bribes may be higher if the individual who makes request is alone with the officer. If there is another community member present, the officer will often request the 'normal' fee.
11. Postmen have been observed insisting on meeting the beneficiary, and not providing the benefit even to a close relative. That the delivery agency ensures that money reaches female beneficiaries is to be appreciated.
12. See Walker and Ryan (1990) and Breman (1993) for details of landlord–worker relationships.
13. See Hulme (2004) for an example from rural Bangladesh.

References

Banik, D. (2002) *Democracy, Drought and Starvation in India: Testing Sen in Theory and Practice*. Oslo: Department of Political Science, University of Oslo.

Blalock, H. M. (1991) *Understanding Social Inequality: Modelling Allocation Process*. London: Sage Publications.

Breman, J. (1993) *Beyond Patronage and Exploitation: Changing Agrarian Relations in South Gujarat*. Delhi: Oxford University Press.

Cornia, G. A. and F. Stewart (1995) 'Two errors of targeting', in D. van de Walle and K. Nead (eds), *Public Spending and the Poor: Theory and Evidence*. Baltimore: Johns Hopkins University Press, pp. 350–385.

Debroy, B. (2003) Mritak Sangh and Lal Bihari. *The Financial Express* (Jan. 7).

Dev, S. M. (1998) 'Government intervention and social security for rural labour', in R. Radhakrishna and A. N. Sharma (eds), *Empowering Rural Labour in India: Market, State and Mobilization*. New Delhi: Institute for Human Development, pp. 173–204.

Drèze, J. and A. Sen (1991) 'Public action for social security: foundations and strategy', in E. Ahmad, J. Drèze, J. Hills and A. Sen (eds), *Social Security in Developing Countries*. Oxford: Clarendon Press, pp. 1–40.

Government of India (GoI) (1997) India's most backward districts: list of 1997 Sarma Committee.

Harriss-White, B. (2004) 'Socially inclusive social security: Social assistance in the villages', in B. Harriss-White and S. Janakarajan (eds), *Rural India Facing the 21st Century*. London: Anthem Press, pp. 429–466.

Harriss-White, B. (1999b) 'State, market, collective and household action in India's social sector', in Harriss-White and S. Subramanian (eds), *Ill-fare in India: Essays on India's Social Sector in Honour of S. Guhan*. New Delhi: Sage Publications, pp. 303–328.

Harriss-White, B. (1995) 'Economic restructuring: state, market and collective and household action in India's social sector', *The European Journal of Development Research*, 7(1), 124–147.

Hulme, D. (2004) 'Thinking "small" and the understanding of poverty: Maymana and Mofizul's story', *Journal of Human Development*, 5(2), 161–176.

Jutting, J. (2000) 'Social security systems in low-income countries: Concepts, constraints and the need for cooperation', *International Social Security Review*, 53(4), 3–24.

Kabeer, N. (1994) 'Gender-aware policy and planning: a social-relations perspective', in M. MacDonald (ed.), *Gender Planning in Development Agencies*. Oxfam: Oxford, pp. 80–97.

Lipsky, M. (1980) *Street-Level Bureaucracy: Dilemmas of the Individual in Public Services*. New York: Russell Sage Foundation.

Mehta, A. K. and A. Shah (2001) 'Chronic poverty in India: an overview study', *CPRC Working Paper 7*. Manchester: IDPM/CPRC.

NCAER (National Council of Applied Economic Research) (2002) *West and Central India Human Development Report*. New Delhi: Oxford University Press.

Pellissery, S. (2005) 'Process deficits or political constraints? Bottom-up evaluation of non-contributory social protection policy for rural labourers in India', *CPRC Working Paper 54*. Manchester: CPRC/IDPM.

Prabhu, K. S. (2001) *Economic Reform and Social Sector Development : A Study of Two Indian States*. New Delhi: Sage Publications.

Sankaran, T. S. (1998) 'Social assistance: evidence and policy issue', in van Ginneken (ed.), *Social Security for all Indians*. New Delhi: Oxford University Press, pp. 57–76.

Singh, R. (1988) *Land, Power and People: Rural Elite in Transition, 1801–1970*. New Delhi: Sage Publications.

Subrahmanya, R. K. A. and R. Jhabvala (2000) 'Meeting basic needs: the unorganised sector and social security', in Jhabvala and Subrahmanya (eds), *The Unorganised Sector: Work Security and Social Protection*. New Delhi: Sage Publications, pp. 17–29.

Walker, T. S. and J. G. Ryan (1990) *Village and Household Economies in India's Semi-Arid Tropics*. Baltimore and London: The Johns Hopkins University Press.

13
Conceptualising the Politics of Social Protection in Africa

Sam Hickey

Introduction

In his study of the New Poor Laws in nineteenth-century England, Karl Polanyi (2001) was centrally preoccupied with the forms of politics that surrounded this initiative, particularly the nature of the parliamentary process that led to Speenhamland being overturned, the new labelling of the poor that this involved, and the impact of such programmes on popular struggles and agency. However, politics has not been accorded a significant role in thinking and policy-making around social protection in Sub-Saharan Africa. The dominance of economics in this field has encouraged a more technocratic focus on social protection, thus overlooking the key role of politics and political economy in raising and shaping this agenda (Niles, 1999: 3; Casamatta *et al.*, 2000: 342). Explanations for the relative paucity of social protection systems and programmes in poor countries tend to suggest that the key problem is simply a lack of financial and administrative capacity. For example, a recent World Bank study focusing on institutional issues in social protection programmes framed the role of national politics in this process as purely contextual, to be examined only 'for the sake of completeness' (Mathauer, 2004: 16). However, there is growing evidence that politics plays a more central role in shaping social protection initiatives than has hitherto been recognised. Given that there 'is no economic law that prevents societies from deciding to allocate more resources to old-age security and less to some other expenditure' (Beattie and McGillivray, 1995: 68, cited in Devereux, 2001: 22), the role of political decision-making regarding public expenditure is clearly central. Indeed, the greater the level of fiscal constraint on a government, the more it is likely to be influenced by the weight of political attitudes concerning who deserves support, and in what form (Graham, 2002: 25). And what else apart from politics can help to explain the radical expansion of the social pension schemes in South Africa and newly independent Namibia in the early 1990s? The challenge, however, is not simply to work towards a greater emphasis on the ways in which politics shapes social protection in Africa, but on a more systematic understanding of these relationships. For example, what are the political pressures or incentives that lead governments to redirect expenditure towards vulnerable and poor groups? Under what conditions might political elites support such initiatives? How important are those aspects of the political conditionality agenda, such as regular elections, multi-party politics and decentralised forms of 'good governance'? What is the role of political 'commitment'? What role do donors play as political actors shaping policy decisions in poor countries? And perhaps most importantly, are countries in Africa close to experiencing what Polanyi termed the 'double movement', whereby a recognition of the problems of unregulated market forces creates an 'impulse for social protection'?

Seeking answers to these questions constitutes an ambitious project, and efforts to seek a systematic understanding of the relationship(s) between politics and social protection are fraught with difficulty. For one reader of Polanyi's work on social protection, virtually any form of politics can be associated with social protection, such that,

> The essential point here is that the impulse for social protection experienced so deeply within society can be mobilized by any number of political tendencies or would-be aspirants to social and political power. This could be a political party of any stripe, a religious movement, a charismatic populist appealing to ethnic or caste identity, a warlord or a fascist. (Putzel, 2002: 3)

At first glance, the African experience might appear to support this position. Very different types of political regime have adopted social protection measures, including colonial regimes, the apartheid regime of South Africa and the much lauded democratic regime – the well-governed state of Botswana. However, a more systematic analysis of the linkages between politics and social protection is lacking. Most work on social protection in Africa makes little mention of political concerns, and studies that do consider only a limited range of variables (for example, political discourse) or makes fairly general references to 'political commitment' or 'political support' without examining how this emerged and might be sustained. Although some studies have sought to develop frameworks of analysis aimed at capturing the influence of politics on social protection within particular country contexts (for example, Graham, 2002; Rothstein, 2002; Pritchett, 2005), these have tended to offer either partial and/or problematic readings of the forms of politics that might shape social protection, and have not been derived from experiences in Africa. Moreover, these approaches have rarely been operationalised (Haddad and Zeller, 1997: 134), leaving them somewhat tentative and less refined than they might be.

Here, an effort is made to bring together the most significant insights from this literature, together with a reading of politics in contemporary Africa, in order to map out the contours of a more holistic analytical framework. The aim is not to be predictive or to produce some kind of blueprint for success that can be applied across the board – politics is highly contextual and the above quote reminds us of the need to recognise the large variations at play. Developing an analytical framework on the basis of an inductive approach to identifying the forms of politics that have been associated with social protection initiatives in Africa may provide the necessary foundation for understanding the role of politics in social protection.

The chapter is organised as follows. The next section outlines the links between social protection and politics, as a first stab at a conceptual framework. The third section discusses how politics shapes social protection in Africa, focusing on institutions, actors and the policy environment. The fourth section suggests the value of a social contract approach, and the final section draws out the main conclusions.

The politics of social protection in Africa: making the links

The linkages between politics and social protection are multi-dimensional and multi-directional (see Figure 13.1). Even the simplest relationship between politics and social protection, which concerns the influence of the former on the latter, is complicated by the fact that different forms of politics shape different dimensions of social protection programmes. For

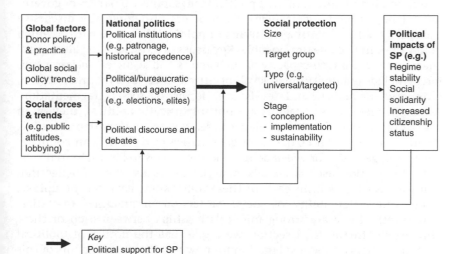

Figure 13.1   The links between politics and social protection: a basic framework

example, the forms of politics that lead to policies being conceived and operationalised may be different from those required to sustain such policies; and different again from the politics of identifying beneficiary groups. The second type of relationship concerns the political impact of social protection itself. For example, social protection programmes may be implemented or boosted with a view to retaining regime legitimacy, or might be associated with increased levels of social solidarity. Finally, and less obviously, the nature of social protection itself shapes the politics of social protection. For example, the design of a social protection programme, for example, whether it is universal or targeted, and its perceived success, might themselves influence the level of political support For reasons of space and also of available evidence, our focus here is predominantly on the first type of relationship.

The approach taken to defining 'politics' here is a broad one, influenced by both political sociology and political economy perspectives.[1] We identify four key aspects of politics in Africa that the literature indicates will be of particular importance in shaping social protection on the continent, namely: political institutions; political actors and agencies; socio-economic forces; and the global dimension. *Institutional* features constitute the historically embedded 'rules of the game' within a given society (North, 1990). Formal political institutions include the rules for elections, and policy legacies that have established accepted ways of doing things, whereas informal political institutions might include patron–client relations. *Actors* include those individuals and agencies that operationalise and contest the rules of the game in ways that shape the distribution of public goods and power, such as political elites, political parties or governmental departments or agencies. Such actors also forge the discursive element of politics, setting the terms of political discourse within which policy options become (im)possible. Key issues here include the ideological character and political capacity of such actors and agencies. *Socioeconomic* forces include public attitudes, levels of citizen voice, levels of urbanisation, economic inequality, and levels and forms of social fragmentation. Although these societal factors are not intrinsically political, they often gain a high degree of political salience in relation to public policy influence. Finally, the particular character of governance in most African countries opens a large space for *global* actors and discourses to be influential. The following section uses case-study material to discuss the influence that political variables within each of these dimensions have on the uptake, forms and sustainability of social protection programmes in Africa. Importantly, there are strong inter-relationships between each of these dimensions. In the final section we argue that the notion of 'political contracts' offers a fuller explanation for how the different elements of this framework become aligned in ways that lead to particular outcomes for social protection in Africa.

How politics shapes social protection in Africa: institutions, actors, socio-economic and global factors

Institutional features: formal and informal

The role of institutions in shaping social protection in Africa encompasses a range of different, and sometimes surprising, relationships, many of them significant. We focus here on the role of elections and political party systems, as well as on the less formal world of patron–client politics. Several studies note the importance of elections in determining public expenditure (for example, Block 2002), and particularly in relation to social policies (Niles, 1999; Schady, 2000; Stasavage, 2003). Block (2002) reveals a strong tendency for African governments both to raise public expenditures in election years (by an average of 4.5 per cent) and to reduce interest rates (by an average of 1–1.5 per cent), as a means of appealing to different constituencies. The study also reveals a tendency for these public expenditures to be in the form of pay rises to public-sector workers, and subsidies to investors. As a consequence, 'welfare programmes do not necessarily target the most needy segments of the population but, rather, the ones critical for the regime's political survival' (Feng and Gizelis, 2002: 220). In Kenya, for example, Daniel Arap Moi distributed food aid selectively in order to secure his regime in power, while denying such aid to some of the most vulnerable groups and areas (de Waal, 1997).

Uganda demonstrates the relevance of 'political cycles' to social-sector spending, with new policies and programmes marking time with the electoral calendar. For example, President Museveni's decision to abolish user fees in Uganda's health sector was timed to coincide with the 2001 elections (Holland and Yeats, 2005). In Botswana, food aid through the Drought Relief Programme was particularly generous in the election years of 1974 and 1979 (de Waal, 1997). The political use of welfare transfers is arguably more likely within authoritarian or semi-democratic regimes that characterised many African states over the 1980s, where the checks on such (ab)uses of power – strong legislature, opposition parties, constitutions – were not well institutionalised (Feng and Gizelis, 2002: 227–228).

Elections, then, can act as a strong incentive towards the initiation of social protection and/or increased expenditure in this area. However, their influence is in turn mediated through other political institutions, most notably political party systems, such that:

> Even limited electoral competition during periods of austerity will create incentives for politicians to broaden their support base, but politicians will only try to take advantage of this opportunity if the party structure helps to reduce the information costs and credibility problems which normally prevent the extension of social programs to the poor. (Niles, 1999: 11)

For Niles (1999), certain forms of party system are more effective than others at creating incentives for regimes to deliver on social protection. Democracies with stable party systems and elected authoritarian systems are likely to be the most progressive here, followed by semi-authoritarian regimes with dominant parties. Those least likely to be associated with social protection policies are non-elected systems and democracies with fragmented party systems. This approach does appear to have a degree of explanatory power, and Feng and Gizelis (2002: 228) note that 'autocratic and semidemocratic governments have much better leverage than their democratic counterparts in using (welfare) transfers to retain office'. In Uganda, the pattern of electorally-driven public expenditure on vulnerable groups by a regime characterised by a 'hegemonic' party system (Carbone, 2003) can be likened to Niles' 'elected authoritarian' system. In addition, none of the main countries to introduce food security measures in the 1970s were liberal democracies (Sudan, Ethiopia and Somalia), but all were committed to a notion of social welfare, to be mobilised through technocratic zeal, and driven by political parties with revolutionary fervour in the latter two countries (de Waal, 1997: 35). On the other hand, while Botswana is usually lauded as the most successful of Sub-Saharan Africa's multi-party democracies, the political sociology of the ruling party (dominated by cattle barons and traders) has ensured that very little effort has gone towards protecting the most destitute groups. For example, the Drought Relief Programme (DRP) increasingly came to serve the interests of large land holders and cattle owners, ignoring the fact that the pressing problem for the destitute was their lack of any formal land rights (de Waal, 1997; Good, 1999).

Much has been written concerning the *informal* character of politics in Africa, characterising the rules of the political game, norms governing the management and distribution of public resources, and the politics of representation (see, for example, Chabal and Daloz, 1999). In discussing more broadly the links between politics and poverty reduction in poor countries, David Booth (2005: 3–4) notes that 'Many or most of the key decisions are made informally, by small groups of politicians linked together by networks of clientelism and patronage', so that 'formal decision-making processes...are...largely "theatre"'. Patron–client politics are cited as a particularly characteristic feature of politics in Africa, and can be linked to social protection programmes in Africa in a number of ways. Patron–client politics can shape the design and targeting of social protection programmes during the planning and implementation phases. For example, the coverage of programmes might be extended to include areas favoured by associated patrons, as with the recent social action fund for Northern Uganda (Brock *et al.*, 2002: 14–15). Where there are strong concerns that funds will be diverted into patronage networks, pressure will arise for arrangements to be put in place to avoid this. These include the establishment of parallel delivery agencies, autonomous project offices within ministries, and a reliance on incentives to ensure that funds reach their intended goal. This was typical during the 1980s and 1990s with the move towards social funds, an approach that arguably undermined the development of more accountable structures of governance. However, this is not to dismiss the progressive role that informal political institutions do and can play. In particular, patron–client relationships provide some of the poorest people with a critical safety net (Wood, 2003).

Political actors and agencies

The key political actors and agencies that might be associated with social protection in Africa are arguably the political elites who set the terms of political and policy debates, and the administrative/bureaucratic agencies that will either lobby for and/or implement social protection initiatives (more popular actors are considered below). Whether political elites consider certain groups to be 'deserving' of social assistance is likely to be a significant factor in the establishment, targeting and size of social protection programmes. Their role in shaping the emphasis on poverty reduction and the terms of engagement has come under particular scrutiny in recent years (Hossain and Moore, 2001), and in the context of chronic poverty (Hickey, 2005; Hossain, 2005). What has been striking here is the extent to which political elites tend to distinguish between groups of the poor, demonstrating a bias towards the productive or economically active poor, who are therefore 'deserving' in ways that are likely to leave some of the chronic poor groups bereft of state support. The experience of social protection in Uganda and Botswana bear this out. The official policy in Botswana is that 'rewards should go to those who make the biggest contribution to Botswana's growth economy' (Good, 1999: 199).

This is a classic statement of a model of economic citizenship rather than social citizenship, with people only fully permitted citizenship status to the extent that they can fully attend to their own economic needs (Fraser and Gordon, 1994), and this is taken up in the later debate on 'contracts'. Precolonial influences may also be of relevance here. Iliffe (1987, in Good, 1999: 199) noted an historical lack of concern towards the poor among Tswana elites, dating back to the nineteenth century.

Once in place, social protection measures themselves become the subject of heated debates between elites. In South Africa, struggles to extend the social pension to Black South Africans were played out through the same form of public discourse over several decades, with criticisms of the system's 'inadequacy and discrimination' ranged against arguments that extending the system would create 'dependency' (Devereux, 2001: 6, box 3). Despite evidence that these transfers have been put to very productive purposes (Devereux, 2002, 2004), the schemes are often criticised by politicians for allegedly creating dependency, fuelling wasteful expenditures such as on alcohol, and helping only those who choose to live off the recipients (Devereux, 2001: 27). This suggests the need for more engagement with political elites by donors, and for linking pro-poor policies to progressive elements of elite political discourse. It is also critical that more resources are put into carrying out and disseminating the results of research into the effects of social protection, including the use of monitoring and evaluation systems.

A more functional but very important set of actors and agencies are the *bureaucrats and bureaucratic agencies* with responsibility for social protection. The argument often put forward here is that, in order for social protection to be a viable policy option, countries must already have high levels of institutional capacity and bureaucratic integrity (de Neubourg, 2002; Besley *et al.*, 2003; Mathauer, 2004). Indeed, it has been argued that, where bureaucratic integrity cannot be guaranteed, it may be better to avoid social safety nets (Iglesias and Palacios, 2000; Besley *et al.*, 2003). However, the mere presence of financial and administrative capacity does not determine the success of social protection in Africa. Moreover, what might be more important is the organisational culture, political commitment and political capacity of bureaucratic actors within government to advocate and implement social protection initiatives. The importance of the implementing agency's organisational culture concerns issues of 'fitness for purpose': for example, the involvement of public works ministries in employment generation schemes, when their *raison d'être* is to 'build stuff' rather than work with people, may be problematic, and suggests that agencies that have a mission to work with the most vulnerable are better-placed here (Pritchett, 2005). However, even here, the inherent universalism of such agencies may clash with a targeted approach that requires them to take a more punitive, disciplinary line. Such departments and ministries tend to be among the weakest in government. Mathauer (2004: 12) underlines the marginality of social-sector ministries, stressing that these suffer from a 'lack of appropriate staff who would be able to make the case for safety net interventions from an economic point of view'. So, beyond a concern to ensure a good 'fit' between public agencies and specific types of social protection (Pritchett, 2005), efforts to enhance not only the institutional but also the political capacity of social-sector ministries might be critical to ensuring strong levels of political support for social protection.

Socio-economic influences on the domestic policy environment

Political institutions and actors, and the policy decisions that emerge from them, are shaped by and respond to a wide range of socio-economic processes and factors. This is well-recognised within political sociology research, and here we draw on such insights to consider the influence that public attitudes, social fragmentation and inequality, and urbanisation may have on the implementation of social protection initiatives in Africa.

The extent of *public support* for social protection in Africa is difficult to gauge, although recent attitudinal surveys into the views of citizens concerning economic and political change suggest that public attitudes on the causes of poverty, the role of the state, and of the procedural justice of public programmes, are important. In terms of how people perceive poverty to be caused, the key issue seems to be whether the causes of poverty are linked to a perceived 'lack of effort' by the poor or 'wider forces' (Gelbach and Pritchett, 1997; Pritchett, 2005). Where it is the former, support is likely to be lower than in the latter. This relates, again, to debates around the 'deserving' and 'undeserving' poor. While evidence of this is rather thin, many citizens in Africa do see a significant role for the state to provide against vulnerability. Attitudinal surveys in southern Africa support Polanyi's thesis in finding that citizens 'are more likely to countenance economic reforms if an effective developmental state provides a safety net against the failure of markets' (Bratton and Mattes, 2003: 318). Here, there may be a distinction between broad-based support for services such as education and health, and assistance to those unable to provide for themselves, especially those who are able-bodied, which are more controversial (Bratton and Mattes, 2003; see also Graham, 2002: 23). The majority of southern Africans approve of the state playing a strong role in terms of education, health and the provision of water and electricity (Bratton and Mattes, 2003: 309), a finding that seems to augur well for states that are seeking popular support for increased levels of social spending.

The extent to which citizens trust the administrative system that delivers social protection to work fairly and effectively and deliver the goods in an impartial way, reflects on notions of procedural justice. Where social protection programmes are associated with elite capture and clientelistic patterns of distribution, they may lose support (Graham, 2002: 15; Rothstein, 2002: 911–912). According to Pritchett (2005), the key points are whether there is a mechanism of appeal beyond the local administration of the project; and, whether the criteria for access change dynamically over time. The effectiveness criterion refers mainly to the 'demonstration effect' of programmes, thus highlighting the importance of effective monitoring and evaluations systems in building virtuous circles between the effects of social protection and the (re)generation of political support for such initiatives (see Figure 13.1).

Levels of inequality and fragmentation, or the political sociology of 'democratic' politics, are likely to be an influential factor concerning social protection, although there are two opposing views on how this might work. Research in Latin America tends to suggest that wide gaps between the middle strata and the poor, both in terms of income gap and social proximity (employment, residence), may reduce the scope for introducing social protection (Graham, 2002). Nelson (2003) also argues that social protection policies require the support of the 'middle-poor', which is itself contingent on there being a large 'range of vulnerability'. Here, the middle/middle-poor strata move in and out of poverty on a regular basis, and feel the need for protective measures to be in place. One implication from this approach would be that, as the gap between poor and wealthy blacks in South Africa grows (Bratton and Mattes, 2003); political support for social protection there may decline.

However, an alternative possibility here is that extreme economic inequality may actually be a driving force behind social protection policies in Africa. One observer notes that such inequalities are a 'pre-condition' for the social pension system in South Africa and Namibia, both in terms of creating the need, and also making it much more feasible in terms of avoiding leakage to the non-poor (Devereux, 2001: 22). The fact that Botswana – another of Sub-Saharan Africa's unusually unequal societies – is one of the few other countries to have introduced a pension system adds further weight to this argument, and may suggest that many African countries have simply not reached the point of economic development and inequality whereby the impulse for social protection becomes pervasive. High levels of income inequality may also indicate the presence of a more viable tax-base for redistributive social policies via the higher earners in society.

However, this issue may hinge on the particular forms of inequality that gain political salience in particular contexts. In Southern Africa, there is a tendency to undertake comparisons intra-group rather than in relation to the whole population (Bratton and Mattes, 2003), suggesting a focus on horizontal rather than vertical inequalities (Stewart, 2002). The issue of relative deprivation is stressed as a key determinate of political behaviour. What counts here are popular perceptions of how 'people like them' will fare under a given programme. Where the boundaries of these types of 'in-group' identification overlap closely with poverty rankings, then the potential for clashes over social protection are clear. Where poverty is associated with a particular group, this may prove to be more intractable, especially where such groups are notably different from either the elites or the middle strata (on whom the elites rely).

The final socio-economic force that appears to shape the politics of social protection concerns *the level of urbanisation*. Although this is closely related to overall levels of development, and industrialisation in particular, there also appear to be a set of more specific political relationships that are worth highlighting. For some, the fact that urbanisation tends to have a positive effect on welfare transfers 'reveals that the welfare system serves the urban areas more than the countryside ... rural residents tend to fall outside welfare transfers in poor countries', not least because urban dwellers are considered by governments to be more politically valuable (Feng and Gizelis, 2002: 228). It is notable that many of the efforts to mitigate the social costs of adjustment were focused on urban areas, such as the GAPVU project in Mozambique (Datt *et al.*, 1997). So, while rural voters are more willing than urbanites to accept a role for the state in development matters (Bratton and Mattes, 2003), urban dwellers are cited as being disengaged from rural poverty issues, and unwilling to extend their social rights to rural areas (de Waal, 1997: 35).

The global politics of social protection

The global politics of social protection cuts across and closely informs the ways in which these predominantly national forms of politics shape social protection. This is especially pertinent in highly-indebted poor countries, where donor agencies play a significant role in influencing domestic policy agendas.[2] The ways in which donor agencies conceptualise social protection and prioritise it in relation to other policies in their lending portfolios and policy advice, are all influential. Here we explore briefly the extent to which there is now a Polanyian impulse for social protection at the global level.

The degree of importance that donor agencies currently place on social protection remains debatable, although there have been significant advances since the rather half-hearted attempt to introduce safety nets via the 'social dimensions of adjustment' initiatives of the late 1980s and early 1990s. This effort was heavily compromised both by the piecemeal and half-hearted efforts of donors, and their concurrent dedication to the rolling back of the state, the only institution capable of delivering widespread forms of social protection in Africa (Putzel, 2002: 3). Such programmes tended to use and even establish parallel structures of governance rather than become embedded within the political system (Parker and Serrano, 2000; de Haan *et al.*, 2002), and were thus unlikely to form part of a general commitment by states to offer systematic forms of social protection to citizens.

The emphasis on social protection has advanced since the late 1990s with the emergence of the 'Post-Washington Consensus' in the aftermath of the economic crisis in East Asia.[3] This revealed the danger of relying on unregulated markets and unfettered growth, seemed to usher in a more genuine 'impulse' for social protection amongst donor agencies. A series of new aid modalities have been introduced – particularly moves towards direct budgetary support and 'poverty reduction strategies' – which promise to offer a more politically-attuned and integrated approach to issues of growth, good governance, and social protection.

However, for Craig and Porter (2005), the Polanyian 'double movement' within international development policy remains unpersuasive, as evidenced by the lowly status of social protection on donor agendas. Social protection effectively constitutes the last and lowliest arrival on an already crowded poverty policy agenda, behind growth, good governance and a broader focus on poverty reduction. This lowly status is reflected in the relative priority given to social protection in the donor-influenced poverty reduction strategy papers (Marcus and Wilkinson, 2002). To the extent that donors shape the politics of what is possible in poor countries through their funding levels and agenda-setting powers, this does not augur well. Moreover, the specific conceptualisation of social protection is also significant here. To the extent that the global discourse on social protection is conceptualised in terms of 'risk management' (for example, Holzmann and Jørgensen, 2000), the relevance for the destitute and chronic poor is likely to remain minimal (McKinnon 2004; Barrientos *et al.*, 2005). As such, the global impulse for social protection remains ambiguous.

From analysis to explanations: a political contract for social protection?

It would be wrong to claim that the foregoing analysis suggests a clear picture regarding the forms of politics that are likely to underpin moves towards social protection in Africa. The discussion suggests that very different regimes may promote social protection for different reasons at different times, or even within the same polity. However, what does seem to be common across these cases is that social protection initiatives have been closely shaped by the existence and particular form of what might be termed a political contract between states and citizens. For example, the social pension programmes in both South Africa and Namibia were transformed into a progressive form of social protection aimed at reversing previous discrimination as the terms of the broader social contract altered. The erosion of apartheid brought more citizens within the contract, a process accelerated and institutionalised in South Africa through the instalment of the African National Congress (ANC). In Namibia, the SWAPO government pledged their commitment to this policy and have increased its coverage significantly. Elsewhere in Africa, it is the lack of a political contract for social protection between states and citizens around issues of social protection that constitutes arguably the greatest barrier. In the absence of a binding contract, social protection policies are liable to be instigated for other reasons – for example, political risk assessments, and ultimately be distorted by other prevailing forms of politics such as patrimonialism. An example here is the Drought Relief Programme in Botswana, whereby 'The duty to prevent famine was closer to an administrative ethic than a directive. Above all, there was never an intention to nurture a corresponding right to relief' (de Waal, 1997: 30). In Uganda, the absence of a contract between the ruling regime and citizens in Northern Uganda arguably informs the tendency to deal with the high levels of chronic poverty in that region through piecemeal social funds that are further diluted by the politics of patronage.

Other dimensions of inclusion and exclusion regarding these contracts are also apparent. Before the 1990s, and with few exceptions, social security schemes in Africa were limited to wage-earners, and often only to civil servants (Gruat, 1990: 409). Certain forms of labour have nearly always been excluded, particularly seasonal or casual labour. De Waal (1997: 29) notes that government employees and townspeople were generally the only ones in Africa to be targeted for food relief during the colonial era. The strongest political contract to emerge was around the right of urbanites to food (ibid.: 31). This again suggests that only certain categories of people are seen as being citizens.

So the notion of a political contract for social protection offers genuine and critical insights into the historical development of social protection in Africa. It also offers a normative purchase. Within current social policy debates, there is an increasing focus on 'contractualism' as a conceptual means of establishing the state's long-term rationale for challenging inequality and injustice (Jayausuriya, 2002), including social protection (Ramia, 2002). This has been reflected increasingly in international development debates concerning social protection. As such, and in addition to offering an analytical tool for understanding the links between politics and poverty reduction, the notion of a social contract can relocate social protection within a project of redistributive justice (Ramia, 2002) that arguably is required to underpin a long-term challenge to chronic poverty (Hickey and Bracking, 2005). Undertaking social protection within the broader remit of social contractualism involves retaining the reciprocity embedded within informal political relations while raising the status of passive beneficiary to that of claimant. As originally understood by Rousseau (1968), the very basis of contractualism is citizenship, and it is along these lines that Jayusiraya (2002: 316) argues that contractualism 'must be conceived as a political relationship that places a premium on the political capacity of the individual to bargain within an adequate range of available choices and options'. In framing the recipient as an actor rather than a passive recipient, the empowering potential of social protection remains intact and transcends the 'hand-out' culture with which it is currently associated in many countries in Africa.

Conclusion

It has been argued here that politics is central to the ways in which social protection is emerging in Africa. Political institutions provide significant incentives for, and barriers to, action; while the ways in which key political actors and agencies engage with those in poverty is also critical. Issues of elite discourses and organisational culture and 'fit' require as much attention as the more technocratic agendas of capacity-building. More broadly, political institutions and actors operate in a policy environment that is clearly shaped by socio-economic forces, particularly concerning public attitudes, levels and forms of inequality, as well as processes of change such as urbanisation. Donor agencies are critical policy actors in many African countries, and need to give social protection a higher priority and ensure its fuller integration with other elements of their policy agendas.

The focus on social contracts can give a broader purpose to the politics of social protection as it reflects existing commitments and responsibilities towards protecting vulnerable members of society, but also offers a normative policy framework through which to promote social protection. In this context, the nexus of politics and social protection in Africa appears to be entering an important transitional phase. For nationally-driven social protection intitiatives, such as the social pension schemes in Namibia and South Africa, the challenge is one of sustaining the political contract that has developed for continued (or expanded) spending and provision in this area. In countries with more imperfect but still nationally-driven efforts to protect people against vulnerability, the issue is one of extending this contract to include the poorest people. The overarching aim for donor agencies should be to strengthen and extend political contracts for social protection where they exist, and to work towards their establishment where they do not, in part through a policy of 'doing no harm'. This means avoiding the temptation to regulate activities where institutional arrangements exist, but rather add material support and political advocacy (de Waal, 1997). A key challenge is to identify and support 'politically progressive constituencies', or drivers of change, that might begin to provide the forms of mobilisation required to secure political contracts for social protection.

Notes

1. From a political sociology perspective, it is important to understand the social bases of institutional and political power, and 'to relate socio-economic conditions to political constitutions and institutional arrangements, and to relate these structural considerations to policy propensities' (Almond, 1990: 24).
2. In Chapter 9 in this volume, Britto notes that the influence of donors on flagship social protection policies in Chile and Brazil has been minimal, although they have played a role in disseminating lessons learnt across Latin America.
3. Chapter 6 in this volume, on Indonesia, discusses the development of social protection there after the financial crisis.

References

Almond, G. (1990) *Separate Tables: Schools and Sects in Political Science*. New York: Sage.

Barrientos, A., D. Hulme and A. Shepherd (2005) 'Can social protection tackle chronic poverty?', *European Journal of Development Research*, 17(1), 8–23.

Beatty, R. and W. McGillivray (1995) 'A risky strategy: Reflections on the World Bank Report *Averting the old age crisis*', *International Social Security Review*, 48(3–4), 5–22.

Besley, T., R. Burgess and I. Rasul (2003) 'Benchmarking government provision of social safety nets', *World Bank Social Protection Discussion Paper No. 0315*. Washington, DC: World Bank.

Block, S. A. (2002) 'Political business cycles, democratization, and economic reform: the case of Africa', *Journal of Development Economics*, 67(1), 205–228.

Booth, D. (2005) 'Missing links in the politics of development: Learning from the PRSP experiment', *ODI Working Paper 256*. London: Overseas Development Institute.

Bratton, M. and R. Mattes (2003) 'Support for economic reform? Popular attitudes in southern Africa', *World Development*, 31(2), 303–323.

Brock, K., R. McGee and R. Ssewakiryanga (2002) 'Poverty knowledge and policy processes: A case study of Ugandan national poverty reduction policy', *IDS Research Paper No.53*. Brighton: IDS.

Carbone, G. M. (2003) 'Political parties in a "no-party democracy": Hegemony and opposition under "movement democracy" in Uganda', *Party Politics*, 9(4), 485–501.

Casamatta, G., H. Cremer and P. Pestieau (2000) 'Political sustainability and the design of social insurance', *Journal of Public Economics*, 75(3), 341–364.

Chabal, P. and J-P. Daloz (1999) *Africa Works: Disorder as Political Instrument*. London: James Currey/International Africa Institute.

Craig, D. and D. Porter (2005) 'The third way and the third world: Poverty reduction and social inclusion strategies in the rise of "inclusive" liberalism', *Review of International Political Economy*, 12(2), 226–263.

Datt, G., E. Payongayong, J. Garrett and M. Ruel (1997) 'The GAPVU cash transfer program in Mozambique: An assessment', *FCND Discussion Paper 36*, International Food Policy Research Institute.

Devereux, S. (2001) 'Social pensions in Namibia and South Africa', *IDS Discussion Paper 379*. Brighton: IDS.

Devereux, S. (2002) 'Can social safety nets reduce chronic poverty?', *Development Policy Review*, 20(5), 657–675.

Devereux, S. (2004) 'Transformative social protection', *IDS Working Paper 232*. Brighton: IDS.

Feng, Y. and T. I. Gizelis (2002) 'Building political consensus and distributing resources: A trade-off or a compatible choice?', *Economic Development and Cultural Change*, 51(1), 217–236.

Fraser, N. and L. Gordon (1994) 'Civil citizenship against social citizenship? On the ideology of contract-versus-charity', in B. van Steenbergen (ed.), *The Condition of Citizenship*. London: Sage, pp. 90–107.

Gelbach, J. B. and L. Pritchett (1997) 'More for the poor is less for the poor: The politics of targeting', *World Bank Development Research Group*. Washington, DC: World Bank.

Gore, C. (2000) 'The rise and fall of the Washington consensus as a paradigm for developing countries', *World Development*, 28(5), 789–804.

Graham, C. (2002) 'Public attitudes matter: A conceptual frame for accounting for political economy in safety nets and social assistance policies', *Social Protection Discussion Paper Series*. Washington, DC: World Bank.

Gruat, J. V. (1990) 'Social security schemes in Africa', *International Labour Review*, 129(4), 406–421.

de Haan, A., J. Holland and N. Kanji (2002) 'Social funds: An effective instrument to support local action for poverty reduction?', *Journal of International Development*, 14(5), 643–652.

Haddad, L. and M. Zeller (1997) 'Can social security programmes do more with less? General issues and challenges for southern Africa', *Development Southern Africa*, 14(2), 125–151.

Hickey, S. (2005) 'The politics of staying poor: Exploring the political space for poverty reduction in Uganda', *World Development*, 33(6), 995–1009.

Hickey, S. and S. Bracking (2005) 'Exploring the politics of chronic poverty: From representation to a politics of justice?', *World Development*, 33(6), 851–865.

Holland, J. and J. Yeats (2005) 'Social protection and health: Experiences in Uganda', *Development Policy Review*, 24(3), 339–356.

Holzmann, R. and S. Jørgensen (2000) 'Social risk management: A new conceptual framework for social protection and beyond', *World Bank Social Protection Discussion Paper No. 0006*. Washington, DC: World Bank.

Hossain, N. (2005) 'Productivity and virtue: Elite categories of the poor in Bangladesh', *World Development*, 33(6), 965–977.

Hossain, N. and M. Moore (2001) 'Arguing for the poor: Elites and poverty in developing countries', *Ids Working Paper 148*. Brighton: IDS.

Iglesias, A. and R. J. Palacios (2000) 'Managing public pension reserves Part I: Evidence from the international experience', *World Bank Social Protection Discussion Paper No. 0003*. Washington, DC: World Bank.

Jayausuriya, K. (2002) 'The new contractualism: Neoliberal or democratic?', *The Political Quarterly*, 73(3), 309–320.

Marcus, R. and J. Wilkinson (2002) 'Whose poverty matters? Vulnerability, social protection and PRSPs', *CHIP Working Paper No.1*. www.chronicpoverty.org

Mathauer, I. (2004) 'Institutional analysis toolkit for safety net interventions', *World Bank Social Protection Discussion Paper No. 0418*. Washington, DC: World Bank.

McKinnon, R. (2004) 'Social risk management and the World Bank: Resetting the "standards" for social security', *Journal of Risk Research*, 7(3), 297–314.

Nelson, J. (2003) 'Grounds for alliance? Overlapping interests of the poor and not so poor', in P. Houtzager and M. Moore (eds), *Changing Paths: International Development and the Politics of Inclusion*. Ann Arbor: University of Michigan Press, pp. 119–138.

de Neubourg, C. (2002) 'Incentives and the role of institutions in the provision of social safety nets', *World Bank Social Protection Discussion Paper No. 0226*. Washington, DC: World Bank.

Niles, K. (1999) 'Economic adjustment and targeted social spending: The role of political institutions'. Background Paper for WDR 2000/1. www.worldbank.org

North, D. C. (1990) *Institutions, Institutional Change and Economic Performance*. Cambridge and New York: Cambridge University Press.

Parker, A. and R. Serrano (2000) 'Promoting good local governance through social funds and decentralization', *World Bank Social Protection Discussion Paper No. 0022*. Washington, DC: World Bank.

Polanyi, K. (2001/1944) *The Great Transformation: The Political and Economic Origins of Our Time*. Boston, MA: Beacon Press.

Pritchett, L. (2005) 'A lecture on the political economy of targeted safety nets', *World Bank Social Protection Discussion Paper No. 0501*. Washington, DC: World Bank.

Putzel, J. (2002) 'Politics, the state and the impulse for social protection: The implications of Karl Polanyi's ideas for understanding development and crisis', *Crisis States Programme Development Research Centre*. http://www.crisisstates.com/

Ramia, G. (2002) 'The "new contractualism", social protection and the Yeatman thesis', *Journal of Sociology*, 38(1), 49–68.

Rothstein, B. (2002) 'Cooperation for social protection: Explaining variation in welfare programs', *American Behavioral Scientist*, 45(5), 901–918.

Rousseau, J. J. (1968) *The Social Contract*. Bucks: Penguin.

Schady, N. R. (2000) 'Seeking votes: The political economy of expenditures by the Peruvian Social Fund (FONCODES), 1991–1995'. Washington, DC: World Bank.

Stasavage, D. (2003) 'Democracy and education spending: Has Africa's move to multiparty elections made a difference to policy?', *LSE STICERD Development Economics Paper*. London: LSE.

Stewart, F. (2002) 'Horizontal inequalities: A neglected dimension of development', *Queen Elizabeth House Working Paper Series, No. 81*. Oxford: QEH.

Turner, B. S. (2001) 'The erosion of citizenship', *British Journal of Sociology*, 52(2), 189–209.

de Waal, A. (1997) *Famine Crimes: Politics and the Disaster Relief Industry in Africa*. Oxford: James Currey/IAI.

Wood, G. (2003) 'Staying secure, staying poor: The "Faustian bargain"', *World Development*, 31(3), 455–471.

14
Political Incumbency and Drought Relief in Africa

Ngonidzashe Munemo[1]

Introduction

For many parts of Sub-Saharan Africa (SSA), droughts are frequent and often severe. The variability of rainfall in the arid and semi-arid regions of the continent, together with the poor capacity of most soils in Africa to retain moisture, has left many parts of the continent food-insecure. Furthermore, in almost all countries prone to recurrent rainfall shortages, the common rural household coping strategies of selling productive assets to smooth consumption and income in the short term not only impedes recovery but has also been shown to increase inequality.

Deepening inequality has not been the worst outcome of drought in Africa. In a number of drought-prone countries, the curse of geography quickly turned into widespread starvation. Because countries in which droughts progressed into famine have captured much of the policy and academic attention over the years, 'it is widely believed that most African countries lack the political structure (perhaps even the commitment) for successful pursuit of comprehensive strategies of entitlement protection' (Dreze, 1990: 127). However, as Dreze himself notes, it would be inaccurate to take this characterization to be truly representative of the situation across SSA.

Since independence, a number of governments have responded to protect their populations from the threat of famine. In these countries, government-initiated responses to drought-induced threats of starvation have included the free distribution of food, and large, income-restoring and workfare-intensive public works programmes for able-bodied adults. Thus, despite similarities in the proximate cause of threats to household food security, both universal food aid and workfare programmes have been used to protect citizens from the 'co-variant risks associated with climatic and systemic shocks' (Subbarao, 2003: 1).

Variation has not just been prominent across countries, but has also been notable *within* them over time. What accounts for the variation in how African governments have typically responded to drought? Why have some governments chosen relief policies that are heavily reliant on free food aid, while others have opted for workfare-based relief? Finding answers to these questions is the main focus of this chapter.

By conceptualizing the choice of one form of drought relief policy over another as involving non-trivial trade-offs between long-run economic benefits but immediate political costs for workfare-based relief on the one hand, and immediate political gains with long-run economic costs for universal food aid, on the other, I argue that variation in the form taken by drought relief programmes results from the relative fragility of political incumbents. My contention is that incumbents who are vulnerable to the loss of power have a preference for policy measures associated with immediate benefits, such as universal food aid. However, when political incumbents are secure in their position and power, the lower discount rates and longer time horizon this produces creates a policy environment in which workfare-based relief is chosen.

The rest of the chapter proceeds as follows. The first section briefly describes the key components of drought relief in Botswana, Kenya and Zimbabwe. The second assesses the debate on the efficacy of universal food aid and workfare-based relief. In the third section I sketch a political incumbency-based framework that guides my analysis of government behaviour. The fourth section examines how the vulnerability of political incumbency shaped the form taken by drought relief in Botswana, Kenya and Zimbabwe. I end with a brief conclusion.

Drought relief responses in Botswana, Kenya and Zimbabwe

Since gaining independence, a number of governments in Africa have sought to protect their populations from the threat of famine. Government responses either involved universal food relief or took the form of workfare-based relief. At different points in their history, governments in Botswana, Kenya and Zimbabwe opted to smooth consumption shocks caused by drought through the universal distribution of food relief. Additionally, workfare programmes have also figured in national drought relief efforts in Botswana and Zimbabwe.

Botswana: from food aid to the institutionalization of workfare relief[2]

Following drought in 1978–9, Botswana adopted its first post-independence drought relief programme (Government of Botswana, 1979). As laid out in President Khama's address, the government's drought relief programme was to involve 'relief in the form of supplementary food ... using the existing distribution points such as clinics, health-posts and primary schools and the village authorities in the districts', the intensification of rations to vulnerable groups, the distribution of seed at subsidized prices through the outlets of the Agricultural Marketing Board, co-operatives and extension services 'to enable the recovery of the arable economy', the scaling-up of operations at BMC abattoirs, and the distribution of free Botulism vaccines and Vitamin A to reduce the risks 'to cattle which will not be marketed' (Khama, quoted in Botswana *Daily News*, 29May 1979: 3).

Between 1981 and 1987, Botswana was once again struck by a serious drought. In response to the crisis, the government adopted a relief programme in which the main component was participation in rural public works programmes (Government of Botswana, 1982; Amis, 1990; Boers, 1990). Following another drought in 1991-3, the government's approach again focused on workfare projects organized by VDC and administered by District Councils. As in 1982-90,[3] individuals *self-selected* to work on the public works projects chosen by the community. Another feature of the 1992-4 response is that it signalled an attempt by the government to institutionalize workfare projects. Specifically, the government's economic blueprint for 1991-7 (National Development Plan 7) built a 3-4 per cent increase in annual expenditure to fund drought relief programmes (Government of Botswana, 1991: 59). All subsequent drought relief programmes in Botswana have involved workfare relief.

Kenya 1984-5: success with universal food aid[4]

In response to what was then the worst drought in 100 years over the 1983-4 season, President Moi announced the establishment of the National Famine Relief Fund (NFRF). The NFRF was to be the main conduit through which private contributions to the relief effort were mobilized and channelled to affected communities (Borton, 1989). More substantively, Kenya's 1984-5 drought relief programme had two key components. First, the Kenyan government used the existing 'commercial distribution channels as the primary means of getting food to people' (Cohen and Lewis, 1987: 281) in the urban areas and those outside the hard-hit eastern and northern areas of the country. For those not able to buy food on the open market, the second component of the government's relief involved the distribution of free food rations (Downing *et al.*, 1989). Under this element of the relief programme, 'District Commissioners were authorized to make free food available wherever needed to prevent hunger' (Cohen and Lewis, 1987: 281). The allocation of resources was the responsibility of the Provisional Administration, which relied on 'famine relief committees and local chiefs to identify those in need of support' (Dreze, 1990: 139).[5]

Zimbabwe 1980-2004: from universal food aid to workfare relief and back[6]

As in Botswana and Kenya, food aid featured prominently in Zimbabwe's drought relief programmes of 1982-4 and 2002-4. The main elements of the government of Zimbabwe's 1982-4 response involved the large-scale distribution of take-home food rations to the adult population in rural areas, plus supplementary feeding for children under five and lactating mothers.[7] The distribution of food aid was the responsibility of Zimbabwe African National Union (ZANU) party cadres at the village and district levels (Leys, 1986; Dreze, 1990; Munro, 2001). Party cadres at branch and district level were the ones who 'identified drought-stricken areas and households and forwarded this information to the DSW [Department of Social Welfare]' (Munro, 2001: 167).

Like its neighbour to the south-west, Zimbabwe also switched to workfare-based relief in its second drought relief programme in 1987–8. However, whereas workfare-based relief programmes in Botswana transferred income to beneficiaries, in Zimbabwe the workers were paid in food rations. The new relief policy adopted by the Government of Zimbabwe had two components: free food distribution (FFD) for households that did not have an able-bodied adult, and food-for-work (FFW) for households with an able-bodied adult (see Government of Zimbabwe, 1986a, 1986b). Under the FFD component of the relief programme, ZANU cadres who had been responsible for the identification of beneficiaries and distribution of food aid during the 1982–4 relief were replaced by *elected officials*, local politicians and *line-staff* in the Department of Social Welfare (DSW).[8] Selection into the FFW component of the government's workfare-based programme was left largely to individuals.[9]

In its third drought relief programme in 1992–3, the government continued with a workfare-based relief programme. The 1992–3 drought relief programme had three key components. First, the government sought to maintain enough grain for the urban food market. Second, the relief effort called for the supplementary feeding of children under the age of 5 and primary-school children designated as being the most vulnerable. Adults in need of drought relief had to register to work on public works programmes through their local DSW offices. Thus the third component of the 1992/3 relief effort was the provision of aid to able-bodied adults through self-selection into food-for-work programmes (Government of Zimbabwe, 1993).

Efficacy of responses

Over the years, the efficacy of each of these response strategies has been the subject of much debate among scholars. Arguments by Dreze and Sen (1989), as well as other accounts by Dreze (1990), Sen (1999) and von Braun *et al.* (1999) suggest that, while free food aid can be commended for its immediate observable benefits by transferring food directly to beneficiaries, overall the policy proves to be *costly and unsustainable*. Specifically, they stress that the distribution of free food aid is intrinsically vulnerable to major administrative and logistic failures, could potentially lead to the spread of infectious diseases,[10] and tends to be wasteful, given its universal coverage. For example, Zimbabwe's

1982–4 relief was characterized by numerous complaints by recipients about delays, uncertainties and fraud (see Leys, 1986; Bratton, 1987a; Saunders and Davies, 1988). The government-operated Central Motor Engine Department (CMED), which had been given the responsibility of moving food to distribution centres, lacked the experience and the capacity to do so. In the end, food delivery was sub-contracted to the private sector in an attempt to unlock some of the logistic constraints in the relief programme.

Because of all these limitations with universal food aid, Dreze and Sen (1989) contend that the most *effective* way for governments to prevent famine is through workfare-based programmes.[11] In support of workfare-based relief, they stressed that the self-selection involved in workfare relief tends to eliminate the indiscriminate distribution of government aid (see also van Braun *et al.*, 1999). Also, if workfare relief pays in cash, as in Botswana, Dreze and Sen (1989) note that rebuilding lost incomes enables affected groups to compete effectively for food at the same time as it encourages trade and commerce. Wage-based protection tends to avoid the social disruption associated with direct food aid.[12] Elsewhere, Subbarao (2003) suggests that another advantage of workfare programmes may include the construction of much-needed infrastructure if they are well designed. According to Subbarao (2003), the construction of infrastructure minimizes the trade-offs between 'public spending on income versus public spending on development' by generating downstream benefits in the form of employment opportunities for the maintenance of the infrastructure.

The limits of instrumental assessments of efficacy

If it is well understood that workfare relief is more effective in poor countries, why, then, has universal food aid bulked large in response efforts in Africa? In response to this question, some scholars impute irrationality, sometimes even pathology, on the part of the African governments for continuing with universal food aid. For example, Benson and Clay (1998: 2), argue that reliance on food aid in Africa 'partly reflect a widespread failure to perceive droughts as a serious and potentially long-term economic problem'.

There are a number of reasons we might not want to place too much weight on explanations of drought relief policy that are wont to attribute 'irrationality' or 'lack of knowledge' on the part of African governments. To begin with, the authors discussed above offer assessments of relief programmes from a very narrow, technocratic and economic perspective. However, as is stressed by Bratton (1987b: 175), 'the insistence that policy be formed only by considerations of economic rationality' fails to appreciate the perspective of political incumbents for whom 'the resources at [their] disposal are the largesse by which political leaders maintain themselves in power'. Thus, policy is not just an economically shaped response, but often a product of political considerations.

My own research into drought relief in Sub-Saharan Africa suggests the need to take into consideration two additional factors: (i) the political gains of each response type; and (ii) the time frame in which incumbents anticipate benefits to accrue. Whereas most assessments, as discussed above, are interested in the economic benefits (that is, a response's appropriateness, cost effectiveness and sustainability) of the two responses, I argue that each response is also associated with a political benefit or cost to responding incumbents. As the number of people who can be a beneficiary of government policy increases, as with universal food aid, so too does the *potential political benefit* to political incumbents. Conversely, a relief programme that is predicated on targeting, as is the case with workfare-based aid, is likely to be associated with a *political cost* as incumbents have to deal with core support groups who find themselves defined-out of the potential beneficiary category.

The second factor that was apparent in researching drought relief policy selection in SSA was the time frame under which incumbents imagined costs had to be 'paid' or benefits obtained. To simplify, I dichotomize this time frame into the short run and the long run. Combining the economic assessments provided by Dreze and Sen (1989) and others,, and with my own assessments of the political benefit/cost of each relief type, I can construct a simple 2×2 table that summarizes the trade-offs incumbents are faced with in deciding on a form of relief.[13] Principally, as Table 14.1 illustrates, there are non-trivial trade-offs between the long-run economic benefits associated with workfare-based relief, on the one hand, and

Table 14.1 Trade-offs between relief responses and vulnerability of incumbents

		Benefit/cost to responding incumbents	
		Short-run	Long-run
Form taken by relief	**Food aid**	*Benefit (political):* Government immediately seen to be doing something Strategy has wide coverage Allows for credit-claiming by incumbents	*Cost (economic):* Administrative problems Spread of diseases Social disruption 'Wasteful' by providing aid to everyone Social disruption 'Wasteful' by providing aid to everyone
	Workfare	*Cost (political):* Takes time to establish Selective coverage cuts out wealthier segments of the population	*Benefit (economic):* Eliminates indiscriminate aid Addresses income shocks of drought May build physical infrastructure

the short-run political benefits produced by the credit-claiming and coalition-building of universal food aid, on the other.

Under circumstances in which free food distribution is associated with immediately identifiable political rewards for incumbents, and workfare relief linked with wider and more diffuse economic benefits, there is good reason to expect drought relief policy choices to be the outcomes of political calculation rather than simply being an instrumental weighing of costs and benefits. The politics-sensitive view of drought relief suggested here is consistent with scholars who have shown that 'political expediency plays a formative role in policy choice, with leaders using the distribution of resources as a device to attract political support, nullify opposition, and remain in control' (Bratton, 1987b: 175). There is good reason, then, to eschew policy accounts that necessarily presume irrationality or lack of knowledge on the part of decision-makers in favour of a framework that takes seriously the interplay between the imperatives of political survival and 'sound' economic reasoning in policy-making. In what follows, I propose a framework for examining this interaction and, subsequently, use it to explain variation in the drought relief policies of Botswana, Kenya and Zimbabwe.

Political incumbency and government behaviour: a brief sketch

Over the years, political scientists have come to take for granted that individuals (and the parties they present) who enter formal politics are united in being motivated by the desire to win and to maintain political office. If rational economic man/woman seeks to maximize utility, his/her political twin is motivated by the explicit desire to acquire and maintain political office. However, after winning political office, the strength of this political incumbency may vary. Even across Africa, where dominant perspectives based on neo-patrimonialism tend to suggest equally weak political incumbency (see Zolberg, 1966; Callaghy, 1984; van de Waal, 2001),[14] variation in the probability that those in power today will remain in power tomorrow can be imagined.

Variation in the probability of losing power may be institutionally embedded in the type of political system within which incumbents find themselves operating. For example, incumbents in countries with elections are at risk each time an election is held.[15] The strength of political incumbency might also reflect a given country's history, with violent challenges by the military, subversive activities or ethnic conflict. Less dramatic and violent, but still signalling the possibility of losing power, declining electoral support may embolden challengers, economic crisis may lead to the defection of political allies, or an unhappy population may take to the streets in protest, and so on.[16]

An awareness of the micro-political conditions faced by political leadership is important because of its impact on government decision-making (Ames, 1987; Geddes, 1994). This is because the way that incumbents view their prospects of being in power in the future in turn affects the policies they are willing to propose and adopt today. For example, the increased attention given to the relationship between governance and economic policy-making in recent years has demonstrated that there is a powerful connection between a government's micro-political condition and the sorts of decisions it is likely to make (see van de Walle, 2001).

Also, as noted by Alence (2004), the 'new institutional economics' paradigm places significant weight on the effect of politics in accounting for differences in growth patterns across states. As Alence puts it,

> Governments facing imminent threats to their hold on power often have shorter time horizons and are more preoccupied with placating the specific groups most pivotal to their survival. They are thus likely to give high priority to the short-term interests of narrow constituencies, at the expense of longer-term social welfare. Such tendencies can lead to myopically self-interested political interventions into policy-making and public administration, with economically damaging consequences. (p. 166)

Accepting the argument that, in unstable political environments, 'rational politicians in office [are forced] to concentrate on activities that lead to quick results and immediate rewards' (Geddes, 1994: 13), the political incumbency framework offered here suggests that vulnerability also affects how governments are likely to respond to threats of famine. Specifically, when incumbents are vulnerable to the loss of position and power, the short time horizons produced by this insecurity leads them to favour free food aid – a policy measure associated with immediate political benefits (see Table 14.1). However, when incumbents are reasonably secure, their longer time horizons create a policy environment in which workfare-based relief and its economic justifications are politically palatable.

Explaining variation in relief policy: political incumbency in practice

In practice, previous research offers two possible explanations of the form taken by drought relief across SSA. Drawing on arguments suggesting a democratic advantage in the choice of socially optimal policy, the first explanation suggests that democracies are more likely than non-democracies to adopt workfare-based relief (Sen, 1981,1999; Holm and Morgan, 1985; Hay, 1988; Dreze, 1990; Thompson, 1993).[17]

My own research suggests that there are number of problems with arguments linking the choice of relief with regime type (see Munemo, defense pending). One of the limitations of arguments along these lines is that they are based on the comparison of Botswana's 1982–90 response with Zimbabwe's 1982–4 relief programme. However, when all responses in these two countries are taken into consideration, along with drought relief responses in other SSA countries, it is quickly apparent that democracy is neither necessary (democratic Botswana has not always adopted workfare relief) nor sufficient (Cape Verde 1976–86 and Zimbabwe 1986–99, among other non-democracies, adopted workfare relief) for the adoption of workfare-based relief. Thus, regime type fails to explain the trajectory of drought relief, not only in Botswana (the *crucial* case), but also in all the other countries.

Similarly sceptical about the explanatory power of regime type, de Waal (1997) argues that differences in drought relief between Botswana and Zimbabwe reflect differences in the domestic availability of food stocks in the two countries. Specifically, de Waal contends that countries that are normally surplus producers of food (such as Zimbabwe) opt to remove the variability in food supply through aid, while countries that are typically net importers of food (such as Botswana) prefer to maintain rural incomes through workfare relief that pays in cash.

As with regime-type arguments, my dissertation reveals that there is no relationship between food stocks held by the government and the form of relief it is likely to adopt.[18] As highlighted in Table 14.2, the holding of large stocks of food (Zimbabwe in 1986–99) did not result in the adoption of universal food aid. Similarly, a number of governments with no food stocks (Botswana 1979–80 and Zimbabwe 2002–4) adopted universal food aid.

What, then, accounts for the variation in the form taken by relief? Why did democratic Botswana in 1979–80 adopt universal food aid instead of workfare relief as suggested by both the regime theory of policy adoption and de Waal's agricultural sector argument? Similarly, why did non-democratic and surplus-food-producing Zimbabwe switch its relief to workfare relief between 1986 and 1999?

The theoretical discussion above suggested that there is good reason to expect that the choice of relief is associated with the vulnerability of political incumbents. Specifically, I argue that political vulnerability produces short time horizons, which lead incumbents to favour policy responses associated with immediate benefits. I contend that universal food aid provides immediate benefits to incumbents in that it provides highly visible transfers, through local elites, to a large group of people. By doing so, universal food aid enables incumbents to benefit by strengthening old coalitions or fashioning new ones. Thus, for insecure incumbents, 'crises of provisioning create opportunities to build national political regimes' (Bates 1989, 138). Conversely, I hypothesize that political security supports longer time horizons, with future benefits not heavily discounted. Under these conditions, I argue that workfare relief was more likely because technocratic arguments predicated on the sustainability and cost-effectiveness of targeted aid are politically palatable.

Table 14.2   First-order matching of dependent and independent variables

Country cases	Workfare-based relief[a]	Universal food aid	Regime type Freedom House country status in the year relief adopted[b]	Structure of the agricultural sector Size of food stocks (+) or deficits (−) in the year relief adopted (kg per capita)[c]
Botswana 1982–90	✔	–	5 (Free)	−132.78
Botswana 1992–94	✔	–	3 (Free)	−135.06
Botswana 1996–98	✔	–	4 (Free)	−121.90
Botswana 2002–5	✔	–	4 (Free)	−136.34
Zambia 1992/3	✔	–	5 (Free)	−7.91
Cape Verde 1976–86	✔	–	12 (Not Free)	−132.10
Zimbabwe 1987/8	✔	–	11 (Partly Free)	201.91
Zimbabwe 1992/3	✔	–	9 (Partly Free)	100.68
Zimbabwe 1997–99	✔	–	10 (Partly Free)	102.95
Botswana 1979/80	–	✔	5 (Free)	−140.38
Kenya 1984/5	–	✔	11 (Not Free)	28.13
Tanzania 1975/6	–	✔	12 (Not Free)	−61.30
Zimbabwe 1982–84	–	✔	9 (Partly Free)	129.69
Zimbabwe 2002–4	–	✔	12 (Not Free)	−85.47

Notes:

[a] Includes public works for food or cash and grain loan programme.

[b] Status based on combining a country's Political Rights and Civil Liberties Score for that year. Countries with a combined score of 2–5 = Free; 6–11 = Partly Free and 12–14 Not Free.

[c] According to WFP and UNICEF, the average yearly requirement to sustain life is about 150–200kg per capita.

Source: WDI Online Available at: http://devdata.worldbank.org.arugula.cc.columbia.edu:2048/dataonline.

Commonalities across food aid governments

To test the relationship between the vulnerability of political incumbents and the form taken by relief, I examined the micro-political environment in cases where universal food aid was used, and those in which workfare based relief was used. As hypothesized, all governments that adopted universal food aid (that is, Botswana 1979–80, Kenya 1984–5, and Zimbabwe 1982–4 and 2002–4) had commonalities in the political milieu faced by incumbents.

Although most accounts of politics in Botswana tend to paint a picture of well-established rules of the political game and an otherwise uncontested Botswana Democratic Party hegemony (du Toit, 1995, 1999), my analysis for the period 1976–9 revealed a fairly uncertain political incumbency for Khama and his Botswana Democratic Party (BDP) (see Munemo, 2007, ch. 5). For example, in April 1977 the government accused the Botswana National

Front (BNF) of training its youth in 'coup tactics' (*Botswana Daily News*, 1 April 1977). The following year, President Khama withdrew the passports of seventeen BNF members headed for a conference in Havana, Cuba, on the grounds that the members were in fact attempting to leave the country to undergo military training (*Botswana Daily News*, 21 June 1978).

In addition to the perceived threat from the BNF, the period was also characterized by significant popular protest. For example, my primary research revealed that, between 1975 and 1978, there were over fifty-six individual strikes and protests directed at the government, compared with only fourteen between 1980 and 1982.[19] Protest directed at the government came from communities affected by the expansion of the mining sector and, significantly, from university students. The rise in protest across Botswana forced President Khama to warn 'political agitators' that he would take action if necessary (*Botswana Daily News*, 26 August 1976).

As in Botswana, my analysis of the political environment in which universal relief was adopted in Kenya revealed that three factors made Moi politically vulnerable (see Munemo, 2007, ch. 4). First, Moi was a 'second' generation leader who lacked the nationalist appeal of a Kenyatta (de Waal, 1997) and more significantly, as a Kalenjin, Moi was not a member of the Gikuyu, Embu and Meru Association (GEMA) – the largest 'faction' in Kenyan African National Union (Widner, 1992). Thus, having only ascended to the position of president after Kenyatta's death in August 1978, Moi's position was extremely tenuous and internally contested.[20]

Second, the fragility of Moi's incumbency was demonstrated most vividly by the coup attempt on 1 August 1982. Although the junior Kenya Air Force officers staging the coup were eventually defeated by loyalist members of the Kenyan Army, the significant public support of the coup by university students (*ViVa*, 1982; Currie and Ray, 1984), the urban poor and large segments of the Lou (Currie and Ray1984; Widner, 1992) revealed that Moi faced a much wider crisis that belied his characterization of the situation as the result of a 'few hooligans and misguided youth' (President Moi, *Standard* (Nairobi), 6 August 1982). As is well summarized by Waruhiu (1994: 81), 'the attempted coup served to point out the shortcomings in the personal status of the new President'.

Finally, the deeper crisis of support that Moi faced in Kenya was evident in the election of 1983. What is significant about these elections is that the majority of registered voters chose not to participate. Turnout in the 1983 elections was only 45.9 per cent. This figure represented a fall in turnout of 21.5 per cent compared with the 1979 elections, which saw 67.3 per cent of registered voters participating (Hornsby and Throup, 1992). While it is likely that the precipitous fall in voter turnout in the 1983 elections was caused by the adoption of *de jure* single-party rule in Kenya, I conjecture that the decision to stay away also signalled popular dissatisfaction with Moi.

When incumbents in Zimbabwe adopted universal food aid (1982–4 and 2002–4), they too faced a political milieu in which they were vulnerable to the loss of power. When Zimbabweans lowered the Union flag on 18 April 1980 and raised their own flag in its place, the sense of achievement that moment marked concealed an uneasy unity government between Robert Mugabe's Zimbabwe African National Union-Patriotic Front (ZANU-PF) and Joshua Nkomo's Patriotic Front-Zimbabwe African People's Union (PF-ZAPU). That the relationship between these two camps was wrought with suspicion was, to an extent, to be expected, given the history between the two parties (see Sithole, 1999) and their conduct during the historic elections of March 1980 (see Sithole 1999; Kriger, 2005).

The acrimonious nature of the independence election meant, in my view, that despite a public face of unity, deep resentment and suspicion still remained between the major players in Zimbabwe. As it was, the discovery of caches of arms around the country, the numerous clashes between former members of ZANLA and ZIPRA in army camps, the beginning of the 'dissident' problem, and the accidental admission by retired Lieutenant-General Walls (former Commander of the Joint High Command) that the Rhodesian forces had considered staging a coup to reverse the outcome of elections all heightened Mugabe's sense of vulnerability.

In addition to the coup fears, dissident and alliance problems that Mugabe's new government faced, the period between 1980 and 1982 also saw widespread protest and strike action. To summarize some of the findings during this period, in examining primary materials I counted forty-nine separate protest or strike actions in 1980, and thirty-one the following year. While the high incidence of protest and strikes could be attributable to the political space produced by independence, this urban 'militancy' was invariably troublesome for political incumbents, who now had to secure their position in both rural and urban areas.

As with other long-standing authoritarian incumbents in SSA in the post-1989 period, the growth of a strong pro-democracy movement (the Movement for Democratic Change-MDC) threatened to unseat the ZANU government at the turn of the twenty-first century (see LeBas, 2005). The strength of the MDC and the vulnerability of incumbents in Zimbabwe were evident in two key votes: the referendum in February 2000 and the parliamentary elections in July 2000. On 26 April, 1999 the ZANU government finally gave in to pressure from civil society and 'appointed a 400-member Constitutional Commission charged with setting in motion a process that would produce a draft constitution to be submitted to a national referendum' (Sithole, 2001). Incumbents received a rude awakening when the MDCs no-vote on the new constitution position carried the day as 54 per cent of the electorate voted against ZANU and only 44 per cent supported ZANU's position. In discussing the implications of the referendum result, Sithole (2001) quite correctly stresses that 'the defeat of the February referendum on the draft constitution marked a turning point in Zimbabwean electoral politics'. It marked ZANU's first-ever electoral defeat in its twenty years in power.

With parliamentary elections due later in the year, the government's defeat in the referendum signalled a real possibility of losing power. I argue that the government's first response to this political vulnerability was to turn to the highly emotive land issue in the hope of immediately strengthening its rural electoral base in the lead-up to the elections. By using land reform and repression, the ZANU government managed to retain its parliamentary majority, but the days of holding 99 per cent of the seats were over. Of the 120 seats that were openly contested in the 2000 elections, ZANU retained 63 and the MDC won 57.

Workfare-adopting governments

As expected from my theoretical sketch of the relationship between political incumbency and government behaviour, when governments in Botswana (1982 onwards) and Zimbabwe (between 1986 and 1999) chose workfare relief there was a noticeable change in the political milieu faced by political incumbents. In both Botswana and Zimbabwe under these conditions of political security, technocratic arguments on the virtues of targeting aid through workfare relief won out in the policy debate.

Although space does do not permit a fuller account of these changes, my examination of the micro-political conditions faced in these two countries when they adopted workfare-based relief revealed that incumbents faced no threats from subversive groups, political protest was minimal and incumbents boasted about super-majorities in parliament. For example, in Zimbabwe between 1986 and 1999, the switch to workfare relief coincided with the end of the ZAPU challenge to ZANU hegemony. In December 1987, ZANU-PF and PF-ZAPU signed a Unity Accord, which effectively ended open hostilities between the two nationalist parties. The merger gave the new party, ZANU, 99 of the 100 seats in the lower House. A General amnesty was declared for all involved in the violence in Matabeleland and the Midlands provinces of the country. A number of senior ZAPU members were given prominent Cabinet posts, including Joshua Nkomo, who became Zimbabwe's second vice-president.

During this same period, the opposition that emerged was quite ineffectual. The weakening of opposition in the country was reflected in the fact that ZANU stood unopposed in 55 of the 120 constituencies in the 1995 elections. The 1995 poll prompted Sylvester (1995: 403), to tease that 'on 8 and 9 April 1995, Zimbabweans turned out for an election that mostly was not'. It is easy to see why Sylvester found humour in the 1995 elections, the fifty-five unopposed seats plus the thirty seats Mugabe could appoint, gave ZANU a majority in parliament even before the polls opened on 8 April 1995. As discussed earlier, the referendum defeat in early 2000 ended fifteen years of political security for ZANU incumbents, and resulted in the government reverting to food-aid-based drought relief.

Conclusion

The basic argument suggested here is that, to explain how governments respond to droughts in Africa, we need to take seriously the micro-political conditions faced by incumbents. This chapter shows that variation in relief policy is not determined by macro-variables such as regime type, nor is it accounted for by mid-range variables such as a country's level of bureaucratic capacity or the structure of the agricultural sector. Rather, the chapter contends that it is micro-political conditions – specifically, incumbent vulnerability to loss of power and position – that explain the form taken by drought relief programmes.

Thus, broadly, the main contribution of this chapter is to extend the famine studies literature beyond the concern with the factors leading to famine in some countries and not others, the working of rural markets during famine, the effects of famine on different groups, and on peasant hunger and coping strategies, by addressing the determinants of social protection. Specific to the argument suggested here, the chapter goes beyond the all-too-blunt macro-level arguments commonly used in trying to explain government responsiveness. In place of such macro-level explanations I offer a micro-level argument that takes seriously the political conditions on the ground to explain the form of anti-famine protection in Africa.

Notes

1. This chapter draws heavily on my dissertation, 'Politics During Dry Times: Incumbent Insecurity and the Provision of Drought Relief in Contemporary Africa'. Field research for the dissertation was conducted under a fellowship from the IDRF Program of the Social Science Research Council, New York, with funds provided by the Andrew W. Mellon Foundation. Preliminary research was conducted under a research grant from the Institute of African Studies, Columbia University.
2. See Chapter 2 of my dissertation for a comprehensive account of drought in Botswana.
3. Although the majority of the country was declared drought-free in 1988, the agricultural recovery component of the relief lasted until 1990.
4. Chapter 4 of my dissertation deals specifically with the form taken by drought in Kenya.
5. Available date indicates that close to 114,000 Mt of food was distributed by the Office of the President between October 1984 and November 1985. In August 1984, nearly 1.4 million (7 per cent of the population) were estimated to be recipients of free food rations. This figure rose to 1.575 million during the following month.
6. I offer a more complete account of drought relief in Zimbabwe in Chapter 3 of my dissertation.
7. In 1982–3, about 850,000 people received a ration of 10.34kg each month, and in 1983–4, 1,462,226 people received a ration of 9.9kg each month.

8. Under the new system, local elected officials assisted DSW staff in identifying households who qualified for FFD. As is well documented by Munro (2001: 175), in making decisions about FFD, DSW staff and local officials were instructed to limit themselves to adults 'over 65 years of age and destitute, or chronically ill or mentally or physically disabled to the extent that they [could not] support themselves, and [had] no family members ... capable of supporting them'.

9. Projects for FFW were drawn from existing projects under Provincial and District Development Plans, with some invention of projects on the spot in some places.

10. On this point see de Waal (1989, 1990, 1997) for a discussion of the relationship between infectious diseases and mortality during a famine.

11. Effectiveness here is understood to mean both sufficient coverage to prevent famine (which free food aid does) and cost-effectiveness and sustainability (which free food aid does not).

12. According to Sen, 'The employment route also happens to encourage the processes of trade and commerce, and does not disrupt economic, social and family lives. The people helped can mostly stay in their own homes, close to their economic activities (like farming), so that these economic operations are not disrupted. The family life too can continue in a normal way, rather than people being herded into emergency camps' (Sen, 1999: 177–178).

13. See Chapters 5 of my dissertation for a less cursory discussion of the short-run/long-run comparison noted above.

14. A more complete list of references to this literature is provided in Chapter 5 of my dissertation.

15. Generally, of course, elections may pose more of a real threat to incumbents in a democracy than incumbents in non-democracies, who may resort to a host of tactics (ballot-stuffing, voter intimidation, harassment of the opposition and so on) to insulate themselves from the insecurity of the polls.

16. Of course, not all of these factors will necessarily result in the fall of incumbents. In the face of challenges, some incumbents hold on to power for extended periods of time, while others last only a few days in office (see Bienen and van de Walle, 1989).

17. See Chapter 2 of my dissertation for a discussion of this literature. The chapter also tests explicitly whether a regime theory of policy choice accounts for the form taken by relief in Botswana and other countries in SSA.

18. In Chapter 3 of my dissertation I test systematically whether the structure of the agricultural sector affects the form taken by relief. As noted above, when all drought relief interventions in Botswana and Zimbabwe are considered, no observable relationship emerges between the size of stocks a government has and its choice of drought relief. In my fuller analysis, it appears the relationship de Waal (1997) points to is an artefact of his limited comparison (Zimbabwe 1982–4 with Botswana 1982–90).

19. Protest counts are based on events that were reported in the local newspapers in Botswana. This, of course, raises the potential problem of missing events that were not covered by the press in Botswana. This potentiality notwithstanding, relying on the reported protests does allow us to focus on those that were political salient.

20. See Karimi and Ochieng (1980), Currie and Ray (1984), Widner (1992) and Waruhiu (1994), among others, on the Change-the-Constitution-Movement and other challenges to Moi in Kenya prior to 1984.

References

Alence, R. (2004) 'Political Institutions and Developmental Governance in Sub-Saharan Africa', *The Journal of Modern African Studies*, 42(2), 163–187.

Ames, B. (1987) *Political Survival: Politicians and Public Policy in Latin America*. Berkeley: University of California Press.

Amis, P. (1990) 'Financial Efficiencies in Drought Relief', *Report on the Evaluation of the Drought Relief and Recovery Programme, 1982–1990*, Vol. 4. Gaborone: Ministry of Finance and Development Planning.

Bates, Robert H. (1989) *Beyond the Miracle of the Market: The Political Economy of Agrarian Development in Kenya*. Cambridge: Cambridge University Press.

Benson, C. & E. Clay (1998) *The Impact of Drought on Sub-Saharan African Economies: A Preliminary Examination*. World Bank Technical Paper No. 401. Washington, DC: World Bank.

Bienen, H. & N. van de Walle (1989) 'Time and Power', *American Political Science Review*, 83(1), 19–34.

Boers, W. (1990) *Botswana Drought Relief Labor Based Relief Programme: Technical Report*. Gaborone: SNV Botswana.

Borton, J. (1989) 'Overview of the 1984/85 National Drought Relief Programme', in T. E. Downing et al. (eds), *Coping with Drought in Kenya: National and Local Strategies*. Boulder, CO: Lynne Rienner, pp. 24–64.

Botswana *Daily News*, Various Issues, 1975–92.

Botswana, Government of (1979) *A Human Drought Relief Programme for Botswana*. Gaborone: Ministry of Local Government and Lands.

Botswana, Government of (1982) *Manual on Human Relief Programme for the Use by District Drought Relief Committees and all Extension Officers as a Reference Document*. Gaborone: Ministry of Local Government and Lands, Food Resources Department.

Botswana, Government of (1991) *National Development Plan 7, 1991/97*. Gaborone: Ministry of Finance and Development Planning.

Bratton, M. (1987a) 'Drought, Food and the Social Organization of Small Farmers in Zimbabwe', in M. Glantz (ed.), *Drought and Hunger in Africa: Denying Famine a Future*. Cambridge: Cambridge University Press, pp. 213–244.

Bratton, M. (1987b) 'The Comrades and the Countryside: The Politics of Agricultural Policy in Zimbabwe', *World Politics*, 39(2), 174–202.

Callaghy, T. (1984) *The State-Society Struggle: Zaire in Comparative Perspective*. New York: Columbia University Press.

Cohen, J & D. Lewis (1987) 'Role of Government in Combating Food Shortages: Lessons from Kenya 1984–85', in M. H. Glantz (ed.), *Drought and Hunger in Africa: Denying Famine a Future*. Cambridge: Cambridge University Press, pp. 269–298.

Currie, K. & L. Ray (1984) 'State and Class in Kenya – Notes on the Cohesion of the Ruling Class', *Journal of Modern African Studies*, 22(4), 559–593.

Downing et al. (eds) (1989) *Coping with Drought in Kenya: National and Local Strategies*. Boulder, CO: Lynne Rienner.

Dreze, J. (1990) 'Famine Prevention in Africa: Some Experiences and Lessons', in J. Dreze & A. Sen (eds), *The Political Economy of Hunger: Volume 2, Hunger Prevention*. Oxford: Clarendon Press, pp. 123–172.

Dreze, J. & A. Sen (1989) *Hunger and Public Action*. Oxford: Clarendon Press.

Geddes, B. (1994) *Politician's Dilemma: Building State Capacity in Latin America*. Berkeley: University of California Press.

Hay, R. (1988) 'Famine Incomes and Employment: Has Botswana Anything to Teach Africa?', *World Development*, 16(9), 1113–1125.

Holm, J. & R. Morgan (1985) 'Coping with Drought in Botswana: An African Success', *The Journal of Modern African Studies*, 23(3) (September), 463–482.

Hornsby, C. & D. Throup (1992) 'Elections and Political Change in Kenya', *Journal of Commonwealth & Comparative Politics*, 30(2), 172–199.

Karimi, J. & P. Ochieng (1980) *The Kenyatta Succession*. Nairobi: Transafrica Book Distributors.

Kriger, N. (2005) 'ZANU (PF) Strategies in General Elections, 1980–2000: Discourse and Coercion', *African Affairs*, 104(414), 1–34.

LeBas, A. (2005) *From Protest to Parties: Explaining Effective Opposition in Democratizing Africa*. Graduate School of Arts and Sciences, Columbia University (unpublished Ph.D. Dissertation, Columbia University).

Leys, R. (1986) 'Drought and Drought Relief in Southern Zimbabwe', in P. Lawrence (ed.), *World Recession and the Food Crisis in Africa*. London: James Currey, pp. 258–274.

Munemo, N. (2007) *Politics During Dry Times: Incumbent Insecurity and the Provision of Drought Relief in Contemporary Africa*. Graduate School of Arts and Sciences, Columbia University (Ph.D. Dissertation, Columbia University). Defense Pending.

Munro, L. T. (2001) *Poverty and Social Safety Nets in Zimbabwe 1990–99*. Institute of Development Policy and Management, University of Manchester (unpublished Doctor of Philosophy Thesis).

Sanders, D. & R. Davies (1988) 'The economy, the health sector and child health in Zimbabwe since Independence', *The Journal of Social Science and Medicine*, 27(7), 723–731.

Sen, A. (1981) *Poverty and Famines: An Essay on Entitlement and Deprivation*. Oxford: Oxford University Press.

—— (1999) *Development as Freedom*. New York: Anchor Books.

Sithole, M. (1999) *Zimbabwe: Struggle Within the Struggle (1957–1980)*. 2nd edition. Harare: Rujeko Publishers.

—— (2001) 'Fighting authoritarianism in Zimbabwe', *Journal of Democracy*, 12(1), 160–169.

Standard (Nairobi), Various Issues, 1980–85.

Subbarao, K. (2003) 'Systemic shocks and social protection: role and effectiveness of public works programs', *World Bank Social Protection Discussion Paper No. 0302*. Washington, DC: World Bank.

Sylvester, C. (1995) 'Whither Opposition in Zimbabwe?', *Journal of Modern African Studies*, 33(3), 403–423.

The *Herald*, Various Issues, 1980–92.

Thompson, C. B. (1993) Drought Management Strategies in Southern Africa: From Relief through Rehabilitation to Vulnerability Reduction. Food Security Unit, Southern African Development Community (SADC).

du Toit, P. (1995) *State Building and Democracy in Southern Africa: Botswana, Zimbabwe, and South Africa*. Washington DC: United States Institute of Peace Studies Press.

—— (1999) 'Bridge or Bridgehead? Comparing the Party Systems of Botswana, Namibia, Zimbabwe, Zambia and Malawi', in Giliomee & Simkins (eds), *The Awkward Embrace: One-Party Domination and Democracy*. Cape Town, South Africa: Tafelberg.

Van de Walle, N. (2001) *African Economies and Politics of Permanent Crisis, 1979–99*. Cambridge, UK; New York: Cambridge University Press.

ViVa. Hours of Chaos and the Aftermath, August 1982.

Von Braun, et al. (1999) *Famine in Africa: Causes, Responses, and Prevention*. Baltimore: The Johns Hopkins University Press.

de Waal, A. (1989) *Famine that Kills: Darfur, Sudan, 1984–1985*. Oxford: Clarendon Press.

—— (1990) 'A Reassessment of Entitlement Theory in the Light of the Recent Famines in Africa', *Development and Change*, 21, 469–490.

—— (1997) *Famine Crimes: Politics and the Disaster Relief Industry in Africa*. Oxford: James Carrey.

Waruhiu, S. N. (1994) *From Autocracy to Democracy in Kenya: Past Systems of Government and Reform for the Future*. Nairobi: Waruhiu and Gathuru Advocates.

Widner, J. (1992) *The Rise of the Party-State: From 'Harambee!' to 'Nyayo!'*. Berkeley: University of California Press.

Zimbabwe, Government of (1986a) *Zimbabwe's Experience in dealing with Drought 1982 to 1984*. Harare: Ministry of Labour, Manpower Planning and Social Welfare.

—— (1986b) *Memorandum on Drought Relief 1986*. Harare: Ministry of Labour, Manpower Planning and Social Welfare.

—— (1993) *The Drought Relief and Recovery Programme, 1992/93*. Harare: Government Publications.

Zolberg, A. (1966) *Creating Political Order: The Party-States of West Africa*. Chicago: Rand McNally.

15
Can Low Income Countries in Sub-Saharan Africa Afford Basic Social Protection? First Results of a Modelling Exercise

Christina Behrendt

Introduction[1]

Close to half of the population in Sub-Saharan Africa still live in extreme poverty on less than US$1 (PPP – purchasing power parity) a day. The 2004 progress monitoring of the achievement of the first Millennium Development Goal (halving poverty by 2015) shows that hardly any progress has been made since 1990 towards attaining this target in this region of the world, while other regions have seen considerable change (UN, 2004a). This outlook is not reassuring.

It is recognized increasingly that social protection is an essential component in addressing poverty in low- and middle-income countries (DfID, 2006; ILO, 2006). National social protection systems providing social security through schemes ranging from basic poverty alleviation to pensions and health-care schemes are one of the most powerful means of alleviating and preventing poverty (ILO, 2001; 2002; 2006). Income transfer schemes for individuals at high risk of poverty (namely, older people, those with disabilities, and children) as well as universal access to basic health care and basic education can help to mitigate the adverse effects of chronic poverty.

It has often been said that social protection was unaffordable to low-income countries, yet this judgement does not hold. Examples from a number of countries show that basic social protection programmes are feasible and have a marked effect on the reduction of poverty. Therefore a strong case can be made for increasing access to health and education as well as providing reliable cash transfers in Africa, in order to reduce poverty and promote social and economic development (Commission for Africa, 2005; Save the Children *et al.*, 2005; DfID, 2006; ILO, 2006).

This chapter summarizes the methodology and main findings of a modelling exercise undertaken at the ILO's Social Protection Sector, which demonstrates that basic social protection benefits are not out of reach of low-income countries in Sub-Saharan Africa, even though some international assistance would be necessary for a transitional period. The model was applied to seven countries in Sub-Saharan Africa: Burkina Faso, Cameroon, Ethiopia, Guinea, Kenya, Senegal and Tanzania, where the required data were available. The next section outlines the approach to modelling adopted. The third section describes the basic social protection package chosen for this purpose. The fourth section presents the main findings, and the final section draws out the main conclusions.

Approach to modelling

In order to estimate the cost of a basic benefit package, a quantitative model was set up. The model takes into account country-specific information on demographic developments as well as macroeconomic developments. The year on which projections were based is 2003. Historical data for the various demographic and macroeconomic variables – that is, population projections, real and nominal gross domestic product (GDP), inflation, exchange rate, government expenditure and government revenue, teacher/medical staff wages and so on were used.

Based on historical trends, various demographic, economic and financial parameters are projected from 2004 till 2034. These are summarized below.[2]

The model is of a simple and robust deterministic 'if–then' type, and treats the key economic variables (that is, economic growth, productivity and inflation) as exogenous. It basically projects expenditure and revenues in the social and public sectors in the form of extended budget scenarios based on exogenous assumptions for key parameters of the model. However, the assumptions are internally consistent (that is, for example, the relationship between population growth, economic growth and productivity) and consistent with observed historical data. The model was built with a view to being flexible, to the extent that it permits sensitivity analysis of some of the main assumptions (that is, GDP growth, productivity, benefit levels and coverage and so on).

The calculations are based on three model scenarios. The first scenario is the base case that reflects methods and indicators used in the Millennium Development Goal indicators and international major reports. Scenario 2 provides a more modest option that is based more closely on country-level data. Scenario 3 is based on a targeted cash transfer that has been tested in a GTZ (Deutsche Gesellschaft für Technische Zusammenarbeit)-sponsored project in Zambia.

Demographic assumptions

For all the countries forming part of this study, country-specific historical data were used as far as they were available. However, for the projections,

Table 15.1   Proportion of population under 15 and over 65 years of age, 2004–34

Country	Age group	2004 (%)	2015 (%)	2034 (%)
Burkina Faso	Under 15	49	48	42
	65 and older	3	2	3
Cameroon	Under 15	42	38	31
	65 and older	4	4	5
Ethiopia	Under 15	45	43	36
	65 and older	3	3	4
Guinea	Under 15	44	42	32
	65 and older	3	3	4
Kenya	Under 15	41	36	30
	65 and older	3	3	5
Senegal	Under 15	43	39	30
	65 and older	2	3	30
Tanzania	Under 15	45	40	31
	65 and older	2	3	3

Source: United Nations (2004c).

the same assumptions were used in all cases. Historical as well as future population estimates are based on United Nations population projections from the *World Population Prospects 2002* (medium variant) (UN, 2004c) (see Table 15.1). Age-specific data were used in order to provide the appropriate demographic basis for the costing of the various basic benefit packages.

The average number of members in the household is based on the most recent Demographic and Health Survey in all countries apart from Tanzania, where more recent census data are used. Average household sizes are kept constant over time.

Economic environment

The model is based on historical data for real and nominal GDP from 1990 to 2003 (World Bank, 2004). Real GDP growth is assumed as working-age population growth plus 1 percentage point for the base case in all countries apart from Ethiopia and Tanzania, where real GDP growth is assumed as working-age population growth plus 2 percentage points.

Historical data on inflation were obtained from the International Monetary Fund's (IMF) International Finance Statistics database, and projections were based on IMF short-term country estimates. Productivity increase is assumed as half of real GDP growth, but the parameter can be modified for eventual sensitivity testing. This automatically means that half of the real economic growth is achieved by increases in the level of employment. Historical exchange rate data of local currency units to US$ and PPPs were obtained from the IMF's International Finance Statistics database. The rates for the projection period are kept constant at their 2003/2004 level throughout the projection period.

Data on government revenue and expenditure were obtained from the IMF Government Finance statistics. Consolidated central government figures were used where general government data were not available. From 2004 onwards, projected levels of government expenditure in percentages of GDP are assumed to increase by half up to a maximum of 30 per cent of GDP by the year 2034 (linear increase). In countries with a government deficit, revenue (excluding grants) is assumed to reach the projected expenditure level by 2014 in order to reach a balanced budget. Thereafter, the budget remains balanced: that is, revenue and expenditure are assumed to be equal. Consolidated government expenditure for education, health, and social security and welfare were also used in order to have a picture of what is currently being spent by the government (IMF, 2002).

It must be noted that expenditure allocated today for a variety of social security, health and expenditure provisions will not and should not be reallocated entirely to financing the basic package of benefits modelled here. Therefore, the fraction of the 2003 expenditure on education, health, and social security and welfare (as provided by the IMF) was included.[3] Because of the lack of statistical evidence, it was assumed that 90 per cent of 2003 expenditure on health care, and 10 per cent of 2003 expenditure on social security and welfare were spent on basic benefits in all seven countries. With respect to 2003 expenditure on education, for Cameroon,[4] Burkina Faso, Guinea and Tanzania, it was assumed that 71 per cent was spent on basic primary education; for Ethiopia this was assumed at 54 per cent; for Kenya, 50 per cent; and for Senegal, 44 per cent. This provides an estimate of the social protection expenditure that is being allocated to finance basic social protection benefits at present.

The model simulates two hypothetical options for the financing of the estimated cost of the future benefit package. The present total government expenditure for these basic social protection functions (health care, education and old age) for 2003 was then used as a benchmark assumption for Option 1. Under this option, expenditure on basic social protection that can be financed by the government for the period 2005–34 is assumed to be equal to the proportion of resources already spent to date on basic social security, health and education in total government expenditure. The residual between the estimated cost of a hypothetical benefit package and the present observed social protection expenditure would then provide a proxy for the theoretical level of external financing.

Under Option 2 it is assumed that in the future one third of government expenditure levels are allocated to the financing of basic health care, education and pensions. Under both options, however, the proportion of total government expenditure allocated to social protection expenditure is capped at the cost of the basic benefit package.

The basic social protection benefit package

The aim of the study conducted by the ILO was to analyse transfers that are not only affordable but that could also have an important effect in reducing poverty. The study focuses on the financial and fiscal feasibility of a basic social protection benefit package consisting of a universal old-age pension provided to individuals over 65 years of age; a universal pension paid to the disabled; universal access to basic education; universal access to basic health care; and a specific child benefit (either to all children or targeted specifically at orphans).

Basic universal old age and disability pensions

According to ILO estimates, only 20 per cent of the world's population benefits from adequate social protection coverage. In Sub-Saharan Africa, coverage for contributory old-age income protection typically is lower than 10 per cent of the labour force. Thus older people are particularly vulnerable to poverty in low- and middle-income countries, where a large proportion of the population is not covered by contributory retirement pensions.

Universal basic pensions could have a strong impact on improving the livelihoods of older people, and could alleviate the most severe forms of poverty at least.[5] Contrary to the widespread view that low-income countries cannot afford universal pension schemes, examples from a number of African, Asian and Latin-American countries show that the provision of universal pensions (sometimes called 'social pensions') are feasible and affordable even in middle- and low-income countries.[6] In Africa, such schemes are found in, for example, Botswana, Lesotho, Mauritius, Namibia and South Africa. HelpAge International, in a recent report, also advocate that the 'social pension should be included as a legitimate part of development spending' (HelpAge International, 2004).

Means-testing would be one way to target the benefit to the most needy, and may thus seem to be an effective way to limit spending. However, existing cross-country evidence has shown that benefit targeting is costly and often does not produce the desired results (Coady *et al.*, 2004). The World Bank also noted, 'screening out the poorest through targeting is a bigger problem than including the non-poor; the poorest may actually lose from too much fine-tuning in targeting' (Subbarao *et al.*, 1997; World Bank, 1997). It is thus assumed that benefits would be universal and would not exclude the non-poor. Benefits would thus also reach those whose living standards are slightly above the poverty line. Spill-over effects to the rich are expected to be very limited if benefit levels are rather modest.

The model calculations are based on a system of universal benefits. As benefit levels are very low, it is assumed that benefits are claimed predominantly by vulnerable groups. The benefits are provided to all people who are 65 years and above, and to working-age disabled persons. It was estimated that approximately 1 per cent of people of working age would be eligible for a disability pension.

The first Millennium Development Goal is based on an extreme poverty threshold of US\$1 a day (PPP). The aim was therefore to take this as a basic starting point for a universal pension. Universal pensions are meant to close the poverty gap for the elderly poor. As the average size of the poverty gap for this group is unknown, it is estimated here as about 50 per cent of the threshold. The base case (Scenario 1) projections therefore take into account a basic universal pension of US\$0.50 (PPP) per day for all the countries involved. This daily value was adjusted for inflation over the projection period in the base case. It should be borne in mind that, when one is assuming a pension based on a specific dollar amount, then exchange rate fluctuation plays a very important role.

In order to see the magnitude of this assumed benefit level, it is important to see its relationship with respect to GDP per capita. This level for 2005 varies from 8 per cent of GDP per capita in Guinea to 28 per cent of GDP per capita in Tanzania. An alternative approach stipulates a basic pension based on each individual country's poverty line or a similar reference as paying more attention to national circumstances (Scenario 2). Based on the relative level of national poverty lines to GDP per capita in the case of Tanzania, Scenario 2 is based on a pension level set at 30 per cent of GDP per capita, with a maximum of 1US\$ (PPP) per day (increased with inflation). This level is equivalent (in 2005) to US\$0.96 (PPP) per day in Burkina Faso, US\$0.59 (PPP) in Ethiopia, US\$0.87 (PPP) in Kenya and US\$0.55 (PPP) in Tanzania.

Basic health care

It is well known that good health, a productive life, economic development and poverty reduction are closely related. Therefore, it is indispensable that the basic social protection package also contains a strong health component. The Commission on Macroeconomics and Health has estimated the per capita costs of scaling-up priority health interventions in low-income countries at US\$34 per year on average in low-income countries by 2007, and US\$38 in 2015.[7] This estimate is based on a detailed costing of the additional expenditure required to extend coverage of 49 priority interventions, focusing largely on communicable diseases, and childhood- and maternity-related interventions (Kumaranayake *et al.*, 2001).

The model provides two options for calculating the cost of universal basic health care. The first uses the estimate of the Commission on Macroeconomics and Health (as above). These figures are indexed in line with inflation. Estimating actual per capita public health-care expenditure based on IMF data, it became apparent that none of the countries forming part of the study were even close to reaching this level at present. Per capita government expenditure on health oscillated in 1999 between US\$1.3 (Ethiopia) and US\$3.4 (Cameroon).

Therefore, an alternative method for estimating the cost of basic health care has been provided in the model. This method proposes a country-specific cost base. Results of this method are provided in Scenario 2. This approximation takes into account the following individual parameters: medical staff ratio to population; wages of medical staff; and overhead non-staff costs. It is assumed that 300 medical staff are available per 100,000 population. This corresponds approximately to the estimates of health personnel in Namibia in 1997 (representing approximately 40 per cent of the level in the United Kingdom at that time).[8]

Basic education

The UNESCO's Education for All (EFA) initiative set out to achieve universal primary education by 2015 (UNESCO, 2003). Within the framework of the EFA Initiative, the cost of achieving universal primary education has been based on estimated recurrent unit costs (costs of one year of primary education per child) plus capital expenditure (Delamonica *et al.*, 2001). As average unit costs vary greatly between countries, country-specific estimates have been used based on current expenditure levels. For the countries included in this modelling exercise, the recurrent unit cost varies from US$26 in Tanzania to US$92 in Senegal.[9] Relative to GDP per capita, the range is from 10 per cent in Tanzania to 37 per cent in Ethiopia. In addition to recurrent expenditure, on average about 15 per cent of expenditure on primary education is allocated to capital expenditure.

The projections of basic education expenditure have been based on the net enrolment ratio (NER), which measures the proportion of children aged 6–11 years who are enrolled in primary education. The latest available data were used for each specific country and it was assumed that the NER would reach a level of 100 per cent by 2015.

An alternative estimate (see Scenario 2) of the cost of achieving universal primary education is based on the average wage of teachers, taking into account that wages make up the largest part of education expenditure. First, the required number of teachers was calculated based on the number of children in the age group 6–11 years of age, the NER and the teacher/pupil ratio.[10] The teacher/pupil ratio was also based on the latest available data from the UNESCO Education Database. It was again assumed that the NER would reach 100 per cent by 2015. Furthermore, the teacher/pupil ratio would also reach 1:40 by 2015. Research has shown that an average teacher/pupil ratio of 1:40/45 is optimal under given economic constraints, and therefore this has been used as the target value for 2015 (Bruns *et al.*, 2003). Furthermore, it was assumed that 10 per cent of the children would be enrolled in private schools by 2015. Where national data on teachers' wages were not available, an estimate based on the ratio of average teacher salary to GDP per capita was used (Mehrotra and Buckland, 1998). The projections of wages of teachers are based on the assumption that these move with inflation plus half of productivity increase (that is, a quarter of GDP growth). Overhead non-staff costs from their actual value were also assumed to reach the target value of 33 per cent of recurrent spending by 2015 (Bruns *et al.*, 2003).

Child benefit

As a further component of the basic benefit package, it was considered that a child benefit (in form of a cash transfer) should also be included in Scenarios 1 and 2, based on the recommendations of The Joint United Nations Programme on HIV/AIDS (UNAIDS), the United Nations Children's Fund (UNICEF) and the United States Agency for International Development (USAID) (UNAIDS *et al.*, 2004). The child benefit broadly follows the example of the South African Child Support Grant.[11] The level of child benefit set in the base case is US\$ 0.25 (PPP) per day. This level of child benefit is equivalent to half of the universal old age and disability pension benefit.[12] Further in-depth studies would be needed to ascertain the level of such a benefit in view of the existence of universal access to basic health care and of access to basic education (primary level). The benefit is paid to all children up to the age of 14.

Even though the more recent 2004 publication by UNAIDS, UNICEF and USAID makes the case for providing programmes for a much 'broader vulnerable children population' and not only for orphans, the cost of providing such a universal child benefit may seem relatively high in certain cases such as Tanzania, where this cost in 2005 is estimated at 6.3 per cent of GDP. Therefore, a more modest option has been chosen in Scenario 2. The level of the projected child benefit in Scenario 2 would be 15 per cent of GDP per capita; that is, half of the basic old age and disability pension in Scenario 2, and be paid to all orphans.[13]

Targeted cash transfers

The model further considers targeted cash transfers following the model of a programme that has been tested in a GTZ-funded project in the Kalomo district in Zambia (Schubert, 2005; Government of Zambia and GTZ, 2006). This programme provides cash benefits of US\$13.71 (PPP) per month to the 10 per cent most destitute households in the district. These households are identified in a community-based targeting mechanism that focuses on those who are unable to support themselves because of a lack of an able-bodied person in the household. Although benefit levels are rather modest (the monthly benefit is equivalent to the cost of a bag of maize), the first results are rather encouraging. Not only the living standards of recipients have improved considerably, but households have also started to save and invest part of the money. Further evaluations of the project will show the effects of the cash transfer on the livelihoods of recipient households in both the short and the medium term. Targeted cash transfers replace universal basic old age and invalidity pensions and child benefits in Scenario 3.

Administrative costs

The model is based on the assumption that 15 per cent of total universal cash benefit expenditure (pensions and child benefit) is spent on administration under Scenarios 1 and 2.[14] This estimate is based on the experience of the basic pension scheme in Namibia, where the cost of reaching the poorer remote rural communities is taken into account (Schleberger, 2002). Because of the higher administrative requirements of a targeted system, the targeted cash transfer under Scenario 3 is based on the assumption that administration costs amount to 33 per cent of benefit expenditure.

The administrative costs for basic health care and basic education are provided for in their overhead costs.

Main findings

For the study, a wide basic social protection package was chosen, consisting of a universal old-age and invalidity pension, universal access to basic education, universal access to basic health care, and a child benefit. Three scenarios for a basic social protection benefit package were analysed, summarized in Table 15.2 below. The base case scenario reflects methods used in the Millennium Development Goal indicators and other major international reports. Scenario 2 reflects levels of benefits and costs in line with specific national circumstances. The basic social protection benefit package modelled in Scenario 3 is identical to Scenario 1 as far as health and education expenditure are concerned, but the cash transfers (old age and disability pensions and child benefits) are replaced by a targeted cash transfer.

Table 15.2   Summary description of Scenarios 1 to 3

Scenario I: Base case	Scenario 2: Country specific	Scenario 3: Targeted transfer
Real GDP growth is assumed as working age population growth plus 1 percentage point. For Ethiopia and Tanzania, it is assumed as working age population growth plus 2 percentage points	Same as base	Same as base
Projected levels of total government expenditure increase by 50 per cent of their current level by the year 2034, with a maximum of 30 per cent of GDP	Same as base	Same as base

Continued

Table 15.2 Continued

Scenario I: Base case	Scenario 2: Country specific	Scenario 3: Targeted transfer
Government revenue (excluding grants) is assumed to reach the projected expenditure level by 2014 in order to reach a balanced budget	Same as base	Same as base
Per capita health care cost equal to the Commission on Macroeconomics and Health estimate of US$34 by 2007 and US$38 by 2015 (indexed with inflation)	Basic health care costs based on ratio of 300 medical staff to 100,000 population; medical staff wages indexed in line with half of productivity and inflation; non-staff overhead costs of 67 per cent of staff costs	Same as base
Per-unit basic education cost based on UNESCO estimate; net enrolment ratio in primary education reaching 100 per cent by 2015; 10 per cent of children in primary in private schools by 2015; 15 per cent capital cost	Basic education costs based on NER in primary education reaching 100 per cent by 2015; 10 per cent of children in primary in private schools by 2015; teacher/pupil ratio would reach 1:40, also by 2015; teacher wages indexed in line with half of productivity and inflation; other overhead recurrent costs reaching 33 per cent of recurrent spending by 2015; capital costs at 15 per cent of recurrent costs;	Same as base
Universal pension benefit at US$0.50 (PPP) per day for all 65 years of age and above and the disabled (i.e. 1 per cent of working-age population)	Universal pension benefit at 30 per cent of GDP per capita (capped at US$1 (PPP) a day; indexed with inflation) for all 65 years of age and above and the disabled (i.e. 1 per cent of working-age population)	Targeted cash transfer to the 10 per cent most destitute households of US$13.71 (PPP) per month in 2004 (indexed with inflation)
Child benefit at 50 per cent of the universal basic pension per child for all children in the age bracket 0–14	Child benefit at 15 per cent of GDP per capita (capped at US$1 (PPP) a day indexed with inflation) provided to all orphans in the age bracket 0–14;	.
Administration costs of delivering cash benefits equal to 15 per cent of cash benefit expenditure	Same as base	Administration costs of delivering the targeted cash transfer equal to 33 per cent of cash benefit expenditure

Source: Author.

Figures 15.1, 15.2 and 15.3 show a comparison of the total cost of such a basic benefit package for the countries forming part of the study under each of the three scenarios.

In all three cases, the costs of a basic social protection benefit package seem within reasonable and affordable limits if countries and donors make a strong commitment to basic social protection as an essential tool of poverty reduction. Ethiopia is the only country in the study with levels above 20 per cent of GDP in Scenario 1 (base case) (see Figure 15.1). In this special case, the availability of donor financing would be essential if internationally-set benefit levels are to be met.

The costs of providing a universal old-age and invalidity pension vary between 0.3 per cent of GDP (in Guinea) and 0.6 per cent of GDP (in Kenya).[15] The single most important component in terms of costs in all these countries is the cost of providing basic health care, which represents between 48 per cent and 60 per cent of the total costs of the basic benefit package (in 2015). In Ethiopia, it represents over 70 per cent of the total cost of the basic benefit package. The cost (at its peak in 2010) of providing health care ranges from 4 per cent of GDP in Cameroon to 11 per cent of GDP in Tanzania (with the exception of Ethiopia, where it represents approximately 31 per cent of GDP). Universal access to basic education, another priority policy area for action in terms of cost levels, also seems affordable. For 2015 (target for achieving the second Millennium Development Goal), costs range from 1.7 per cent of GDP in Tanzania to 6.2 per cent of GDP in Ethiopia. The cost of a child benefit paid to all children up to the age of 14 ranges (at 2005 prices) from 1.8 per cent of GDP in Guinea to 6.3 per cent of GDP in Tanzania.

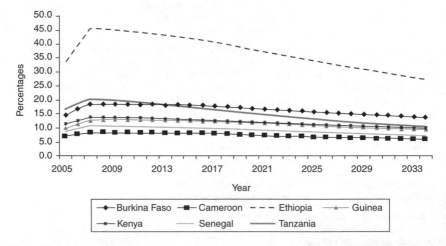

Figure 15.1   Cost of basic social protection package in percentage of GDP (Base case) for selected Sub-Saharan countries, 2005–34

Source: ILO calculations.

However, the level of an adequate child benefit would need to be studied in more depth in order to reflect the education and health care benefits that are being provided.

The share of government expenditure allocated to basic social protection will determine the level of external financing required. If countries were able to maintain the current proportion of government expenditure allocated to financing basic social protection benefits constant over the projection period, the level of international financing required would vary for 2005 from 91 per cent (Ethiopia) to 61 per cent (Kenya). However, if countries were to reallocate 33 per cent of government expenditure to the financing of a basic social protection benefits package, then in 2005 Ethiopia would need 74 per cent and Kenya 15 per cent of the cost of the benefit package to be financed by external sources. Under such an option, Senegal would be able to finance entirely through domestic sources the full cost of the basic benefit package by 2021 and reduce the proportion of government spending to a level of approximately 25 per cent by 2034.

Scenario 2, once again, also shows that universal old-age and invalidity pensions can be provided and still be affordable, representing less than 1.5 per cent of GDP throughout the projection period for all the seven countries. The overall level of the cost of a basic benefit package are much lower than under the base case scenario as these levels are anchored to much more country-specific details (such as medical and education staff wages and so on). Ethiopia shows this very clearly. Whereas under the base case in 2005 and 2034, the total expenditure on the benefit package in terms of GDP is 34 per cent and 27 per cent, respectively, under Scenario 2 the cost is 8 per cent and 7 per cent, respectively (see Figure 15.2).

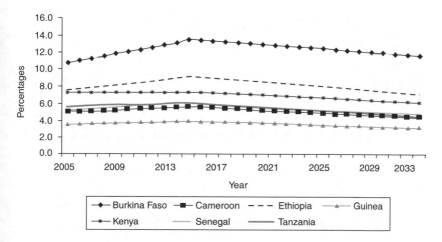

Figure 15.2 Cost of basic social protection package in per cent of GDP (Scenario 2) for selected Sub-Saharan countries, 2005–34

If countries were to maintain the current proportion of government expenditure allocated to financing basic benefits constant over the projection period, the level of international financing required would vary (for 2005 from 73 per cent (Burkina Faso) to 4 per cent (Tanzania). However, if countries were to reallocate 33 per cent of government expenditure to the financing of a basic benefits package, then in 2005 Burkina Faso would need 52 per cent to be financed by external sources and Tanzania could finance the cost of the benefit package entirely with 25 per cent of government expenditure.

Scenario 3 was inspired by a GTZ (Deutsche Gesellschaft für Technische Zusammenarbeit)-sponsored cash transfer programme that has been tested in one district in Zambia. It provides a cash benefit of US$13.71 (PPP) per month to the 10 per cent most destitute households. In the model, this benefit replaces the basic universal old-age and invalidity pensions as well as the child benefits assumed under the base case and Scenario 2. The health and education benefits are the same as assumed in the base case. As Scenario 3 is based on much lower levels of cash transfers, in four of the countries (Burkina Faso, Cameroon, Guinea and Senegal), expenditure on a targeted cash transfer providing the same purchasing power parity as the benefit provided in Zambia would require between 0.15 per cent and 0.30 per cent of GDP. Expenditure would reach about 0.7 per cent of GDP in Ethiopia and Tanzania, and 0.5 per cent of GDP in Kenya.

The projected expenditure on the total basic social protection package is driven mainly by the health care and education expenditure. Expenditure levels reach 5–15 per cent of GDP in all countries except Ethiopia, where expenditure would quickly rise to almost 40 per cent of GDP before slowly decreasing to 24 per cent of GDP by 2034 (see Figure 15.3).

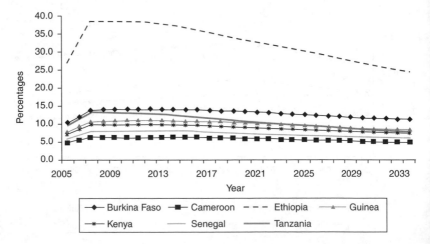

Figure 15.3 Cost of basic social protection package in per cent of GDP (Scenario 3) for selected Sub-Saharan countries, 2005–34

Under the assumption that countries would maintain their current spending levels on basic social protection at their 2003 level, between 8 per cent (Ethiopia) and 47 per cent (Kenya) of total expenditure could be covered from domestic sources in 2010, during the peak expenditure period. If countries were to devote a third of their government budgets on basic social expenditure, between 24 per cent (Ethiopia) and 100 per cent (Kenya and Senegal) could come from domestic resources by 2010. By the end of the projection period, five of the seven countries – Cameroon, Guinea, Kenya, Senegal and Tanzania – would be able to afford the basic social protection package from their own resources.

Two sensitivity tests were also undertaken in order to ascertain the effects of variations of main macroeconomic variables. Sensitivity Test 1, with GDP growth linked to total population growth rather than working-age population growth, shows lower average annual GDP growth rates in all countries with respect to the base case. The relative cost of the basic benefit package in all seven countries is higher than in the base case, as absolute benefit amounts do not change (with the exception of expenditure on education). Sensitivity Test 2, with higher government expenditure with respect to GDP by 2030 for Burkina Faso, Cameroon and Tanzania would increase the share of the basic benefit package that could be financed by domestic sources.

The projections provided in this chapter can be a starting point to further explore the affordability of basic social protection in low-income countries.

Conclusions

A basic social protection package is a powerful instrument to reduce poverty and social insecurity (ILO, 2006). Microsimulations have shown that a combination of a universal old age and disability pension and child benefit would cut poverty rates by some 40 per cent in the cases of Senegal and Tanzania (Gassmann and Behrendt, 2006). While more difficult to quantify, similar effects on the reduction of poverty are expected by providing access to health care and education.

As the model results have shown, a basic level of social protection could be affordable within a reasonable time-frame in the selected countries if a more modest option were to be chosen (Scenario 2 or 3 for the cash transfers component) for even low- and middle-income countries. The results found for African countries can also be applied to other parts of the world, as the application of a similar modelling approach to five Asian countries has shown (Mizunoya *et al.*, 2006). It is also evident that – if one were to introduce such a basic level of social protection immediately – many low-income countries would need assistance in terms of financing from international donors in most of the countries for some transitional period. If the national commitment exists and a third of total government expenditure could be reallocated to meet basic social protection needs, then the necessity for international financing would steadily decline in the medium-term.

This is a commitment that each individual nation needs to make. The share of their budgets devoted to basic social protection benefits would have to be fixed at a higher level than today. In addition, at least for some time to come, the richer nations would be required to support that commitment by direct financial aid. But with increased government commitment and under reasonable economic conditions over the coming decades, such external support would be substantial in only three of the seven countries considered: Burkina Faso, Ethiopia and Guinea. What these calculations also show is that, without such support, some of the countries are not likely to reach the first Millennium Development Goal (MDG) even with increased government commitment. More important is that the increased government commitment to social transfers can go a long way towards achieving the MDGs on their own. Intense national dialogues on public spending priorities in the context of comprehensive social budget-cum-public expenditure reviews in the context of Poverty Reduction Strategy Papers (PRSPs) are needed.

The projections provided in this chapter can be a starting point to further explore the affordability of basic social protection in low-income countries. This chapter does not aim to prescribe any standard basic benefit package for all countries; rather, it seeks to raise awareness of the feasibility of providing basic social protection. As the chapter concludes, this is within the reach of even low-income countries. However, further studies would be needed to assess the affordability and impact of such programmes in more depth in the specific country context, based on national data. This would also include a more detailed discussion of how a basic social protection package could be designed, how it would fit into the broader national social protection strategy – including contributory schemes and other programmes, what effect it would have on poverty reduction, how it could be organized and administered, and how it could be financed.

Notes

1. This contribution is based on a paper written jointly with Karuna Pal, Florian Léger, Michael Cichon and Krzysztof Hagemejer (Pal *et al.*, 2005). Armando Barrientos' generous support is gratefully acknowledged.
2. Full methodological explanations are found in Pal *et al.*, 2005.
3. It is assumed that the cost of non-basic social protection measures would move in line with inflation, GDP or GDP per capita growth and the respective population sub-group growth where appropriate, and that these expenditures would not be financed by external sources.
4. Source: UNDP, 2004. Corresponds to proportion in 1990.
5. See, for example, Charlton and McKinnon, 2001; Barrientos, 2002; Barrientos *et al.*, 2003; Barrientos and Lloyd-Sherlock, 2003.
6. Some of these pension schemes are universal in a strict sense; others operate with some form of means test.
7. See Commission on Macroeconomics and Health (2001), pp. 55, 165–7. Amounts are expressed in 2002 US$. The respective estimate for least developed countries

is US$34 for 2007 and US$41 for 2015. For low- to middle-income countries, the estimate is US$36 and US$40, respectively. The authors note that 'at purchasing power parities...the minimum cost of the essential package would probably be above $80 per person per year' (fn 79, p. 120).

8. World Health Organization Statistical Information System (WHOSIS).
9. Data not available for Cameroon.
10. UNESCO Education Indicators.
11. Targeted at giving additional income support to poor children, the Child Support Grant is a means-tested child benefit for children under the age of nine. The benefit level of 110 Rand per month (2001) is equivalent to 6 per cent of GDP per capita – or US$ 12.78 (US$55 PPP) per month, or US$ 0.42 (US$1.83 PPP) per day). See Hunter *et al.*, 2004, own calculations.
12. The assumed relationship between the child benefit and the old age and disability pension is based on the equivalence scale calculations for Tanzania in Lancaster *et al.*, 1999.
13. The number of orphans is based on estimates from UNAIDS *et al.* (2004).
14. The existing basic old-age pensions in Southern Africa provide interesting blueprints. The experiences in Botswana, Namibia and South Africa show that the main administrative problems are the delivery of benefits to the population, mainly in respect of long distances and security requirements, and, in the case of Namibia, the lack of up-to-date registry information about pensioners' deaths (Fultz and Pieris, 1999).
15. See Pal *et al.*, 2005 for the full results.

References

Barrientos, A. (2002) 'Old Age, Poverty, and Social Investment', *Journal of International Development*, 14, 1133–1141.

Barrientos, A., M. Gorman and A. Heslop (2003) 'Old Age Poverty in Developing Countries: Contributions and Dependence in Later Life', *World Development*, 31(3), 555–570.

Barrientos, A. and P. Lloyd-Sherlock (2003) *Non-contributory Pensions and Social Protection*, Issues in Social Protection Discussion Paper, Geneva: International Labour Office.

Bruns, B., A. Mingat and R. Rakotomalala (eds) (2003) *Achieving Universal Primary Education by 2015 – A Chance for Every Child*. Washington, DC: World Bank.

Charlton, R. and R. McKinnon (2001) *Pensions in Development*. Aldershot: Ashgate.

Coady, D., M. Grosh and J. Hoddinott (2004) *Targeting of Transfers in Developing Countries: Review of Lessons and Experience*. Washington, DC: World Bank.

Commission for Africa (2005) *Our Common Interest: Report of the Commission for Africa*. London: Commission for Africa.

Commission on Macroeconomics and Health (2001) *Macroeconomics and Health: Investing in Health for Economic Development*. Geneva: World Health Organization, <http://www.cid.harvard.edu/cidcmh/CMHReport.pdf>. Accessed April 2006.

Delamonica, E., S. Mehrotra and J. Vandemoortele (2001) *Is EFA Affordable? Estimating the Global Minimum Cost of 'Education for All'*, Innocenti Working Paper. Florence: UNICEF Innocenti Research Centre.

DfID (2006) *Eliminating World Poverty: Making Governance Work for the Poor*. DfID White Paper. London: Department for International Development, United Kingdom.

Fultz, E. and B. Pieris (1999) *Social Security Schemes in Southern Africa*, ILO/SAMAT Discussion Paper Series, 7. Harare: International Labour Office – Multidisciplinary Advisory Team for Southern Africa.

Gassmann, F. and C. Behrendt (2006) *Cash Benefits in Low-Income Countries: Simulating the Effects on Poverty Reduction for Senegal and Tanzania*. Issues in Social Protection Discussion Paper 15. Geneva, International Labour Office.

Government of Zambia and GTZ (2006). Evaluation Report – Kalomo Social Cash Transfer Scheme. Lusaka, Zambia – Ministry of Community Development and Social Services (MCDSS) and German Technical Cooperation (GTZ).

HelpAge International (2004) *Age and Security: How Social Pensions Can Deliver Effective Aid to Poor People and Their Families*. London: HelpAge International.

Hunter, N., I. Hyman, D. Krige and M. Olivier (2004) *South African Social Protection and Expenditure Review (Draft)*. Geneva: ILO.

ILO (2001) *Social Security: A New Consensus*. Geneva: International Labour Office.

ILO (2002) *A Global Social Trust Network: Investing in the World's Social Future: Report and Documentation of a Feasibility Study*. Geneva: International Labour Office.

ILO (2006) *Social Security for All: Investing in Global Social and Economic Development: a Consultation*. Issues in Social Protection Discussion Paper. Geneva: ILO.

International Monetary Fund (2002) *Government Finance Statistics Yearbook 2002*. Washington, DC: International Monetary Fund.

Kumaranayake, L., C. Kurowski and L. Conteh (2001) *Costs of Scaling up Priority Health Interventions in Low-income and Selected Middle-income Countries: Methodology and Estimates*, Background paper of Working Group 5 of the Commission on Macroeconomics and Health: Improving Health Outcomes of the Poor, W5–18. Geneva: World Health Organization.

Lancaster, G., R. Ray and M. R. Valenzuela (1999) 'A cross-country study of equivalence scales and expenditure inequality on unit record household budget data', *Review of Income and Wealth*, 45(4), 455–482.

Mehrotra, S. and P. Buckland (1998) *Managing Teacher Costs for Access and Quality*, UNICEF Staff Working Papers: Evaluation, Policy and Planning Series, EPP-EVL98–004, New York: UNICEF.

Pal, K., C. Behrendt, F. Léger, M. Cichon and K. Hagemejer (2005) *Can Low Income Countries Afford Basic Social Protection? First Results of a Modelling Exercise*. Issues in Social Protection Discussion Paper, Geneva: International Labour Office.

Save the Children UK, HelpAge International and Institute for Development Studies (2005) *Making Cash Count: Lessons from Cash Transfer Schemes in East and Southern Africa for Supporting the Most Vulnerable Children and Households*. London: Save the Children UK, HelpAge International, Institute for Development Studies.

Schleberger, E. (2002) *Namibia's Universal Pension Scheme*, Extension of Social Security (ESS) Paper Series, 6. Geneva: International Labour Office.

Schubert, B. (2005) *The Pilot Social Cash Transfer Scheme: Kalomo District – Zambia*, CPRC Working Paper, 52. Manchester: Chronic Poverty Research Centre.

Subbarao, K., *et al.* (eds) (1997) *Safety Net Programs and Poverty Reduction: Lessons from Cross-Country Experience*. Washington, DC: World Bank.

UNAIDS, UNICEF and USAID (2004) *Children on the Brink 2004: A Joint Report of New Orphan Estimates and a Framework for Action*. New York: UNICEF, <http://www.unicef.org/publications/files/cob_layout6–013.pdf>. Accessed April 2006.

UNDP (2004) *Human Development Report Statistics*. New York: UNDP, <http://hdr.undp.org/statistics/data/>, accessed April 2005.

UNESCO (2003) *Education for All: Global Monitoring Report 2003/04*. Paris: UNESCO.

United Nations (2004a) *Implementation of the United Nations Millennium Declaration*, Report of the Secretary-General, A/59/282. New York: United Nations.

United Nations (2004b) *Millennium Indicators Database.* New York: United Nations, <http://millenniumindicators.un.org/unsd/mi/mi_goals.asp>.

United Nations (2004c) *World Population Prospects: The 2002 Revision.* New York: United Nations. Accessed April 2006.

United Nations (2005) *In Larger Freedom: Towards Development, Security and Human Rights for All,* Report of the Secretary-General, A/59/2005. New York: United Nations. Accessed April 2006.

World Bank (1997) 'Designing Effective Safety Net Programs', *Poverty Lines,* 7, 1–2.

World Bank (2004) *World Development Indicators Database.* Washington, DC: World Bank, <http://www.worldbank.org/data/onlinedbs/onlinedbases.htm>. Accessed April 2006.

16
Financing Social Protection

Armando Barrientos

There is a consensus emerging among international organizations and national governments in developing countries that social protection provides an effective policy framework for addressing rising poverty and vulnerability in the global economy. Social protection can be defined as all interventions from public, private, voluntary organizations and informal networks, to support communities, households and individuals in their efforts to prevent, manage and overcome a defined set of risks and vulnerabilities. Social protection is an extension of anti-poverty policy. It is grounded in the view that vulnerability, understood as the limited capacity of some communities and households to protect themselves against contingencies threatening their living standards, is a primary factor explaining poverty. It is also a key factor explaining the low levels of human capital investment observed among households in poverty, which prevent them from taking advantage of economic and social opportunities.

In line with this emerging consensus, many national governments and international organizations are taking steps to establish and strengthen social protection institutions and policies. In the context of middle-income countries, these efforts involve the strengthening of existing institutions and policies, and a renewed focus on poverty and vulnerability. This is very much in evidence among Latin-American countries that have recently introduced income transfer programmes focused on strengthening consumption and human capital investment by the poor and poorest (Morley and Coady 2003; Barrientos and Holmes 2006). In low-income countries, social protection institutions and policies are scarce, and the main emphasis is on establishing these. This applies especially to countries in Sub-Saharan Africa (Commission for Africa 2005).

There has been much discussion and debate on the kinds of institutions and policies that could best address poverty and vulnerability, and considerable activity and innovation on the ground. In these discussions, financing has emerged as a key constraint on the development of social protection. There are different sources of financing for social protection. These include aid from international donors, revenues of national governments, private, community and NGO financing, and household saving and out-of-pocket expenditure. The problem is to put in place an effective and sustainable financing mix for social protection institutions and policies (ILO 2001; Holzmann et al. 2003). This is a complex problem, in that the issues involved are as much to do with economics as with politics, and the background is one of rapid social and economic transformation.[1] An optimal financing mix is essential to (i) generating the resources needed to establish and strengthen appropriate social protection systems; (ii) ensuring the incentives generated by the financing modalities reinforce poverty and vulnerability reduction; and (iii) securing legitimacy for social protection institutions and policies.

The main purpose of this chapter is to consider the nature and constraints of the financing mix for social protection in developing countries, and in particular the low-income countries among them. The chapter is divided into four sections. The next section provides a brief and informal discussion of the main elements of the financing mix, and their linkages. The following two sections focus on two key components of this mix – national governments' and international organizations' funding for social protection. The last section reviews the key issues ahead and concludes.

The financing mix for social protection

As indicated above, the sources of finance for social protection are many and the focus should be on the financing mix. The dynamics of this mix has a direct relationship to economic development. Comparative data on the financing of health care provides us with an insight into the differences in the financing mix across regions, and the dynamics associated with development. Summary information is presented in Table 16.1.[2] The data in the Table show the differences in the financing mix across different regions.

Table 16.1 Regional comparison of health services financing mix, 2002 (percentage of total health expenditure)

	Public			Private		
	Revenue financed	Externally financed	Social insurance	Pre-paid plans	NGO/ Occupational	Out of pocket
OECD	47.2	0	25.3	7.1	2.1	18.3
Latin America and the Caribbean	38.8	3.9	13.8	6	2.8	34.7
South Asia	37.6	10.1	1.4	0	1.5	49.4
Sub-Saharan Africa	40.7	16.4	0.1	2.8	4.6	35.4

Source: Own calculations using country data from The World Health Report (2002). (World Health Organisation 2003), classified according to regional classification from the World Bank website. The residual in public expenditure is general government expenditure. The residual in private expenditure is NGOs and occupational plans financed health expenditure.

The share of health expenditure financed by government revenues is dominant in the OECD region, but less so as we move to less-developed regions. Another key difference is the large share of social insurance financing in developed nations, in particular when compared to lower-income regions. Among less developed regions, out-of-pocket financing is substantial, and external sources of finance are important in SSA and Asia.

The dynamics implicit in the data in the Table apply fully to social protection. In OECD countries, social protection is financed primarily through tax revenues and social insurance contributions. Broadly, the task ahead for low-income developing countries is to reduce the share of out-of-pocket financing and raise the share of government revenue financing and, perhaps in the short run, external financing too. The changes in the financing mix need to take place in the context of an increase in the overall volume of resources available for social protection. In middle-income developing countries, the role of social insurance financing also needs to be considered.[3]

While setting out the task ahead appears to be relatively straightforward, outlining a road map is a difficult undertaking. As noted above, an appropriate financing mix needs to raise the required resources for social protection, but also ensure that, at the same time, the incentives for poverty and vulnerability reduction are strengthened, and the legitimacy of social protection institutions is reinforced. Microeconomic and political economy perspectives on the financing mix for social protection provide essential road signs for developing income countries. Space restrictions mean that only the briefest of outlines is possible here.

How do households respond to contingencies that might threaten their living standards? Gill reviews and updates a simple model of households' demand for insurance developed originally by Ehrlich and Becker (Ehrlich and Becker 1972; Gill and Ilahi 2002), which helps to pinpoint three main strategies. Households could take steps to reduce the likelihood that the contingencies might occur. For example, investment in health checks, nutrition, and schooling will improve their human capital and reduce the likelihood of unemployment or low wages. Alternatively, households could focus on reducing the losses that might result in the event that the contingencies materialize. There are, broadly, two strategies that ameliorate these losses. Households may protect themselves by accumulating assets or entitlements that could compensate them in the event of losses. They could save some of their income to survive periods of unemployment. A third strategy would be to join an insurance scheme covering households threatened by a similar contingency, in which a small premium would ensure a measure of compensation for associated losses, as in unemployment insurance schemes. The three main strategies are: self-protection, saving, and insurance.

The insights provided by the model into the way households respond to contingencies have important implications for the financing mix for social protection. First, households are better off if they are able to use the full range of strategies noted above. Extending the range of available social protection instruments to meet households' demands should facilitate household financing as well as improve their protection. Second, insurance solutions are more effective for large losses/low-frequency contingencies, while savings solutions are more effective for small losses/high-frequency contingencies. This implies that community or trade insurance schemes may have limited scope, and therefore constitute a limited source of financing for social protection. Micro-saving schemes, on the other hand, are a potentially important source of finance in low-income countries. Unfortunately, in many developing countries, micro-finance institutions make savings compulsory and discourage easy access to withdrawals. As a result, many of these schemes provide only limited social protection.

Third, trade-offs between the different strategies also have implications for the financing mix. Savings and insurance are substitutes, with the implication that improving the availability of insurance will reduce precautionary saving. Compulsory insurance may be sub-optimal if it 'crowds out' optimal levels of precautionary saving, and especially so if it packages in a mix of desirable and undesirable insurance. Self-protection, on the other hand, can be complementary to saving and insurance, with the implication that improving the provision of insurance, either public or private, may not necessarily involve a reduction in households' self-protection efforts, a concern commonly expressed by policy-makers.

There is much less clarity on the insights from political economy models for the financing of social protection. Public-choice models suggest that self-interested taxpayers would be more inclined to finance social protection if it benefited them directly (Gelbach and Pritchett 1995), or if the indirect benefits, from a reduction in social unrest or crime, say, are large. However, these models would also be consistent with taxpayers seeking to 'truncate' social protection institutions, as in Latin America, or invest in law and order instead. Public understanding and values, on the causes of poverty and vulnerability, and the effectiveness of potential remedies, are also important in generating support for financing social protection institutions and programmes. In the context of external financing for social protection, the latter are significant in persuading taxpayers in different jurisdictions to finance social protection in developing countries. Factors of political economy are important in explaining public financing of social protection. This goes some way to explaining regional and sub-regional differences in the evolution of social protection institutions. In Southern Africa, cash transfers are the main policy instrument, whereas other Sub-Saharan countries favour in-kind transfers (see Chapters 13 and 14 by Hickey and Munemo, respectively, in this volume).

A less precise but perhaps more informative framework for assessing political support for social protection considers a country's 'social contract'. As Graham suggests, the extension of social protection 'ultimately requires the development of a politically sustainable social contract' (Graham 2002).

Countries that have expanded publicly financed social protection since the 1980s, such as Brazil, have achieved this on the basis of a renewal of the social contract (Barrientos and Lloyd-Sherlock 2003).

To sum up, an understanding of the factors determining the dynamics of the social protection financing mix, including microeconomic and political economy perspectives, is essential to set current trends in an appropriate context. The next two sections focus on two key components of social protection financing: national governments' and international organizations' financing.

Government financing of social protection

National governments can support social protection through macroeconomic policy, public expenditure, tax policy, and regulation. Macroeconomic policies that ensure sustainable growth and fiscal stability are important in reducing vulnerability, and in securing the resources needed for social protection. Public expenditure on basic and social services are in the main directed towards social protection.[4] Tax policy helps to ensure that resources for social protection are adequate and can encourage household social protection expenditure through 'tax expenditures' – that is, tax exemptions applied to self-protection, savings or insurance expenditure. Regulation covers a wide area: labour standards, employee benefits, financial regulation and access, and price regulation (utilities, foodstuff, merit goods and so on). Key issues for discussion below are whether public expenditure on social protection is adequate, the constraints on tax financing, and the significance of distortionary effects from taxation and regulation.

Are governments spending enough on social protection? In theory, increases in public expenditure on social protection should stop at the point where the marginal benefits of that expenditure equal the marginal cost of raising public funds. In practice, it is a hard question to answer precisely.[5] Taking a positive approach and examining current levels of expenditure across countries and regions suggests a number of stylized facts. Table 16.2 shows public expenditure on social security across different regions of the world. There is considerable global, regional and intra-regional variation but, broadly, a positive association exists between the level of economic development and public expenditure on social protection. Political economy factors, the nature of the social contract, and path dependence are also important, as the contrast between Europe and North America reveals. In low-income and middle-income countries, donors play an important part in financing social protection expenditure and in setting the priorities for policy (Smith and Subbarao 2003).

What are the options facing developing countries wishing to raise their social protection spending from domestic revenue? Growth can generate additional revenues, but it is hard for low-income countries to rely solely on this. Without growth, additional domestic revenues would require either increased

Table 16.2 Public expenditure on social security (as percentage of GDP), 1999

Region	GNP per capita (1997 PPP)	Pensions	Health	Other[a]	Total
Africa	1,868	1.4	1.7	1.2	4.3
Asia	4,713	3.0	2.7	0.7	6.4
Europe	13,040	12.1	6.3	6.4	24.8
Latin America and the Caribbean	6,695	2.1	2.8	3.9	8.8
North America	28,346	7.1	7.5	2.0	16.6
Oceania	15,461	4.9	5.6	5.6	16.1

[a] Includes work injury, sickness, family, housing, and other social assistance benefits in cash and kind.

Source: World Labour Report, ILO (2000) .

tax revenues or deficit financing. Finance ministers are reluctant to borrow to finance social protection, and in most plausible scenarios they would be ill-advised to take this route. There are hard constraints on the capacity of developing countries to increase tax revenue collection. These constraints are associated with the structure of the economy, but also administrative capacity and political economy institutions. For the period 1995–7, tax revenue was 37.9 per cent of GDP among developed countries, but only 18.2 per cent in a sample of developing countries (Tanzi and Zee 2000). There are also differences in the composition of the tax revenues. Developing countries rely to a greater extent on consumption and trade taxes, whereas developed countries are able to finance their social protection programmes with payroll taxes. See Figure 16.1 for a comparison of the composition of tax revenue for both developed and developing countries. Nevertheless, sustainable social protection institutions and programmes will need to be financed domestically, at least in the medium term. The weight of evidence on this suggests that regressive, but efficient, taxation, coupled with progressive social protection expenditure could be more effective in supporting the extension of social protection in low-income countries. Greater efficiency in the collection of existing taxes should have priority over efforts to extend the tax base.

The potentially distortionary effects of taxation need not be exaggerated. Concerns over whether this will exacerbate market distortions in developing countries need to be balanced by the fact that the excess burden of taxation is lower there (because it is broadly proportional to the level of tax revenues as a proportion of GDP), and markedly lower for income taxes. The perceived benefits from improved social protection, especially in the context of missing insurance markets, could generate conditions for a 'double dividend'.[6]

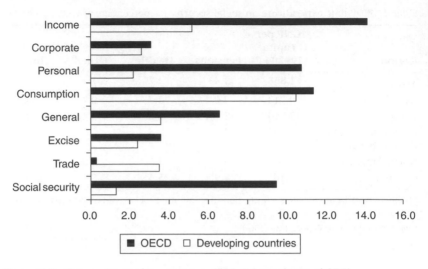

Figure 16.1   Composition of tax revenue, 1995–7 (percentage of GDP)
Source: Tanzi and Zee (2000).

There is also scope to shift expenditure from other areas towards social protection, but there are also practical obstacles to this shift. The time-frame for shifts in public expenditure is usually a long one, making this at best a medium-term objective.[7] The political economy literature on public sector reform suggests that, the greater the number of losers, and the more upfront the losses are, shifting public expenditure will be more difficult. Among developed countries, raising public expenditure on social protection has been achieved by shifting the composition of tax revenues towards income, especially payroll taxes. Tax exemptions on foodstuffs, school materials, agricultural tools and so on are very common in developing countries. They tend to show large leakages to the non-poor while at the same time diminishing the tax base. In sum, the options for low- and very low-income countries wishing to expand social protection are very limited, they involve improving the efficiency of tax collection and shifting resources from less effective programme, and external finance is crucial.

International organizations' financing of social protection

The ILO has largely been responsible for the development of social protection instruments and institutions in the developing world (Usui 1994). The extension of the scope of social protection in the 1990s has meant that a number of other multilateral organizations that finance development programmes are also involved in social protection – for example, the World Bank, UNDP, WHO, UNICEF, and others. In addition, regional organizations have developed and adopted social protection policy frameworks (IADB 2000; ADB 2001), or are in the process of doing so.

Are different forms of aid support more or less appropriate for social protection? It will be useful to focus on three main aid modalities: structural adjustment finance, provided by the IMF and World Bank to support a programme of policy reforms; general budget support, provided through the government budget, either as general support or targeted on specific sectors; and programme or project aid, providing finance earmarked for expenditure in pursuit of specific programmes or projects managed either by government/ government agencies, or donors. In terms of financing social protection, there are advantages and disadvantages with the different aid instruments. They are summarized in Table 16.3, which pays special attention to conditionalities and earmarking as potential avenues for securing resources for social protection.

Table 16.3 Modalities of aid support and social protection

Aid type	Social protection?	Conditionality?	Earmarking?
Structural adjustment	• Scope for supporting social protection is low • Social protection introduced in the midst of a crisis is unlikely to be effective • Polarization is highest during a crisis and unlikely to result in a new social contract	• Targets macro-variables • Policies that may be effective in dealing with crises may not be those that best protect the poor and vulnerable, and conditionality may involve a trade-off • Need to ensure that adjustment lending does not *increase* vulnerability • Macro and fiscal stabilization rules may contribute to reducing vulnerability after the crisis	• Not appropriate
Budget support	• Requires a vulnerability assessment • Effective only if aid is a significant share of budget and there is agreement on policy priorities between donors and government • Requires effective institutions for policy reform and co-ordination across ministries and provinces • Requires civil society monitoring and participation	• Appropriate to ensure financing is additional to current government budgetary support • Appropriate to ensure co-ordinated policy priority • Appropriate to ensure the right instruments are targeted on vulnerable groups But: • Difficulty in identifying indicators; indicators deteriorate over time • No clear link between public expenditure and outcomes	• Effective only if fungibility of government spending is limited • More effective in sectoral budget support, but at this level the boundaries with conditionality become blurred

Continued

Table 16.3   Continued

Aid type	Social protection?	Conditionality?	Earmarking?
Programme or project aid support	• Vulnerability assessment a pre-requisite • More 'expensive' in terms of political support and co-operation with stakeholders • Scope for 'co-funding' with government and other donors • Requires investment in technical capacity first • Enables multi-country and regional scope • Can have large demonstration effects	• Appropriate to the use of the funds	• Appropriate and effective • Direct monitoring of disbursement and outcomes by donors

Sources: DFID (mimeo); Collier and Dollar (2002); Cordella and Dell'Ariccia (2003).

The UK government's DFID, which has taken a particular interest in social protection, has stated its intention to rely to a greater extent on budget support in the context of its poverty reduction objectives (DFID 2004). The expectation is that budget support will provide a partnership-based, predictable and transparent mechanism for establishing a more productive policy dialogue that supports institutional development, and in particular government policy ownership and leadership, in the recipient countries. For our purposes, the issue is how budget support can best be used to strengthen social protection.

The effectiveness of budget support aid is dependent on the quality of the partnership between donors and the national government. PRSs and vulnerability assessments enable a process of learning and understanding within government and civil society, and provide the basis for achieving a common understanding on poverty reduction goals, objectives and targets.

Strengthening institutional capacity through budget support suggests a number of advantages with this aid modality in the context of social protection. Social protection will be more effective if it integrates interventions across sectors, and co-ordinates the efforts of a range of providers within the public, voluntary and private sectors. Budget support can more easily identify these linkages, and support them effectively, in particular compared with project aid. Budget support is also, on paper, more flexible in responding to changes in the pattern and significance of risks. Disbursement is more flexible.

The term structure of social protection is an important issue. Social protection interventions are most effective in the medium and long term. This is in stark contrast to the short-term horizon favoured by donors, and the term structure of aid support, leaving infrastructure projects aside. The optimal length of time of a social protection programme may extend beyond the maximum period to which a donor may be willing to commit. For longer-term programmes, establishing partnerships with government and other donors will be important. Donors may be in a position to finance in full the start of a programme, but rely on the commitment of the government to take over the financing of the programme gradually after it has been established successfully.[8]

Key issues and conclusions

The objective of this section is to discuss some remaining issues and underscore others. The section ends with some conclusions.

What are the costs of raising domestic revenue for social protection? The public finance literature suggests there are costs to a market economy of raising revenue through taxation. Payroll taxes may reduce the incentives to work among marginal workers, and taxes on non-labour income may reduce incentives to save.[9] This implies that, in order to finance US$1 for public expenditure, it may be necessary to raise US$1.25, say, in revenue. The marginal cost of social funds may be greater than the amount needed for expenditure.[10] At the same time, taxation may bring additional benefits to the economy, a social dividend, if, for example, carbon taxes reduce environmental damage in addition to raising revenue for public expenditure. There is an expectation that a social dividend might be available where taxes correct market imperfections. In this situation, the marginal cost of raising social funds may be less than the revenue collected. To the extent that social protection corrects market failures, in insurance, skills and time preferences, it can be argued that the marginal cost of raising funds for social protection may be less thanactual spending. This implies that evaluating the returns of social protection programmes is important.

It was remarked above that the term structure of aid might be too short for the time framework involved in social protection programmes. It was also noted that external financing may provide the start-up funds needed, which are substantial. Persuading governments to commit to absorbing a social protection programme gradually can be facilitated if it can be shown that the programme is effective, and political support for it is forthcoming. This involves, necessarily, a partnership with governments and a dialogue with civil society to engender the basis for a new social contract.[11]

To conclude, there is an emerging consensus that social protection provides a framework for addressing rising poverty and vulnerability. Financing an extension of social protection requires that attention is paid to the financing mix. Achieving an appropriate financing mix is essential to ensure that the resources required are available, but it is also important in strengthening the incentives for poverty and vulnerability reduction, and in reinforcing the legitimacy of social protection institutions and programmes. The task for developing countries is to raise the share of domestic revenue financing, in the context of increasing the volume of resources for social protection. There are important constraints to the capacity of national governments to achieve this, especially in low-income countries. Constraints on revenue-raising are strong, and switching expenditure is a protracted process. International organizations have an important role to play in supporting an enlargement of fiscal space for social protection. Their preference for lending to short-term, sectoral and infrastructure projects, and the ineffectiveness of conditionality in structural adjustment and budget support are important restrictions on their ability to support the extension of social protection. Strengthening social protection in developing countries may require sustained financial support and engagement with civil society, around integrated policy interventions.

Notes

1. In low-income countries, for example, donors had been traditionally resistant to engage with long-term social protection programmes, such as old-age pensions or child benefits, on the grounds that these countries would not be able to finance these programmes in the medium term. Changes in the pattern of vulnerabilities – for example, those brought about by the incidence of HIV/AIDS and migration – and in the focus of development organizations and national governments on poverty reduction, are helping to develop partnerships for long-term social protection.
2. Comparative and reliable data on social protection expenditure is sorely lacking. Recent changes to the IMF's guidelines on the reporting of public expenditure on social protection will facilitate comparative analysis in the future, but estimates of out-of-pocket household expenditure on social protection are scarce.
3. It is debatable whether increasing the share of social insurance financing is realistic, even for middle-income countries, especially as the share of social insurance financing is in decline among OECD countries. This important issue will not be discussed further below, as our focus here is on low-income countries.
4. Public expenditure primarily directed at social protection includes expenditure on early childhood interventions, primary education, primary healthcare and public health, nutrition programmes, social services, social assistance, and disaster preparedness.
5. Although in rough terms this is a 'no-brainer' – needing little or no effort to understand. Take an income transfer supporting schooling. Psacharopulos estimates that the returns to education in Africa are 24 per cent, 18 per cent and 11 per cent, respectively, for primary, secondary and tertiary education (Psacharopoulos 1994), while according to Warlters and Auriol the marginal cost of social funds for 38 countries in Sub-Saharan Africa average at 1.17 (it is necessary to collect US$1.17 to make a US$1 available for public expenditure) (Warlters and Auriol 2005). Any intervention with a rate of return at or over 17 per cent is welfare-enhancing.
6. To the extent that increased taxation provides a corrective instrument for market imperfections that cause inefficiencies, the tax 'burden' could become a 'benefit' – for example, as a result of introducing a carbon tax (Atkinson 2003). The burning of hydrocarbon fuels is an important factor in global warming, and because the fuels contribute in proportion to their carbon content, a tax on their use in proportion to the amount of carbon burned would generate significant revenues, and a reduction in the use of environmentally harmful fuels (Clunie-Ross 1999).

7. A shift of this nature could be facilitated by conditionality. The ILO has championed social budgeting as a tool for identifying potential gains from switching public expenditure, and to facilitate their implementation.
8. The term structure for this contract may be an issue. The Global Social Trust programme, for example, envisages the provision of start-up capital and know-how for open-ended projects, with a gradual withdrawal of the trust after ten years. There is also a political economy dimension to this. Once a programme becomes established, and evaluations show its effectiveness and impact, it becomes easier to ensure its political sustainability.
9. In addition, there are costs associated with administration and enforcement of tax rules.
10. The marginal cost of public funds is 'the multiplier to be applied to the direct resource cost in order to arrive at the socially relevant shadow price of resources to be used in the public sector' (Sadmo 1998).
11. This is in line with the findings of *Assessing Aid*, about what makes aid successful (World Bank 1998).

References

ADB (2001) *Social Protection Strategy*. Manila: Asian Development Bank.

Atkinson, A. B. (2003) *Innovative Sources for Development Finance – Global Public Economics*, Mimeo. Oxford: Oxford University.

Barrientos, A. and R. Holmes (2006) *Social Assistance in Developing Countries Database*. Brighton: Institute of Development Studies.

Barrientos, A. and P. Lloyd-Sherlock (2003) *Non-contributory Pensions and Poverty Prevention. a Comparative Study of Brazil and South Africa*, Report. Manchester: IDPM and HelpAge International.

Clunie-Ross, A. (1999) *Resources on Global Development*, Mimeo. New York: UN.

Coady, D. (2003) *Alleviating Structural Poverty in Developing Countries: the Approach of Progresa in Mexico*, Mimeo. Washington, DC: International Food Policy Research Institute.

Commission for Africa (2005) *Our Common Interest*, Report. London: Commission for Africa.

DFID (2004) *Poverty Reduction Budget Support*, Policy Paper. London: Department for International Development, U.K. Government.

Ehrlich, I. and G. S. Becker (1972) 'Market insurance, self-insurance and self-protection', *Journal of Political Economy*, 80, 623–648.

Gelbach, J. B. and L. Pritchett (1995) 'Does more for the poor mean less for the poor? The politics of targeting', *Policy Research Working Papers* 1799. Washington DC: The World Bank.

Gill, I. S. and N. Ilahi (2002) *Economic Insecurity, Economic Behaviour and Social Policy*, Mimeo. Washington, DC: The World Bank.

Graham, C. (2002) 'Public attitudes matter: A conceptual framework for accounting for political economy in safety nets and social assistance policies', *Social Protection Discussion Paper* 0233. Washington, DC: The World Bank.

Holzmann, R., L. Sherbourne-Benz and E. Tesliuc (2003) *Social Risk Management. the World Bank's Approach to Social Protection in a Globalizing World*. Washington, DC: Human Development Network, The World Bank.

IADB (2000) *Social Protection for Equity and Growth*. Washington, DC: Inter-American Development Bank.

ILO (2001) 'Social security: issues, challenges and prospects', Report VI. Geneva: International Labour Office.

Morley, S. and D. Coady (2003) *From Social Assistance to Social Development: Targeted Education Subsidies in Developing Countries*. Washington, DC: Center for Global Development and International Food Policy Research Institute.

Psacharopoulos, G. (1994) *Returns to Investment in Education: A Global Update*, Report. Washington, DC: The World Bank.

Sadmo, A. (1998) 'Redistribution and the marginal cost of public funds', *Journal of Public Economics*, 70, 365–382.

Smith, W. J. and K. Subbarao (2003) 'What role for safety net transfers in very low income countries?', *Social Protection Discussion Paper* 0301. Washington, DC: The World Bank.

Tanzi, V. and H. H. Zee (2000) 'Tax policy for emerging markets: developing countries', *IMF Working Papers* WP/00/35. Washington, DC: IMF.

Usui, C. (1994) 'Welfare state development in a world system context: event history analysis of first social insurance legislation among 60 countries, 1880–1960', in T. Janoski and A. M. Hicks (eds), *The Comparative Political Economy of the Welfare State*. Cambridge: Cambridge University Press, pp. 254–277.

Warlters, M. and E. Auriol (2005) 'The marginal cost of public funds in Africa', *Policy Research Working Paper* WPS 3679. Washington, DC: The World Bank.

World Bank (1998) *Assessing Aid. What Works, What Doesn't, and Why*. Oxford: Oxford University Press.

World Health Organisation (2003) *The World Health Report*. Geneva: WHO.

Part V
Conclusion

17
Embedding Social Protection in the Developing World

Armando Barrientos and David Hulme

Introduction

The chapters in this volume provide evidence of the rapid spread and evolution of social protection concepts and practices in developing countries, with much innovation and experimentation occurring in the design and implementation of social protection programmes. It is now clear that, in many poor countries, social protection policies can reduce short-term human suffering and at the same time help to create a basis for long-term human development. These medium- and longer-term impacts make it possible for social protection to contribute to national development through economic growth and strengthened social and political cohesion. Moreover, the recent initiatives are contributing to developing and extending knowledge of poverty and the reduction of vulnerability that can be deployed to strengthen existing activities and improve social protection policies in other regions or for social groups excluded from existing policies and programmes. While policy transfers are part of this process, social protection has managed to avoid the 'silver bullet' syndrome and naïve replications that characterise social funds and much microfinance in the 1990s.

To date, discussion on social protection has been dominated by concerns over the effectiveness of alternative instruments and their design. However, as the contributions to this volume signal, an emerging body of literature is beginning to investigate the conceptual frameworks that underpin social protection. This literature looks into the linkages between social protection and social theory, and between social protection and ethics. Social protection as a policy framework is unlikely to be effective if it is insufficiently grounded on knowledge about the factors and processes that produce and reproduce poverty and vulnerability, and the factors and processes that facilitate or hinder social transformation. It is therefore important to link policy back to theory. This is a two-way process, as social protection practice and experimentation can make an important contribution to this body of knowledge. There is also increasing awareness and discussion of the linkages existing between social protection and ethics. Sometimes these concern design issues such as the selection of beneficiaries, or the setting of programme conditionalities. At other times, these are more abstract, and discussion about social protection reflects, to an important extent, the shared or competing views we hold about what is a fair society. Potentially, there are large gains from connecting social protection to social theory and ethics, as this can help us to appreciate that social protection is not only about the reduction of poverty and vulnerability but also about developing stable and productive societies with a capacity to adapt to the changes induced by globalisation, climate change, and other external factors.

The contributors to this volume also point out the need to supplement discussions of social protection as a policy framework, with an understanding of the specificity of social protection institutions and practices in different parts of the developing world. While it is important to seek to identify policies and programmes that work, and to learn from 'best practices' and institutional frameworks, it is perilous to do so on the assumption that there are universally effective models of social protection. As the cases in this volume revealed (Britto, Hulme and Moore, Munemo, Sumarto *et al.*) social protection programmes are to an important extent grounded in specific national and historical experiences: they need 'acting out' as much as they need 'thinking through' (Johnston and Clark, 1982). Capacity and institutional development are also important. Policy prescriptions are easy to advance, but the capacity to implement policy needs to develop in specific contexts at specific times. The task now is not to homogenize social protection around the developing world but to promote and support learning from fully contextualised and carefully monitored experiments. It is only on this basis that interventions showing clear evidence of effectiveness in reducing poverty and vulnerability can be expanded systematically, both geographically and across social groups.[1] We need social protection to evolve not as the next development aid fad but rather as a set of context specific policy experiments that are carefully scaled up (Rondinelli, 1993).

Moving from policy to theory and back again to policy describes the kind of learning cycle that is needed to take social protection forward. It is with this in mind that this chapter will aim to bring together the different strands in the debate about social protection examined in this book. The chapter has three main sections. First, a brief discussion of the features and trends in social protection in the main developing regions will consider the immediate antecedents of existing social protection policies, and the linkages existing between these and new initiatives. Second, a review of the major issues facing contemporary social protection policies that are common to current policy innovations, including issues of programme design, affordability, beneficiary selection, the setting of conditionalities, and implementation capacity. Finally, the chapter speculates on the potential trajectories for future social protection. In the latter, there is a particular need to focus on sub-Saharan Africa, where the extension of social protection is so urgent and the contemporary capacity to provide it so limited.[2] The overarching theme of this conclusion is the need to see social protection not merely as a set of programmes reducing vulnerability but also as a set of institutions embedding new and stronger social contracts.

Regional perspectives

Latin America's recent experience with innovative poverty and vulnerability reduction programmes – *Bolsa Escola/Familia,* followed by *Progresa/ Oportunidades,* followed by *Chile Solidario* – has mobilised international interest in social protection policies. The acute economic crisis in the early 1980s, followed by structural adjustment and economic liberalisation, marked a dramatic policy shift from the import-substitution industrialisation developmental model – which had dominated in the region from the 1950s – to export-led growth. The immediate outcome of the crisis and adjustment was rising vulnerability, poverty and inequality. Reform of social insurance institutions that protected workers in formal employment was seen as being essential to controlling fiscal deficits, but in the context of labour market liberalisation it helped to fuel the growth of informality. Workers in informal employment and their dependants – a majority in the region – remained excluded from formal social protection institutions. Liberalisation also weakened the capacity of public agencies to address rising poverty, opening the way for fragmented, often externally financed, safety net and social fund programmes run by parallel agencies. By the mid-1990s, it was clear that more comprehensive and permanent public responses were needed. The move away from military and emergency governments ensured that democratic governments engaged with the strong demand for social protection.

The origins of *Bolsa Escola* are to be found in the innovative approach to multi-dimensional and persistent poverty adopted by the Municipality of Campinas in Brazil, in the mid-1990s, and later extended to the rest of the country. Similarly, Mexico's *Progresa* reflected both systematic learning from the politicised and ineffective anti-poverty programmes that preceded its introduction in 1997, and the need to address the human development deficits that ensured the intergenerational persistence of poverty in rural communities. The new human development programmes aimed to meet both short-term needs – namely, improved consumption and nutrition; and longer-term aspirations – namely, improved schooling and health, and a more productive population.

While international development agencies have played a role in financing, providing technical assistance and supporting policy transfers of such programmes, the Latin-American dynamic for social protection is strongly national and regional. Relatedly, the capacity of Latin-American countries to finance social protection is high, dependence on external financing is lower than in other regions, and the capacity to design and monitor experimental programmes was in place.

South Asia has a quite different historical and contemporary experience. The deep-seated informal social protection of pre-colonial 'Indian' societies have been added to by colonial programmes of food for work and public assistance for destitutes, especially the elderly, and by the social welfare initiatives of newly independent national governments and the programmes of national and international NGOs. In many cases this means that social protection is now a morass of often poorly funded, and weakly implemented, overlapping programmes. These are overseen by welfare ministries that have limited capacity for policy analysis or evaluation and are marginal to the mainstream debates of prime minister, presidential office and treasuries. While historically the political elites in South Asia have been ideologically inclined to pursue social welfare through public policy, there are clear differences between countries and sub-regions. Sri Lanka has been more successful in financing and delivering social protection policies than have Bangladesh and Pakistan. The southern states of India – Kerala, Karnataka, Tamil Nadu and Andhra Pradesh – have been much more effective at implementing national social protection policies than the north and north-eastern states.

In the late 1990s and early 2000s there has been much donor-financed activity, ranging from the World Bank's Janasaviya Trust Fund to BRAC's Targeting the Ultra Poor programme in Bangladesh, alongside domestic initiatives – for example , old-age pensions in Bangladesh, India and Nepal. However, since 2004 India has taken a regional leadership through its National Rural Employment Guarantee Scheme (NREGS) and, in 2007, with the preparatory studies and discussion of the Unorganised Sector Worker's Social Security Bill (USWSS). These two schemes are quite different in their aims and scope (Kannan 2006). The National Rural Employment Guarantee Scheme is a social assistance programme, with the objective of ensuring basic income security for vulnerable households in rural areas with economic capacity. It extends, on a national scale, the approach to social protection tested in the Maharashtra Employment Guarantee Scheme. The USWSS Bill aims to incorporate the majority of urban workers into a basic social insurance scheme. It seeks to extend social insurance to workers in informal employment. Potentially, these two schemes promise to reduce substantially the insecurity of India's vast rural and urban informal labour forces. In practice, early reports on the NREGS suggest that, in relatively well governed states, such as Kerala (Jacob and Varghese, 2006), the policy is being implemented effectively, but in poorly governed states, such as Bihar, it has stalled (Louis, 2006). The role of international agencies and aid donors also varies geographically. Donors have substantial influence in smaller, more aid-dependent countries (for example, Nepal), less traction in larger countries experiencing economic growth (for example, Bangladesh), and minimal influence in India. In Bangladesh in particular, donor support has greatly strengthened the microfinance and related programmes that have replaced emergency food support programmes introduced after the 1975 famine. Lessons learnt from microfinance and asset building programmes have led to the design and implementation of integrated anti-poverty programmes such as BRAC's Targeting the Ultra Poor programme, discussed by Hulme and Moore in Chapter 10 of this volume.

South-East and East Asia demonstrate a common reliance on family-based social protection, but with different policy pathways reflecting different responses to rapid social transformation. Among the more economically advanced countries in North-East Asia, Korea, Taiwan, Malaysia, Thailand and Singapore, social insurance is the core of social protection institutions. Interestingly, the 1997 financial crisis served to strengthen the social insurance pathway here (Cook and Kwon 2006). In Korea, for example, it led to the Minimum Living Standards Guarantee Scheme, and in Thailand to the introduction of a universal health insurance scheme. By contrast, among lower-income countries in South-East Asia – the Philippines and Indonesia in particular – the routes to extending social insurance were severely undermined by the 1997 crisis. The immediate response to the financial crisis was the expansion of temporary safety nets (the expansion of these safety nets into more permanent forms of social assistance in Indonesia was covered in some detail in the Sumarto *et al.*'s Chapter 6 in this volume). Transition countries had a different starting point and evolution, especially China and Vietnam, and the recent changes in social protection are directed primarily towards addressing rapid economic transformation and liberalisation. In urban China, economic liberalisation has led to a rapid decline in the strength and coverage of social insurance based around productive units, and an equally rapid rise in social assistance through the Minimum Living Standards Scheme, which covered more than 22 million households by 2006. In rural China, the main social protection innovation has been the introduction of mixed-provision health insurance schemes, but there is rising concern about the increasing vulnerability of rural dwellers.

As a consequence of the diversity in initial conditions and institutions, the region has not developed a dominant social protection model, but in general terms the emphasis in higher-income countries has been on strengthening social insurance institutions, while in lower-income countries it has been on social assistance. The latter also appears to be the main focus of social protection in transition economies. In very low-income countries in the region, such as Laos and Cambodia, social protection is incipient, and restricted to fragmented programmes that usually externally funded (Cook and Kwon 2006).

Sub-Saharan Africa has a legacy of social protection institutions akin to South Asia: deeply-embedded, informal systems of social protection, especially in rural areas. This is overlain by under-funded, fragmented and partially implemented social insurance institutions for civil servants; and by a patchwork of (mainly externally funded) social assistance programmes focused on emergency support. Emergency food aid, famine relief, and humanitarian assistance have been central to social protection for many African countries since the 1970s. Attempts at shoring up social insurance schemes have not proved successful in the region, given fiscal constraints and the decline of public-sector employment. More recently, a concern to shift from a focus on emergency aid into more permanent social protection programmes has led to the spread of pilot cash transfer schemes, financed by international institutions. Such initiatives are under way in Zambia, Kenya, Malawi, Uganda, Ghana and Nigeria. These countries are piloting cash transfer programmes targeted at the poorest and most vulnerable, and the majority of schemes include human development objectives. The Protective Safety Nets Programme in Ethiopia provides an example of a food security programme incorporating cash-based public assistance components.

The wealthier countries of the Southern Cone, South Africa, Namibia and Botswana are the exception, with a stronger social assistance focus relying on grants for vulnerable groups, especially the elderly and children. More recently, social pensions have been introduced in Swaziland and Lesotho, perhaps signalling the emergence of a distinct approach to social protection in the sub-region. Social pensions in South Africa and Namibia reflect the successful adaptation of colonial forms of social protection, once focused on providing a minimum income floor for whites and coloureds, but later extended to the population as a whole, and providing vital income redistribution to poorer black households against the background of the end of apartheid. The impact of HIV/AIDS on household structures, the rise in the incidence of households with 'the missing middle', suggest a further adaptation of the social pension to address a new problem. The introduction of the Child Support Grant in South Africa constitutes an extension of social assistance with human development objectives. While the evolution of social protection in South Africa is closely related to its political history, the country's experience shows the way in which a deeply embedded programme, the social pension, has been adapted over time to address changing vulnerability, including most recently the rise in the incidence of households with the 'missing middle' as a result of AIDS or migration.

A number of policy experiments are under way with cash transfers and, despite the problems of service delivery in many African countries, recent experiments with conditional cash transfers. More than any other region in the world, Sub-Saharan Africa's social protection trajectory is likely to be heavily dependent on donor design and financing. Moreover, the capacity of African intelligentsia (think-tanks, universities, policy advisers to political parties and so on) to engage with multilateral agencies and donors to debate policy choices and implementation options and propose alternatives, is lower than in other regions.

This outline of trends in social protection in developing regions suggests that responses to poverty and vulnerability will follow a range of pathways in different regions, depending on the nature of their existing institutions (determining path dependence), level of economic development (determining their fiscal space), and features of their economic transformation (especially the interactions between longer-term transformations such as ageing and short-term fractures such as transition or change in the development model). Some shared issues and dilemmas emerge.

In this book we have focused on social protection for the poor and poorest. With few exceptions, developing countries are addressing the vulnerability of the poor and poorest through strengthening social assistance institutions and programmes. This applies to low-income countries, in which social insurance institutions are in any case absent, but also in middle-income countries in Latin America or Southern Africa. It is interesting that the strengthening of social assistance institutions in most developing countries has focused on time-defined programmes, such as pilot programmes in sub-Saharan Africa, and cash transfer programmes in Latin America. Some important countries buck this trend: China's Minimum Living Standards Scheme, India's National Rural Employment Guarantee Scheme, and Brazil's *Bolsa Família*. In these countries, the extension of social protection is taking place through more permanent policies and institutions. Only a handful of countries have attempted to address the vulnerability of the poor and poorest through social insurance programmes or policies. These are in North-East Asia, Thailand and Korea. This is intriguing, especially in view of the fact that Latin America's social insurance institutions, the oldest and comparatively strongest in the developing world, have not been able to make progress along this path. These issues will be taken up in the next section.

Key policy issues

There are many issues associated with the extension of social protection in developing countries which are widely discussed and strongly contested. In this section we discus very briefly a few that are especially important in the context of determining the future trajectory of social protection.

Programme design. Discussions around instrument design options have had a very high profile, especially as the main area of expansion in developing countries is in social assistance rather than social insurance. The basic design of social insurance models can be adapted to the conditions present in developing countries, but it is unlikely to depart in significant ways from social insurance institutions in place elsewhere. The situation is very different when considering social assistance. In developed countries, social assistance is largely a residual safety net charged with protecting a small minority of individuals and households from the effects of poverty after all the other components of social protection (social insurance, basic services, labour market regulation) have proved to be unsuccessful. In developing countries, where social insurance covers, at best, a minority of the labour force, basic services are highly stratified, and labour market regulations are thin and poorly enforced, and where the incidence of poverty and vulnerability are high, social assistance is far from residual.[3] The primary role of social assistance in developing countries calls for fresh approaches and models.

In developing countries, social assistance is called on to play a broader role than in developed countries. As in developed countries, it aims to ensure minimum levels of consumption that protect poor households from the worst effects of deprivation. In addition, social assistance in developing countries is expected to strengthen productive capacity, whether through investment in human or physical assets. It is also expected to bridge access to basic services and therefore weaken social exclusion, advancing the participation of the poorest in their communities and societies. Given the high incidence of poverty and vulnerability in developing countries, social assistance programme are sometimes also charged with reducing inequality. By comparison with its essentially residual and compensatory role in developed countries, social assistance in developing countries is a very different type of animal.

Much discussion within social protection in developing countries has focused on the advantages and disadvantages of specific instruments – for example, whether cash or in-kind transfers work best. On occasion, valid concerns with establishing the effectiveness of different design options can become distorted into an unproductive search for a 'silver bullet'. It is highly unlikely that a single social protection instrument can achieve the manifold objectives of protecting household consumption, promoting asset accumulation, strengthening productive capacity and inclusion, and reducing poverty, vulnerability and inequality. It is therefore vitally important that discussions around design options shift from a current focus on single instruments to a broader focus on integrated programmes or a mix of programmes,[4] capable of progressing the different objectives of social protection among the poor and poorest.

There is no question that income transfer programmes are spreading rapidly in most developing countries. In Latin America, conditional cash transfer programmes with human development objectives now reach a significant proportion of the poor and poorest in the region. Income transfers are also expanding in East Asia. The growth in unconditional income transfers, such as social pensions and child grants in Southern Africa, is also noteworthy. Income transfers have a number of advantages relative to alternative design options. They can be implemented and scaled-up relatively quickly, have an immediate impact on consumption, and are capable of reaching the very poorest. The experience from Latin America shows that they can be effective both in improving consumption and in facilitating human development objectives. It also demonstrates that their effectiveness is raised where complementary interventions adding skills, employment, savings and participation dimensions are included progressively (see Hulme and Moore's Chapter 10 in this volume). Moving progressively towards integrated social protection programmes for the poor and poorest is the main challenge for the future.

Selection. The extent to which social protection interventions should select beneficiaries based on their poverty status has attracted some attention in the literature. It is important to distinguish carefully the different levels in which the issue of selection is relevant. A great deal of discussion about this is pitched around the effectiveness of selection, with those arguing against selection emphasising the costs associated with selecting beneficiaries, in terms of administration and stigma. On the other hand, the high incidence of poverty in developing countries makes the selection of beneficiaries a necessity where resources for poverty reduction are insufficient to reach everyone. At this level, assessing the advantages of selection is specific to the programme and the programme's resources.

A second level considers selection in the context of the dynamics of poverty reduction in a political economy context. Gelbach and Pritchett develop versions of public-choice models in which budgetary decisions on social protection depend on voter coalitions, and conclude that selection undermines support for programme budget allocations (Gelbach and Pritchett 1995). This echoes Titmuss's dictum that 'a programme for the poor soon becomes a poor programme' (Titmuss 1968).[5] Several chapters in this book approached this issue directly, and suggested that alternative dynamics are possible for developing countries. In many developing countries, and in Latin America in particular, the selection of beneficiaries through sophisticated methods ranking households according to the extent of their poverty has constituted a response to widely held concerns that anti-poverty programmes in the past proved ineffective because of political clientelism and corruption. The selection of beneficiaries through agreed and transparent methods can build credibility and political support for social protection interventions.

A third level in which discussions around selection need to be rehearsed are related to the ethics of assistance. In the influential description of a just society provided by Rawls, all persons have equal rights to the 'most extensive scheme of basic liberties', but 'social and economic inequalities' must be arranged to the benefit of the least advantaged (Rawls 1971). As a result, a fair society is one in which public policy is judged from the perspective of its least advantaged members. This would be consistent with social protection programmes that take the poorest to the level of the next poorest, progressively, until poverty is eradicated. Selection of beneficiaries might be required to ensure that anti-poverty programmes meet ethical precepts.

Paying due attention to the distinctiveness of these three levels of analysis is important for the future of social protection. It is perfectly reasonable to agree with Rawls' principles of a just society, and to be persuaded that the least advantaged may not be well served by selection, either because it is inefficient or because it blocks the path to further extensions of social protection that will favour them. These judgements depend on the specifics of the programme and its resourcing. It is less helpful to confuse judgements of efficiency with those of principle.

Some argue that selection of beneficiaries in social protection programmes is in conflict with universalism. It depends on what is meant by universalism. If by universalism it is meant that no one should be excluded from protection against poverty, those concerns are not justified. South Africa's social pension is means-tested, while Namibia's is paid to all persons over the age of entitlement. The description of universalism given above would easily apply to both. However, to the extent that selection is arbitrary, or distorted by political clientelism or unwarranted distinctions between deserving and undeserving poor, those concerns would be justified. To the extent that the selection of beneficiaries arises from resource constraints, and is done on the basis of transparent and agreed criteria, those concerns are misplaced. Selection does necessarily conflict with a universalism, nor with a rights perspective, provided that the right in question is the right to protection against poverty, as opposed to the right to a given benefit.

Looking into the future of social protection, linking through the three levels in this discussion of selection will be a central concern. Advances in the techniques and technology of selection have reduced its administrative costs significantly, with important benefits to other operational aspects of social protection programme implementation, such as information systems and monitoring. Nevertheless, combining attention to the costs of selection, to the influence of programme design on the dynamics of social protection expansion, and to strengthening solidarity and supporting shared values of social justice, are crucial challenges for social protection in developing countries.

Affordability. Many have questioned whether developing countries, and especially low-income countries, can afford social protection. It is useful to weave together the different points emerging from the discussion in earlier chapters. First, it is important to acknowledge that the lack of effective social protection has significant costs in terms of poverty and vulnerability. These generate long-term restrictions on the development of human capital and supportive institutions that themselves become a constraint on growth and development. Second, establishing social protection involves shifting the financing mix from one based mainly on households and informal provision to a more diversified mix. This is clearest in the context of the introduction of health insurance institutions. In their absence, out-of-pocket household expenditure on health care is often inefficient as well as insufficient, because responses to health shocks can crowd out investment in preventative care and because they are rationed by available resources. Health insurance instruments can improve the efficiency of households' health expenditures and make resources go further.[6] Thirdly, the costs of social protection programmes focused on the poor and poorest are small in absolute terms, income transfers in Latin America are below 1 per cent of GDP. These suggest that establishing social protection is affordable, even in low-income countries (see Barrientos's Chapter 16 in this volume).

There are, however, important constraints to financing social protection in poorer countries (Smith and Subbarao 2003; Barrientos forthcoming). In the low-income countries in Sub-Saharan Africa, poor revenue mobilisation is an important barrier to social protection. In countries where 15 per cent of GDP or less is mobilised for public spending, the fiscal space for an extension of social protection is limited, even if social protection programmes for the poorest are kept below 1 per cent of GDP. The route to the expansion of social protection followed by today's developed countries was through payroll taxes to finance social insurance, but this is an unlikely route for countries in which the majority of the labour force works informally. The short-term structure of international development assistance means that international donors can contribute to financing the start-up costs of social protection, but that in the medium and longer run, domestic financing is essential. New aid modalities such as general budget support could extend the time-frame for external support for social protection in low-income countries. However, strengthening domestic revenue mobilisation remains a significant challenge to the future of social protection.

Implementation capacity. Capacity limitations are a further barrier to the extension of social protection in low-income countries. These apply at several points in the policy cycle, beginning with the capacity to study, measure, and analyse poverty and vulnerability, the capacity to design and implement appropriate policies, and the capacity to deliver and evaluate social protection programmes. On the ground, a successful extension of social protection will involve the horizontal integration of poverty researchers, policy analysts, political scientists, financial experts, programme managers, information systems analysts and developers, accountants and field officers. Developing these capacities in low-income countries has not been an explicit objective of policy-makers, research institutes or international organisations. In many low-income countries, government restrictions on recruitment and salaries, 'and departmentalism' make it unlikely that government agencies could grow these networks and ensure their integration. Engaging international NGOs to fill in this gap provides a short-term palliative solution, but not a longer-term one. This is an area in which technical fixes may be feasible, through donor support for the development of the appropriate skills, and there is also the potentially significant role of inter-governmental transfers of information, knowledge and know-how across the developed and developing world, and within the latter.[7]

Future trajectories for social protection

Extending social protection to the poor and poorest involves raising dramatically the analytical, planning and implementation capacities of social assistance institutions in countries that have them, or establishing them in countries that lack them. Among the former, a range of design options have been tried, reflecting local conditions and institutions. The types of trajectory that need to be pursued vary between countries and regions. The historical record in high-income and middle-income countries demonstrates that effective social protection is not simply achieved by a good programme or policy. It needs to be embedded in its society to ensure continued public and political support for financing it and adapting it to changing domestic circumstances (population age structure, patterns of disease, levels of human development) and external conditions (globalisation, security, climatic change). What might this mean for the world's major regions?

- In Latin America, the recent focus (one might say breakthrough) has been on conditional transfer programmes which link income transfers with human development objectives (see above). The design of these programmes reflects widely shared concerns with multi-dimensional poverty that persists across generations. It also reflects low public confidence in government-supported anti-poverty interventions, which quickly become captured by client groups. In addition, the elites and middle classes of Latin America are not keen to support indefinite social assistance programmes because they want to ensure that the poor do not become dependent on welfare. The spread of similar programmes in Latin American countries is also a response to the threat to social cohesion posed by high levels of poverty and vulnerability. Aided by technical and financial support from the World Bank and the Inter-American Development Bank, future development in social protection for the poor and poorest will involve the expansion of the scope of these programmes to include additional dimensions (as in Mexico's *Oportunidades* or Chile's *Solidario*). The main challenge will be to developed integrated anti-poverty programmes, and to better integrate social assistance and social insurance components.
- In South Asia, several trajectories are evident from the expansion of public social assistance programmes in India, Sri Lanka and Nepal, to experiments with conditional income programmes in Bangladesh and Pakistan, and the extension of social insurance to the unorganised sector in India. The challenge will be to integrate and consolidate these different developments with a focus on the poor and poorest; to scale-up such programmes without a loss of quality; and to extend these programmes into poorly governed

regions and remote areas. Much will depend on the performance of the vast NREGS and USWSS in India. If these perform well, social protection policies will move to centre stage across the regions, but if they are judged negatively, interest in social protection will weaken as national elites and middle classes withdraw their support.

• In the more developed countries of East Asia, the trajectory involves extending social insurance institutions to cover the poor and poorest, as in the extension of health insurance in Thailand and the Minimum Living Standards Scheme in Korea.

• In South East Asia, the challenge will be to continue along the trajectory of consolidating temporary safety net programmes introduced as a response to the financial crisis, and widening their scope to support investments in education and health care among poor households. The Latin-American experience may have especial relevance in this region.

• Last, but not least,[8] in sub-Saharan Africa, two separate trajectories can be observed. Among Southern African countries, the extension of social assistance is taking place through the strengthening of cash grants focused on vulnerable groups – pensioners in particular. In countries in West Africa, and increasingly East Africa, a rapid expansion of income transfers with a human development component is under way – in Ethiopia, Kenya, Uganda, Tanzania, Malawi, Nigeria and Ghana. The main challenge will be to build the epistemic and administrative capacity needed to scale-up these programmes and to improve domestic resource mobilisation to ensure their medium-term financial consolidation and reduce dependence on donors. In part, these are technical tasks but there is also a need to engage with the social and political processes of the region to ensure that social protection is not treated as a donor interest and responsibility but becomes central to national debates about development (see Hickey's Chapter 13 in this volume).

These varying trajectories reveal the different rates of progress and forms of evolution in developing countries. They suggest the possibility that, within a relatively short time – perhaps fifteen to thirty years – social protection institutions will be in place in most low-income and middle-income countries.[9] We can speculate on the challenges involved.

The scale and speed of the changes involved are astounding. In the course of less than a decade, a raft of social assistance programmes have been put in place across the different regions, with the capacity to reach large numbers of households in poverty in the South. A conservative estimate, based on the rough numbers listed in the Introduction, suggests that these programmes combined have the capacity to reach in excess of 100 million households in poverty – perhaps over half a billion individuals. This is an extraordinary achievement. The rapid scaling-up of social assistance in developing countries will change substantially the mix of anti-poverty policies in the South, and hold the promise of making a significant dent in global poverty. Even more astounding is the fact that the majority of these programmes are focused explicitly on the poor and poorest. This is a feature that sets them apart from the direction of anti-poverty and development policies of the past (Barrientos *et al.* 2005).

Their effectiveness in reducing poverty and vulnerability in the short run is supported by the weight of evidence from evaluation studies, but in a sense this is to be expected, given that the bulk of social assistance consists of transfers in cash which directly bolster consumption among poor households. A large proportion of the social assistance programmes introduced since the mid-1990s also have the medium- and longer-term objectives of strengthening the productive capacity of poor households, in particular through investment in nutrition, health and schooling. It will be some time before we can be certain that these objectives have been met. Investment in the human capital of poor and poorest households is intrinsically a risky undertaking. Even among non-poor households, the risks involved in investing in education are such that few, if any, financial institutions are prepared to lend in support of this investment. Changes in the demand for skills, macroeconomic crises, social unrest, migration, or increased natural hazards through climate change, have the potential to wipe out the returns from the investment in human capital. These contingencies could also affect investment in the productive capacity of poor households. The medium- and longer-term returns to social assistance are more difficult to predict with any degree of accuracy.

The medium- and longer-term effectiveness of social assistance also depends on the extent to which current programmes and policies are sustained into the future, and expanded with the integration of complementary interventions. The emerging consensus around social protection needs to be nurtured and strengthened through long-lasting partnerships, involving a wide range of stakeholders – civil society, political elites, national governments, NGOs, bilateral aid donors, multilateral agencies, national and international research institutes. There is a strong role for multilaterals and bilaterals in supporting the implementation of appropriate social protection interventions in low- and middle-income countries, especially in financing start-up costs, providing technical assistance, ensuring effective monitoring and evaluation processes, and supporting capacity building. In undertaking this role, strong partnerships with national governments are essential – social protection must be owned by national governments and civil society. Civil society organisations and domestic NGOs play a key role in advocacy and ensuring government accountability. At one level, extending social protection is a technical and financial challenge to spearhead a sustained reduction in poverty and vulnerability, but at a deeper and more fundamental level, it is about generating the kind of social contract that can embed and nurture sustained improvements in opportunity and well-being for all. In this context, national governments have the mandate and responsibility for leading the development of social protection, in terms of both concrete programmes and the promotion of an ongoing public debate about the ends and means of social protection. There are growing indications that in many developing countries these partnerships for social protection are already hard at work.

Notes

1. The concern with strengthening the evidence base of poverty reduction programmes through robust impact evaluation involving randomised trials is a very welcome development. The knowledge these can generate is essential to the extension of effective and sustainable social protection in developing countries. It is worth keeping in mind that, in European countries, securing this level of evidence to support domestic programmes remains an aspiration. It is therefore important that strengthening the evidence base for social protection is not turned into an obstacle that discourages programme experimentation in order to support failed orthodoxies.
2. Informal social protection, from relatives, friends, neighbours and informal local institutions, remains important in all regions of Sub-Saharan Africa, and the central pillar for managing vulnerability.
3. In some African countries, the majority of the population could plausibly be supported by social assistance.
4. We are tempted to say that it is necessary to think in terms of social protection systems, but this term is already associated with technocratic approaches that eschew institutional and political analysis. An alternative is to focus on the need for integrated programmes or a programme mix.
5. However, he also noted that selection was required to compensate for hazards, luck and inequalities in opportunity. As he put it, 'universalism is not, by itself alone, enough: in medical care, in wage related social security and in education. This much we have learnt in the past two decades from the facts about inequalities in the distribution of incomes and wealth' (Titmuss 1968, pp. 134–5).
6. A particular problem for the poorest and most vulnerable households is assessing the quality of private providers in the unregulated health markets of Africa and South Asia. Health insurance schemes play an important role in directing poor people to providers who are both competent and ethical (see Dercon *et al.*, Chapter 3 in this volume).
7. See Hulme (2007) for the argument that India is now in a position to make the development of capacities for poverty analysis a major component of work of the newly established India International Development Agency (IIDA).
8. The Chronic Poverty Reports (Chronic Poverty Research Centre 2004 and 2008, forthcoming) show that Sub-Saharan Africa has the deepest concentration of persistent poverty and vulnerability in the world.
9. As revealed above, the biggest questions are about prospects for institutional development in Sub-Saharan Africa.

References

Barrientos, A. (forthcoming) 'Introducing basic social protection in low income countries: Lessons from existing programmes', in P. Townsend (ed.), *Challenging The Development Paradigm: Rethinking the Role of Social Security in State Building*. Geneva: ILO.

Barrientos, A., D. Hulme and A. Shepherd (2005) 'Can social protection tackle chronic poverty?', *European Journal of Development Research*, 17(1), 8–23.

Chronic Poverty Research Centre (2004) *The Chronic Poverty Report 2004–2005.* Manchester, IDPM, University of Manchester (www.chronicpoverty.org)

Chronic Poverty Research Centre (2008, forthcoming) The Chronic Poverty Research Report 2008–2009. Manchester, IDPM, University of Manchester (www.chronicpoverty.org). Accessed June 2007.

Cook, S. and H.-j. Kwon (2006) *Economic Development and Social Protection in East Asia,* Mimeo. Brighton: IDS.

Gelbach, J. B. and L. Pritchett (1995). *Does More for the Poor Mean Less for the Poor? the Politics of Targeting,* Policy Research Working Papers 1799. Washington, DC: The World Bank.

Hulme, D. (2007) *Inclusive Globalisation: India's Role in Tackling Global Poverty.* Exim Bank of India Annual Commencement Day Lecture. Mumbai: Exim Bank. (www.eximbankindia.com). Accessed May 2007.

Jacob, A. and R. Varghese (2006) 'NREGA Implementation I – Reasonable beginning in Palakkad, Kerala', *Economic and Political Weekly* Dec 2 2006, 4943–5.

Johnston, B. F. and W. C. Clark (1982) *Redesigning Rural development: A Strategic Perspective.* Baltimore: Johns Hopkins University Press.

Kannan, K. P. (2006) *Employment And Social Security for the Working Poor. Two Major Initiatives in India.* New Delhi, National Commission for Enterprises in the Unorganised Sector, Government of India.

Louis, P. (2006) 'NREGA Implementation II – Birth pangs in Bihar', *Economic and Political Weekly* Dec 2 2006, 4946–7.

Rawls, J. (1971) *A Theory of Justice.* Cambridge, MA: Harvard University Press.

Rondinelli, D. A. (1993) *Development Projects as Policy Experiments: An Adaptive Approach to Development Administration.* London: Methuen (2nd edition).

Smith, W. J. and K. Subbarao (2003) *What Role for Safety Net Transfers in Very Low Income Countries?,* Social Protection Discussion Paper 0301. Washington, DC: The World Bank.

Titmuss, R. M. (1968) *Commitment to Welfare.* London: Allen & Unwin.

Index